COMPETITORS IN ALLIANCE

Industry Associations, Global Rivalries and Business-Government Relations

Andrew A. Procassini

QUORUM BOOKS
Westport, Connecticut • London

Library of Congress Cataloging-in-Publication Data

Procassini, Andrew A.
  Competitors in alliance : industry associations, global rivalries,
and business-government relations / Andrew A. Procassini.
     p.   cm.
  Includes bibliographical references and index.
  ISBN 0–89930–962–3
  1. Commercial associations—United States.   2. Foreign trade
promotion—United States.   3. Commercial associations—Japan.
4. Commercial associations—Germany.   5. Competition, International.
I. Title.
HF296.A164   1995
338.6—dc20   94–39659

British Library Cataloguing in Publication Data is available.

Library of Congress Catalog Card Number: 94–39659
ISBN: 0–89930–962–3

First published in 1995

Quorum Books, 88 Post Road West, Westport, CT 06881
An imprint of Greenwood Publishing Group, Inc.

Printed in the United States of America

The paper used in this book complies with the
Permanent Paper Standard issued by the National
Information Standards Organization (Z39.48–1984).

10 9 8 7 6 5 4 3 2 1

To Dorothy Cornelius, my wife

Contents

Figures and Tables

FIGURES

TABLES

Preface

In the past decade, a great number of books and articles have been written about the competitiveness of American industries in the global marketplace. Their emphasis has ranged across a number of industries, including steel, automobiles, computer systems, and semiconductors. These publications have also covered the global geography by analyzing the industrial policies of many nations, including the United States, Japan, France, and Korea, as well as others. The variety of forms have included the general press, magazines, trade publications, academic studies, and government reports. Despite this broad coverage, only a few of these works describe the role of trade associations in helping their nation's industries achieve a high level of global competitiveness, and even these few do not treat the subject of trade associations comprehensively. The purpose of this book is to focus primarily on the role of trade associations in bringing about a higher level of competitiveness for U.S. high-technology industries. Therefore, it will not cover the broader aspects of global competitiveness but only the one area that has not been adequately addressed.

The role of an industry trade association is seldom clearly understood by Americans. Moreover, even when the role is understood, there are no guarantees that it is being implemented as well in the United States as it is in the competitor nations of Japan and Germany. One area in which American trade associations seem to lag behind their foreign competitors is in forming effective partnerships with government. This book, therefore, attempts to shed a brighter light on the issue of global competition as related to industry associations and their involvement in industry-government partnerships.

The approach taken here is fairly simple. Following an introduction, the second part of the book provides a look at the history of the trade association movement in the United States, Japan, and Germany against the background of each nation's socioeconomic and political experiences. It also serves as a preliminary foundation for further explanation and recommendations. The countries of Japan and Germany were chosen because they are the chief competitors of the United States in the battle for global industrial supremacy.

Part 3 is written to provide real-world examples of associations at work. Rather than dwell on more mature industries, which are discussed to some degree in other books, Part 3 focuses on specific high-technology industries, including their global competition and primary associations. The high-technology industries selected were microelectronics, computer systems, aerospace, and biotechnology. Finally, Part 4 recommends a new approach that will improve the efficiency and effectiveness of U.S. trade associations in achieving America's industrial goals.

This book, which is based on past history and present-day experiences, describes the future directions that industry associations must follow to perform their competitiveness functions. At the beginning of most chapters, an anecdotal section is presented. The purpose is to keep in perspective a subject that may appear academic or even arcane by relating it to everyday events that demonstrate association activity. This book, via several approaches, concludes by proposing specific changes in industry associations that will improve the position of U.S. firms and industries in global competition.

Acknowledgments

I am truly thankful for the time and talents of the many individuals who helped create this book. Although as the author, I must be solely responsible for its contents, I could not have completed these efforts without the help of others. Among them I would first point to those whose extensive reviewing and suggestions were invaluable. They were Andre Delbecq, Jeffrey Hart, Hunter Hale, Dan Okimoto, Michael Borrus, Ed Steinmueller, Tom Howell, John Stern, John Young, Warren Davis, Jerry Arnold, and Gunther Moller. I especially wish to thank Dr. Philip A. Mundo of Drew University, not only for his review and suggestions, but also for his authorship of research reports describing specific associations' organizations, which were incorporated, with few modifications, into Chapters 7, 8, and 10.

I also wish to thank my assistants, Helen Harris and Robin Mahan, who worked hard to produce the interim, as well as final, versions of the manuscript. I am also grateful to my publisher, Eric Valentine, and others at Quorum Books, including Marsha Goldstein, Elisabetta Linton, and Denise Van Acker. Moreover, I must consider myself fortunate to have been associated with many capable and knowledgeable persons at the Semiconductor Industry Association (SIA) and other business organizations. They have been the source of my motivation to write this book, and their words of encouragement often provided the necessary incentive.

Finally, Dorothy, my patient and understanding wife, made all the family inconveniences that come along when writing a book seem easy to overcome. I could not have finished this endeavor otherwise.

Additionally, to all those who helped but were (inadvertently) not mentioned, I offer my sincere thanks.

I

INTRODUCTION

Chapter 1

Association Foundations: Past, Present, and Future

THEN TO NOW, BRIEFLY

In seven short years, from 1864 to 1871, the present-day economic and sociopolitical foundations of the seven major industrial world powers came into being. With the end of the Civil War in 1864, "these United States" became "the United States." In 1868, the Meiji Restoration began the development of modern-day Japan, while at about the same time, Great Britain granted autonomy to the Dominion of Canada. In 1870, Italy became a unified nation instead of a collection of kingdoms. Germany became unified in 1871 under Otto von Bismarck as its first chancellor, and that same year, France saw its last emperor deposed and the Third Republic established.

These events, although brought about at the culmination of conflict—civil unrest, wars, or the clash of political ideologies—were also the beginnings, in each of these nations, of a tremendous acceleration in the world's industrialization. This resulted in these economies requiring large amounts of capital investment funds; new technologies and innovations; an educated, creative, and skilled work force, including a managerial class; and an increased degree of interorganizational behavior among firms, industries, and governments.

In fulfilling their needs, these economies—the United States, Japan, Germany, the United Kingdom, France, Italy, and Canada—became the world's most wealthy and powerful nations, but not without the turmoil of an industrial revolution. The revolution was led by the impact of the new infrastructure industries, the railroad and the telegraph. These industries themselves were the economic drivers: they required other new industries, technologies and innovations, new means for accumulating and allocating capital funds, and new managerial knowledge and worker skills. The concomitant paradigm shift in infrastructure concepts, which continued beyond the lifetime of these nineteenth-century industries, became the bedrock for the later industries of the automobile, airplane, and the telephone, as well as multitudes of other dramatically new products. The industrial revolution also brought about new kinds of alliances between firms, between industries, and even between governments. Among these key alliances are the business and trade (or industry) associations, which affected industry structure, the overall economy, and the highest levels of government policy in all nations.

Since the 1950s, the Information Age, a new and modern era, has been unfolding and affecting all areas of business activity, including trade associations. There are four major aspects of this new age. The first, rapid technological progress, has brought about the development of new high-technology industries such as aerospace, biotechnology, computer systems and software, and semiconductor chips. The second aspect is the globalization of industrial activity, which has not only spread the new technologies across the world, but has also raised the level of international transactions to the point that national borders appear to provide few barriers to trade and investment. The third aspect is the high degree of interorganization activity between governments and business, and last, the combination of high-tech growth, globalization of industrial activity, and the interorganizational behavior of government and business is characteristic of a new world competition. Each nation views these aspects as important elements in the determination of its global competitiveness.

Industry trade associations, an important factor in the interorganizational behavior of government and business, must therefore be closely observed as global competitiveness increasingly becomes the national goal of the industrialized nations of the world.

A VARIETY OF OPINIONS

Associations have been considered by some observers to be essential to the national interest, but they have also been designated by others as harmful to the general public. They have been deemed to be necessary for economic and political order, and yet they have been also described as underutilized in their application to public policy matters. Examples of these various opinions can be shown in the following short passages with regard to the United States, Japan, and Germany.

The most often-quoted writer in America on economics is Adam Smith. Regarding businessperson meetings, his thoughts are given here:

"People of the same trade seldom meet together, even for merriment and diversion, but the conversation ends in a conspiracy against the public, or in some contrivance to raise prices."[1] In the 1980s Murray L. Weidenbaum, chairman of the Council of Economic Advisors during the Ronald Reagan administration, wrote, "Trade associations may be one of the most underutilized mechanisms for improving public policy."[2] Later, in 1990, George Lodge wrote his view:

Industry associations are crucial to the organizing of business leadership for new and more creative relationships with government. . . . These associations manage cooperation, set visions and make strategy. Industry associations are the bridge between business specialists on one side and politicians and government on the other. That bridge . . . is becoming increasingly crucial to competitiveness.[3]

With respect to Germany, a report to the U.S. Congress provided the following comments:

The relationship between German industry and government is cooperative, i.e., based on negotiation and consensus building. . . . German ministers are required to consult with industry and union representatives when drafting legislation. . . . Furthermore, industry groups play a direct role in administering public programs of industrial relevance. For example, government program applications and state subsidies are sometimes administered by trade associations.[4]

An American observer of differences between the United States and Germany stated:

It is a well-organized private sector that is the prime motor for communitarian policies in modern Germany. . . . Most of German industry falls under the Federation of German Industry (BDI) and the German Chamber of Commerce (DIHT). There are many trade associations that actively help companies to strengthen their competitive standing.[5]

At a 1984 business history conference in Tokyo, a Japanese university faculty member addressed Japan's associations:

"It is often said that a feature of Japan not found in other countries is that there are few clashes between business associations, the zaikai, and the government. Both parties cooperate mutually, almost as if in a military pact, and initiate activities to achieve the same goals."[6] An American professor, Daniel L. Okimoto of Stanford, wrote in 1989:

In Japan, where the challenge of organizing for collective industries or sector-specific interests has been achieved with greater frequency and success than in the United States or most European states, industrial associations (IAs) have played a big role in aggregating individual company interests, building intra-industry consensus, and serving as a vehicle of communication between industry and government.[7]

These or similar statements from different eras and countries may confuse, puzzle, or even bias interested observers. The present volume considers and clarifies these statements in order to point the way to a new era and a new role for American trade associations.

A HISTORICAL PERSPECTIVE

To better understand how the world's most advanced nations have been affected by business and industry associations in reaching their present status, a brief historical outline is essential. The history of these organizations as related to the United States, Japan, and Germany will help explain why Japan and Germany seem able to function today with greater strength and speed than the United States in a number of specific global industries. Finally, an understanding of the unique historical basis of American trade associations will enable us to suggest ways to reconstitute them for both the public interest and the global competitiveness of American industries.

History does more than merely describe events. It also provides an understanding of the forces that brought business organizations and industry associations to the fore by the beginning of the twentieth century. It explains the reactions of governments, business, and other interested groups to the associations' growing influence in formulating public policy as well as business policy.

History explains not only the broader issues but also the methods employed by the associations to achieve their purposes. Among these methods were activities that ranged from setting price schedules to bargaining with labor unions and promoting exports. Overall, history provides a basis for understanding change, thereby improving the level of knowledge for future actions.

THE PRESENT ROLE OF HIGH-TECH ASSOCIATIONS

Although a historical review is necessary for planning the future role of associations, it is not, by itself, sufficient. An understanding of how high-tech industry associations work today is also essential. Therefore, several high-tech industries and their associations will be closely examined to learn how future associations may be made to operate more effectively and efficiently. The present linkage of industry competitiveness and association activity must be considered if future associations are to assist their respective industries in achieving success in global competition. The high-tech industries and their corresponding associations that are described and analyzed in these pages include:

Industry	Associations
Aerospace	• Aerospace Industries Association
Biotechnology	• Industrial Biotechnology Association
Computer Systems	• American Electronics Association
	• Computer and Business Equipment Manufacturing Association
	• Computer Systems Policy Project
Semiconductors	• Semiconductor Industry Association

The final result of the analysis is a characterization of U.S. high-tech associations and their comparison to the associations of Japan and Germany. This comparison provides a glimpse of the alternatives available in the design of American associations.

A NEW ERA FOR ASSOCIATIONS

Global competitiveness and its elements (technology, globalization, and business-government partnerships) will be felt by every industry association. These business organizations must respond in assistance to their industries or else they will be abandoned in favor of new organizations. Whether an association is reformed or a new association is established, each must reflect an appropriate response to a changing world. The new era association will be formed and focused in a manner that will make it more effective and efficient in its assistance to its industry.

To ignore the need for newly designed associations will result in the loss of an essential national factor for international industrial success.

Within what kind of a world must the newly designed association be capable of operating? What kind of world has been developing, and will continue to evolve, as we approach the turn of the century? The answer is that the new, globalized, technologically oriented, and industrially competitive environment will be configured as follows:

- Global competitiveness will be a key factor in maintaining a nation's standard of living, and a nations industrial leadership will be essential in achieving this goal.

- Strong government-industry partnerships will be necessary in order to develop the high-tech industries necessary for maintaining the living standard of a nation's citizens.

- Greater emphasis on equal partnerships—not only of government with industry, but also of companies with other companies, associations of companies in an industry, and environmentalists with industrialists—will increase. There will be less emphasis on mandated relationships and greater emphasis on the need for individuals and organizations to voluntarily cooperate.

- Along with global competitiveness and a rising national living standard there will be a renewed concern for domestic affairs, namely, health reform, welfare reform, environmental conditions, and economic security. Military security will be of lesser concern.

- Organizations in all phases of organized activities, whether government, industry, associations, education, or medical services, will become broader, more efficient, and quicker to respond.

- Knowledge-based industries, technology-developing organizations, and educational and training institutions will all contribute to an ever-increasing fund of technical advances and progress in products, services, and activities for the enhancement of personal well-being.

- A middle sector (comprised of trade associations, consortia, informal groups, and interest groups) will be of greater importance in every nation that leads in global competitiveness, because the private and public sectors will no longer be so clearly separated.

SUMMARY

The ultimate objective of this book is to help in the design of American associations for today's world competition. To accomplish this, however, requires the lessons of history, the practices of present-day associations, and a synthesis of all the best forward-looking ideas, whether American or foreign. The work required to present all three facets—history, current activities, and the synthesis of the best ideas—is embodied in these pages.

NOTES

1. Adam Smith, *The Wealth of Nations* (Chicago: University of Chicago Press, 1976), 144.

2. Murray L. Weidenbaum, *Business, Government and the Public* (Englewood Cliffs, NJ: Prentice Hall, 1981), 386.

3. George C. Lodge, *Perestroika for America: Restructuring U.S. Business-Government Relations for Competitiveness in the World Economy* (Boston: Harvard Business School Press, 1990), 209.

4. U.S. General Accounting Office, *Competitiveness Issues: The Business Environment in the United States, Japan, and Germany, a Report to Congressional Requestors* (Washington, DC: U.S. General Accounting Office, August 1993), 105.

5. Jeffrey E. Garten, *A Cold Peace: America, Japan, Germany and the Struggle for Supremacy* (New York: Random House, Twentieth Century Fund Book 1992), 113–114.

6. Juro Hashimoto, "Comments," in *Trade Associations in Business History*, ed. H. H. Yamazaki and M. Miyamoto (Tokyo: University of Tokyo Press, 1988), 46.

7. Daniel L. Okimoto, *Between MITI and the Market: Japanese Industrial Policy for High Technology* (Stanford, CA: Stanford University Press, 1989), 165.

II

LEGACIES OF THE PAST AND PRESENT

Chapter 2

Japan

THE MINISTRY OF INTERNATIONAL TRADE AND INDUSTRY MAKES A U.S. VISIT

President Reagan had announced in March 1987 that the U.S. government would levy duty sanctions of $320 million on imports from Japan for that nation's failure to meet the terms of the U.S.-Japan Semiconductor Agreement, signed on September 2, 1986.[1] These terms included the cessation of dumping of computer chips by Japanese companies and access to the Japanese chip market. It was now the fall of 1987 and the Japanese visitors to the Semiconductor Industry Association (SIA) offices in Cupertino, California, included Yukiharu Kodama and three of his associates.[2]

Kodama held an important Japanese government post, serving as the director-general of the Machine and Information Industries Bureau of the Ministry of International Trade and Industry (MITI).[3] He was concerned, therefore, with industrial and trade matters regarding computers, consumer electronics, and other electronic equipment, as well as components such as semiconductor integrated circuits ("computer chips" or simply "chips," as they are popularly called by the worldwide news media). It was Kodama's branch of MITI that was most directly involved with the signing of the semiconductor agreement.

Kodama is a soft-spoken, sophisticated man with a good command of English and a long tenure at MITI, the primary instrument of Japan's industrial policy. He graduated from Tokyo University and had been in progressively higher posts since joining MITI after graduation. In the early 1980s, he had participated in joint informal discussions with semiconductor industry and government representatives from the United States and Japan. The informal meetings had attained a few successes, such as the removal of import tariffs on chips in both countries. However, they had not addressed the major repeated American complaints.

These complaints were based on the inability of the American semiconductor industry, which was highly successful in the world outside Japan, to penetrate the

Japanese market, and also on the practice by Japanese chip manufacturers of "dumping" in foreign markets, that is of selling their output below cost, with the effect of driving non-Japanese competitors from the marketplace. Since almost all Japanese firms are part of huge conglomerates (keiretsu), with great amounts of resources, the managers of many American firms believed that Japanese firms could drive almost any chip-dedicated manufacturer out of business through the use of their financial power.[4]

The U.S.-Japan Semiconductor Agreement was not the outcome of an informal set of discussions, but the result of negotiations between the two governments with regard to dumping and access issues raised by individual American companies as well as by the SIA. After a year of effort, the agreement was signed by both governments.[5]

Now, twelve months after the signing of the five-year agreement, Kodama had come to the United States for a series of visits to convince the U.S. semiconductor industry and the government that the sanctions imposed by President Reagan had served their purpose and should now be lifted. His visit to the SIA office, as he stated it, was key to accomplishing his purpose. (The details of his request and the SIA's corresponding response are not essential here.)

As the discussion came to an end, Kodama asked for a tour of the SIA office facilities. The group left the meeting room and walked about a hundred feet down the corridor, past several small offices. In all, the entire space was no more than 3,000 square feet, the size of a large family home. On completing the brief tour, Kodama and his entourage stood at the exit, with the SIA executives following to bid them good-bye. As he recognized the exit door, Kodama turned about, looked at his SIA hosts with surprise on his face, and asked, "Is this all there is?" He had evidently made a mental comparison between SIA's political success and the relatively scarce resources at its command and had been shocked by the discrepancy.

My reply was that these facilities were a small and insignificant part of the association, and that the real strength was with the joint consensus of the thirty member companies' chief executive officers (CEOs) and their senior executives. Kodama-san left the premises shaking his head. Obviously, he had completely overestimated the resources located at this trade association headquarters. He appeared to feel that any organization powerful enough to convince the Reagan White House to effectively take on Japan's bureaucracy, which was highly experienced in industrial policy and international trade negotiations, and ultimately force them to sign an agreement more onerous to them than any in their postwar history, must have great resources. The entire incident brought out the international differences in how trade associations are viewed and utilized.

This book addresses these kinds of differences in organizations, their history, their strengths and weaknesses, and their roles and relationships in nations' international and domestic economic affairs. It suggests their potential impact on issues of industrial policy and the future of American high-technology industries in a global marketplace where foreign governments are more often partners with their industries than the industries' impartial regulators.

JAPAN: FROM RESTORATION TO OCCUPATION

The importance of the period from the Meiji Restoration to the American occupation in relation to the formation of Japanese business organizations cannot be underestimated. It was then, when modern Japan was emerging on the world scene, that most of Japan's present business institutions were defined and their foundations laid. In order to understand the industry associations of today's Japan, an awareness of this history is essential. It was to catch up with the West that Japanese rulers began the rapid, mandated, organized drive that still characterizes Japan's economic endeavors.

Using Japan as the first national example in this book is appropriate because its utilization of associations in both global and domestic industries is broader than that of most other nations. In 1603, the Tokugawa family was successful in uniting Japan and establishing a strong central government. Its rule lasted for 250 years, most of which were peaceful. This long period of peace allowed for the building of an effective infrastructure based on the then current technologies, a strong economic policy, a disciplined social system, and a broad spectrum of educational activity, especially for the samurai, a warrior class that no longer had wars to fight.

The period was marked by a prosperous agrarian economy based on rice, silk, and foodstuffs, but there were also enough merchants and artisans to form large cities such as Osaka. Those cities, which were based on trade and pre-factory production, were the commercial core of the national economy. The commercial activity required currency, and a monetary system based on national gold and silver coins as well as local paper currency was put in place. Agriculture was more highly esteemed than trade and, as a result, more heavily taxed. This lack of esteem worked to the advantage of the merchant class, since the eventual outcome was its ability to accumulate capital faster than the other classes, namely, the landholders (including peasants) and the artisans and warriors. The merchants became the personal capitalists of Japan, just as the merchants of England and America had become their countries' capitalists.[6]

The Tokugawas, in their desire to maintain power, had concluded that foreigners and foreign nations should be prohibited from dealing with the Japanese. The government's experience with the Jesuit missionaries, who preached Christianity, and the Dutch merchants, who proposed new, unfavorable terms of trade, had turned them toward a policy of isolation exemplified by the execution of Christians, the limiting of trade boundaries for foreigners, and the prohibition of foreign travel by Japanese subjects. By the 1830s, with the forty four-year rule of the shogun, Ienari, almost at an end, social and political conflicts peaked.[7] This was the beginning of the decline of the Tokugawa regime.

In 1853, the black ships of Admiral Mathew Perry arrived and Japan was opened to foreign trade under unfavorable treaty terms. Another period of civil unrest followed, which put the Tokugawa regime in a dilemma over whether to attempt to keep the foreigners out and fall prey to their superior military technology or open the country and fall victim to their greater commercial knowledge. The final result of civil unrest was the fall of the Tokugawa shogunate itself and the restoration of the Emperor Meiji to the imperial throne in 1868. Not only was the emperor restored, the nation's store of private wealth had permanently shifted from the landowners and peasants to the merchants and traders.[8]

Although Japan had a developing economy prior to Meiji, the restoration put into motion a set of events that was to modernize the country and put its political and economic system on a course to match that of the Western nations. The Meiji government's two popular slogans were *fukoku-kyohei* ("a wealthy nation and strong army"), and *shokusan-kogyo* ("industrialization by government planning"). The first goal came to pass when the Japanese army successfully won the war in China (1894–1895) and defeated the Russian forces (1904–1905). The results included large gains in reparations and control over Taiwan, Korea, the southern part of the island of Sakhalin, and the Manchurian Railway. The concept of "industrialization by government planning," and the efforts that the slogan represented, was to have far greater long-term impact, however, than all Japan's military actions.[9]

Although Meiji instituted a parliamentary form of government similar to that of Great Britain, the government retained the concept of strong central control. A national compulsory education law was introduced in 1879, and it was totally effective by 1905. Mobility of labor, both in upward employment promotion and geographic location, began to take place. Foreign travel was allowed and, in fact, was utilized to obtain information about the West. Fiscal reform including new tax policies and a central bank, the Bank of Japan, were put in place by 1882. The government actively introduced foreign technology in agriculture and in industry, and scarce foreign currency was used to hire foreign technical advisors and purchase foreign machinery. With regard to manufacturing, the government went so far as actually to build and operate factories, such as textile mills, for a short period of time.

The transportation and communications infrastructure was improved, and the first railroad, consisting of twelve miles from Yokohama to Shinbashi (present-day Tokyo), was built in 1872. Telegraph service from Tokyo to Yokohama began in 1870, and a postal system was established in 1871. The underlying basis of modern industry, namely, transport and communication, was being laid in Japan along the same lines as their earlier development in the Western world.

The Meiji government also took an active role in the development of manufacturing industries and, in effect, began Japan's long history of industrial policy. It subsidized key industries and built modern factories such as the Tomoku silk factory and the Sakai spinning mill. It also trained technicians and sent them to private factories to run newly acquired modern European equipment, sold or leased public land for a discount to manufacturers, and protected target industries such as shipbuilding from foreign competition via implicit and explicit regulations.[10]

The commercial economic activities of the early Meiji era were, in a sense, a carryover of the Tokugawa period. The pre-Meiji period had an economy in which merchants, although considered lower class, were active and successful and where artisans operated on a pre-factory-era basis. These merchants and artisans congregated in cities and formed guilds for each of their activities in ways similar to those in Europe at that time. The merchant guilds in Japan, as in Europe, attempted to provide protection against competition through controlled prices and quality standards, assure a labor supply at agreed wages, obtain joint facilities such as warehouses, make credit available, and also act as an important group in social matters.[11]

The merchant guilds were essential to the economy because the Tokugawa government, which did not place a great deal of emphasis on trade, had failed to establish many rules for mercantile practices or laws to regulate business transactions. The guilds were themselves forced to do so, and commercial activities became grounded in the guild system. However, the Meiji government later attempted to wipe out all feudalistic practices and mistakenly attempted to destroy the guilds, which it condemned for acting in a private, monopolistic manner. Chaos followed: established credit systems, commercial procedures, business conduct, and other aspects of an orderly business environment began to decline.

At the same time, foreign governments criticized the Meiji regime for failing to elicit the opinions of the Japanese business community in regard to foreign trade matters. The two concerns—businessmen's concern for order in their working lives, and the government's concern that its voice be heard abroad in foreign trade circles—led to the formation of the new business associations to replace the guilds.

In the 1870s, the Japanese government requested that several prominent Japanese businessmen set up chambers of commerce similar to those in Europe and America, which would become the focal point of business opinion. In order to accelerate the organization, the government subsidized the project. Although strong government sentiment was present here, Japanese businessmen also felt the need for a businessmen's association. Consequently, the result from the beginning was not only a locally oriented business association, but also one with a national purpose.

At that time, however, the organization was set up in a manner similar to that of the Anglo-American type, as a private voluntary body with membership open to all propertied businessmen. It was not set up as a Continental European type organization, which tended to be a publicly chartered, self-governing body with compulsory membership for all businesses. Although most of the members of these organizations represented typical finance, transportation, and merchant businesses, their leading members were generally former government officials or men from the newly emerging industries, who tended to be unusually enlightened on the national interests. Many of the chambers' activities were centered on specific issues such as business practices, commercial law, relief works, and product standards. They also included a provision for advising the central government in such areas as tariffs, treaties, the effect of monetary and fiscal policy on the supply and demand of products, prices, and national transportation networks, such as the railroads and shipping.[12]

By 1880, however, it was becoming clearer that the structure of commerce and manufacturing was to change. The larger firms, which had stressed banking, coal and copper mining, shipping, and foreign trade, were expanding into heavy manufacturing industries of a capital-intensive nature, which were larger in scale and scope than the traditional manufactures of textiles, pottery, and other housewares. These newer industries were in areas such as iron, steel, chemicals, and electrical machinery. They were to begin a period of dramatic growth, which was especially great during and after World War I, when imports from Western countries declined. The small- to- medium-sized manufacturing industries in cotton and silk fabrics, ceramics, household items, toys, glassware, and lacquerware continued to flourish and be modernized; however, the traditional commercial merchant trade interests began to decline in terms of influence.

The chambers, therefore, became polarized into a structure that was primarily dependent on the size of firms. The smallest firms were represented by merchants and owners, while the largest, which were private joint-stock companies, were represented by managers and executives. Light manufacturing firms, often of a small to medium size, fell between these two extremes. This phenomenon, in which personal capitalism was being replaced by managerial capitalism (as it was in most of the industrializing Western nations during the late nineteenth century), was now beginning to become evident in Japan. The large Japanese firms, in a similar fashion to the Continental European ones, were primarily financed by banks rather than by personal funds (as in Great Britain) or by a combination of personal funds and the sale of equities (as in the United States). Consequently, one of the basic similarities in the financial-industrial underpinnings of Japan and Germany was the use of large banks. The fact that the Japanese banks were also owned by the largest firms in Japan, however, is dissimilar from both Germany and the United States, but in different ways.

The changing structure of industry resulted in a movement toward industry-by-industry associations, in other words, associations dedicated to firms in the same trade, as opposed to merchants who dealt in commerce across many lines, especially those manufactured by light industry. Some of the products of these early industries were candles, umbrellas, hemp, and indigo.[13] In 1882, the president of the Kyoto Chamber of Commerce asked the governor of Kyoto prefecture for permission to form local trade associations for various kinds of industry such as textiles, silk, pottery, and lumber and, with some expansion of membership criteria, the plan was adopted. Many other local governments across the country soon carried out the same policy. The national government established regulations for the new industry associations and stipulated that the local government must report any new formation of associations. Some of these government regulations involved the improvement of product quality for export purposes. The regulations also required mandatory membership after three-quarters of existing industry entities had joined. They also allowed the associations to fix quality standards, set prices, prohibit sales at a loss, expand markets, prohibit the stealing of customers by prices or terms, issue bills of exchange, prohibit sales to those not paying or beating down prices, teach and train apprentices, and punish apprentices for unjust deeds or quitting (that is, they could basically regulate terms of employment).[14]

Although the association activity with respect to commercial matters was increasing, the level of attention to national interests with regard to industrial growth did not satisfy the central government. The cause for its dissatisfaction was founded on the fact that the voluntary nature of the initial membership resulted in a small group that was uneven in terms of representation, and there was still greater organizational emphasis on merchants than industrialists. On the other hand, the merchants were dissatisfied because they felt they were being reduced to government advisory bodies rather than private business associations. These issues were addressed after 1889 when the new national constitution was in force and the first Japanese Diet (parliament) was convened. These actions set the stage for the events of the next year, when a new commercial code was enacted. As part of the new code, the Chamber of Commerce Ordinance was passed, which defined the chamber as a self-governing, chartered organization based on regional lines and with mandatory membership defined as all manufacturers, builders, bankers, and warehousers, as well as merchants.

Other major revisions of the regulations stated that the chamber was granted the official privilege to levy compulsory dues on members; managers of companies and corporations, as well as individuals, were given the right to vote; and the chambers were compelled to represent manufacturing companies as well as commercial firms. The law, in essence, provided the legal foundation for the chambers' development as the representative voice of the overall Japanese business world. The activities of the chamber included the promotion of exports, the proposal of solutions for national economic problems, and the obtaining of government support for favorable terms of trade by lowering duties on raw material and increasing tariffs on imported competitive processed goods. The promotion of exports is an interesting aspect since it included requests to the government to appoint men with business acumen as foreign consuls, send commercial graduates abroad for experience in foreign trade, establish a specialized import-export bank, promote import substitution, and institute a system of quality standards to improve the reliability of Japanese exports. The government vigorously adopted all measures.[15]

From 1860 to World War I the Chamber of Commerce played the most important organized business role, even though associations by industry, such as the Japan Spinners Association and the Japan Paper Association, were operating in parallel. By the end of World War I, the chamber was still the sole, formal general business association in Japan; however, its influence had begun to wane for several reasons. A decided change in industrial structure had occurred because of the remarkable growth in heavy industry—chemicals, electrical machinery, and metals such as steel, iron, and aluminum—which required large-scale operations and highly intensive capital investments. The *zaibatsu*, Japan's largest commercial-industrial-financial combines, which previously had stressed banking, trade,

shipping, and mining (mostly of copper and coal), had expanded into new, growing manufacturing industries. The combined control of banking and the high
growth of heavy industry resulted in a great strengthening of the zaibatsu. Big
business became the dominant influence in national affairs, and the large emerging industry-by-industry associations were operating in parallel with the chambers of commerce. Many of these industry associations were essentially cartels,
and between 1902 and 1920 more than tnirty-five new associations were formed,
including those in textiles, paper, food, chemicals, iron and steel, and petroleum.
The eventual split of large business interests from the Chamber of Commerce
occurred in 1917 with the establishment of the Industry Club of Japan involving
185 large companies as members.[16]

The Chamber of Commerce attempted to counteract this movement by explicitly making rules that disproportionately encouraged membership by industrial corporations and industry-by-industry trade associations. However, the problem of
divergent interests between large industrial manufacturing concerns and the small
and medium firms in the light and traditional industry group was not solved by the
chamber actions to the satisfaction of both groups. The Industry Club of Japan
(ICJ) became the dominant trade association of the first group, while the chambers
continued to champion the needs of small and mid-sized businesses. In 1922, the
Japan Economic Federation was formed to take on the direct activities of the ICJ,
which then became a social club. In a counter move by the chamber, a new law in
1928 changed its name to the Chamber of Commerce and Industry (its present-day
title), and made revisions to membership rules that significantly revised upward the
number of members that must be corporations or other associations. Despite the
chamber's rule changes, the split was maintained and the Industry Club remained
apart. The operation of the Industry Club of Japan, which eventually caused the formation of the present-day Keidanren (Federation of Economic Organizations), was
therefore the result of the disaffection of industrialists and big businesses which
lacked an organization to represent their interests.[17]

The period between 1880 and 1917, however, is an illustrative one in terms of
the development of the sector-specific industry trade associations. Among the first
of these was the Japan Cotton Spinners Association. This association, which was
formed in 1882, represented private firms and, by 1932, as part of Japan's textile
industry, became the world's largest exporter of cotton goods. The Meiji government had attempted to set up government factories but had failed and by 1882 had
sold them all to private parties. The Japan Cotton Spinners Association became
Japan's most famous and representative prewar association and cartel organization, although it had been preceded by the Japan Paper Manufacturing Federation
in 1880. Other associations were soon set up in petroleum, coal mining, linen
yarn, and many other industries. By 1900, over 20 manufacturing industry associations had been established, by 1931, over 100, and by 1937, over 800. Today
there are well over 3,000 manufacturing industry associations in Japan.[18]

While the associations established from 1880 to 1900 were primarily in industries such as textiles, food, and paper, by the end of World War I, the iron, steel,

chemicals, and electrical machinery associations were by far the larger and more influential. However, all the associations, in both light and heavy manufacturing, were able to function in very broad areas, including the cartelization of their industry. They also performed functions that improved the internal efficiency within the firms and the industry, in addition to those that restricted competition. The internal or functional manufacturing efficiency, as well as the external efficiencies related to products and markets, were therefore association concerns.

The functions of the associations that improved internal efficiency included labor relations, joint purchasing of raw material, expansion of distribution outlets, acquisition of capital, and collection of operational and market information. These efforts tended to improve the internal operation of the industry since no one firm could affect the degree of positive internal economics that the industry enjoyed collectively. The function of the associations that restricted competition included the reduction of capacity, exclusive distribution agreements, and agreements stabilizing prices. However, there is no conclusive history with regard to these associations' ability to restrict competition totally. In fact, it appears that cartels and competition coexisted.[19]

The restriction of competition appeared to operate effectively only during recessions, and even during these periods, the stabilization of prices allowed marginal firms to survive. As economic recovery occurred, these firms often improved their efficiency and remained more than marginal during the next recession. Price control also encouraged new entrants who did not abide with the same price controls and, therefore, instigated partial competition. Although the opinions on uses of cartel actions by associations is divided, the overall impact in Japan was to raise the productivity of the firms and strengthen their international competitiveness. In a nation dependent on international trade for its raw materials and large markets, it appears that the development of cartels may have been economically rational, especially since it did not appear to discourage the development of downstream products.[20]

In the 1920s, the Japanese established export associations similar to the U.S. Webb-Pomerene associations (authorized by the Webb-Pomerene Act of 1918), which allowed American exporters to organize approved associations for conducting export trade without being subject to the U.S. antitrust laws. The Japanese export organizations focused on enforcing quality standards for goods to be exported and often provided a collective response to foreign complaints about Japanese exports. Voluntary export limitations similar to the voluntary restraints of the 1980s on autos and other products into the United States were implemented by these associations for export products of that period.[21]

By 1930 the government had begun to make a historic turnaround from indirect to direct control of association affairs. Regulatory statutes that had depended primarily on the self-control of associations and had enabled the government to give the appearance of supporting free trade were changed. The new government policy and statutes allowed direct and explicit intervention in association affairs.[22] In 1931, two laws were passed to promote the cartelization (or organization of) industries—one law for large-scale industries (Important Industries Control Law) and another for smaller-scale manufacturers (Manufacturers Association Law). These laws, which may have been the result of a war for power between the electric utilities, had dual, but not necessarily reinforcing, purposes.[23] They were intended to improve the efficiency of Japan's industries in international competition by fostering cartelization and interfirm cooperation, while on the other hand protecting the interests of smaller businesses and consumers from any abuses by giving the government authority to intervene in association agreements when it was in the public interest. The laws, therefore, were directed toward an industrial policy, while at the same time they encompassed a social policy. As a result of the law, twenty-six industries, including silk, paper, cement, coal, iron, and steel, were designated as important and organized into cartels.[24] By 1936, these laws had resulted in over 800 associations, of which three-quarters had cooperative inspection, over half regulated products and price, and over one-third cooperated in equipment use, purchasing, and sales.[25]

The Industry Club of Japan (ICJ) grew from 500 firms in 1920 to about 800 companies by 1942. Of the 800 firms, 150 were from the machinery industry, 50 from the chemical field, 60 from electrical power or gas, 60 from transportation, 50 from textiles, and 70 from insurance and banking. It is no wonder that the ICJ favored the large firms, and in fact, executives from the zaibatsu of Mitsui, Mitsubishi, Furakawa, and Sumitomo, among others, formed the early ICJ boards of directors. Initially, the stated purposes of the ICJ had been relatively modest. They included surveys of and research on industry-related matters, encouragement of industrial invention, dissemination of industry data and information, and interindustry communication and coordination. The true primary goal, however, was to influence public policy for the benefit of "big industry." ICJ became the prototype of the *zaikai*, which, in Japanese, means "economic circles," implying a powerful pressure group representing the interests of big business.[26]

The efforts of the large business associations to control labor should not be overlooked. Just as business in the United States fought the labor unions in the 1930s, so did the manufacturers' associations in Japan. The business associations of Japan were successful in 1931 in defeating a law that would have given legal rights to the unions. In a follow-up to this success, the National Federation of Industrial Organizations was formed by business firms to handle in the future labor-related activities previously led by the ICJ, the predecessor to the Keidanren. The final outcome was a labor force whose demands, even up to the present day, are primarily brought forth by company unions organized by business.[27]

With the coming of World War II, many trade associations were transformed into official "control associations" for the wartime allocation and control of supplies of labor, capital, products, and raw materials. The large business firms dominated these organizations and eventually won out over the military, which had attempted to gain direct control over the associations.[28] The fact that "big business" prevailed is significant in that these same firms maintained continuity of association control from before World War II, through the hostilities, and right through to the postwar period. Before the end of World War II, there were more than 1,500 control associations at the national level in Japan, and three special peak associations were especially established to control the wartime economy. These were the Council for Vital Industries (1941), the Economic Association for Commerce and Industry (1943), and the Association of Industries for National Strength (1943).[29]

The U.S. occupation planned to eliminate the control associations, but some were still active until 1949. As they were eliminated between 1946 and 1949, most reverted to operating as trade associations. New peak organizations were also organized, the most prominent of which was the Keidanren, established in 1946 to replace the Council for Vital Industries. It is the most prestigious of all trade associations in Japan and is an organization of large firms and trade associations. It is dominated by respected figures from a number of industries and appears to be well balanced in terms of firms and associations. The Nikkeiren, the employers association, was established in 1948 to replace the Association of Industries for National Strength and is responsible for business's relationship with labor. It has as members individuals who are top managers of the major firms rather than representatives of the corporations themselves.

Finally, the Economic Association for Commerce and Industry was replaced by the Japan Chamber of Commerce and Industry, which was originally established in 1892 and then reestablished in 1949. Its major function, not unlike that of the U.S. Chamber of Commerce, was to represent small- and medium-sized businesses. However, some major firms have been members and contributed leaders from their firms. Another peak association, which is not related to any prewar group but was founded as a forum for young individual executives, was established in 1946 under the name Keizai Doyukai (Japan Committee for Economic Development). This group, which was encouraged by the U.S. Occupation Forces, was meant to raise the consciousness of rising executives to broader public policy issues.[30] A useful diagram of the historical development of Japan's trade and business associations up to 1950 is shown in Figure 2.1, which provides a chronology for the period discussed thus far.

In summary, the period of 1845 to 1945 served as the baseline for all subsequent business organization formation in Japan until even after World War II. A strong central government controlled, supported, and encouraged the economic development of business, and especially big business. By the beginning of hostilities in the 1930s, the Japanese could feel they had succeeded in large measure in attaining the Meiji objectives of *fukoku-kyohei* ("a wealthy nation and strong army") and *shokusan-kogyo* ("industrialization by government planning").

RECONSTRUCTION

World War II resulted in the utter destruction of the cities and the major industrial facilities of Japan. The strong, imperial central government was replaced by

Figure 2.1
Development of Trade and Business Associations in Japan

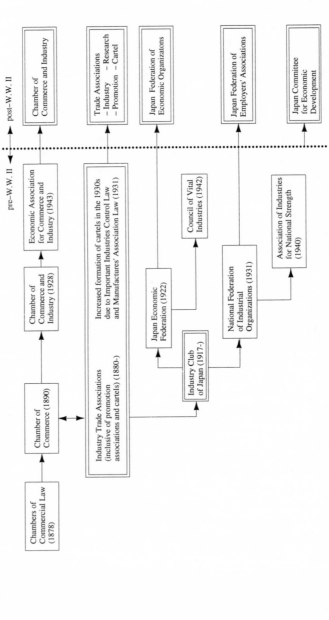

Source: Based primarily on the time chart in Matao Miyamoto, "The Development of Business Associations in Prewar Japan," in *Trade Associations in Business History*, edited by Hiroaki Yamazaki and Matao Miyamoto (Tokyo: University of Tokyo Press, 1988), p. 4.

Note: The double lines enclose existing associations; single lines enclose associations that have been dissolved.

an administration of the country overseen by an American general, Douglas Mac-Arthur, and his occupation forces. Along with the American military came American advisors on various aspects of the political and economic issues that faced the occupied country. All came with their views of how the nation should be reconstructed and, with little guidance from Washington, D.C., began to put their ideas into motion. Among the American actions were the demilitarization of the country, political reform based on a perfection of the British parliamentary form of government, enfranchisement of women, creation of a new supreme court, increases in local government powers, and elections for provincial governors. Further laws and regulations were instituted by the occupation forces, including land reform, encouragement of labor unions, and revision of the education system. The actions taken with regard to the industrial system of Japan, however, were eventually to prove ineffectual. The Americans attempted to disband the zaibatsu firms, dispossess landowning families, and break up the large commercial and industrial combines. However, whatever the social and political motives for this action, they were soon outweighed by the economic realities of maintaining a viable nation—and one that could support the United States in its conflicts with the USSR.

The role of associations was also redefined by the occupation authorities, but within a short period of time, they began to function as they had in the earlier periods. A large number of wartime officials and managers still played an important role in the corporations, the associations, and the government. The purging of wartime figures was apparently limited primarily to zaibatsu families, military leaders, and other figures thought to have militaristic influences. As a part of the intended breakup of the zaibatsu, over 325 companies were identified as candidates to be dissolved; however, only 18 were eventually dismantled, and most of these had been reconstituted by the 1960s. The important fact, though, was that although the zaibatsu families were removed from control of the companies, the managers were not removed. A form of managerial capitalism seems to have been instituted through the circumstances of war and occupation reforms. As the last of the control associations left the scene in 1949, the former associations returned to perform the same prewar functions and the prewar managers resumed the practices of earlier years.[31]

THE POSTWAR CARTELS

In 1947, under pressure from the occupation authorities, the Japanese government passed the first antimonopoly law (AML) in the history of Japan. It was drafted by the Americans and was based on a combination of the U.S. antitrust laws; in some ways, it was even more stringent than American law. It made monopoly illegal, outlawed cartels, prohibited overlapping ownership or control through shareholding, and required preapproval of all mergers. It was believed by the Japanese that the U.S. imposition of the law was intended to keep the Japanese economy weak.[32] By 1953, however, just one year after the end of the occupation, an amendment to the AML again allowed depression cartels. The logic of depression or recession cartels was that industries faced with capacity adjustment problems should not be forced into price cutting. Soon other cartels were also allowed, such as the rationalization cartel and the promotion cartel.[33] The rationalization cartels attempted to bring about a more efficient allocation of industry resources by limiting the use of technology, thereby restricting the production of certain types of products. They have also been used to limit access by foreign firms to the Japanese market, while the promotion cartels were used primarily to promote exports, as well as control imports. The cartels were planned, implemented, and administered largely through the use of trade associations, which worked closely with government. Quite often, the views of the Industrial Structure Advisory Council, an advisory group made up of private organizations but chartered by MITI, would assist in the selection and formation of the cartels. The Industrial Structure Advisory Council and other such councils will be further described as the interrelationship of MITI with other economic entities comes into focus later in this volume.

By 1973, the total number of cartels exempted from the antimonopoly law (AML) numbered 979 and divided as follows:[34]

Depression cartels	2
Rationalization cartels	10
Export cartels	180
Import cartels	2
Cartels under small and medium enterprises organization act	607
All others	178

It is now believed that this number has been declining and that antimonopoly investigations of illegal behavior have been increasing. By 1990, 180 cases had been probed by the Japan Fair Trade Commission, and the number of warnings and advisories issued in that year were 145 and 22, respectively.[35] According to the 1992 annual report of the Japan Fair Trade Commission, the number of legal cartels had dropped to 219 by March of that year. It appears that both foreign pressure, principally from the United States, and internal pressure have served as the impetus for the recently increased enforcement activity.[36] However, it is much too early to tell if any serious anticartel enforcement will be forthcoming.

Two practices in direct violation of the AML—*dango* and *saihan*—have recently received attention in the press. The first of these, dango, or bid-rigging, was applied to construction contracts. One of the most publicized examples was a case in which Japanese contractors were found guilty of price rigging that resulted in excess payments of millions of dollars by American armed forces for construction on their bases in Japan.[37] The construction cartel and its impact were felt again in the controversy over the participation by foreign firms in the construction of the Kansai airport.[38] The second practice, saihan, is the system of fixing minimum retail prices. In July 1988, NEC Corporation received a letter of warning from the Japan Fair Trade Commission (JFTC) with regard to the company's practice of setting a minimum price on its personal computer when sold through retail outlets.[39]

The depression associations or cartels are particularly interesting. These associations represent firms whose product offerings are part of a declining market at home and abroad. At the declining end of the product and industrial life cycle, the requirement in terms of business in Japan is that industries withdraw from the market in an orderly way so that investment and employment are not brutally decimated. An orderly withdrawal allows employers sufficient time to relocate their redundant employees into other commercial endeavors within the firm, or within the keiretsu, or even into quasi-government enterprises. In addition, the capital equipment investment will be withdrawn in such a manner that the least efficient plants are closed first, despite individual interests that may be involved, and at termination, the sacrifice of industry capacity in terms of cost is shared by industry members. Finally, the stockholders' equity and the banks' loans are satisfied over time in some agreed-upon manner. The entire process can be encapsulated in the phrases making an "orderly withdrawal" in an attempt to avoid "excessive and ruinous competition." The benefit to the consumer and the producers is subject to a great deal of debate, although conventional Anglo-American economic thinking would suggest that the identity of the surviving producers should be determined by free competition; that is, competition should continue until producers who are forced to withdraw should do so regardless of the timing of the impact on all stockholders. The Japanese view, as expressed by one author, is that the depression cartel is not efficient but that it is better than employing subsidization, as in Western Europe, and moreover is the best solution considering all economic circumstances.[40]

The depression cartel, which provides the orderly withdrawal, is not new to Japan. The Japan Cotton Spinners Association (JCSA), mentioned earlier, became just this kind of cartel and was singularly successful in its operations until the time of its disappearance, in 1942. The association operated for almost sixty years to curtail production, supply workers, purchase materials, obtain capital, and provide industry statistics. Its control of production was implemented by eleven reductions in operations between 1890 and 1930, all undergone as a legal cartel.[41] A present-day story of depression cartels can be told with regard to the steel industry in Japan, which utilized a modification of the depression cartel. The 1953 amendment allowed manufacturers to impose limits on the quantity of products made and the technologies used in their manufacture. Manufacturers were also allowed to procure raw materials jointly and, therefore, an effective monopsony was also put in place. The leading campaigner for this amendment was the Japan Iron and Steel Federation, an association representing the steel industry. This action, taken in 1953, has been called the beginning of the postwar cartel trend.[42]

The subject of "associated activities," although not involving formal cartels or associations, is equally important in any description of Japanese business. Keiretsu are the primary example of such activity. The former zaibatsu of pre–World War II became the keiretsu of post–World War II—organizations with long-standing relationships on either an ownership, financial, supplier, or purchasing basis arranged in such a way that they operate primarily to the benefit of their business partners. The Japan Fair Trade Commission estimated that nearly 90 percent of all domestic trade activities in Japan are carried out among parties involved in some sort of long-standing relationship.[43] Some of the larger keiretsu today, such as the Mitsui, Sumitomo, and Matsushita groups, are made up of hundreds of companies, and these in turn control other thousands of business units in Japan. The keiretsu that controls all inputs from suppliers through the manufacturing of hundreds of products to virtually all the distribution outlets can, in essence, operate as a vertical cartel. These cartels, in turn, may cooperate with other firms in the industry to effectively form horizontal cartels. The nature of Keiretsu, including their behavior and structure, has been one of the most frequently studied facets of Japan's industrial economy. Keiretsu continue to be singled out by business and academic journals as unique business organizations, and many related articles with various views are continually published on the topic.[44]

THE RESEARCH ASSOCIATION

Our attention now turns to a unique form of association that appeared early and often in postwar Japanese business—the research association. These associations are part and parcel of Japan's industrial policy. Research associations (*kenkyu kumiai*) are generally formed as the outcome of government deliberations that indicate that the development of a specific technology is vital to the nation's economic well-being or, in military terms, its security. The government will attempt to have companies from the related industries make proposals for technology development and then determine which corporations appear most likely to be successful. A research association of these corporations, which also may include government agencies, is then formed to develop the specific new technology. The selected firms may be allowed to operate in this area without being subject to antitrust laws, and thus may be considered cartels. They also generally receive partial funding, as well as tax breaks, from the government. These associations, although common, are still prestigious in the structure of Japan's industrial organizations. They have been formed in the fields of computers, integrated circuits, new materials, automotive technology, biotechnology, and aircraft engines, as well as many others. A published work on associations listed sixty-three research associations that were formed between 1961 and 1983 in Japan.[45] An additional thirty-two research associations, covering the years 1983 to 1993, were obtained for this work from a list provided by MITI and are shown in Table 2.1. The technologies covered range over a broad spectrum and involve hundreds of corporations.

Table 2.1
Japan's Research Associations, 1983–1993

Associations	Date Established	Members
New Uses for Light-Weight Oil	1983	Asahi Kasei, Idemitsu Kodan, Kobe Seiko, Cosmo Sekiyu, and Showa Shell Sekiyu, plus seven others
High-Efficiency Manufacturing of Synthetic Textiles	1983	Kanebo, Clare, Toyo Boseki, Mitsubishi Rayon, and Teijin, plus twelve others
Bio-Processing Technology	1983	Ajinomoto, Kao, Mitsubishi Kagaky Kogyo, and Dainippon Ink Kagaku Kogyo, plus two others
Conductive Inorganic Compounds	1983	Sumitomo Denki Kogyo, Nihon Ita Glass, Hitachi, and Matsushita Electric Corporation
Manufacturing Technology for High-Efficiency Resins	1983	Mitsui Toatsu Kagaku, Kurare, Sekisui Kagaku Kogyo, Mitsubishi Kasei, and Mitsui Sekiyu Kagaku Kogyo
Development Manufacturing Technology for Aluminum-Utilizing Powder Metallurgy	1983	Kobe Seiko, Showa Aluminum, Sumitomo Keikinzoku Kogyo, Sumitomo Denki Kogyo, and Toyo Aluminum, plus three others
Research in Form-Memory Alloys	1983	Furukawa Denki Kogyo, Tonen, Sumitomo Tokushu Kinzoku, Mitsubishi Material, and Dowa Kogyo, plus one other
Utilization of Bacteria in the Production Processing of Alcohol Fuel	1983	Kirin Beer, Takara Shuzo, Nikki, Hitachi Zosen, and Suntory, plus four others
Large-Size Heat-Pump Systems	1985	Asahi Glass, Ishikawajima Harima Jukogyo, Ube Kosen, Ohbayashi-gumi, and Kyshu Denryoku, plus thirteen others
Development of New Materials and Systems for Multiple-Unit Housing	1985	Asahi Glass, INAX, Shimizu Construction, Takenaka Komutem, and Nippon Kokan, plus twenty-five others
Light-Water Reactors for Nuclear Power Plants	1985	Ishikawajima Harima Jukogyo, Kawasaki Seitetsu, Kobe Seiko, Showa Denko, and Sumitomo Denki Kogyo, plus twenty-six others

Table 2.1
Japan's Research Associations, 1983–1993 (Continued)

Associations	Date Established	Members
Processing Hydrogen from Coal for Use as an Energy Source	1986	Idemitsu Kosan, Dengen Kaihatsu, Osaka Gas, Tokyo Gas, and Toho Gas, plus four others
Joint Coal-Gas-Chemical Power Plant	1986	Hokkaido Denryoku, Tohoku Denryoku, Chuba Denryoku, Kansai Denryoku, and Chugoku Denryoku, plus six others
High-Efficiency Gas Turbine Power Supply Systems	1986	Ishikawajima Harima Jukogyo, Kawasaki Jukogyo, and Mitsubishi Jukogyo
Manufacturing Systems for Textile Products	1986	Maeda Computer Service, Mitani Komputer System, Emori Shoji, Sakai Elcom, and Hanabusa Sangyo, plus ten others
Precision Machining and Surface Processing Utilizing Laser Beams and Ion Beams	1987	Canon, Kobe Seiko, Komatsu Seisakusho, Toshiba, and NEC, plus sixteen others
Atomic Vapor Laser Separation Method for Uranium	1987	Hokkaido Denryoku, Tohoku Denryoku, Tokyo Denryoku, Chuba Denryoku, and Hokkaido Denryoku, plus seven others
Advanced High-Efficiency Co-Generation Systems	1987	Tokyo Denryoku, Chuba Denryoku, Kansai Denryoku, and Tokyo Gas, Osaka Gas, plus seventeen others
Equipment and Materials Related to Superconductive Power Supply	1987	Tokyo Denryoku, Chuba Denryoku, Kansai Denryoku, Mitsubishi Electric, and Fujikura Densen, plus eleven others
Composite Materials Product Development	1987	Daiko Rozai, Kuroki Kogyosho, Yawata Denki Seiko, Honda Kiko, and Nishi-Nippon Computer, plus three others
Carbon-Based Fuel Cell Power Supply	1988	Denryoku Chuo Kenkyuji, Hitachi, Mitsubishi Electric, Fuji Electric, and Toshiba, plus nine others
Basic Research in Fuzzy Logic and Its Application	1989	Intec, NTT Data Communications, Omron, Toshiba, and Mitsubishi Electric

28

Table 2.1
Japan's Research Associations, 1983–1993 (Continued)

Associations	Date Established	Members
Manufacture of Factory-Built Homes	1989	Asahi Kasei, Asahi Glass, Osaka Gas, Kyocera, and Komatsu, plus thirty-one others
Propulsion System for Ultra-sonic Transport	1990	Ishikawajima Harima Jukogyo, Kawasaki Jukogyo, and Mitsubishi Jukogyo
Solar Battery Power Supplies	1990	Asahi Glass, Oki Electric, Kawasaki Seitetsu, Kyosera, and Sanyo, plus twenty-one others
Advanced New Material Technology	1990	Mitsubishi Material, Asahi Kasei, Nippon Kogyo, Mitsubishi Electric, and Ricoh, plus eighteen others
Phosphoric Acid Type Fuel Cell Power Supply	1991	Hokkaido Denryoku, Tohoku Denryoku, Chuba Denryoku, Hokuriko Denryoku, and Kansai Denryoku, plus nine others
Robot System for Improving Galvanizing Conditions	1991	OM Kogyo, Shinsei Kogyo, Toho Renkin Kogyo, Nankai Renkin Kogyo, and Nankai Aen Rekin, plus three others
New Information Processing Systems for the 21st Century	1992	Oki Electric, Sanyo, Sharp, Toshiba, and NEC, plus eight others
Lithium Cell Reserve Batteries	1993	Osaka Gas, Sanyo, Toshiba, Nippon Denso, and Nippon Denchi, plus six others
System for Observation of Individual Atoms and Molecules	1993	Oki Electric, Kobe Seiko, Olympus, Sharp, and Sony, plus twenty-five others

Source: Japan, Ministry of International Trade and Industry (MITI), Agency for Industrial Science and Technology, "Summary of Research Associations in the Mining and Manufacturing Industries" (Tokyo: Agency for Industrial Science and Technology, April 1, 1993).

Another type of cooperative research organization is the research and development (R&D) support-subsidy foundation (*shien dantai*), which was funded by industry and government to work on seed technology that will grow into future industries. Often these efforts require interindustry and interdisciplinary research that no one single industry can address. They are closer to the usual industry trade associations than the research associations, but classified as scientific or technical organizations and, at times, posses the capability to do in-house research within the association. Some of these foundations—often called associations—are incorporated (*zaidan hojin*), and examples of these are shown in Table 2.2.[46]

Among the key characteristics of Japan's industrial economy is the cooperation of government, industry, and academia in research and development. This activity started as early as the 1950s and is projected to continue into the twenty-first century. Some of the specific areas of research and development that are designated to be worked on jointly are the preservation of the environment and the development of a sophisticated global information networking system.[47]

THE TRADE PROMOTION ASSOCIATIONS

Also among the unique associations of Japan are the export promotion associations. As with the antimonopoly law, no sooner had the occupation forces left Japan than the Diet passed the Export Transactions Law of 1952, and within a year, the Exports Imports Transaction Law (EITL) was enacted, which also included imports. This law allowed cartels to promote exports and impose standards of price, quality, quantity, and design on its members. They also may handle foreign complaints and disputes related to exports, lend and borrow on members' behalf, establish facilities and offices to promote their products, and develop the necessary statistical data for their efforts. These privileges can be broadly interpreted to open the door to behavior resulting in the control of competition, not only of other domestic companies outside the association, but also of foreign firms attempting to serve the Japanese market. A number of examples of this type of association are shown in Table 2.3.[48]

ASSOCIATIONS AND THE LIFE CYCLE

As we review the various types of trade associations in Japan (research associations, export-import promotion associations, and the general industry trade associations, including those functioning as depression cartels), their roles with respect to the industry life cycle, specific industries, and government intervention appears to be related, as shown in Table 2.4.[49]

The extent of parallel and collaborative activities is such as to attempt to reinforce the competitiveness of the industry by focusing on technology, investment, and productivity in relationship to growth rather than profitability. The relative activity level at the various stages of industry life is different for each organiza-

Table 2.2
Partial List of MITI's Incorporated Foundation-Type Institutions

Name	Year Established	Corporate Members	Budget ($U.S. Millions)
Engineering Advancement Association of Japan	1978	136	$ 5.1
Research and Development Association for Future Electron Devices	1981	25	$ 8.2
R&D Institute of Metals and Composites for Future Industries	1981	36	$ 7.1
Japan Fine Ceramic Center	1985	n.a.	$40.0
The Materials Process Technology Center	1985	431	$ 3.3
International Robotics and Automation Center	1985	103	$ 4.7
Electro-Mechanic Technology Advancing Foundation	1988	n.a.	$ 0.4

Sources: Zenkoku Kakushu Dentai Meiken, 1989 (Directory of all types of national associations) (Tokyo: Shiba, 1989), vol. 1; Dick K. Nanto and Glenn J. McLoughlin, "Japanese and U.S. Industrial Associations: Their Role in High technology Policy Making," (Washington, DC: Congressional Research Source, Library of Congress, June 26, 1991), p. 13.

Notes: n.a. = not available. Incorporated foundations = "zaidan hojin."

tion in the business-government structure. As an example, the government, through MITI, is most interested in the initiation of an industry and in its decline. As an MITI official once said, the government is most interested in the "bow and stern of the industry ship." Research associations, on the other hand, are closely involved in the initial and early phases of the product life cycle, while their interest declines with the onset of maturity. The trade and export associations have

Table 2.3
Selected Export Promotion Associations of Japan

Japan Bicycle Exporters' Association

Japan Chemical Exporters' Association

Japan Cotton Textile Exporters' Association

Japan Electric Line and Cable Exporters' Association

Japan Iron and Steel Exporters' Association

Japan Non-Ferrous Metal Exporters' Association

Japan Pharmaceutical Medical and Dental Supply Exporters' Association

Japan Rolling Stock Exporters' Association

Japan Ships Exporters' Association

Japan Special Steel Exporters' Association

Source: MITI Handbook (Tokyo: Japan Trade and Industry Publicity, 1992), pp. 294–304.

Table 2.4
Relative Activity Levels of Government, Associations, and Corporations in Japan during Stages of a Typical Product/Industry Life Cycle

Activity Involved	Product/Industry Stage				
	Early	Growing	Mature	Declining	Late
Government Ministries: MITI, Finance (MOF), etc.	High	Decreasing	Low	Increasing	High
Research Associations	High	Low	None	None	None
Trade Associations	Low	Increasing	Stable	Increasing	High
Export/Import Promotion Associations	Low	Increasing	Stable	Increasing	High
Corporate Investment in R&D	High	Decreasing	Low	None	None
Corporate Investment in Capital Equipment	High	Increasing	Stable	Decreasing	None

parallel increasing efforts while corporate investments and R&D decline. The table, therefore, provides a broad guide for understanding the longitudinal relationship of the various government, association, and corporate activities. The next section focuses on the most important government ministry, MITI.

MITI AND THE ASSOCIATIONS

Due to the kinds of activity and their relationship to growth, as described in Figure 2.2, the various roles of Japanese trade associations in industrial policy have become highly publicized and been frequently discussed in many written works. These writings often relate association efforts and their success to the manner in which the government of Japan and, specifically, the Ministry of International Trade and Industry involve themselves with trade associations. The relationship between government and trade associations in Japan has existed since the Meiji Restoration. Indeed, government in Japan has often been the initiator and the guide of the association movement overall, as well as for specific industry associations.

In today's Japan, the key government ministry for industrial policy is MITI, and a discussion of its organization is key to understanding how industry associations fit into Japan's industrial structure. MITI's broad, private sector scope

Figure 2.2
Relationships between Japan's Government, Industries, and Councils

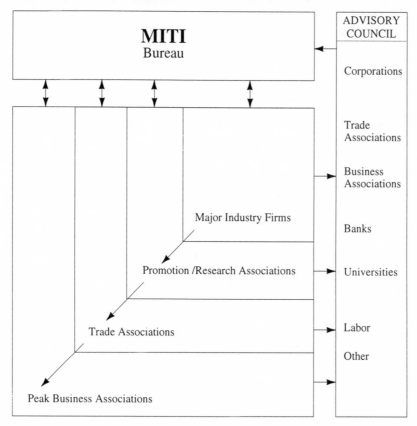

includes all organizations involved in the production of consumer and industrial goods and services as well as those in the production and use of natural resources and energy. Other government ministries are responsible for: foreign affairs; finance, including banking; insurance and securities; agriculture, and construction, transportation, and communications, as well as other national economic sectors. The MITI organization has a vertical component, a horizontal component, and an external or advisory component. The vertical component consists of bureaus responsible for various industry categories. The Basic Industries Bureau covers iron and steel, nonferrous metals, chemicals, biotechnology, and similar industries. The Machinery and Information Bureau's responsibilities include industrial electronics, consumer electronics, data processing, aircraft, autos, and space applications. The Consumer Goods Industries Bureau handles fibers and spinning, textiles, paper and pulp, ceramics, household goods; and the Agency of National Resources and Energy is concerned with electrical power, gas, petroleum, coal, and nuclear energy. The Industrial Policy Bureau is dedicated to commercial, service, and trade activities. All the vertical categories listed here are overseen horizontally by groups that include agencies, offices, and bureaus for technology, intellectual property, small and medium enterprises, international trade, and research and statistics, among the most important.[50]

In addition to the direct supervision of these departments, MITI also appoints various organizational members from external economic activities to sit on advisory councils related to specific industries or issues. The councils act as discussion groups and provide a forum for the discussion of ideas. They supplement the internal MITI activities and include as members trade associations, large corporations, labor unions, trading companies, banks, universities, and the public media. No seated civil or legislative members may sit on the councils. There are advisory councils for textiles, mining, aircraft and machinery, and data processing, among those that are industry specific. Advisory councils for cross-industry issues include the categories of industry structure, small industry modernization, international trade transactions, and product safety and quality. In all, there are over thirty advisory councils.[51]

The representation by trade associations in the councils is very high. In 1979, of sixty-nine members of the Aircraft and Machinery Council; twenty-nine were trade association members, nine were corporations; thirteen were quasi-government institutions such as banks, utilities and research institutes; and the rest were universities, labor unions, and newspapers. The largest group, trade associations, accounted for over 40 percent of the members. In the Industrial Structure Council in 1979, the largest number of members were again trade associations, with twenty-eight of eighty-two members, or almost 35 percent. The list of members by name and by council capacity and present or past employment affiliation was described in 1984 by Ouchi.[52]

By 1992, the name of the Aircraft-Machinery Council was changed to the Aircraft Industry Council. The type of membership for this council and the Industrial Structure Council, as well as the total membership, are shown in Table 2.5. Again,

Table 2.5
Membership in Two Specific Advisory Councils in Japan, 1992

Type of Member	Aircraft Industry Council	Industrial Structure Council
Trade Association	7	16
Manufacturer	1	5
Trading Company	1	-
Commercial Bank	1	5
University	2	6
Newspaper	3	2
Labor Union	1	2
Consumers' Union	-	1
Other	7	7
Current Membership Total	23	44
Total Members Allowed	25	150

Source: Data were taken from Japan, *Government Council Directory '92* [based on information as of May 31, 1992], Tokyo:1992.

Notes: The Aircraft Industry Council was called Aircraft Machinery Council during 1978–1986 and had wider coverage thus the larger membership in1979. Figures shown under the Industrial Structural Council are for its General Committee, besides which there are thirteen other committees. Members of those committees are not made public.

the trade associations account for the largest single type of member, with about 30 percent of members being trade associations on the Aircraft Industry Council and over 36 percent, trade associations on the Industrial Structure Council.

The number and variety of trade associations serving as advisory council members are impressive when the breadth and depth of the corporations are considered. Each association can represent up to hundreds of corporations from the same manufacturing industry. In addition, peak business associations such as the Chambers of Commerce and Industry and the Keidanren are generally included on the advisory councils. Council members are invited for a two-year period, although many remain for a number of terms. Most councils are divided into committees and study groups of twenty to forty members, with more than two thirds generally attending. These smaller groups may meet as often as two to three times per month for three or four hours at a stint. A diagram that illustrates the interrelationship of MITI, the corporations, the associations, and the councils is shown in Figure 2.2. The arrow in the figure shows the tendency of influence.

This interaction in a formal fashion, as well as through multitudes of informal ties, gives the impression to the casual observer of virtual unity in purpose and action by industries. This simplification is partially true, since all individuals and organizations participating in the process will make compromises and may modify, for some purposes, the implementation of any resulting regulations or activities. However, the most important interactive aspect is the total openness of discussion, the study of various questions, the description of alternatives, and the willingness to reach consensus. Only if and when no consensus can be reached, as in cases in which none of the private parties directly involved are willing to make decisions perceived as unfavorable to their self-interest, will MITI apply "administrative guidance."[53]

This interaction in a formal fashion, as well as through multitudes of informal ties, gives the impression to the casual observer of virtual unity in purpose and action by industries. This simplification is partially true, since all individuals and organizations participating in the process will make compromises and may modify, for some purposes, the implementation of any resulting regulations or activities. However, the most important interactive aspect is the total openness of discussion, the study of various questions, the description of alternatives, and the willingness to reach consensus. Only if and when no consensus can be reached, as in cases in which none of the private parties directly involved are willing to make decisions perceived as unfavorable to their self-interest, will MITI apply "administrative guidance."[53]

THE JAPAN FAIR TRADE COMMISSION (JFTC) SURVEY

In order to present a current view of trade associations in Japan, a review of a recent survey of 1,002 trade associations, of which 844 responded, will be presented.[54] It is believed by the Japan Fair Trade Commission (JFTC) that a grand total of over 15,000 trade associations, including very small groups such as local shopkeepers, exist in Japan. The salient points of the survey were:

- In 32 percent of the groups surveyed, group members controlled a greater than 90 percent share of the market for the members' products. In 54 percent of the groups surveyed, group members controlled a greater than 75 percent share of the market.

- Among the various activities of groups, 83 percent of the groups identified the transmission of information from government to industry as part of their activity, and 38 percent dealt with Japanese reaction to international issues.

- For a new member to be admitted to the group, 23 percent of the groups required sponsorship by an existing member, 17 percent required the permission of the Japanese government, 16 percent required it to own manufacturing facilities in Japan, 11 percent required the member to be a Japanese juristic person, 7 percent required a certain number of years of business experience in Japan, and 7 percent required a certain volume of business. Multiple requirements were common.

- A survey of 275 companies with 50 percent or more foreign capital revealed that 68 percent of the companies belonged to a Japanese group. Of those companies that belonged to a group, 77 percent said that a benefit of group membership was easier access to information about government regulation of their industry. Of those companies that belonged to a group, 18 percent said the dues or entrance fees were a burden.

- Among the 32 percent of foreign companies that were not members of Japanese groups, 55 percent complained of lack of access to industry information and 38 percent complained that they were at a disadvantage in addressing the Japanese government.

- In 1991, 21 percent of the JFTC findings of restriction of competition in violation of Article 8 of Japan's Antimonopoly Law were against groups. In 1990, it was 41 percent and, in 1989, it was 30 percent. Since 1981, there have been 39 cases of violations of Article 8 involving groups.

The report provided a view of the activities and functions of Japan's trade associations, and these are shown in Table 2.6. This table is enlightening in its degree of detail regarding association efforts in relation to government, international, and technology issues. Later in this volume, American associations in response to a National Association of Manufacturers survey presented a similar list of activities that will allow an interesting comparison.

This and previous sections have described a broad range of specific forms of industry associations and organizations as well as their roles and activities. The unique ones covered included cartels, research associations, and the trade promotion associations. All these organizations are designed to perform unique roles in the industrial economy so that they will assist, not only the firms' business goals, but also the goals agreed-upon through government-business discussion via the advisory councils and other means.

The high degree of collaboration by business with government can be easily recognized in the roles of each organization.[55] The close actual interactions between business and government in Japan have led to a form of capitalism aptly called collaborative capitalism.

COLLABORATIVE CAPITALISM

In reviewing the past, but with emphasis on the more recent decades, a number of trends with regard to industry associations in Japan can be noted.

If the thesis is true that associations among businesses and government are formed and operate effectively only after times of crisis, such as revolution or defeat after war, and if their formation and effective operation is observed to be fairly constant, one can only conclude that the crisis has to be perceived as constant as well.[56] This conclusion may be the same as expressed by Leonard Lynn and Timothy Mckeown: "In some respects, the Japanese have for the past 120 years regarded themselves as being in a chronic state of emergency vis-à-vis foreign competition."[57] This chronic and constant crisis would certainly, according to theory, have strengthened the use of associations in Japan's industrial policy, at least insofar as they contribute to international competitiveness.

The functions of Japanese industry associations are very broad, and they are supported by law as well as by the ministries' regulations and directives. Over time, they also range from research to commercialization, production and sales,

Table 2.6
Activities and Functions of Japan's Associations
(Survey of 1,002 Associations, Yielding 844 Respondents)

Activity/Function	% Responding "Yes"
Transmitting information about government rules, regulations and policies	83.5
Public relations	71.4
Market research and surveys	67.5
Other government activities (schedules meetings with government regulators)	64.0
"Friendship" (industry networking)	62.7
Formulating official standards and granting official legal certifications	55.3
Studying laws and regulations	55.2
Formal advisory opinions given to government	53.7
Other overseas/foreign-related activities	45.4
Technical/worker training	43.5
Response to international issues/problems	38.0
Self-regulation (codes of ethics)	25.2
Assisting in preparing MITI and other official "Visions" for the industry	22.4
Labor relations issues	20.7
Research on technology and technical issues	19.1
Conferring qualifications and certifications (i.e., professional certifications)	17.9
Voluntary product standards	16.6
Guidance on company management	16.5
Finance and debt guarantee	4.4

Source: Trade Associations Activities and Problems under the Antimonopoly Act [Survey] (Tokyo: Japan Fair Trade Commission, March 1993).

and finally to decline and eclipse for any product or industry life cycle. Their functions appear to be, not only broad, but perhaps in conflict with those performed by foreign associations in many other industrialized capitalist nations. However, similar to most foreign associations, Japanese associations are managed by corporate executives who may not have a high level of ownership stake in the businesses themselves and are, therefore, not too different in means, education, and skills from their international counterparts.

The interrelation of government and business, with the tacit agreement of the general public, is deeper in Japan than in most nations; moreover, the number and kinds of personnel and organizational interrelationships between them also is much greater in Japan than in other countries. It is this aspect of the closeness of businesspeople in formal and informal associations, as well as closeness between them and government, that has caused observers to denote them as "collaborators."[58] The term "Japan Inc." has been utilized to describe the closeness.[59] The word "communitarianism" has also been used.[60] Chalmers Johnson called the Japan system a "capitalist developmental state," and Pat Choate, the economist and public policy spokesperson, called it "network capitalism."[61] More recently, the term "Alliance Capitalism" has been used.[62] I would choose a different term, not as a stand-alone term, but as one to be used later on in comparison with the capitalism of other industrialized nations. The term I would use is "collaborative capitalism." It is a descriptor that will be of further value as the capitalist systems of Germany and the United States come into focus and are compared as the background from which associations and their function and value should be judged. It is also an extension of the terms already developed in describing the United States as employing competitive capitalism and Germany, cooperative capitalism.[63]

Collaborative capitalism is a system in which government and business work together in unison and in a defined manner toward a common understanding of the national economic goals that can be achieved through meeting business objectives. To go further, this form of capitalism assumes that business goals are an essential element in reaching national goals. Collaborative capitalism in Japan can be described by a number of nation-business characteristics, which have come about because of history and tradition, population homogeneity, cultural preferences, and other circumstances, including the American occupation. These characteristics can be related to trade association roles past and present, as well as the general business and economic success of Japan, and can be listed as follows:

1. A close stable government-business relationship whereby the national interests are agreed upon and then passively accepted by a trusting general public.

2. Strong intermediate organizations and practices that interweave the private and public sectors. These include associations, industry councils, and foundations, which may legally act in a joint manner as cartels if so required.

3. The existence of large, efficient corporations with core competitiveness supplemented by keiretsu relationships and other collective or associative behavior.

4. Comparative weakness of labor unions at the level of public policy and national issues. Their strength lies within the firms due only to consensus decision making.[64]

5. Relatively weak influence of consumer groups, citizen interest groups such as environmentalists, and other nonbusiness interest bodies in terms of central government policy.

6. Subordination of foreign interests, including foreign corporations and professionals, that will interfere with the five previously listed characteristics.

This system of collaborative capitalism definitely requires the building of consensus and the collective execution of goals. The use of benchmarks is another aspect of the system.[65] Therefore, the essential value of intermediate organizations such as trade, business, and peak associations is in providing these functions. On this basis one can conclude that the role of associations, as well as other intermediaries in Japan, is an essential ingredient to the exercise of collaborative capitalism.

A small but growing group of observers believe that the basis of collaborative capitalism is producer economics. A recent article by James Fallows provided interesting insights into producer economics as espoused by the German writer Frederich List.[66] The theory and practice of producer economics is found in many countries of Asia, such as Japan, Korea, and Singapore, and many of its influences also exist in France and Germany. In his book *Head to Head*, Lester Thurow provided an easily understood basis for producer economics in Japan as compared to the United States.[67] It can be concluded from his remarks that producer economics depend on society placing a much higher value on group participation, incentives, and rewards than on individual values and benefits. The group orientation in itself assures a much higher probability of success of any group activity, including the need for the extensive use of associations, which provide a group orientation, not only within the firm, but also between firms in an industry, between industries, or in joint industry-government relationships.

The industry trade associations and their diversity and applicability in Japan reflect that nation's focus on producer economics and, especially, collaborative capitalism.

THE CHARACTER OF JAPAN'S TRADE ASSOCIATIONS

The character of associations is, to a large degree, determined by the historical foundations of business organizations. Therefore, it is appropriate after relating the past history of these organizations to describe their present character.

Trade associations in Japan are government sanctioned; that is, if any firms wish to form an incorporated association for trade, they must obtain permission from the ministry with jurisdiction over the industry. In most cases, this is MITI, which gives life to every proto-trade association within its jurisdiction and is in a position to dictate association activities and personnel as a condition of permission to incorporate. MITI can also prevent competition among trade associations by setting the boundaries of activity of each association, unlike in the United States, where associations split up and regroup at their members' whim. The only alternative for a group of Japanese companies that wish to form a trade association but cannot obtain ministry approval is to become an unincorporated association. Such associations exist, but they can be dissolved at any time and most Japanese creditors require guarantors for significant obligations such as rent.

Trade associations in Japan communicate overall industry interests and mobilize industry programs. Industry associations therefore build intraindustry and interindustry consensus. They also provide a pipeline between government and association members. Moreover, associations receive early information from the government on loans, projects, regulatory changes, industrial policy, and other matters. All these comments relate equally to specific associations for cartel activity, research, and trade promotion, as well as to trade associations with a broader role.

In conclusion any U.S. industry competition with its Japanese counterpart must contend with the assistance and strength that Japanese organizations receive from business and government through their trade associations.

NOTES

1. Clyde V. Prestowitz, Jr. *Trading Places: How We Allowed Japan to Take the Lead* (New York: Basic Books, 1988), 67.

2. Philip A. Mundo, *Interest Groups: Cases and Circumstances* (Chicago: Nelson Hall, 1992), 41–66.

3. *MITI Handbook: Profile of MITI Senior Officials* (Tokyo: Japan Trades and Industry Publicity, 1988), 3.

4. Thomas R. Howell, William A. Noellert, Janet H. MacLaughlin, and Alan W. Wolff, *The Microelectronics Race: The Impact of Government Policy on International Competition* (Boulder, CO: Westview Press, 1988), 58–59.

5. Prestowitz, *Trading Places*, 61.

6. Edwin O. Reischauer, *The Japanese* (Rutland, VT: Charles Tuttle, 1977), 71–72.

7. J. W. White, "Economic Development and Sociopolitical Unrest in Nineteenth-Century Japan," *Economic Development and Cultural Change* 37, no. 2 (January 1989): 231–260.

8. Reischauer, *The Japanese*, 71.

9. Takatoshi Ito, *The Japanese Economy* (Cambridge, MA: Massachusetts Institute of Technology Press, 1992), 13.

10. Ibid., 13–23.

11. Leonard H. Lynn and Timothy J. McKeown, *Organizing Business: Trade Associations in America and Japan* (Washington, DC: American Enterprise Institute for Public Policy Research, 1988), 10.

12. Matao Miyamoto, "The Development of Business Associations in Prewar Japan," in *Trade Associations in Business History*, ed. H. H. Yamazaki and M. Miyamoto (Tokyo: University of Tokyo Press, 1988), 5–10.

13. Ibid., pp. xi, xx, nn. 3–5.

14. Teiichiro Fujita, "Local Trade Associations (Dongo Kumiai) in Prewar Japan," in *Trade Associations in Business History*, ed. H. H. Yamazaki and M. Miyamoto (Tokyo: University of Tokyo Press, 1988), 89–92.

15. Miyamoto, "Development of Business Associations," 11–16.

16. Ibid., 25.

17. Ibid., 19–20.

18. Lynn and McKeown, *Organizing Business*, 11–14.

19. Takeo Kikkawa, "Functions of Japanese Trade Associations Before World War II: The Case of Cartel Organizations," in *Trade Associations in Business History*, ed. H. H. Yamazaki and M. Miyamoto (Tokyo: University of Tokyo Press, 1988): 71–73.

20. Ibid., 77–78.

21. Lynn and McKeown, *Organizing Business*, 34.

22. Harumi Matsushima, "Wartime Economy and the Consolidation of the Government Control of Industries in Japan" (in Japanese), *Shakai-Keizai-Shigaku* (Socioeconomic history) 41, no. 6 (1976): 70–94.

23. Takeo Kikkawa, "The Electric Power Federation and the Committee on Electricity: The Electric Power Industry, Cartels, and Consumer Regulations," *Shakai-Keizai-Shigaku* 48, no. 4 (1982): 29–53.

24. Chalmers Johnson, *MITI and the Japanese Miracle: The Growth of Industrial Policy, 1925–75* (Stanford, CA: Stanford University Press, 1982), 110.

25. Hideaki Miyajima, "Comment," in *Trade Associations in Business History*, ed. H. H. Yamazaki and M. Miyamoto (Tokyo: University of Tokyo Press, 1988): 115–116.

26. Miyamoto, "Development of Business Associations," 26.

27. Ibid., 29–30.

28. Matsushima, "Wartime Economy," 70–94.

29. Lynn and McKeown, *Organizing Business* 13.

30. Jeffrey A. Hart, *Rival Capitalists: International Competitiveness in the United States, Japan and Western Europe* (Ithaca, NY: Cornell University Press, 1992), 41.

31. Lynn and McKeown, *Organizing Business*, 24.

32. Ibid., 39.

33. Toshiaki Nakazawa and Leonard W. Weiss, "The Legal Cartels of Japan,"*Antitrust Bulletin* 34, no. 3 (Fall 1989): 641–653.

34. Richard Caves, "Industrial Organization," in *Asia's New Giant: How the Japanese Economy Works* ed., Huch Patrick and H. Rosovsky (Washington, DC: Brookings Institute, 1976) 487.

35. "FTC Gets Tough," *Tokyo Business Today* 60, no. 4 (April 1992): 26–28.

36. Nigel Holloway, "Freeing the Watchdog: Japan Gives More Teeth to Fair Trade Laws," *Far Eastern Economics Review* 145, no. 42 (19 October 1989): 48–49; A. E. Cullison, "U.S. Presses Japan to Increase Fines for Illegal Cartels," *Journal of Commerce* 27,398, no. 387 (18 January 1991): 3; "Up, Fido, Up," *Economist* 312, no. 7,620 (16 September 1989): 80–81.

37. R. L. Cutts, "Capitalism in Japan: Cartels and Keiretsu," *Harvard Business Review* 70, no. 4 (July-August 1992): 48–55.

38. R. L. Cutts, "The Construction Market: Japan Slams the Door (Kansai)," *California Management Review* 30, no. 4 (Summer 1988): 46–65.

39. Tokutaro Imogawa, "FTC Takes Aim at Japan's Own 'Big Three'—Keiretsu, Dango and Saihan," *Tokyo Business Today* 60, no. 4 (April 1992): 29–30.

40. James C. Abegglen and George Stalk, Jr., *Kaisha: The Japanese Corporation* (New York: Basic Books, 1985), 23.

41. Kikkawa, "The Electric Power Federation," 39.

42. Thomas R. Howell, William A. Noellert, Janet H. MacLaughlin, and Alan W. Wolff, *Steel and the State: Government Intervention and Steel's Structural Crisis* (Boulder, CO: Westview Press, 1988), 203–224.

43. Cutts, "The Construction Market," 49.

44. C. Rapoport, "Why Japan Keeps Winning," *Fortune* 124, no. 21 (15 July 1991): 76–77; Michael L. Gerlach, "The Japanese Corporate Network: A Blockmodel Analysis," *Administrative Science Quarterly* 37, no. 1 (March 1992): 105–139; Angelina Helou, "The Nature and Competitiveness of Japan's Keiretsu," *Journal of World Trade* (Law-Economics-Public Policy) 25, no. 3 (June 1991): 99–131; Fusae Ota, "Debunking the Keiretsu Myth," *Journal of Commerce* no. 391 (24 February 1992): 8A; A. E. Cullison, "Japan's

'Old Boy' Network," *Journal of Commerce*, no. 387 (9 January 1991): 8A; Yoshi Tsurumi, "Don't Beat the Keiretsu. Join Them," *New York Times* 144 (2 August 1992): F11.

45. Lynn and McKeown, *Organizing Business*, 147–152.

46. Dick Nanto and Glenn McLoughlin, *Japanese and U.S. Industrial Associations: Their Role in High Technology Policy Making* (Washington, DC: Congressional Research Service, Library of Congress, 26 June 1991), 13.

47. Y. Takeda, "Cooperation of Government, Industry and Academia in Research and Development Activities in Japan, Looking toward the 21st Century," *International Journal of Technology Management* 6, nos. 5–6 (1991): 450–458.

48. Lynn and McKeown, *Organizing Business*, 129–131.

49. Daniel L. Okimoto, *Between MITI and the Market: Japanese Industrial Policy for High Technology* (Stanford, CA: Stanford University Press, 1989), 50.

50. Ibid., 113–119.

51. MITI Handbook: *Profile of MITI Senior Officials*, 199–215.

52. William Ouchi, *The M-Form Society: How American Teamwork Can Recapture the Competitive Edge* (Reading, MA: Addison-Wesley, 1984), 235.

53. Okimoto, *Between MITI and the Market*, 93–95.

54. Japan Fair Trade Commission, *Trade Association Activities and Problems under the Antimonopoly Act* [Survey] (Tokyo: Japan Fair Trade Commission, March 1993).

55. Ito, *The Japanese Economy*, 177–208.

56. Mancur Olson, *The Rise and Decline of Nations: Economic Growth, Stagflation, and Social Rigidities* (New Haven, CT: Yale University Press, 1982).

57. Lynn and McKeown, *Organizing Business*, 32.

58. Reischauer, *The Japanese*, 191.

59. Karel Van Wolferen, *The Enigma of Japanese Power: The First Full-Scale Examination of the Inner Workings of Japan's Political/Industrial System* (New York: Alfred A. Knopf, 1989), 44.

60. George C. Lodge, *Perestroika for America: Restructuring Business-Government Relations for Competitiveness in the World Economy* (Boston: Harvard Business School Press, 1990), 15.

61. Johnson, *MITI and the Japanese Miracle*, 310. Pat Choate, [Luncheon Address], (Address presented at the Semiconductor Industry Association Conference, San Jose Fairmont Hotel, 26 October 1992).

62. Michael L. Gerlach, *Alliance Capitalism and the Social Organization of Japanese Business* (Berkeley: University of California Press, 1992).

63. Alfred D. Chandler, Jr., *Scale and Scope: The Dynamics of Industrial Capitalism* (Cambridge, MA: Belknap Press of Harvard University Press, 1990), 47, 383.

64. Okimoto, *Between MITI and the Market*, 121.

65. Richard Meyer, "Preserving the Wa," *Financial World* 160, no. 19 (17 September 1991): 52, 54.

66. James Fallows, "How the World Works," *Atlantic Monthly,* December 1993, 61–87.

67. Lester Thurow, *Head to Head: The Coming Economic Battle Among Japan, Europe and America* (New York: William Morrow, 1992), 117–124.

Chapter 3

The United States

THE FEDERAL TRADE COMMISION OPENS AN INQUIRY FILE

Over the years, the American semiconductor industry has attempted by many means, including company-to-company as well as informal industry-government meetings, to persuade Japan's electronic equipment makers to purchase more U.S. chips. Finally, in 1983, a high-technology working group made up of American and Japanese government officials and supported by their industries' executives attempted to reach agreement on opening the Japanese semiconductor market. Although the meeting produced other beneficial results to both nations' industries in the areas of import duties and intellectual property, it failed to solve the "Japan access problem," as described by the Americans.[1]

The American position was that for many years Japan had protected, subsidized, rationalized, and guided its electronics firms in the production of chips as the "rice of the electronics industry." The result was a share of market in Japan of 8 percent by U.S. and foreign firms, when these same firms held an overwhelming 52 percent share of market in the world markets outside the United States and Japan and over 80 percent in the United States. Japan's reasons were many and varied, and whether true or not, they were often considered excuses by the American makers.[2]

By 1984, the American chip makers, through the Semiconductor Industry Association, had petitioned the U.S. government to take action, which it did in 1986 via Section 301 of the 1976 U.S. Trade Law, branding the Japan chip market as a closed market. This charge, along with others by private companies in the area of dumping product in the United States, brought the trade friction between the two countries and their respective industries to the boiling point. After months of negotiation, the U.S.-Japan Semiconductor Agreement was signed in September 1986. The terms of the agreement addressed the Japan market access problems, as well as Japanese dumping of chips, which affected the U.S. firms. Many economists have argued about the short- and long-term effects of this trade agreement. The best discussion from the economist's viewpoint was presented by Laura Tyson, now chair of the U.S. Council of Economic Advisors.[3]

In an early effort to stave off this Section 301 action and, in particular, to resolve the market access conflict without the long delays and accusations involved in an intergovernment negotiation or the complex procedural aspects of an interassociation negotiation, Akio Morita, chair of the board of Sony Corp., called on Robert Galvin, chair of the board of Motorola, Inc., to discuss convening an interindustry meeting of senior Japanese and American executives. The discussion resulted in the organization of a meeting to be held on March 15, 1986, in Los Angeles, California, with representation, not only of the two countries' industry leaders, but also of several antitrust counsels, observers from MITI, and the necessary language interpreters.[4] Representatives of the U.S. government, namely, the U.S. Trade Representative's Office and the Department of Commerce, were invited to attend but declined.[5]

No members of the staff of the Electronics Industries Association of Japan or the Semiconductor Industry Association, of which the American chip makers were members, attended. The attempt was to have individual industry members meet with each government's knowledge and approval and to allow others in attendance to act as observers.

The meeting took place at the Beverly-Wilshire Hotel on March 14 and 15 and was attended by ten American chip maker executives; three American antitrust and trade attorneys, including the former dean of the University of Chicago Law School and a former Justice Department antitrust prosecutor; ten Japanese chip and electronic equipment makers; six Japanese industry observers; three officials from Japan's Ministry of International Trade and Industry; and, finally, two interpreters—in all, thirty-four persons. The antitrust counsel approved the agenda in advance, overriding any request for off-the-record discussion. Galvin and Morita were scrupulous to demonstrate that they were obeying the law at every step.

The result of the two-day meeting was reported to U.S. Trade Representative (USTR) Ambassador Clayton Yuetter and to Bruce Smart, undersecretary of the Department of Commerce. It was reported that the meeting was cordial and productive and that the American interest was not to criticize, but to overcome past obstacles to improving sales in the Japan market. It was also reported that the meeting was conducted in a manner that met the requirements of the U.S. antitrust law. The report from the American contingent to U.S. government officials was also that the meeting could result in a meaningful conclusion to the U.S.-Japan government talks on chip access, to be held in Washington, D.C., starting March 27, about two weeks after the Los Angeles meeting.[6]

The conduct of the meeting was to provide the U.S. and Japanese government negotiators with the necessary industry backing to solve a difficult problem in the Japanese commercial market. The American contingent felt that some good might come from the Los Angeles meeting if it was of assistance in smoothing the way for the upcoming Washington meeting of the two governments. The Japanese contingent felt the same since it did not seek either open conflict or a resultant punitive tariff from the U.S. government. Both sides left Los Angeles feeling that the American government could now speak in agreement with a Japanese side that appeared ready to reach a common understanding of what was required. Both sides looked forward to meeting on March 27 in Washington.

Although the Los Angeles meetings were announced to the press in advance[7] and a press release was issued following them,[8] on March 18 a headline in the *Financial Times* of London screamed, "US and Japan plan a cartel."[9] The following day, in spite of the wide publicity given the talks, the same paper referred to a "secret, informal" meeting in Los Angeles.[10] Three days later, *the Economist* of London, after discussing the government talks, went so far as to speculate: "The chip makers may just take matters into their own hands. On March 15-16 [*sic*], the heads of the five leading American and six Japanese chip makers—who produce nearly 90% of the world's semiconductors between them—met in a Los Angeles hotel to talk prices."[11] This totally false report of price fixing was enough to set off a formal U.S. Federal Trade Commission (FTC) investigation.

On April 4, just three weeks after the Los Angeles meeting, the FTC notified all the American participants that they were to account for their presence at that meeting. The response required, among other things, submission of all documents relating to the meeting discussion. Some of the Japanese participants, having subsidiaries in the United States, were also required to respond to the FTC. The FTC document demands were broadly worded and made it clear that the investigators wanted proof that no illicit conversations had occurred in hotel corridors or over lunch. The former Justice Department prosecutor who acted as antitrust counsel for the meeting met with the FTC staff on April 29 and convinced them that the meetings were structured so that complete and accurate records existed and no practical opportunity existed for conspiracy. On the contrary, the meetings were clearly focused discussions aimed at improving the operation of the Japanese market. The following day, the FTC closed its investigation, and on May 1 it withdrew its document demands, less than a month after they were mailed.[12]

The political-economic beliefs that support the inquiry actions of the federal regulatory agency appear to be the same as those represented by the 200-year-old admonition of Adam Smith that any meeting of merchants is potentially detrimental to the public. The reality of U.S.-Japan trade is that buyers and sellers can, and should, meet to improve the operation of the market and thereby benefit the consuming public, Adam Smith notwithstanding.

POST–CIVIL WAR EXPANSION

When the case of the Los Angeles chip makers' meeting is viewed in the light of American business history it is easy to understand why Americans are skeptical about some trade association meetings. The emergence of big business in the latter part of the nineteenth century brought with it various kinds of associated and collusive behavior by industrialists, to the detriment of the public. Because of these roots of suspicion with regard to associations, Americans must keep this history in mind if they are not to succumb to the same dangers in the twenty-first century while organizing business for world competitiveness. A return to predatory practices by associations of corporations would be forcefully rejected.

The period of time that resulted in the suspicion of associations by Americans occurred just after the Civil War. The Civil War period is most often considered the beginning of the U.S. expansion that was to culminate in that nation becoming the world's greatest industrial power by the early twentieth century. The period from 1860 to 1920 is applauded in American economic history for its spectacular growth. The United States in 1870 was responsible for 23 percent of the world's industrial production, second to Germany, but by the beginning of World War I, in 1914, it was 36 percent, equal to that of Britain, Germany, and France combined.[13]

In this period American associations had already been established based on earlier roots in the guilds of Medieval Europe, which were of two types: the guilds of the artisan or craftsman, whose use of skill transformed raw material into products, and the guilds of merchants, who bought the artisans' output and sold it in the marketplace. The craft guilds were often differentiated into varieties such as tanneries, carpenters, and iron workers, and they generally restricted their membership to various levels of skill—masters, journeymen, and apprentices. The main objective of the craft guilds was to produce high-quality goods and obtain a price that would support the accepted quality. With the introduction and development of the factory system, which began in light industries, many of the craft guilds died. However, their vestiges can be found in the craft unions of the twentieth century. The merchants, on the other hand, continued to thrive with the change to the factory system. Although their source of goods changed, their markets were the same, or similar, to those of the past. Their commercial skills were sufficiently general and less product related, and these guilds became the basis for later commercial associations. The merchants, therefore, were able to maintain their contributions to commerce and continued to enjoy high positions in society as well as government.

Both kinds of guilds continued to serve their previous functions, but as a different kind of organization. The changing structure of the economy and industry began to modify the character of these bodies so that they soon became associations—voluntary membership organizations where merchants could seek out members in the same trade or in other trades where interchange was of value, and thereby improve their business positions because of the communications and cooperation that were forthcoming. Some of the earliest associations still in existence today in America are such important institutions as the New York Chamber of Commerce (1768), which was formed by twenty merchants,[14] and the New York Stock Exchange (1792), which literally began trading in the street.[15] These precursors were obviously much simpler versions of today's complex associations, but their functions were essentially the same. The fact that they are over

200 years old merely provides a historical perspective to the continuing values reflected in the history of the commercial association in America.

Prior to the Civil War, agriculture, mining, shipbuilding, furniture, foodstuffs, textiles and transportation were included among the major American industries. The railroads had begun to spring up, the first telegraph lines were built, iron forges were extensive, simple manufacturing operations utilizing interchangeable parts were in operation, and the nation was being opened to the settlement of a vast region. The rapid growth rate of population and the opening of extensive lands were preliminary to the oncoming economic expansion. The major impetus for the late-nineteenth-century industrial growth, however, sprang from the railroad, which provided the technology to move goods on a scheduled basis, and the telegraph, which allowed instantaneous communication between distant points. These basic industries promulgated a broad variety of new industries as well as technologies and commercial change. Technological and commercial change, in turn, brought about great changes in governmental regulations and private institutions.

Previous to these tremendous changes, merchants had formed their trade associations primarily on the basis of their needs to regulate business transactions, improve quality, and support prices, wages, standards, and terms of credit. The associations made requests to government as issues arose, and they made significant contributions to collective social endeavors when needed. Consequently, they were employed to blunt intense competition, influence government, and appear socially responsible. Intervention in commercial activities by government was considered to be as great an evil as ruinous competition. One left the merchant powerless, while the other left him poor.

The American business association movement did not flourish as it did in Japan, with central government impetus. Rather, it grew as the businessman felt his own local interests to be at stake. The chambers of commerce sprang up as local organizations in a few cities such as New York, Chicago, and Boston; however, no nationwide U.S. Chamber of Commerce was established until 1912.[16] The specific industry associations were developed at about the same time, with some of the earliest being the National Association of Cotton Manufacturers (1854), the American Iron and Steel Institute (1855), and the American Brass Association (1853). Among others formed later in this period were the American Bankers' Association (1876), the American Paper and Pulp Association (1878), and the American Transit Association (1882). These tended to have local beginnings before expanding nationally. One example is the Ohio Salt Manufacturers, which banded together as a local trade association in 1851 before expanding into other states and regions. Therefore, although the word *American* appeared in many of their names, these early associations were American only in the sense of nationality, and not in the sense of a nationwide association with broad pervasive strength. In addition, their membership was essentially formed of proprietors and partnerships, with corporations being only a minor portion. Even in the iron industry, which required a relatively higher level of investment, corporations were in the minority.[17]

With the period of the Civil War and its great expansion in commerce and industry, there began a corresponding increase in the charter of corporations, the regulation of banking institutions via the National Banking Act, and the formation of trade associations. Also at about this time, oil was discovered in Pennsylvania (1859), the Bessemer Process for making steel was being transferred to America by Andrew Carnegie (1863), the Homestead Act and the Pacific Railway Act were signed in 1862, and the Western Union telegraph company was incorporated in 1856. The economy was beginning to build on the foundations of large-scale permanent enterprises, and new corporate legal institutions were integral to the new industry structure.

The individuals who were the prime movers of many of the new industries were hard-driving men of modest means who took risks, manipulated people and events, and were talented in at least one functional aspect of the business, whether it be production, marketing, or finance. They included the elder John D. Rockefeller, Andrew Carnegie, Leland Stanford, and Cornelius Vanderbilt. These men proceeded to focus on the basic industries of oil, steel, railroads, and telegraph, while financing and banking fell under the influence of J. P. Morgan and others.[18] They invested, acquired, merged, intimidated, and used all available means to compete intensely in large-scale businesses and basic industries. Often the goal was to cooperate with chosen allies to drive others out of the market. In some cases, the objective was to control market share through control of prices, rebates, profit sharing, and many other means. Although legal at the time, these practices caused their own social dislocation and raised a great deal of ire, first at the state level and then, eventually, at the national level. Before the period of regulation began with the Interstate Commerce Act (1887), trade associations were a favorite mechanism among many other businessmen for controlling production and restricting market environments, thus working against the public interest.[19]

In order to control markets, the first attempt was "to reach informal agreements as to price and output, and then to make more formal agreements (enforced by trade associations) to reduce output, set prices, [and] allocate regional markets."[20] By the 1880s the trade association was the favorite way of organizing markets, and over fifty associations in the United States were essentially serving as cartels for many different specialized product lines.[21] Among the cartels and associations of this time were the Pittsburg and Wheeling Goblet Company, a small, short-lived, glassware cartel, in existence from February 1877 to September 1877;[22] the Gunpowder Trade Association, formed in 1872 through the influence of the DuPont family and dissolved in 1912;[23] the Western Flint and Lime Glass Protective Association of 1874–1877;[24] the American Paper Makers Association of 1878;[25] the Southern Railway and Steamship Association of 1875–1897, which was notable for a fairly successful system of dividing up profits; [26] and finally, another organization that achieved some stability and uniformity in pricing, the American Wholesale Hardware Association of 1870–1900.[27] The incentive to form associations was particularly great in industries where several entrepreneurs had adopted innovative production technologies and organizations requiring high levels of capital and energy.[28] In the period from before the Civil War to 1890, the trade association, along with other vehicles such as informal gentlemen's agreements, formal pools, trusts, and holding companies, were used to restrict competition.[29] These methods resulted in very high levels of corporate concentration and at times led to dominant firms achieving 85 to 100 percent of their market.[30] Some of the best known associations of the period from 1860 to 1890 included those representing large-scale manufacturing industries such as iron and steel, brass, paper and pulp, textiles, meat packing, flour milling, sugar, and chemicals, as well as the specialized product lines.

The government response against the collective and predatory practices of business not only affected the corporations' behavior but also affected their business-related organizations, such as trade associations and labor unions. The response was written into laws that included the Interstate Commerce Act (1887), the Sherman Antitrust Act (1890), and, in 1914, the Federal Trade Commission Act and the Clayton Antitrust Act. All these were designed to either regulate broad business behavior or specific industry activities.[31] The presence of these new U.S. laws made anticompetitive agreements reached within trade associations (or by any means) unenforceable under the law and subject to civil and criminal sanctions. These events were to have a profound impact on the evolution of American business institutions and practices in the United States and abroad from that time forward. After the enactment of these laws, the growth of trade associations slowed since their original purpose of blunting intense competition and protecting against government actions was no longer performed as earlier.[32] Since other means of collective action such as trusts and pools were also now illegal, American business began to undergo one of the highest rates of consolidation in history under the new state incorporation laws, such as those of New Jersey.

After passage of U.S. antimonopoly and anticartel laws, the reaction of American corporations and associations was to begin to recast trade associations as being procompetition and beneficial to the overall good of the consumer by reducing industry costs through higher efficiency. This rather interesting switch helped save the trade association movement from total decline. Another reason why the trade associations remained intact was that many of the participating members were represented by salaried managers and not proprietor-owners or new entrepreneurs. These managers had been developed by the earlier entrepreneurs in order to run the large-scale enterprises which required technical and managerial skill. In fact, the term "managerial capitalism," as used by Chandler, results from this activity. The managers had met to establish professional associations in prior years and their ability to represent corporations as "professionals" made it easy to meet as "management" and to begin to develop services that were the outgrowth of their professional skills. Two of the earliest of these professional societies or associations were a result of the first American large-scale enterprise, the railroads. These were the Society of Railroad Accounting Officers and the American Society of Railroad Superintendents.[33]

One can conclude by looking back in history that associations in existence up to the pre–Civil War period were formed by proprietors and owners working in an informal, ad hoc, "dinner club" manner to take up specific, relevant problems of business, government, and society. This could be called the "club association" period. The period after the Civil War, from about 1860 to 1887 (the time of the Interstate Commerce Act), could be called the period of the "collusive associations." The period from 1888 to the 1920s was that of the "service associations," a description in keeping with their claim of performing activities whose end result was the members' benefit by providing a menu of services to each member firm. Since the antitrust laws affected the competitive behavior of the large business enterprises in such a way that associations would have to assume new roles, the functions they took on reflected these changes. Although they could not set future prices, the new service organizations could gather statistical information on past prices in an open fashion available to all, as well as information on capacity utilization and foreign trade, including imports and exports. Other areas of continued effort included product promotion, setting of standards, economic services such as group insurance and credit bureaus, educational services, conventions, and public relations. In the period between 1887 and the passage of the Wagner Act (1936), associations were also involved in labor relations, with attempts to maintain "open shops" and other antiunion organizational positions. From 1895 to 1904, for example, the National Association of Manufacturers sparked militant employer opposition to the unions and helped significantly slow the labor union movement.

Another area where associations acted, but not from a uniform position, was international trade. In fact, foreign markets were not of major concern. An anecdote related to me by a General Electric Co., Ltd., executive many years ago was that when the General Electric Company was established in the United States in 1892, its president then wrote to the managing director of the General Electric Co., Ltd., in Great Britain to indicate that he saw no problems with the use of the same name by both companies because it was highly unlikely that, with markets an ocean apart, the companies would ever have an identity problem. The American public visiting Great Britain, today, however, would now easily recognize the problem. The areas of labor relations and international trade did affect trade associations in later years, however, especially after 1932.

As the suppression of illegal activities by associations occurred, the founding entrepreneurs became less heavily involved in cooperative activity and managers took over from the leaders in the association activity revolving around services. This tendency to leave association activity to managers rather than entrepreneurial founders unless a crisis occurs appears to continue in some of today's association activities in America. This tendency may also have worked to the detriment of most association activity ever since, although in high-tech associations the entrepreneurs often have remained as active participants.

THE PEAK ASSOCIATIONS

With the increasing interest of government in the behavior of business, the growth of the organized labor movement, the expansion of the international market, and the ascendancy of professional managers as replacements for entrepreneurial owners came the organization of two key American umbrella, or peak, associations, the U.S. Chamber of Commerce and the National Association of Manufacturers. The U.S. Chamber of Commerce, which was established in 1912, is one of the oldest business groups in the United States. The local chambers of commerce of Chicago and Boston played key roles in the establishment of the U.S. chamber, and the membership by this time included local, state, and regional chambers, trade associations, business enterprises, and individuals. The specific concerns of the businessmen-founders were antitrust laws, unionism, and international trade.

In the 1920s, businessmen also received encouragement from the U.S. government in terms of political support from a president and two successive cabinet members, namely, Oscar Strauss, followed by Charles Nagel, both of whom served as the secretary of commerce and labor and both of whom emphasized the need for a closer relationship between business and government. This particular encouragement from government is unique. In later decades, such a move would have been condemned by many as a movement in the direction of an industrial policy.

The U.S. Chamber of Commerce from its beginning was partly a federated organization of local chambers and trade associations; however, individual firms could also be members. To this day, the U.S. Chamber of Commerce has these types of members and still maintains the position that was the basis of its foundation. It has probusiness political objectives and is national in scope. In addition, its focus tends to be on those issues on which there is broad agreement, since any attempt to meet all the needs of different constituents in such a broad organization would be impossible.[34]

The National Association of Manufacturers (NAM) began in 1895 when a group of Ohio machine tool builders became concerned about the possible abandonment of reciprocal international trade treatment by Congress. They were concerned that outright protectionism would be promoted by other businesses. The machine tool makers were often successful exporters, and protectionism was not in their interests.[35] The NAM has attempted to be an umbrella-like structure, which is not unlike the organizational objective of the U.S. Chamber of Commerce. It represents thousands of companies and hundreds of state and local associations of manufacturers, as well as national trade associations. The focus of the NAM is on large organizations numbering in the thousands rather than many other smaller geographical units, such as those in the Chamber of Commerce which number in the 100,000s. However, the NAM is also faced with conflicting views among members because of its broad membership. Partially due to these conflicts caused by the broad spectrum of members in the NAM and the Chamber of Commerce, other associations were later formed to represent various groups. The National Federation of Independent Business (1943) and the National Small Business Association (1937) focused on small business, while large corporations created their own organizations such as the Business Roundtable (1972) and the Committee for Economic Development (1942). However, no mechanism or procedure has existed in any period to reconcile the positions of all these organizations. In fact, the final reconciliation takes place within governmental institutions such as the Congress, for legislative programs, rather than at the level of national industries. This is different than the situation in both Japan and Germany.

By the 1920s, a number of new large industries had developed. Henry Ford formed his automobile manufacturing company in 1903, and Alfred Sloan had completed the corporate formation of today's automotive side of General Motors by 1918. Charles Pillsbury in flour, Alfred Dupont and Herbert Dow in chemicals, Thomas Edison in electrical machinery, and others laid their personal imprint on the structure of huge corporations in large new industries. By the end of this period, the federal government also had made the major changes in regulatory laws that would affect American firms, not only domestically, but eventually also in the global markets of today.

The associations had gone from being entrepreneurial means for market conquest in the latter part of the nineteenth century to serving management tools for improving industry efficiency and shaping public opinion by 1920—a dramatic change that came about in only forty years. It is well worth looking back and noting the national business characteristics in the latter part of the nineteenth century:

1. An expanding domestic market, both geographically and in population growth, was becoming a reality. Rapid exploitation of the nation's geological resources resulted in a high level of world trade.[36]

2. Development of capital-intensive technologies of transportation and communications had accelerated, and these in turn were initiating or accelerating, new basic industries of steel, oil, chemicals, and electrical machinery, along with the financial requisite of investment banking.

3. Enterprises were initially driven by individual entrepreneurs, who were intensely centered on their own corporate interest and yet, at the same time, developed specialized managers and organizations.

4. The legal environment in terms of corporate structure and financing, as well as government regulations, was changing rapidly, and the business-government relationship had eventually turned adversarial.

5. Labor unions were actively opposed by large corporations and their associations, with neither group affecting a final outcome at this time.

This period, which is often referred to in business history as the period of the industrial barons or the rise of the modern corporation, redefined association actions in the United States from collusion to competition and from coercion to cooperation, although this newer form of cooperation within the association was to be closely watched by government. This period in American history is considered the underlying historical basis of America's competitive capitalism.

THE COMMONWEALTH OF BUSINESS

The interwar era of 1918–1945 is one of the most studied boom-bust periods of U.S. economic history. It was a period of postwar recession and then prosperity, which was followed by depression and, finally, war. It also involved rapid shifts in the supply and demand of America's goods and services, as well as in the kinds of goods produced and consumed.

By 1920, the changes brought about by the technological, economic, and political forces in play at the turn of the century were affecting all aspects of corporate life, and the trade associations served as an integral part of a rapidly evolving practice of management. The associations were now functioning as professionally run service organizations that attempted to shape public policy as well as generally upgrade the efficiency of their client firms. The new emphasis was a turnaround from the internal industry collusion of the late 1800s to an open activity that not only served the industry internally, but also focused on affecting public policy. These efforts were domestically focused, well-financed, systematic programs managed by professionals.

The new service organizations directed themselves toward internal or external concerns depending upon the issues, not on ad hoc interests as did the club associations, and yet were more public minded and systematic than the collusive associations. The causes for this change in the character of the associations were several. The new federal antimonopoly laws required a change in business behavior, which in turn was responded to by the use of corporation offices to run businesses instead of being headquarters posts to run pools, trusts, holding companies, and associations. Now, the corporation was the production and marketing firm itself. Parallel to this change was the development of managers who did not normally have ownership in the firm, but whose contribution was the human capital of professional skills. Another significant change was in the nature of the products produced by industry. By the turn of the century, a plethora of commodities based on the internal combustion engine, electrical and communications equipment, and electronics began to make a significant impact on the nature of economic activity. The 1920s was the time of the automobile, radio, telephone, and household electricity. The new products made family life easier and more enjoyable by the personal choice of consumer products, as well as more convenient and better through the greater choice of public transportation and utility services. If the earlier twentieth-century industrial economy was characterized by basic materials, industrial products, and infrastructure, the decade of the 1920s was the beginning of a massive consumer products age. It was an age of roadsters, radios, and movie reels; an age characterized by scale in the mass production of personal commodities and scope in their broad distribution and application.

The 1920s were a period of intense product competition, not only in terms of the price, quality, and service of a given item, but also in the plethora of different products available as well as different makers of the same generic product. There were hundreds of automobile companies that existed between 1900 and 1940, and at least as many local telephone companies. Not only were the robber barons followed by the corporate managers of their firms in terms of management, but in terms of impact, the process-oriented engineers were followed by the product innovators—Thomas Edison, Henry Ford, Alexander Graham Bell, George Westinghouse, Cyrus McCormick, George Eastman, and their like. Consequently, the structure of industry changed as well. While the older industries began a process of corporate elimination, resulting in oligopolies whose members were remarkably the same as those today (including U.S. Steel, DuPont, and Dow, among others), the newer commodity and consumer products industries engaged in an intense competition for market position. The names of the 1950s were just emerging in the 1920s—General Electric, Kodak, Ford, and others.

New trade associations sprang up representing new industries, and the older peak business associations such as the Chamber of Commerce and NAM, gained new members. The new associations were in the same mold as the pre–World War I groups in terms of functions, but now the product content of their services had changed. For example, standards for automotive products were now being developed, as well as standards of basic material testing, which had emanated from the larger, earlier basic metals industries. Although the product focus and the production and marketing aspect of industries had changed the basic functions of trade associations remained essentially the same. Perhaps the only function that received greater emphasis was the determination to confront unionism and to address international trade issues, but this related to most businesses and not merely the newer industries. The 1920s were also a period when government appeared friendly to the association movement. Several secretary of commerce appointees continued to encourage the formation of the U.S. Chamber of Commerce. Herbert Hoover, as candidate and president, was also friendly to the association movement, and finally, even the Supreme Court appeared to be siding with the associations and their activities to a greater degree than in the past.[37]

Some of the newer trade associations, designated by their present-day names, were:[38]

   The Computer & Business Equipment Manufacturer Association (1916)
   The Motor Vehicles Manufacturing Association of the U.S. (1913)
   The Aerospace Industries Association of America (1921)
   The National Electric Manufacturing Association (1926)
   The Electronic Industries Association (1924)
   The Graphic Arts Technical Foundation (1924)

New tests, however, faced the associations with the market crash of 1929 and the subsequent Great Depression. Stock prices plunged, construction was in the midst of a decline, agriculture was depressed, world trade had broken down, labor had not shared in the productivity gains, many business leaders had engaged in unhealthy corporate practices, the market for some products (such as the automobile) began to slow, knowledge and leadership with regard to monetary and fiscal policy were inadequate, the financial system was in disarray, and finally, while all this happened, the U.S. government maintained a confirmed laissez-faire attitude, and thus, a leaderless role in recovering from the blows.[39]

The only depression measure that the Hoover administration approved was establishment of the Reconstruction Finance Corporation, which lent money to banks, railroads, and the insurance companies, but not to manufacturing industries or for public works. Industrial leaders were of mixed opinions. W. Gilford of AT&T, as head of the Emergency Committee for Employment, decided it was bad for the government to intervene. Just months before he laid off thousands of workers, Henry Ford said that there was enough work and that people were just lazy. W. Tragle of Standard Oil suggested that antitrust laws be suspended, and finally, G. Swope, the president of General Electric, put forward a daring proposal known as the Swope Plan.[40] The plan involved the use of associations to cartelize the industries to ensure profits while remaining sensitive to labor and consumers. The associations would self-regulate themselves and participate in economic planning.

The New Deal took over at the depth of depression in 1933 and, in response to its devastating impact, began to move in new and ground-breaking directions. These included devaluation of the dollar, with an abandonment of the gold standard, an artificial increase in the price of silver, enactment of farm price supports, strengthening of the Federal Reserve System, regulation of the banking and securities industries, and the establishment of Social Security. Most pertinent to this area of interest, the New Deal established the National Recovery Administration (NRA).

The National Industrial Recovery Act (NIRA), which was passed in 1933 was an original and bold step to lift the country from the depths of the depression. It was an attempt to affect the recovery of an industrial economy by focusing on the major industries of the nation and on their organization and operation. The attempt to create and manage the NRA created conflicts of ideology in much the same way as the other New Deal initiatives, which were approved to help the small farms, small businesses, and the "working man" of the labor force and included farm price supports, the regulation of banks, and Social Security. However, the NIRA was meant to help companies in major industries, many of which were very large corporations. Although these firms employed tens of thousands of workers, purchased goods from thousands of small businesses, and often bought enormous amounts of agricultural products for processing into food and industrial products, they were still distrusted as "big business."

The act brought forth a great deal of debate. It was a departure from the "rugged individualism" and the ideals of "free competition," and brought back images of the trusts of only fifty years earlier. The arguments and debates went on primarily between three groups, each of which had its own beliefs and opinions, which focused on different versions of business structure.[41] The first view was of an alliance or commonwealth of business. The industrialists would form rational cartels, which would plan the economy and ensure profits, but not at the expense of the consumer or labor. Government as a party to these agreements of business would not only oversee the activity from the viewpoint of business, but would be sensitive to consumer and labor concerns. The government would also penalize the "chiselers," as those who did not abide by the cartel agreements were called. This vision had a resemblance, some felt at that time, to the cooperatives of European fascists. Today, perhaps, it would be likened to the depression cartels of Japan.

The second vision was one of a cooperative economic democracy, a system under which groups consisting of business, labor, and consumer members would organize themselves and rationalize their behavior and activities so that all could achieve the benefits of the resulting better economy. This vision was supported by those to the left of center politically, and it appeared to have a slight similarity to the 1930s Soviet ideal of collectivism. On the other end of the spectrum, the third vision was far to the right politically and represented the most rigorous and intense enforcement of free competition. It foresaw the economic improvement coming from an atavistic economy in which the largest corporations and their practices would be attacked for forestalling recovery by their monopolistic and oligopolistic practices. The National Recovery Act, depending on interpretation, could be used to implement any one of these three visions: industry cartelization, joint national planning, or the aggressive enforcement of competition.[42]

There were many precursors to the NRA. Not insignificant among them was the Swope Plan, which represented the first view, that of cartelization. In 1931, Gerald Swope, president of General Electric Co., authored the plan, and his vision was of an economy based on a cartel system managed by trade associations.[43] It was to be a forum of industrial democracy that would lead to equitable returns to all sectors of society. However, President Hoover (who earlier, as secretary of commerce, as well as while president, had been a leading supporter of trade associations) condemned the Swope Plan as being beyond his idea of voluntary cooperation. He felt that mandated structure and management of an industrial economy by business was too orderly and rigid a rationalization.[44]

From the work of Swope and others, however, came the support by the New Deal for a cooperative economic activity. The administration quickly put a bill together incorporating the central ideas: self-governing trade associations that would write their own codes of compliance and enforce them through public agencies with minimum government modification or supervision.[45] Within a year, codes of fair competition for 450 industries covering 23 million workers were passed. Before the law was declared unconstitutional in 1935, a total of over 550 codes had been passed, covering the entire range of nonagricultural industry.[46]

Among the provisions of the codes were minimum prices that were fixed either directly or indirectly; legalized and regulated open price systems, covering not only past price statistics but also current and future prices, with identification of the sellers; regulation of nonprice competition such as advertising, credit terms, and trade-in allowances; control of production; and last, code authorities to enforce the codes.[47]

Soon, however, the entire process began to have among its critics consumers and farmers who thought prices were being raised, economists and sociologists who saw free competition and consumer sovereignty being destroyed, small businessmen who saw themselves as being eliminated, administrators within the NRA itself who argued about how far the codes should go, and finally, U.S. senators siding with critics who charged that monopolies had been formed. By 1934, the NRA was being scaled back, and finally, in 1935, it was declared unconstitutional and the attempt at an industrial self-governing democracy was over.

From 1935 on, the association movement in the United States declined. Countering associations, labor received a boost from the Wagner Act (1935), the courts had declared the association work of the NRA unconstitutional (1935), the academic world publicly condemned the association practices as encouraging monopoly, and farmers and small businessmen, who distrusted associations based on their NRA experience, were finally relieved. Only in 1939, with the coming of World War II and the need to mobilize wartime industrial production, were the associations able to present themselves as contributing positively to overall national purposes.

POST-WAR COMPETITIVE CAPITALISM

In terms of association activity, the years immediately following the war's end in 1945 were tied to the new peacetime economic conditions and to the completion of the political programs of the New Deal. The association movement continued its immediate prewar level of service organization activity in industry and government matters. The antitrust laws, the 1930s labor laws, and the pervasiveness of government regulations had given associations less latitude to perform their functions. The formation of new associations had been declining from the 1930s peak caused by the enactment of the National Recovery Act. By the 1980s, the number of association formations appears to have steadily declined to less than half the formation of the mid-1930s, as shown in Figure 3.1.

In addition, the rapid development of new products within older industries and the specialization of new products within industries had led to many name changes among existing associations. Since 1970, it has been estimated that over 60 percent of the existing associations have changed their names and that name changes have occurred in all the Standard Industrial Code (SIC) industries, as defined by the U.S. department of commerce. The rapid development of the electronics, aerospace, chemical products, and energy industries brought about new expansion activity and new names in these areas.[48] It should be noted that this trend of increasing expansion and proliferation of new names while formations declined is suspected to have happened in the professional societies as well. The

Figure 3.1
Association Formation in the United States by Decade

Number of Associations

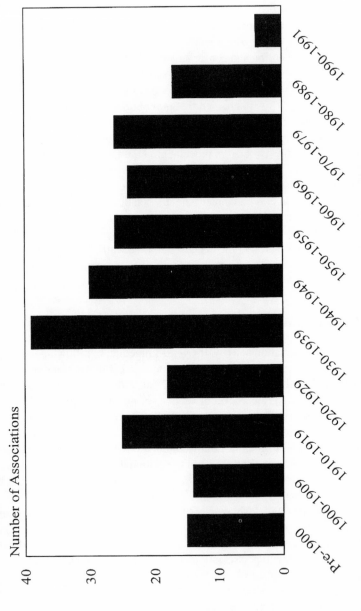

Source: "Manufacturing Trade Associations," A survey conducted by the National Association of Manufacturers, Washington, D.C., 1991.

reasons are also related to changes that occurred in U.S. industries, their firms, and their parallel associations.

By the late 1970s, the sense that the economic circumstances of the United States had changed and the country was in economic decline was being shared by a number of observers. Among the many reasons given for decline were the energy crises of 1973 and 1979–1980, accelerated world inflation after the ending of fixed exchange rates in the 1970s, underinvestment in the private sector while overspending occured in the public sector, overexpansion of the money supply, decline in personal savings, increased regulation of business, high cost of defense, reduction in civilian R&D spending and increased time to commercialize research, deterioration of the nation's infrastructure, decline in educational accomplishments and, finally, deterioration of the American value system.[49]

In itself, the number of reasons given indicates that the problem may not be easy to define; however, the precise definition is not necessarily essential to an approximate solution that may help reverse the decline in the U.S. economic position. The nation's economic decline, however, has become a concern of many trade associations because they believe that their industries must proactively participate in a national solution if they are not to be overwhelmed by the myriad of problems facing the nation as a whole. Associations, in keeping with all responsive organizations, are attempting to react to these changes in the business environment that have occurred since the mid-1970s. The conditions that American businesses would characterize themselves as confronting today are:

1. An expanding global base for production and marketing in which goods, services, capital, and people appear to move easily and in increasing numbers across national borders.

2. Foreign competitors working closely with their governments, with the result that American businesses feel a need for closer liaison with the U.S. government if a "level playing field" is to be obtained.

3. Knowledge-intensive industries, requiring high R&D and capital equipment costs, especially in intermediate products, and enabling technologies that are central to global competitiveness, have undergone rapid growth and a pervasive economic and social impact.

4. Older managerial hierarchies in transformation in an attempt to implement efficiencies from newer managerial philosophies such as "lean production," "first to market," and "flatter organizations."

5. Greater government involvement in areas such as the environment, health, and safety; international trade; and dual-use technologies.

6. Labor unions, consumer groups, and other external interest groups that tend to combine on an ad hoc basis by issue, making the industries' response more difficult and costly.

When viewed in total, association changes in the 1970s and 1980s were a result, in large degree, of changes in industry structure, new technologies, international trade and competition, industry-related interest group concerns, and government involvement. With regard to industry structure in the United States, the mature industries appear to be consolidating. Many basic industries, such as steel, textiles, and rubber, appear to have matured and been consolidated through mergers and acquisitions, with the result that their association formation has declined and association membership has vastly changed. While some basic industry trade associations have declined in number, those in the electronics, chemicals, machinery, and transportation industries, and especially in their high-technology segments, have expanded in the number of members, and the specialization is reflected in name changes and breakaway segments. Thus, changes in the U.S. industrial structure in terms of products, scale of production, growth, concentration, competition, and the like have affected the formation and structure of trade associations.[50]

As an example, the U.S. electronics industry revenues of the mid-1920s were less than $100 million per year. The industry had few associations, the most prominent being the Electronic Industries Association (EIA) (1924), the Computer and Business Equipment Manufacturers Association (CBEMA) (1916), and perhaps to some degree, the National Electrical Manufacturers Association (1926). Today, the U.S. electronics industry revenue is over $300 billion per year, and the membership in the American Electronics Association (1943) is about 3,500 firms, the Electronic Industries Association, 1,000 members, and CBEMA, over forty members. These are only three of the ten or more electronics associations that can be named today. Famous electronics manufacturers names of the past—Radio Corporation of America, Philco, Emerson, Burroughs, and many others—are gone, having either been acquired, merged, or failed. Industry concentration ratios have changed, as have the identities of the firms making up the top ten in any industry. For example, the top ten firms in the computer and semiconductor industries ten years ago and those of today are substantially different. The comparisons are shown in Tables 3.1 and 3.2, respectively.

Major segments of the electronics industry, such as computers and semiconductor products, are only two of the examples of structural change. The same analysis can be applied to many other industries and trade associations. The name change frequency is only one such measure; another, more comprehensive means is an input-output table of the United States, which identifies the sources of such changes.[51] A study of the effect of mergers, acquisitions, and takeovers on associations has shown a dwindling membership base, a reduction in dues income, the loss of executive participation and its attendant institutional memory, and loss of loyalty to the industry. Associations have responded by creating new services, becoming niche marketers, and finding new ways to recruit members.[52]

Technological change has come to the fore in several areas, including precompetitive technology cooperation within an association, in terms of lowering costs but also in terms of competing globally with industries based in countries where the collective civilian R&D per capita is high, as in Japan and Germany, and cooperative civilian R&D is common. One of the results of this concern in the

**Table 3.1
Top Ten U.S. Computer System Companies, 1980 and 1990
(Ranked by Revenue)**

Rank	1980	1990
1	IBM	IBM
2	Digital Equipment	Digital Equipment
3	Burroughs	Apple
4	Control Data	Hewlett-Packard
5	NCR	Unisys
6	Sperry	Compaq
7	Hewlett-Packard	Sun Microsystems
8	Honeywell	Amdahl
9	Xerox	AT&T
10	Wang Laboratories	NCR

Source: Provided by Thomas Burns, Computer Service Director, Dataquest, April 1992.

Note: Unisys was formed by the merger of Burroughs and Sperry.

**Table 3.2
Top Ten U.S. Merchant Semiconductor Companies, 1980 and 1990
(Ranked by Revenue)**

Rank	1980	1990
1	Texas Instruments	Motorola
2	Motorola	Intel
3	National Semiconductor	Texas Instruments
4	Intel	National Semiconductor
5	Fairchild	Advanced Micro Devices
6	Mostek	Harris
7	RCA	AT&T
8	Advanced Micro Devices	LSI Logic
9	General Instruments	Analog Devices
10	Harris	VLSI Technology

Source: Dataquest, April 1992.

United States was the passage in 1983, at the urging of several electronics industry associations, of the National Cooperative Research Act, which allows pre-
competition cooperative research by private corporations without violation of the
antitrust laws.[53] It encourages companies to undertake joint research that is too
risky to be undertaken by a single firm. The result of this change in the United
States, where fear of the antitrust laws had previously deterred such a formation,

was the rapid establishment of R&D consortia. Most notable among these are the
organizations listed in Table 3.3.

Table 3.3
Prominent American Research and Development Consortia

Consortium	Established	Industry	1992 Budget (Millions of U.S. Dollars)
Bellcore	1984	Telecommunications	$1,200
Great Lakes Composites Consortium	1990	Advanced Composites	20
Microelectronics and Computer Technology Corporation	1983	High-Value Electronics and Information Systems	45
MCNC	1980	Electronics and Information Technology	30
National Center for Manufacturing Sciences	1986	All Industries	175
Ohio Aerospace Institute	1990	Aerospace	7
SEMATECH	1988	Semiconductors	200
Semiconductor Research Corporation	1982	Semiconductors	37
Software Engineering Institute	1984	Software	36
Software Productivity Consortium	1985	Aerospace and Electronics	15

Source: List obtained from L. Sumney, president of the Council of Consortia CEOs, 1990.

Since the enactment of the NCR Act, over 250 cooperative research consortia
have been created in the United States, representing many segments of U.S. industry. The consortia are organized in many different ways and work on projects
ranging from basic research to applied technology. Some are based on an alliance
of industry, government, and academia.[54] The research consortia efforts have only
been recent, and insufficient time has pased to evaluate the overall impact.

Changes in international trade and competitiveness became the major concern
of some associations that compete with major national industries in other countries, such as chemicals and machinery in Germany and electronics and automobile equipment and products in Japan. The result of these concerns has been an
intense level of activity involving governments, industry associations, and inter-

national bodies with regard to product dumping, foreign access, and intellectual property rights. Although a single firm may take action against foreign governments and firms through federal laws that require the U.S. government to act, the likelihood of one company alone succeeding in such an approach is not very high. However, as firms join in associations, their actions with regard to international issues is strengthened and the likelihood of success increases substantially.

One special effort to improve international trade and foreign access is the Trading Company Export Law. The law, passed in 1982, allows companies to form associations with functions that are not subject to antitrust laws. Although there were high expectations, with regard to companies formed under this law, no notable degree of success has been reported.

The recent post-war period in the United States has been characterized by intense competition with a higher level of association activity including technology consortia in response to competition from foreign firms both here and abroad. Government actions have assisted industry groups but not to the collaborative degree existing in Japan. Business-government relationships in the United States are still rooted in competitive capitalism.

THE FUNCTIONS OF TRADE ASSOCIATIONS

It is a major task for trade associations to assimilate and accommodate to the wishes of their members with respect to all public policy issues of vital interest. Despite the criticality, little data exists with regard to how effectively American associations evaluate or act on these issues. There is even less data on how effective each association has been in achieving these objectives, and reported results indicate a wide variation in the success of associations in achieving these public policy goals. However, some indications can be noted if the actual overall functions or activities of associations are reviewed. The functions of U.S. associations are often divided into "traditional" and "government relations." A listing of functions does not result in a determination of the objectives of an association, but it does aid in assessing where their efforts are applied. The objectives of trade associations are usually industry specific, although more general areas of public policy are sometimes included. It is this latter area that will receive further discussion in the last part of the book. In order to complete that picture of the U.S. trade association movement, a review of the typical current trade association functions is shown in Figures 3.2 and 3.3, which depict traditional and government-relations functions, respectively.

The traditional functions shown in Figure 3.2 are familiar to most business managers and are found in most American associations. They tend to consist of services that can be provided to member firms because of their willingness to share these types of data and tasks.

The government functions shown in Figure 3.3 primarily involve the monitoring and lobbying of state and federal officials and agencies. These functions receive a great deal of attention in American associations since the formal resolution of industry concerns only occurs when the relevant associations learn of the existence of key issues for debate.

Last, a major impact on trade associations has been made by other external interest groups who have become concerned with the behavior of the industries and the associations that represent them. Quite often these groups consider the trade associations themselves, as well as the individual company members, to be their adversaries. Groups representing the environment, workers' health and safety, and workers' benefits, including insurance and pensions, consumer health, and economic rights fall into this category. The number of these types of groups is extremely high. The American Society of Association Executives has publicized the fact that trade associations are only a part of the American interest group representation. One writer even indicated that business groups represent only 17.4 percent of the interest groups in the United States, as is shown in Table 3.4.[55] However, a closer analysis would indicate that organized business is vastly underestimated in a figure such as 17 percent. Organized business not only employs trade associations, the individual firms belong to a number of associations, employ lobbyists, retain law firms, and hire public relations experts to press their case. Overall, one could argue that although business may appear to be represented by a small percentage of groups, it has a very high profile in matters relevant to its interests.

One other trend has exhibited itself in recent years: the formation of alternative, ad hoc alliances by firms that choose not to use their associations. A recent survey by the American Society of Association Executives (ASAE) lists 180 Washington coalitions in 1988, up from 128 in 1986.[56] It would appear that these ad hoc groups actually compete with associations in the representation of organized business.

Today, the U.S. trade associations; their broader, peak associates, the chambers of commerce and NAM; and their narrower associates, including the new research consortia, appear to have similar structures and functions to the corresponding Japanese and German associations. There are, however, a number of major, key areas of difference. These differences include, among others, legalized and formalized member and association privileges and responsibilities, antitrust or antimonopoly laws and their application, the characteristics of the hierarchal aspects of peak associations, and finally, and perhaps most important, the nature and degree of government relationships.

THE CHARACTER OF U.S. TRADE ASSOCIATIONS

The character of associations is, to a large degree, determined by the historical foundations of business organizations. Therefore, it is appropriate, after relating the past history of these organizations to describe their present character. At the end of the previous chapter, Japan's trade associations were characterized in

Figure 3.2
Frequency of Selected Traditional Functions

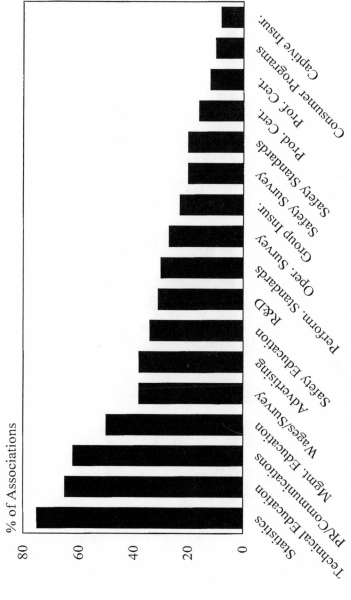

% of Associations

Source: "Manufacturing Trade Associations," A survey conducted by the National Association of Manufacturers, Washington, D.C., 1991.

Figure 3.3
Frequency of Selected Government Relations Functions

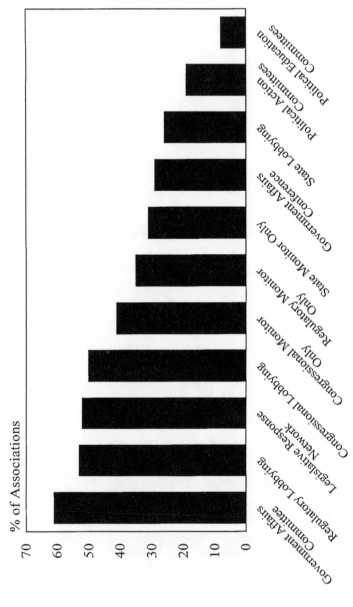

Source: "Manufacturing Trade Associations," A survey conducted by the National Association of Manufacturers, Washington, D.C., 1991.

Table 3.4
Types of U.S. National Associations: Quantity and Percentage of Total Associations

Type of Allocation	Number	Percentage
Trade, business, commercial	3,806	17.4
Public affairs	2,292	10.5
Health and medical	2,162	9.9
Cultural	1,872	8.5
Social welfare	1,686	7.7
Hobby	1,471	6.7
Scientific, engineering, and technical	1364	6.2
Educational	1,268	5.8
Religious	1,169	5.3
Agricultural and commodity exchanges	914	4.2
Athletic and sports	838	3.8
Legal, governmental, public administration, and military	775	3.5
Fraternal, foreign interest, nationality, and ethnic	570	2.6
Fan clubs	561	2.6
Veteran, hereditary, and patriotic	404	1.8
Greek and non-Greek letter societies	337	1.5
Labor unions, associations, and federations	254	1.2
Chambers of commerce	168	0.8
Total	21,911	100%

Source: Leonard Freedman, *Power and Politics in America* (Pacific Grove, CA: Brooks/Cole Publishing Co., 1991), p. 77. Reprinted by permission of Wadsworth, Inc.

order to best understand their roles. The same type of description is now given for American associations.

American trade associations are essentially private and voluntary. They are also closely scrutinized for collusive behavior that may be considered detrimental to the public interest in terms of their industry's pricing, quality, safety, and other marketplace factors. The emphasis on antitrust enforcement in this country has greatly influenced the way in which associations are viewed.

American firms easily join and leave associations, form new ones as they abandon others, set up competing, ad hoc business interest groups, and take all the actions with regard to business organizations that are expected in our pluralistic society. Consequently, association membership tends to be unstable and association actions tend to be uncertain. Government does not administer their formation nor oversee their activities. In recent years, however, there is a tendency for private firms to join together in research consortia to provide precompetitive research. These consortia are cost-effective as well as excellent time savers, and they increase the speed of knowledge diffusion. Although joint manufacturing is permissible now by law, little activity has taken place in this area as yet.

Overall, U.S. trade associations are unstable, redundant, and limited rather than expansive, due to the laws and regulations. On the other hand, they are private, voluntary, and flexible, as befits a pluralistic society.

NOTES

1. Thomas R. Howell, William A. Noellert, Janet H. MacLaughlin, and Alan W. Wolff. *The Microelectronics Race: The Impact of Government Policy on International Competition* (Boulder, CO: Westview Press, 1988), 102.

2. *Japanese Market Barriers in Microelectronics* (San Jose, CA: Semiconductor Industry Association, 14 June 1985).

3. United States trade representative, *Arrangement between Government of Japan and Government of the U.S.A. Concerning Trade in Semiconductor Products* (Washington: U.S. Government Printing Office, 1986).

4. "Japan, U.S. Semiconductor Industry Leaders to Meet" (Kyodo News Service, 8 March 1986).

5. Invitations were sent to Ambassador Clayton Yuetter, U.S. trade representative, and Malcolm Baldridge, secretary of commerce.

6. The March 27 meeting in Washington, DC, did not result in any significant progress.

7. "Japan, U.S. Semiconductor Industry Leaders to Meet."

8. "U.S., Japanese Semiconductor Delegates Meet in Los Angeles," [Press release by meeting council] (Los Angeles; 15 March 1986).

9. "U.S. and Japan Plan Cartel," *Financial Times* [London], 18 March 1986; 24.

10. "U.S., Japanese Chip Industry Leaders Meet," *Financial Times* [London], 19 March 1986, 7.

11. "A Cartel to Stop America's Chip Makers from Feeling Dumped Upon," *Economist*, 18 March 1986, 70.

12. Author's correspondence with attendees.

13. Alfred D. Chandler, Jr., *Scale and Scope: The Dynamics of Industrial Capitalism* (Cambridge, MA: Belknap Press of Harvard University Press, 1990), 4.

14. *Association Fact Book* (Washington, DC: American Society of Association Executives, 1992), 11.

15. Nathan Rosenberg and L. E. Birdzell, Jr., *How the West Grew Rich* (New York: Basic Books, 1986), 220.

16. Philip A. Mundo, *Interest Groups: Cases and Circumstances* (Chicago: Nelson Hall, 1992), 68–69.

17. Daniel E. Diamond and John D. Guilfoil, *U.S. Economic History* (Morristown, NJ: General Learning Press, 1973), 290.

18. Ben B. Seligman, *The Potentates: Business and Businessmen in American History* (New York: Dial Press, 1971), 114–177.

19. Chandler, *Scale and Scope*, 72.

20. Ibid., 71–72.

21. Alfred D. Chandler, Jr., *The Visible Hand: The Managerial Revolution in American Business* (Cambridge, MA: Belknap Press of Harvard University Press, 1977), 317.

22. James S. Measell, "The Pittsburg and Wheeling Goblet Company," *Western Pennsylvania Historical Magazine* 71, no. 2 (June 1988): 191–195.

23. Donald A. Grinde, Jr., "The Powder Trust and the Pennsylvania Anthracite Region," *Pennsylvania History* 42, no. 3 (1975): 207–219.

24. James S. Measell, "The Western Flint and Lime Glass Protective Associations, 1874–1887," *Western Pennsylvania Historical Magazine* 66, no. 4 (October 1983): 313–334.

25. Willard S. Bromley, "The Making of Forest Policy in Pulp and Paper Trade Associations, 1878–1986," *Journal of Forest History* 30, no. 4 (October 1986): 192–196.

26. David A. Argue, "Dividing Cartel Profits: The Southern Railway and Steamship Associations," *Essays in Economics and Business History,* 9 (1991): 277–293.

27. William H. Becker, "American Wholesale Hardware Trade Associations, 1870–1900," *Business History Review* 45, no. 2 (1971): 179–200.

28. Chandler, *Scale and Scope*, 72.

29. Rogene A. Buchholz, *Business Environment and Public Policy* (Englewood Cliffs, NJ: Prentice Hall, 1992), 31.

30. Alex Groner, *The American Heritage History of American Business and Industry* (New York: American Heritage Publishing Company, 1972), 68–70.

31. Buchholz, *Business Environment*, 32.

32. Chandler, *Scale and Scope*, 73–75.

33. Chandler, *Visible Head*, 130.

34. Mundo, *Interest Groups*, 67–101.

35. Leonard H. Lynn and Timothy J. McKeown. *Organizing Business: Trade Associations in America and Japan* (Washington, DC: American Enterprise Institute for Public Policy Research, 1988), 7.

36. Gavin Wright, "The Origins of American Industrial Success, 1879–1949," *American Economic Review* 80, no. 4 (September 1990): 651–688.

37. Browning M. Carrott, "The Supreme Court and American Trade Associations, 1921–1925," *Business History Review* 44, no. 3 (1970): 320–338.

38. Gale Research, *Encyclopedia of Trade Associations* (Chicago: Gale Research, 1991).

39. Diamond and Guilford, *U.S. Economic History*, 80.

40. Seligman, *The Potentates*, 316–317.

41. Ellis W. Hawley, *The New Deal and the Problem of Monopoly* (Princeton, NJ: Princeton Press, 1966), 35.

42. Ibid., 35–50.

43. In J. George Frederick, ed., *The Swope Plan: Details, Criticism, Analysis; Plan by Gerard Swope* (New York: Business Course, 1931).

44. Hawley, *The New Deal*, 42.

45. Ibid., 37–42.

46. Michael M. Weinstein, "Some Microeconomic Impacts of the National Industrial Recovery Act, 1933–1935," in *The Great Depression Revisited*, ed. K. Brunner, (Boston: Martinus Nijhoff, 1981): 263.

47. Hawley, *The New Deal,* 57–62.

48. National Association of Manufacturers, *A Survey for Manufacturing Trade Associations* (Washington, DC: National Association of Manufacturers, 1991), 11.

49. Robert U. Ayres, *The Next Industrial Revolution* (Cambridge, MA: Ballinger Publishing, 1984), 11–45. Anthony Harrigan and William Hawkins, *American Economic Pre-Eminence: Goals for the 1990's* (Washington, DC: U.S. Industrial Council Educational Foundation, 1989), i-ii.

50. Nancy Davis, "Restructuring America's Trade Associations," *Association Management* 41, no. 8 (August 1989): 50–61.

51. Stanley J. Feldman, David McClain, and Karen Palmer, "Sources of Structural Change in the United States, 1963–78," *Review of Economics and Statistics* 69 (August 1987): 503–510.

52. Davis, "Restructuring America's Trade Associations," 50–61.

53. George C. Lodge, *Perestroika for America: Restructuring Business-Government Relations for Competitiveness in the World Economy* (Boston: Harvard Business School Press, 1990), 68.

54. Ibid., 69–72.

55. Leonard Freedman, *Power and Politics in America* (Pacific Grove, CA: Brooks/Cole Publishing, 1991), 77.

56. Kirk Victor, "Step under My Umbrella," *National Journal* 20, no. 17 (23 April 1988): 1063–1067.

Chapter 4

Germany

THE EUROPEAN ELECTRONIC COMPONENTS MANUFACTURERS TAKE A STAND

It was November 1987 in Paris, and the international industry event taking place was called the Composants Electroniques (Electronics Components) Conference and Exhibition. It was a convenient time to arrange a meeting of representatives of the European Electronic Components Manufacturers Association (EECA) and of an American association, the Semiconductor Industry Association (SIA). The highest executive officers of the semiconductor products divisions of several European corporations, including SGS-Thomson (French-Italian), Philips (Netherlands), Plessey (United Kingdom), and Siemens (Germany) were meeting with the highest executive officers of American firms such as Intel, Motorola, Texas Instruments, Advanced Micro Devices, National, LSI Logic, and others. Cochairing the meeting were Jurgen Knorr from the Siemens company, who was also chair of the Semiconductor Public Policy Committee of EECA, and Gordon Moore, of Intel, chair of the SIA board of directors. This meeting had been preceded by smaller and lower-level executive meetings in the United States and Europe in the previous year.

The European manufacturers were in a quandary as they faced two strong national challengers—Japan and the United States. The Americans, the Europeans' older adversaries in the semiconductor market, had recently been successful in their quest for a U.S. government semiconductor agreement with the government of Japan which opened the Japanese market to foreign chips, had promised to curtail dumping by Japanese chip firms, and provided for the suspension of dumping duties levied by the United States.[1]

The Europeans were highly suspicious of this arrangement, believing that the European Commission of the European Community in Brussels had not been adequately informed during the bilateral negotiations and that the terms held dire consequences for them. They felt that the agreement would result in the world chip markets being dominated by the Japanese and American companies. They also believed that the agreement held secrets, since the public statements regarding Japanese access and cessation of dumping were not conditions that they believed Japan would readily enforce. In both meetings the Europeans proclaimed that it was not possible, considering Japan's industrial policy, for Japan to really meet the terms of the U.S.-Japan Semiconductor Agreement. They appeared to believe that the true focus of the agreement was a division of world markets through managed trade.

The Europeans and the Americans had competed over a period of the past thirty years, and the Americans had captured over 50 percent of the European markets, while building numerous facilities and factories within the European boundaries. The Europeans, however, failed to attack globally and remained in possession of less than 5 percent of the U.S market and less than 1 percent of the Japanese market, while holding less than 40 percent of their own home market.[2]

That day in November, the Europeans presented their position, as follows. European chip companies had higher social costs and fewer legally allowable labor hours per year expended in their chip plants than their American or Japanese counterparts. Consequently, they stated that their manufacturing costs would necessarily be higher. Despite this fact, the Europeans also believed that the size of the European chip market was such that European firms must maintain, or be allowed to maintain, at least 50 percent. The intrusion of the Japanese into the European market would upset even the existing disproportionate American-European balance. In addition, the general worldwide use of dumping by the Japanese chip companies to gain market share would continue, which they believed would be devastating to the Europeans. To offset the possibility of dumping, the Europeans insisted on maintaining their import tariffs of up to 14 percent ad valorem. The Europeans also believed that their joint intra-Europe technology programs, supported by government funds such as the Joint European Submicron Silicon Initiative (JESSI) and European Strategic Programs for R&D in Information Technology (ESPRIT) would help them only partially to advance their technology. In addition to these European consortia, the Europeans wished to join an American chipmakers consortium called SEMATECH, which was established specifically to raise manufacturing capabilities for the American industry. At this time, non-Americans were not allowed to join SEMATECH for various reasons, but primarily because of its relationship to the U.S. Defense Department Advanced Research Projects Agency (DARPA) and because U.S. government funding was based on the support of the American industry.

After hours of discussion, the Europeans would not agree to the request by the Americans that their tariffs should be lowered despite the fact that the United States and Japan both had zero import duties on chips. They insisted on keeping JESSI closed to American subsidiaries in Europe unless the United States opened SEMATECH membership to European companies. They did agree, however, to work on a common antidumping cost-analysis protocol. They did not wish to join SIA in any joint access program to Japan, since they felt it would be unproductive, and they definitely wanted either an implicit or explicit agreement from the Americans that Europeans would be allowed to maintain or improve their share of their home markets. Paradoxically, they appeared to want an agreement in which the American industry would limit its access to the European chip market.

The American side, put simply, wanted zero import tariffs into Europe; contracts, but not memberships, for Europeans in SEMATECH; open markets without market sharing or any "reverse access" agreements; and cooperation in developing an antidumping protocol for common applications to Asian producers.

One further European suggestion was that a three-way meeting of EECA, SIA, and the Electronic Industries Association of Japan (EIAJ) be held within one year. (The meeting eventually was held, but it had no significant impact on public policy, commercial market competition, or international trade related to semiconductors.)

Three years later, in 1992, after seeing American firms virtually double their share of market in Japan through the cooperation of American and Japanese firms within the framework of the 1986 U.S.-Japan Trade Agreement, the Europeans, though EECA and the European Community (EC), began to approach the Japanese government and electronics industry to have them agree to a separate access agreement.[3] The discussions were still continuing as of the start of 1993.

The European chip industry's attempt to solve its international trade problems by favorable association agreements on protective tariffs, reciprocal cooperative national research, and implied share of market stipulation for its home markets, all beyond the competitive nature and legal standards of U.S. firms and beyond the collaborative, export-driven nature of Japanese firms, was stalled without progress. Jurgen Knorr, EECA's committee chair and the leader of the largest and most prestigious German electronics and electrical products firm, was not able to formulate a cooperative industry association strategy in Paris, despite his background of success in the utilization of associations to form public policy.

Although this is a first-person account of an interassociation meeting, it seems quite surprising that a published description of the SIA-EECA meetings, written a year after the account, is remarkably similar:

> There are also cooperative efforts between American and European semiconductor companies at the industry level. The SIA and the European Electronic Components Association (EECA), for example, have been holding regular talks to develop common positions on trade policy issues. Not surprisingly, their greatest success to date has been in developing common proposals on questions of dumping—in particular, how to construct costs to measure dumping, how to speed up the dumping and remedy process, and what kinds of remedies to impose. In some areas, however, trade conflicts continue to divide American and European producers. For example, American producers would like to see the elimination of European tariffs, while European producers would not. In addition, the Europeans have lobbied for balanced regional trade in semiconductors, proposing what would amount to a regional managed trade arrangement. But American companies, committed to improved market access rather than managed trade, have rejected such proposals.[4]

THE SECOND EMPIRE

The historical basis of business institutions and trade associations in Germany is distinct from that of the United States. America's associations ranged from the tools of the robber barons to the cartels of the NRA, and then back to private, but restricted, groups. Germany's trade associations from the beginning were cooperatively instituted by business and government, first at the regional level and then at the national level, and were part of a mandated chambers system. Furthermore, the associations themselves became part of a hierarchy of associations. These unique aspects of the German associations, as distinct from those of the United States, are a part of German political, economic, and business history. This history begins here with the German Second Empire.

Although 1871 marks the beginning of the Second Empire in Germany and the subsequent establishment of that nation as an economic power, the period for five decades preceding it had been one of accelerating economic development in the multitude of individual region-states of Germany.[5] Historians have claimed that prior to 1871, as many as 1,800 political entities existed in the preunified Germany, with perhaps as many as seventy-five major secular principalities.[6] In 1820, Germany appeared to have few qualities of a future economic power. The country appeared to lack fertile, tillable land and easily accessible natural resources; politically, it was fragmented into many authoritarian entities; and economically, it lacked a pool of private commercial capital. Transportation and communication networks were rudimentary, and each principality had its own customs barriers, which held broad economic development in check.

Among all these German states, however, Prussia was the largest and most organized in its political aspects. It had possessions in the west as well as in the eastern German territories, and its resultant attempt to take active steps to improve transportation and communication between its unconnected territorial possessions within the German borders resulted in the negotiation of trade treaties, the building of roads, and the securing of technical information from abroad to overcome its industrial shortcomings. The tariff law, which was enacted in 1818 (Maasen's Tariff Law), was one of the decisive actions that affected the future unification as it facilitated the economic expansion by enticing the small German states into customs unions in return for a share of the revenues. Eventually, by 1834, the major principalities had joined Prussia in a great customs union, the Zollverin, which included nearly 24 million people.[7]

Prior to 1871, the various German states, dominated by the efforts of Prussia, had begun to develop an advanced transportation network of hard surface roads, river steamships, canals, and most important, railroads. The railroads shook the nation out of its economic stagnation, completing what the Zollverin had surely begun. "So vigorously did they influence all habits of life that by the 1840's Germany had already assumed a completely different aspect."[8] Along with the railroads, the telegraph communications network grew in parallel, exceeding its initial applicability to railroad scheduling.

The capital for this expansion was provided primarily by the Prussian state. In fact, the state also capitalized mines and factories, although some individuals and families, such as the Krupps at Essen and the Borsigs in Berlin, also built factories, for steel and locomotives, respectively. Joint-stock companies were formed in which the state was also a partner. The state, at the national, state, and local levels, joined in these company ventures and established banks along the lines of the then-existing Credit Mobiliere and Credit Foncile in France. These banks provided funds for capitalizing ventures on an investment basis as well as by providing loans against property and land as security. The Credit Mobiliere became the model of the German *Kreditbank*. The dominant financial institutions in Germany, these were a combination of commercial, development, and investment banks, and investment trusts.[9] By 1860 there were over 320 recently founded joint-stock or partnership companies, and by now Frankfurt had become an international center for the exchange of state bonds. Foreign capital from England, France, and Belgium also played a part in German development at this time.

Along with foreign capital, foreign technology flowed into Germany from many countries. Prussia attempted to learn of new technologies from outside sources, and in 1821 the Association for the Promotion of Industrial Knowledge was formed. Technical schools were established in Berlin and the provinces, and technical education was highly regarded.[10] The education system, which was based on Prussian reforms, was producing one of the most literate and appropriately educated work forces in Europe, and German universities were already producing highly qualified graduates at the leading edge of research in the natural sciences and in the traditional areas of law, theology, and literature.[11]

Along with trade, transportation, communication, capital, and education came the exploration of Germany's coal and lignite resources and the subsequent development of its heavy industries, namely iron, steel, other metals, and machine making. Following these industries came two other industries of great importance to Germany's future economy: chemicals and electrical equipment. Germany's combination of mineral resources and technical research was the basis of the chemical industry, while the invention and development of the dynamo by Werner von Siemens became the basis of the electrical machinery industry.[12]

In agriculture, the lessons of scientifically developed methods in farming, including chemicals, resulted in a dramatic improvement in commercial crops. The new knowledge was spread through university experimental stations, agricultural schools, and other special courses for new young farmers. The combination of improvement in agriculture and industry led to growth and mobility of the population, so that by 1865, Germany held 40 million people, with a very high proportion being relatively young.[13]

Despite the structural economic growth, trade cycles, financial panics, harvest failures, and other catastrophes continued to occur. Prussia still had not unified Germany, and Bismarck's three wars, against the Dutch, the Austrians, and the French, were still the essential future events for unification. After these did occur however, and unification did take place, the authoritarian-feudal outlook of the governing classes remained unchanged. Prussia's conservative society maintained the controlling leadership where the nobility held sway, not only in governing and politics, but also in the army, the civil administration, and the economy as well. The resulting effect was to be felt by capitalist entrepreneurs, financiers, and landowners alike.[14]

The association movement in Germany during the decades before unification bore the stamp of the political and economic conditions of the times. In 1819, an association along the lines of today's chamber of commerce, called the Commercial and Industrial Union, made up of merchants and manufacturers was established in the southern and central states of Germany. It was established to promote a system of free commerce between rival German states. Ten years later, in 1829, the Industrial Association of the Kingdom of Saxony was founded to deal with technological developments, trade policies, and economic legislation. However, it was the railroads that provided the impetus for the initial trans-German association activity.[15]

The Association of German Railway Administrations was established in 1846 in Prussia and quickly spread to include railway organizations in the other German states. Its initial concern was the need for changes in the railroad laws and the need for better financial-reporting standards. Later, it began to draw up regulations, procedures, and standards that started to build the system that was to become the central portion of the European Continental Railway System. At about the same time, in 1850, a professional organization of railway civil engineers was formed. The two—the association of firms, represented by managers, and the association of professionals, represented by engineers—were complimentary and reinforcing in their efforts. In 1871, the German Railway Traffic Association was established to set uniform rates and classifications, and in the same year, the unification of Germany under Bismarck hastened the integration of all state railway systems. The telegraph and postal systems, which had been owned and operated by the separate German states, were integrated under the new nation's post office system. The state's presence in the transportation and communication networks was to determine Europe's future patterns.

At the same time, as state interests were becoming evident in transportation, communication, agriculture, and banking, the private interests also accelerated in these fields, as well as in manufacturing and trade. The overlap between state and private interests was substantial. Consequently, Germany's government bureaucrats and its private professionals and managers were to have a great deal in common, a fact that clearly distinguished nineteenth-century Germany from the United States. The joining of private and public interests at this point in German history led to economic methods, such as pricing mechanisms (i.e., rate systems and schedules) that were more of a public regulatory nature compared with the legal confrontation of private interests and public interests in the nineteenth-century United States.[16] This joining of private and public interests in Germany prior to the antitrust movement in the United States probably forms the starting point of a German economy that economic historians have called "organized capitalism."[17]

By 1861, the various merchant organizations that had already begun had achieved a fairly uniform profile, and the German Commercial Parliament (Deutsche Handelstag) was formed as the central forum and leading organization (Spitzenorganization) for the chambers of commerce. It was the common voice for both merchants and manufacturers. The chambers of commerce of Germany were functionally similar to those established in the United States and Japan, but in Germany, they were self-governing bodies, publicly chartered, and with mandatory membership for all businesses in the chamber region.[18]

By the second half of the nineteenth century, specific industry trade associations began to find that their special interests required greater attention. By the turn of the century, the Association of German Iron and Steel Industrialists (1873), the Association for the Maintenance of Interests of the German Chemical Industry (1877), the Association of Machine Builders (1889), the Association for the Maintenance of Common Economic Institutions in the German Electrical Industry (1902), and others had been formed. By 1900, another 500 associations were in existence. Each emphasized its specific industry interests, which might include transportation policies and rates, capacity, tariffs, labor unions, or social security laws.[19]

The cartel was the third form of association to develop in Germany. Cartels are business associations that can be horizontal, whereby all firms produce the same product, or vertical, whereby the cartel represents the various stages of production, such as the transformation of coal to steel, and then to rails. Generally a cartel will attempt to control prices, output, and marketing procedures. In some cases, only the marketing arms of the firms are part of the cartel. It should be noted that the vertical cartels of Germany were similar to the zaibatsu of Japan.[20]

The reasons for cartel formation were varied. Some were formed to handle depressions and the concurrent excessive capacity and employment, some for tariff protection in order to maintain profits, some to resist foreign penetration into the domestic market, and some to raise capital more easily for initial research or even for joint production facilities. There is little hard evidence that the cartels achieved their long-term objectives, but despite this fact, the German Cartel Commission in 1905 enumerated over 350 cartels and by 1925, counted over 3,000. Only 4 cartels, however, achieved dominant positions—in coal, steel, chemicals, and electrical machinery. Not inconsequently, these were, and continue to be, Germany's leading industries.[21] Cartels in Germany received legal protection in that their members' agreements were treated as binding contracts. In Great Britain, at the time, agreements in "restraint of trade" were not legally enforceable, while in the United States these cartel agreements would be specifically illegal. Some of the well-known cartels at the time were the Potash Syndicate (1881), which was formed to maintain profits, especially of exports to the United States, the Rhenish-Westphalian Coal Syndicate (1897), the Steel Works Association (1904), the International Rail Makers Association (IRMA) (1883), and the Association of German Machine Builders (1892). By the 1890s, additional cartels had been rapidly formed and by 1914, the cartelization of German industry peaked. The important relationship of cartels to associations in Germany was that the cartel was often formed within an association or was the association itself.[22]

The cartel idea appeared to work best in industries where there were relatively few firms, possibly because of their high-capital or knowledge-intensive character: for example, steel and chemicals; relatively homogeneous products such as iron ingots, steel rolls, and tanks of general-use chemicals; and highly reactive business climate for their product due to the nature of their derived demand under cyclical business conditions. Not all cartels were totally effective, since they did not have the characteristics mentioned above, but occasionally they helped their members earn a better-than-competitive profit in the short term.[23]

The fourth major type of association was the employers associations, which dealt exclusively with labor union matters. They paralleled the unionization movement in Germany and were organized around specific industries. The intent was that the unions and the employers associations would reach agreement on wages, hours, and other general terms, while the individual firms and their local union members would handle the implementation and maintenance of the agreements. These various employers associations finally amalgamated into the League of German Employers Associations (Vereinigung Deutschen Arbeitgeberverband), or the VDA.[24]

Finally, peak associations representing a number of specific associations began to form about 1876, with the establishment of the Central Association of German Industrialists (Centralverband Deutschen Industrielle) (CDI), the Federation of Industrialists, in 1895, and the Hansa Federation, in 1909. Each held various public policy positions at the national level in regard to trade and worker benefits. The peak association, CDI, arose out of protectionist sentiments in regard to tariffs on iron. Its primary focus was on trade matters, including tariffs, and second, on labor matters as well as proposed social and economic legislation. The CDI did pursue a policy of initiating worker benefits such as accident and health insurance, social security and disability laws. However, its motives were to remove the incentives for labor to organize itself, which was the primary goal of organized labor.[25]

The Federation of Industrialists, Bund der Industdriellen (BI), was formed with opposite views to those of the CDI in some areas. The CDI primarily tended to the interests of large-scale industry, while the BI wished to further the interests of firms smaller than the typical CDI member. It attempted to forge an antitariff position but was unsuccessful in doing so. The Hansa League, the other peak organization, tended to focus on political movements rather than industry interests and did not attain the stature of the CDI or the Federation. Consequently, the BI and the CDI were essentially national rivals, particularly in the area of trade policy. Neither side was interested in absolute free trade, but they differed in the degree of government action desired. Moreover, as the labor union movement became more important, the CDI promoted confrontation with the labor organizers while promoting government labor progress. The BI favored a different line, which was neither as confrontational nor as promotional. Obviously, the different structure of their membership was the major determinant of their policies.

In the German association movement to the turn of the century, there existed overlapping networks of firms for marketing, production, purchasing, labor, and public policy purposes. The associations included the chambers of industry and commerce, which where the broadest in membership; the peak organizations such, as the CDI and the BI; the industry-specific trade organizations; the employer associations; and finally, but certainly among the most important, the cartels.[26]

Integral to these networks were the major Kreditbanken of Germany, which were essential to Germany's industrial development. They were also joint-stock holders as well as marketers of company stock. By 1918, four banks, the "Four D's" had virtually absorbed all others—the Darmstader (founded 1853), the Diskontogesellschaft (1850), the Deutsche Bank (1870), and the Dresden Bank (1872).[27] They lent money, helped float companies, gave long-term credit terms, and in effect became corporate partners. They were represented on company boards of directors and encouraged the formation of cartels.

With this industrial-government-banking partnership in place, Germany expanded its economy greatly enough between 1871 and 1914 to surpass Great Britain and France in production. Being a latecomer to the modern industries of the time allowed Germany to learn from the mistakes of other nations. Germany had matched Great Britain in coal, surpassed it in iron and steel, and dominated the world's chemical industry, and was generating over one-third of the world's trade in electrotechnical equipment by 1914.[28] This model of Germany's capitalism, which is based more on industrial concentration and cooperation than on classical economics, has been called "organized capitalism."[29] The term is based, however, not only on interfirm cooperation, but on the entire economic system.

Its characteristics describing Germany before 1918 include:

1. A strong central government based on an imperial system consisting of a privileged class, autocratic administration, strong army, efficient bureaucracy, and paternalistic autocracy.

2. State ownership of the infrastructure, namely, railroads, the telegraph, post offices, canals, utilities, and some factories and mines.

3. Industrial growth and technological advances funded by state investment, foreign investment, and broad banking firms.

4. Associations of all kinds whereby peak associations, industry-specific trade associations, cartels, employer's organizations, and similar groups took an active part in economic planning and execution. The association structure was deeply embedded in the very heart of the industrial economy.

5. A state that, true to its paternalistic nature, ruled that the workers' needs in health insurance, workers' compensation, social security, and other social programs must be met but did not look favorably on organized unions.

6. Citizen interest groups (outside of inept attempts to form political parties) concentrated in cultural activities, such as music, art, and festivals, and not on economic or social welfare issues.

THE ASSOCIATIONS AND THE ECONOMY, 1918–1945

The German desire to catch up to the economies of England and France is not unlike the Japanese goal. This desire, plus the increasing prosperity that seems to be forthcoming from combining the smaller states and their resources, continued to be the driving force for cooperation. The associations of all types were the vehicles of the cooperative nation. The authoritative force of government driving a cooperative state of industry was an early form of industrial policy, again not too dissimilar from that of Japan. The inclination for associations to join peak associations in order to achieve a hierarchy indicates that the command-and-control organizational form of the imperial government was applied to business organizations as well.

In Germany, the motives were the drive to catch up economically and the assignment of authority and control, in order to regulate and maintain order in business. The end of World War I and imperial rule were to change the character of Germany, especially the prevailing view toward unions and citizen interests. However the primary focus of the economy after World War I still remained the production capacity of the industrial structure, including the ancillary functions of the banks, the associations, and the cartels.

World War I was the catalyst that affected the eventual unification of the rival peak organizations in Germany. In 1914, the War Committee of German Industry was established to help in the war effort, and in 1916, the Council of German Industry was established to aid in the transition to peace. Both groups were made up the CDI, the Federation of Industries (BI), and the Chemical Association, and eventually the need and benefits of working together became clearer.

In February 1919, these rival organizations founded the National Association of German Industry (Reichsverband der Deutchen Industrie) (RDI). The RDI was headquartered in Berlin and was "a super-association of 26 trade groups, subdivided into 400 national associations and cartels, 58 regional and 70 local associations, over 1,000 individual members and firms, and 70 chambers of industry and commerce." The central power lay with a thirty-six-member presidential board, which met monthly to work out its approach to various issues. The RDI also had a general assembly which met every one or two years with 2,000 to 3,000 delegates in attendance. The main committee of the general assembly consisted primarily of trade association members and met more frequently. The interests of big business, although small in terms of number of firms, was well represented at the level of the thirty-six-member presidential board.[30]

The RDI attempted to shape public policy to its interests and mold public opinion through the media. It opposed any socialist movements and supported conservative causes. In addition, industry offered its own members as candidates to state and national political office, and these tended to form a single block in the Reichstag, the German Parliament. By 1928, they numbered 76 out of the 490 deputies, or 16 percent of the total. Another tie between industry and government existed in that, of the 490 deputies, 58 held seats on 275 corporate boards of directors.[31]

Although the RDI appeared to be a monolithic organization, there existed no united support for a given party. Rather, the RDI interacted with all levels of government and various parties and "served as a national forum where disparate industrial interest groups could seek to reconcile differences."[32]

Just as the United States had experienced recession, prosperity, depression and war during the period of 1918 to 1945, the economic periods in Weimar Germany between the wars were also volatile. The period from 1919 to 1923 was dominated by inflation; 1923 to 1929 brought an unprecedented boom; 1929 to 1932, as in the United States, was marked by financial, industrial, and agricultural crisis; and finally, beginning in 1932, there was a period of full employment brought about by the Nazis' complete control of the economy, which continued until the German defeat in 1945.

With the defeat of World War I and the institution of the Weimar Republic, Germany had lost all its colonies, the Saar, Alsace-Lorraine, and a portion of Upper Silesia. In addition, the reparations to the allies were severe, including their right to confiscate all German private property in their countries. Only the United States eventually returned sequestered private property to German citizens. In fact, the transfer of ships, railroads, materials, and property to its former enemies made the postwar economic situation catastrophic for Germany.[33]

Inflation ran out of control as Germany resorted to the printing press to solve the currency and debt problems. Chaos occurred in industry, with some industrialists building huge conglomerates based on paper funds while others lost virtually everything due to receiving worthless paper for formerly solid physical assets. The nation was in chaos.[34] In 1923, the Dawes Plan, which restructured Germany's reparations, ushered in a recovery of unprecedented proportions based on a process usually called "rationalization" in Germany—a process employing economic and technological policies that included American production methods. One Oxford professor defined rationalization simply by stating that "to rationalize an industry is to remove all the duplication and overlap which can be avoided, and introduce as much unity of purpose as is practicable without loss of economy." There is no doubt that the cartels as an ideal could practice rationalization to the most complete degree when compared to any other industry structure. Rationalization was the application of new technical and management skills to large-scale, large-volume production in such a way that specialized mass production was the outcome. The cartels and the associations, including the association of German trade unions, lauded the rationalization movement.[35]

Starting in 1923 and up until 1930, Germany's industries—chemical, electrical, optics, textiles, and engineering—attained leading positions in the world economy. At the same time, excellent urban housing, playgrounds, schools, and hospitals were built. Electric power was extended, while highways were modernized. Germany rebuilt its entire commercial fleet, and exports in 1929 exceeded the pre–World War I numbers by 34 percent.[36]

This period of Weimar prosperity was not only to be unequaled in the sense of growth but in addition, probably in no other period was the high degree of development of business association–government cooperation achieved. The period also featured a great degree of vertical integration; a high level of industrial concentration; a multiplicity of organizational ties, with banks, cartels, corporations, cross-holdings, well-financed and professionally managed verbands (trade associations); two major peak associations (one, the employers' association, the VDA, and the other, the RDI); and many other special-purpose industry associations, all tied together within the Chambers of Commerce and Industry.[37] During this period, there was a high degree of concentration. About 158 joint-stock companies, or 1.3 percent of the firms, accounted for 46.7 percent of all capital stock values in Germany. At the top were the newly formed chemical and electrical equipment industries, followed by coal, iron, steel, and banking. Despite this broad industrial base, one observer believed that although Germany had developed into an industrial state, it was not essentially a capitalist one.[38]

This prosperity, which was built, to a large degree, by foreign as well as domestic investment in Germany, finally came to an end in 1930 with several crises. Although an agricultural crisis occurred, of greater import was a banking and industrial crisis, which led to controls on foreign credit and currency exchange to the point that Germany's exports, which had previously constituted about one-third of high-production output, now fell dramatically by almost two-thirds (i.e., from 13.5B marks in 1929 to 4.8B marks in 1933). With industry's exports badly affected and its domestic demand now its only driver, the Weimar government made the mistake of forcing a general reduction of "fixed prices" for the cartels it controlled by law rather than allowing flexibility to be exercised by the firms according to product demand, supply capability, and other market factors.[39] By 1931, unemployment had reached 4 million persons and a year later, 5 million. Germany, too, was now fighting the Great Depression, with a government very new to democracy and a fatal flaw in its constitution: the right given its president to invoke emergency powers. President Paul von Hindenburg chose to do so and thus fell under the influence of forces aiding the Nazi party, and Adolf Hitler finally became the chancellor of Germany on January 30, 1933.

On July 14, 1933, Germany became a one–political party nation ruled by Adolf Hitler. Prior to this event, a group of industrialists had financially supported the Nazi party, but probably not to any greater degree than other industrialists supported more conservative parties. However, in a February 1933 meeting including Adolf Hitler, Herman Goering, Hajalmar Schact, and Wilhelm Frick, who were all at the top of the Nazi party, as well as about twenty-five leading industrialists and bankers, Krupp von Bohlen und Hallbach, president of the RDI, expressed hope for a politically strong, independent state in which industry and commerce could flourish.[40]

When the Nazis came to power, they did not wish to have free and independent business associations, but on the other hand, they needed the cooperation of business and industry. They set up an authoritarian Organization of Trade and Economy to streamline the association structure, and at the same time, expanded the associations to include all businesses. This new organization reported directly to

Hitler's minister of Economic Affairs and the National Economic Chamber, and the RDI was submerged within its organization to be reformed into the Reichsgruppe Industrie.[41] Despite these authoritative organizational structures, the Nazis eventually returned state monopolies back to the private sector and gave individual firms a great deal of freedom. Permission to consolidate and operate cartels was granted, and high tariffs and other import restrictions were put in place. Representation in state-owned war industries was also allowed. Consequently, the seeming paradox of strict government authoritarian control with broad freedom of action by industrial firms appeared to exist for the benefit of both.

The 1930s ended with Germany's 1939 invasion of Poland and the beginning of World War II. The efforts of industry accelerated to meet the needs of the military, and for all practical purposes, all commercial action by the firms and the other members of the economy ceased. The end came in 1945, with the devastation of the industry and land of Germany as the nation was defeated by the Allies.

THE ASSOCIATIONS SINCE 1945

With the end of World War II, the employers, their firms, and the associations were discredited by the victorious Allies. Leading industrialists were put on trial for war crimes, and many business enterprises were dismantled. However, three reasons have been proposed as resulting in the consequent reversal on the part of the Allies. First, the quick emergence of the Soviet Union as an enemy forced them to move Germany quickly toward reconstruction. Second, the fact that businessmen and workers united in order to save their jobs, and thus their livelihoods, in a common action of strength gave the Allies a greater sociopolitical problem than had existed at the beginning of the occupation.[42] A third reason suggested has been American business pressure.[43]

The Allies reacted positively to the situation but agreed on the necessity of limiting the power of associations and restricting the concentration of monopolies and cartels. As would be expected, however, the Soviets, the Americans, the British, and the French would probably take different steps in each of their zones. The Soviets banned all associations. The Americans allowed only local associations with voluntary membership to provide advisory counsel, but without any public power. The British allowed organizations to go beyond the local districts to the entire zone, while the French adopted the American approach. As soon as the organizations were allowed in any of these forms, German businessmen attempted to reach across the zones and establish suprazonal groups. With time, unions, associations, and chambers of commerce were all allowed, and by May 1949, delegates from thirty-five industrial associations, representing 90 percent of industry, met in convention in Cologne. The result was that by early 1950, the successor to the RDI had been set up, called the Federation of German Industry (Bundesverband der Deutschen Industrie) (BDI). Within time, the industrial associations all reverted to the jurisdiction of the German state and federal authorities.

The DIHT (Chamber of Industry and Commerce) was also reconstituted in 1949 and comprised over eighty local and district chambers of industry and trade. All membership was compulsory, as before World War II, giving the DIHT a quasi-public status with a central committee, a board, and a president. The organization primarily serves the regional interests by analyzing economic development, fostering vocational training, establishing fair trade practices, and lobbying at the local, state, and federal levels. Today, the DIHT is to the U.S. Chamber of Commerce as the BDI to the National Association of Manufacturers, but only in the general sense of their constituents and interests, not in their legal and formal standing or their extensive membership. The Federation of German Employers Associations (Bundesvereinigung der Deutschen Arbeitgeberverbande) (BDA) was also reorganized in 1949, replacing the VDA, which Hitler had disbanded in 1933. It acts as a coordinating and advisory center for employers in regard to labor and social policies. Collective bargaining is not a BDA function, but it does recommend policies that are followed by national associations in industry, banking, insurance, and transportation. The BDA has accepted the concept of a unified trade union movement and attempts to work toward a market economy where labor is a recognized bona fide participant.

By 1964, the BDI was possibly greatest in influence and strength in the area of business organizations. Its membership was restricted to federally structured associations of various industries such as textiles, steel, and chemicals, which at that time numbered thirty-nine. It was claimed that of these member associations, none had less than 80 percent of the firms in the industry. No individual firms could be members of the BDI. By comparison, BDI compromised 98 percent of all German firms, while the American National Association of Manufacturers (NAM) at that time could only claim 6 percent of 324,000 manufacturing firms in that country.[44] The individual associations in the BDI, with their number in parentheses, are representatives of mining (two), basic and production goods (ten), investment goods (ten), consumer goods (twelve), food and related products (four), and construction (one). The industrial economy is, therefore, well represented in the BDI. A list of BDI associations is shown in Table 4.1. The BDI without a doubt is the peak organization in Germany whose power is unparalleled.

THE LEGAL CARTELS

In order to complete the picture of German associations, three additional types are described: cartels, German research institutes, and European research consortia in which German firms are members.

With regard to cartels, they continue to be, as in the past, a legal role for associations. The German Federal Cartel Office is in charge of antitrust administration, and as yet there is no evidence of any firm national policy opposing cartels, despite rhetoric about free markets. In fact, the office at times aids German industrial policy and industrial concentration by placing barriers in the path of foreign

Table 4.1
List of BDI Member Associations

A. *Mining*
   Mining Association
   Petroleum Extraction Association

B. *Basic and Production Goods*
   Stone and Gravel Association
   Iron and Steel Association
   Association of Steel Works and Rolling
     Mills
   Association of Nonferrous Metals
   Association of the Foundry Industry
   Mineral Oil Association
   Association of the Chemical Industry
   League of German Sawmill Associations
   Bureau of the Cellulose and Paper Industry
   Association of the German Rubber Industry

C. *Investment Goods*
   Steel and Iron Construction Association
   Association of German Machine
     Construction
   Automobile Industry Association
   Association of German Shipyards
   Central Association of the Electrotechnical
     Industry
   Association of the Precision Tool and
     Optical Industry
   Steel Fabrication Association
   Association of Iron-, Tin- and Metal-
     Finishing Industries
   Association of the Bicycle and Motorcycle
     Industry
   Federation of the German Air and Space
     Industry

D. *Consumer Goods*
   Association of the Ceramics Industry
   Federation of the Glass Industry
   Association of the German Wood and
     Related Products Industries
   Industry Group Association
   Association of Paper and Allied Products
     Industries
   League of Graphic Associations of
     Germany
   Association of the Synthetic Fabrics
     Industry
   Association of the German Leather
     Industry
   Association of the Leather Goods and
     Suitcase Industry
   Association of the German Shoe Industry
   Federation of the Clothing Industry
   Association of the German Textile Industry

E. *Food and Related Products*
   Federation of the German Food Processing
     Industry
   Association of the Sugar Industry
   German Brewers League
   Association of the Cigarette Industry

F. *Construction*
   Association of the German Construction
     Industry

Source: Gerard Braunthal, *The Federation of German Industry in Politics*, Appendix A, pp. 357–358. Copyright © 1965 by Cornell University. Used by permission of the publisher, Cornell University Press.

firms attempting to acquire German ones. German firms will often acquire another firm that is failing rather than let it be acquired by foreign interests. The cartels, although perhaps more closely scrutinized today than in the past, are still able to continue operations. German cartels may also appeal to the minister of economics, who can overrule the Federal Cartel Office on a ruling.[45] Among the types of legal cartels of Germany are those listed in Table 4.2.[46] They number over 300 in total.

Table 4.2
Types of Legal Cartels in Germany

Types of Cartels	Legal Definition	Number in Existence, 1986
Condition	Uniform application of general terms of business, delivery and payment	50
Rebate	Uniform granting of rebates and discounts	5
Crisis	Coordinated adjustment of productive capacity to demand in the case of a decline in sales due to a lasting change in demand	2
Rationalization	Uniform application of standards or types, sometimes in conjunction with price agreements including the establishment of joint purchasing or selling organizations	20
Specialization Cartel	Rationalization of economic activities through specialization	44
Cooperation	Rationalization of economic activities by cooperation between enterprises other than those above	136
Export	Protection and promotion of exports	56
Import	Regulation of imports only	0
Minister (emergency)	Cartel agreement does not satisfy any of the conditions for exemption provided for in previous categories	0

Source: David B. Audretsch, "Legalized Cartels in Germany," *Antitrust Bulletin* 34, no. 3 (Fall 1989): 591 (Table 2).

It should be noted, however, that with the development of the European Community and Union, acquisitions of German companies by foreign companies is occurring at an increasing rate and with less interference by federal agencies.

THE RESEARCH INSTITUTES

Research associations in Japan and research consortia in the United States are reflections of the technology policies of government, industry, universities, and other institutions. In the case of Germany, however, a different model of cooperation in research and development comes into focus.

The German federal government has, at the ministry level, a federal Ministry for Research and Technology, for which there is no direct counterpart in the United States or Japan. The ministry provides a statement of goals every five years. The 1988 research report stated that the German government has four general objectives:[47]

- Deepening scientific knowledge;
- Developing technology to promote humane living and working conditions;
- Promoting innovation to improve the efficiency of industry; and
- Using technology to promote international cooperation.

In addition, other related principles are:[48]

- A greater emphasis on basic rather than programmatic research;
- The principal funding of industry;
- Improvement of the conditions for small high-technology firms;
- A high degree of international cooperation is involved;
- Long term infrastructure questions are involved;
- Technologies have an effect "across the board through a multitude of sectors" so that the market incentive for individual industries is small; and
- Technologies affect the quality of life (e.g., environmental technologies).

In 1987, a total of 56 billion DM ($37 billion U.S.) were spent in research and development. Of this amount, about 21 billion DM were provided by federal and state governments, and 35 billion DM by industry. Of these amounts, 40 billion DM were used by industry, 7 billion DM by universities, and 8 billion DM by research institutes. Of all government funding, approximately one-third goes to industry, one-third to universities, and one-third to public research centers. These public research centers are unique in that they emphasize applied research and maintain ties with both universities and industries.[49]

Among the research institutes in Germany that bring universities, industry, and government together are the Fraunhofer Institutes, which provide for the development of new knowledge and alternative channels for the diffusion of information and technology. There are thirty-five Fraunhofer Institutes associated with major universities and directed by faculty members in science, engineering, or the social sciences, each with a specific research specialty. The institutes form a bridge between universities and industry, where by any firm or industry group can contract for specific applied research. According to one report, the Fraunhofer Institutes played a major role in helping German industry make the transition from older, mechanical engineering–based manufacturing to electronic semiconductor–based automation.[50] A list of Fraunhofer Institutes is shown in Table 4.3.

Table 4.3
Fraunhofer Institutes, by Department

Microelectronics Department	Information Technology/ Production Automation Departments	Production Technologies/ Materials and Components Departments	Process Engineering/ Energy Technology and Construction Engineering Departments	Environmental Research and Health Department	Studies and Technical Information Services Department
Fraunhofer Institutes:	Fraunhofer Institutes:	Fraunhofer Institutes:	Fraunhofer Institutes:	Fraunhofer Institutes:	Fraunhofer Institutes:
Applied Solid State Physics	Applied Optics and Precision Engineering	Applied Materials Research	Applied Polymer Research	Atmospheric Environmental Research	Technological Trend
Solid State Technology	Industrial Engineering	Applied Polymer Research	Buildings Physics	Biomedical Engineering	Systems and Innovation Research
Integrated Circuits	Factory Operation and Automation	Strength of Structures under Operational Conditions	Chemical Technology	Toxicology and Aerosol Research	Information Center for Regional Planning and Building Construction
Integrated Circuits Device Technology	Computer Graphics Research	Electron Beam and Plasma Technology	Surface Technology and Biochemical Engineering	Toxicology and Aerosol Research	Patent Center for German Research of the Fraunhofer-Gesellschaft

Table 4.3
Fraunhofer Institutes, by Department (Continued)

Microelectronics Department	Information Technology/Production Automation Departments	Production Technologies/Materials and Components Departments	Process Engineering/Energy Technology and Construction Engineering Departments	Environmental Research and Health Department	Studies and Technical Information Services Department
Microelectronics Circuits and Systems	Information and Data Processing	Hydroacoustics	Wood Research Group "Wilhelm-Klauditz-Institut"	Environmental Chemistry and Ecotoxicology	
Silicon Technology	Material Flow and Logistics	Ceramic Technologies Sinter Materials	Food Process Engineering and Packaging		
	Physical Measurement Techniques	High Speed Dynamics "Ernst-Mach-Institut"	Silicate Research		
	Production Systems and Design Technology	Laser Technology	Solar Energy Systems		
	Manufacturing Engineering and Automation	Production Technology			
	Software Engineering and Systems Engineering	Thin Films and Surface Engineering			

Table 4.3
Fraunhofer Institutes, by Department (Continued)

Microelectronics Department	Information Technology/ Production Automation Departments	Production Technologies/ Materials and Components Departments	Process Engineering/ Energy Technology and Construction Engineering Departments	Environmental Research and Health Department	Studies and Technical Information Services Department
	Technology Development Group Stuttgart	Silicate Research			
		Forming Technology and Machine Tools			
		Mechanics of Materials			
		Material Physics and Thin-Film Technology			
		Non-Destructive Testing Methods			

Source: Fraunhofer-Gesellschaft, "Research Establishments—Services, Research Fields, and Addresses" (Munich, Germany, August 1992).

Germany has also participated in various consortia and joint ventures with other European nations. Three consortia are illustrative of the many that Germany has joined: Joint European Submicron Silicon Initiative (JESSI), European Strategic Program for Research in Information Technologies (ESPRIT), and Research and Development in Advanced Communications (RACE).[51]

COOPERATIVE CAPITALISM

With the establishment of the Federal Republic in 1949, the economy was intended to be based on private enterprise with industrial interests strongly considered. The 1950s were a decade of rapid growth led by exports. Economic growth was based on a number of factors, including an abundant supply of low-cost labor, a high rate of industrial investment, and the rapid reconstruction of industrial capacity.[52] The 1960s, which was supposedly a period of normalcy, began with labor demanding higher wages and industry and the government, including the federal bank, being brought together to deal with the cyclical behavior of the economy through the Stability and Growth Act of 1967. The 1970s and onward to the reunification of West and East Germany has been a period of slower economic growth and a high level of foreign trade dependency. This is not unrelated to Germany's falling behind the United States and Japan in several high technology sectors. The export-driven economy has been based on manufacturing industries, which employ over 40 percent of the work force (specifically chemicals, automobiles, and electrical and nonelectrical machinery). Crisis cartels still exist, for example, in steel. There are strong trade unions, and two of the largest (the metal workers and chemical workers unions) are active participants in modernizing their industry, at the expense of less competitive industries if need be. The banks continued in the 1970s to have important roles in the structure of industry. In 1979, they represented 62 percent of the vote at the general stockholders' meetings of seventy-four key companies.[53]

In the postwar period, Germany has shown itself to be more democratic, liberal, and free trade–oriented than ever before in its history as a unified nation. However, ingrained still in its economic patterns is the existence of large firms in basic industries such as chemicals and steel, and in capital goods industries such as transportation, electrical machinery, and industrial electronics. Further, the tendency to cooperate through a structure of industry, banks, and governmental networking at the association level still exists. Actual legal coownership of businesses at the corporate level is also extensive. The term *cooperative capitalism*, as a synonym for *organized capitalism*, is as apt today as in the latter part of the nineteenth century, albeit it now has a freer and more subtle nature.[54] Growth economics and industry concentration and structure, rather than the maximization of profits, still appear to be the focus of industrialists. Even the cartel movement in Germany often points to its nature—not one of rising prices to extract high profits, but of increasing efficiency to lower costs and prices in order to promote growth.

One interesting analysis of Germany's post–World War II success indicated that the factors that explain it are training, labor harmony, product quality and improvement, niche markets (often supplied by midsized companies), export orientation, innovation, and fiscal conservatism.[55] It failed to list associations and cooperative activity, but many of the factors mentioned are strongly dependent on the support of association activity, such as labor harmony by the VDA; niche markets, mid sized companies, and innovation by the research institutes; and export orientation by the export associations. The term *cooperative capitalism* is apt in describing the business economy in today's Germany. The corporations, associations, and banks, in cooperation with the regional and federal governments, have achieved a level of cooperative industrial effort greater than that of the United States, but not as close or directed as the collaborative effort of Japan.

THE CHARACTER OF GERMAN ASSOCIATIONS

The bedrock of all German association activity is the government's treatment of the chambers of commerce and industry. The reason for this statement is the fact that for over 100 years, German laws have mandated that firms belong either to a chamber of commerce and industry or a chamber of artisans. This mandatory requirement has provided the basis for the almost 100 percent membership of firms in industry-specific associations despite the fact that they have only a voluntary membership requirement. Voluntary trade associations include over 90 percent of all firms eligible for membership, while employers' associations for collective bargaining with labor unions have over 80 percent membership. This high level of membership in the key associations and the associations' membership in peak associations are not duplicated in any other advanced industrial nation. *Cooperative capitalism*, an apt term for Germany's industrial economy, is again exemplified by business being organized into associations. The extension of industry or trade associations into employers' associations, research associations, and cartels, with the same extensive degree of overlapping memberships along with the maintenance of a hierarchy by industry is not found anywhere in the G-7 nations—United States, Japan, Germany, United Kindom, France, Italy, and Canada—except perhaps Japan.

In addition to the all-encompassing German association structure, there also exists a cooperative attitude between German business and government. The relationship is based on the knowledge that negotiation and consensus, rather than edicted laws or regulations, will be the governing rules. In some cases, German government agencies are required to consult with industry representatives and peak associations. For example, the BDI has an official status when in consultation with government. Furthermore, associations may directly administer government programs, including program applications and awards of state subsidies. These programs cover areas that include labor training and technology projects. The Fraunhofer Institutes, the primary facility for applied research in Germany, receives half their funds from industry and half from government, on a matching funds basis.

The legal cartels in Germany continue to have support. Today, however, their activities are being modified as the European Union rules and regulations begin to be observed. The essential character of the German association structure is its all-encompassing role in industry, coupled with a cooperative role with government.

NOTES

1. United States Trade Representative, *Arrangement between Government of Japan and Government of the U.S.A. Concerning Trade in Semiconductor Products* (Washington, DC: U.S. Government Printing Office, 1986).

2. "European Semiconductor Market Share, by Supplier Base," *Dataquest* (January 1992), reprinted in *Electronic News*, 22 June 1992, 9.

3. J. Robert Lineback and Elizabeth de Bonny, "Europe Eyes Its Own Japan IC Market Share," *Electronic News*, 22 June 1992, 9.

4. Laura d'Andrea Tyson, *Who's Bashing Whom? Trade Conflict in High-Technology Industries* (Washington, DC: Institute for International Economics, 1992), 151.

5. W. R. Lee, "Economic Development and the State in Nineteenth-Century Germany," *Economic History Review* 41 (August 1988): 346–367.

6. Ernest Passant, *A Short History of Germany, 1815–1945* (New York: Cambridge University Press, 1959), 1.

7. M. Fullbrook, *A Concise History of Germany* (New York: Cambridge University Press, 1990), 115.

8. Passant, *Short History,* 73.

9. Alfred D. Chandler, Jr., *Scale and Scope: The Dynamics of Industrial Capitalism* (Cambridge, MA: Belknap Press of Harvard University Press, 1990), 416.

10. Passant, *Short History,* 76.

11. Fullbrook, *Concise History,* 110.

12. Gustav Stolper, *German Economy, 1870–1940* (New York: Cornwall Press, 1940), 43–44.

13. Passant, *Short History,* 80.

14. Ibid., 83.

15. G. Braunthal, *The Federation of German Industry in Politics* (Ithaca, NY: Cornell University Press, 1965), 4.

16. Chandler, *Scale and Scope,* 414.

17. Ibid., 395.

18. Toni Pierenkemper, "Trade Associations in the Late Nineteenth and Early Twentieth Centuries," *in Trade Associations in Business History,* ed H, H. Yamazaki and M. Miyamoto (Tokyo: University of Tokyo Press, 1988), 236.

19. Ibid., 240–241.

20. Stolper, *German Economy,* 83–88.

21. Passant, *Short History,* 111.

22. Gerald D. Feldman and Ulrich Nocken, "Trade Associations and Economic Power: Interest Group Development in the German Iron and Steel and Machine Building Industries, 1900–1933," *Business History Review* 49, no. 4 (1975): 413–445; Lon L. Peter, "Managing Competition in German Coal, 1893–1913," *Journal of Economic History* 49, no. 2 (1989): 419–433; Steven B. Webb, "Tariffs, Cartels, Technology and Growth in the German Steel Industry, 1879–1914," *Journal of Economic History* 40, no. 2 (1980): 309–

329; Werner Troesken, "A Note on the Efficiency of the German Steel and Coal Syndicates," *Journal of European Economic History* 18, no. 3 (1989): 595–600; Stolper, *German Economy*, 85–88.

23. Pierenkemper, "Trade Associations," 237.

24. Braunthal, *The Federation of German Industry*, 8.

25. Pierenkemper, "Trade Associations," 243–247.

26. Archibald J. Wolfe, *Commercial Organizations in Germany* (Washington, DC: U.S. Department of Commerce and Labor, 1914), 9–19.

27. Passant, *Short History*, 111.

28. Chandler, *Scale and Scope*, 410.

29. Ibid., 395.

30. Braunthal, *The Federation of German Industry*, 9–10.

31. Ibid., 12.

32. Henry Ashby Turner, Jr., *German Big Business and the Rise of Hitler* (New York: Oxford University Press, 1985), 36.

33. Stolper, *German Economy*, 136–137.

34. Ibid., 157–162.

35. Hermann Levy and A. H. Kelley, *Industrial Germany: A Study of Its Monopoly Organizations and Their Control by the State* (New York: Kelly Bookseller, 1966), 32.

36. Stolper, *German Economy*, 178.

37. Turner, *German Big Business*, xix.

38. Ibid., 4.

39. Stolper, *German Economy*, 210.

40. Braunthal, *The Federation of German Industry*, 16.

41. Ibid., 19.

42. Ibid., 23.

43. Carolyn Eisenberg, "U.S. Policy in Post-War Germany: The Conservative Restoration," *Science and Society* 46, no. 1 (1982): 24–38.

44. Braunthal, *The Federation of German Industry*, 31.

45. Jeffrey A. Hart, *Rival Capitalists: International Competitiveness in the United States, Japan, and Western Europe* (Ithaca, NY: Cornell University Press, 1992), 185.

46. David B. Audretsch, "Legalized Cartels in West Germany," *Antitrust Bulletin* 34, no. 3 (Fall 1989): 579–600.

47. David Rubenson, *Technology Policy in the Federal Republic of Germany* (Santa Monica, CA: Rand Corporation, January 1990), 14.

48. Ibid., 15.

49. Ibid., 17.

50. Hart, *Rival Capitalists*, 186.

51. Warren Davis, Thomas R. Howell, and Brent L. Bartlett, *Creating Advantage* (San Jose, CA: Semiconductor Industry Association, 1992), 313–321.

52. Simon Bulmer and William Patterson, *Federal Republic of Germany and the EC* (London: Allen and Unwin, 1987), 86.

53. Ibid., 90–91.

54. Chandler, *Scale and Scope*, 393–395.

55. Tom Peters, "The German Economic Miracle Nobody Knows: The Japanese May be Getting the Press, but the West Germans Are Getting the Business; Why Aren't We Paying Attention?" *Across the Board* 27, no. 4 (April 1990): 16–23.

Chapter 5

The Leaders

THE MANDALA

It was 1986 when we met in a hotel conference room in Washington, D.C. Each of us was the president of a trade association representing a segment of the American electronics industry. Among the associations represented were the American Electronics Association, the Electronic Industries Association, the Computer and Communications Industries Association, the Computer and Business Equipment Manufacturers Association and others, perhaps ten in all.

The group was to call itself the Electronics Roundtable (ERT). This was one of its early meetings, and my first. As the discussion started, I began to feel comfortable with this group of professionals, who were all more experienced in association management than I. At one point in the meeting, I asked a question that I felt was important to address, based on my several years working abroad in Japan and Germany, where I had been exposed to the cooperative aspects of their electronics industries. The question was, "Should we not describe a national vision of progress for the American electronics industry since our global competitors from Japan and Europe are doing so on a cooperative national basis?" As soon as I had tabled the question, the response was virtually explosive—that is, negatively so. The responses were varied depending on the viewpoint of the individual. They included:

- Associations exist to provide services to company members, not indulge in cooperatives as if they were farm granges.
- This is a global marketplace and, therefore, American companies must be free to operate with complete freedom. A national "vision" would tend to restrict individual efforts.
- U.S. productivity is the highest in the world despite Japan and Germany's higher rates of productivity growth, and, therefore, America has no need to plan out of fear.

- Japan and Germany are our friends and customers, not our enemies, and have invested in American companies and the nation.

- American corporations do not believe in shaping industrial policy through government intervention.

These were a few of the responses that were meant to convey a deep sense of support for the American ideal of free competition on a global basis without any governmental intervention. The answers implied or stated opinions that a common industry vision would work against American free trade principles and the free enterprise system. Reverend Adam Smith's ghost was certainly shaking his finger at me for suggesting actions that nonetheless worked in the common interest of the U.S. electronics industry.

Within three years, in 1989, data from various market research firms began to show that the U.S. electronics industry was losing its share of market in virtually all its market segments; the consumer electronics segment was a disaster, microelectronics was on the defensive against Japan, and the computer industry was beginning to feel substantial international competition. A number of steps involving U.S. industry-government joint activities were now being proposed by some associations, and they had been approved by the Congress and the administration. In fact, some cooperative consortia, such as SEMATECH, had already been formed by 1988.

Six years after the initial meeting, in September 1992, another Electronics Roundtable meeting took place. At that meeting a national technology policy (actually, an industry-led industrial policy) was to be voted on, and it was planned to be adopted by all associations. The associations now represented by the ERT were:

> American Electronics Association
> Computer and Business Equipment Manufacturers Association
> Computer and Communications Industry Association
> Electronic Industries Association
> Electronic Representatives Association
> Information Technology Association of America
> Institute of Electrical and Electronics Engineers
> Institute for Interconnecting and Packaging Electronic Circuits
> National Electronic Distributors Association
> Semiconductor Equipment and Materials International
> Semiconductor Industry Association
> Software Publishers Association
> Telecommunications Industry Association

The headings on the glossy three-page, American Electronics Association (AEA) document, titled *Call to Action: U.S. Technology Leadership Policy*, read:

- The Opportunity
- Establishing a National Vision
- Identifying a Strategy[1]

It was printed by the AEA for the fiftieth anniversary of its founding and had been adopted by the board of directors of that association. The AEA represents over 3,500 electronics firms in the United States, and included among them are virtually all the largest and smallest electronics firms in America. Every association took the brochure by AEA under serious consideration, and almost all accepted it. As a symbol of a unified electronics industry, the short AEA brochure had an illustrated geometric figure which presented the segments of the U.S. electronics industry and their employment in the form of a mandala (i.e., geometric forms within a geometric form). It is shown in Figure 5.1.

The road from Washington, D.C., in 1986, where the first meeting took place, to San Diego, California, in 1992 was a difficult one. It was difficult in terms of the decline in U.S. business revenues and job losses that had occurred in the electronics industry due to global competition. Nonetheless, it was also positive in the sense that constructing a common vision for America's electronics industry in 1992 was no longer deemed an inappropriate activity by trade associations.

ORGANIZING FOR COMPLEXITY

When we look at Japan, the United States, and Germany for the period of 1870 to 1940, which is virtually coincident with the second industrial revolution, several common experiences are evident. Each nation began the period with a reconstituted central government authority that had the capability of governing to every corner of its national borders. Each had experienced war or civil disturbances just prior to the establishment of its government—Meiji Japan, the U.S. Civil War, and the Second Empire in Germany. Each nation rapidly introduced major transportation and communication networks to the maximum extent that the technology of the time would allow, namely, railroads, steamships, telegraph lines, hard surface roads, and the new materials required to put them in place, such as steel and specific chemicals. By the beginning of the twentieth century, the distribution of electrical power, the production of gasoline combustion engines, the installation of telephone systems, and the mass production of consumer goods were beginning to change the nature of the economy and society.

The second industrial revolution may be considered as having two phases. The first was one of building new national networks that moved people and dispatched goods, distributed energy, and communicated voice and data. These networks were often funded or assisted by governments as well as by private investors, and they were primarily available for use by the general public. The services they provided did so at speeds and with capabilities that had never before been experienced. These networks, often called the infrastructure, increased the effectiveness and efficiency of economic activity not only by their use but also by their very construction. The periods of infrastructure creation are periods of both accelerated consumption and rapid investment, both interrelated and reinforcing. The early period of 1870 to 1914 brought forth great growth in

Figure 5.1
The AEA Mandala

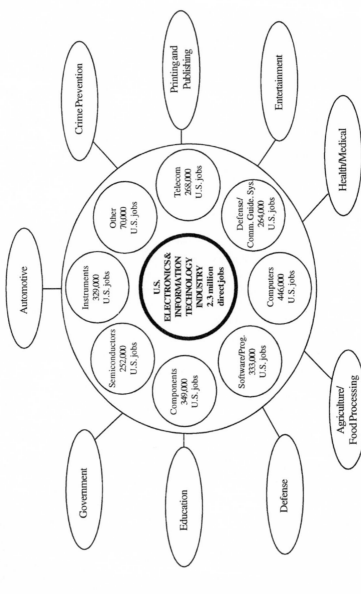

Crime Prevention

Printing and Publishing

Entertainment

Health/Medical

Automotive

Other 70,000 U.S. jobs

Telecom 268,000 U.S. jobs

Defense/ Comm. Guide. Sys. 264,000 U.S. jobs

Instruments 329,000 U.S. jobs

U.S. ELECTRONICS & INFORMATION TECHNOLOGY INDUSTRY 2.3 million direct jobs

Computers 446,000 U.S. jobs

Semiconductors 252,000 U.S. jobs

Components 349,000 U.S. jobs

Software/Prog. 333,000 U.S. jobs

Agriculture/ Food Processing

Government

Education

Defense

Source: American Electronics Association (AEA), *Call to Action: U.S. Technology Leadership Policy* [Brochure] (Washington, DC: AEA, 1992).

cooperative economic ventures, whether they were partnerships, joint-stock companies, corporations, cartels, or associations, because no organizations of lesser size or influence could bring together all the essential capital, labor, management skills, and required knowledge. In terms of capital, for example, each nation utilized a mix of government assistance, private investment institutions, and personal fortunes. However, the degree of government involvement in the formation of infrastructure in all three countries has remained high ever since the 1870s.

By the early twentieth century, the second phase of the industrial revolution, industrial activity began to shift toward the mass production of consumer goods and, in the vernacular of the times, "flivvers, flickers, and fones" (i.e., automobiles, motion picture theaters, and telephones) were becoming commonplace. To these, many other consumer items can be added, such as those that make up the list of small household appliances, including radios and electric and gas stoves. Coincident with the period of mass production, government continued to be involved with infrastructure development as parts of the infrastructure developed further; for example, transportation shifted in emphasis from railroads to airports and modern roads for the use by increasing numbers of airplanes, trucks, and busses.

Beginning in the 1870s, there also occurred dramatic changes in human services. For example, in education, the United States, through the Morrill Act, made possible the rapid establishment of many state universities; the German government continued to build upon the Prussian educational systems established in Berlin and elsewhere; and the Meiji rulers adopted the Western concept of universal education. The resulting educational institutions must be considered as part of the infrastructure and should, perhaps, be called enhancement institutions. In addition to educational institutions, dedicated research, and medical facilities, other societal services should be included within this category. The human intellect and the overall physical well-being of individuals are the focus, which is becoming increasingly evident, of the enhancement networks of today's infrastructure.

An analysis of the forms of infrastructure in place, but changing progressively, through the period of 1870 to 1940 would bring to the fore five basic networks: transportation, communication, energy, information, and enhancement networks. The first three had a dramatic impact in the nineteenth century, while the other two were of lesser prominence until after 1940.

One can readily look at each network and trace a path of development. For example, in transportation, we can begin with railroads and steamships and track the new applications to trucks and autos and then airplanes, and perhaps in the future to rocket-type, supersonic aircraft. Energy production and distribution began with distribution networks of electricity based on coal and then petroleum and on to power-generating dams and eventually, after 1950, to atomic power plants. One can trace the various infrastructure networks through time, and it can easily be recognized that fundamental to all these progressions in the networks are the basic technologies necessary for their construction. All enabling technology development is essentially created by human intellect working with basic earth materials or earlier discoveries to solve real problems. There are no inputs more fundamental than these.

Tracing a path for consumer products and services, as opposed to those products and services utilized by business and government, leads to the recognition that the path was similar in the sense of increasing complexity. The progression from early audio entertainment devices, namely, the radio of the early twentieth century, to today's audio systems, with their great breadth of capabilities, is one simple example. The technologies, manufacturing, services, and distribution of these modern household and personal products are highly complex relative to the products of old.

With this degree of increasing complexity of technology and infrastructure, shifts in product demand in capital goods and consumer goods, changing demographics and organizations, and the impact of a global economy, it is easily understood that the required socioeconomic interrelationship of government, business, households, and persons has also become increasingly complex. It is within these increasingly interactive economic activities that businesses and governments have found it necessary to deal, not only with each other as distinct firms and agencies, but also in more recent decades for each of them to deal with each other on an organized basis. Government and business have also found it necessary to deal with individuals and households, not as single units but as organized, collective consumer or citizen interest groups. It is neither possible nor efficient for every unit in the economy to deal with every other individual unit, that is, households or government officials.

It is essential, then, that business must organize itself in order to deal with two major forces: government and the marketplace of consumers and citizens. The attempts to organize themselves into intermediate organizations result in the organizations that are the primary subject of this book, the trade association. Associations can be considered organizations that operate in a region between the seemingly immovable, impenetrable rock of government and the risky, hard place called the marketplace. In an American colloquialism, in representing business interests the trade association is truly "between a rock and a hard place."

THE INFORMATION AGE

The decades since 1940 have been called the Atomic Age, the Space Age and, more recently, the Information Age. This last label is due to the extensive applications of microelectronics, computers, and telecommunications to all phases of daily activity. The first commercial delivery of computers, in the early 1950s by Univac and International Business Machines (IBM) accelerated their data-processing applications, while the microelectronic inventions in 1948 and 1958, of the transistor and integrated circuit, respectively, led to much higher performance in information technology than the vacuum tube–based applications of earlier years.[2]

The story of computers and semiconductor devices has been told many times before. The amazing improvements in speed of computation, reduction in size and power, and dramatic lowering of costs have all been broadly recounted. The progress in telecommunications during the 1940s, 1950s, and beyond has also been recounted by many sources. These accounts describe the progression from one-wire, one-channel lines to the most recent microwave, cellular, and fiber optics lines, which carry hundreds of thousands of telephone calls simultaneously. The combination of computers, microelectronics, and telecommunications has resulted in new products such as network computer systems, satellite communications, cellular telephone systems, and interactive television. The merging of these major inventions and innovations has resulted in such a pervasive range of electronics applications that terms such as *information highway* are now being used to represent its employment and future potential. The application of these information highway and electronic superhighway systems has allowed the rather rapid development of all other aspects of infrastructure activity and every related economic and social activity as well.[3] Today's infrastructure is consequently more complex, efficient, and effective than the world has ever seen. The interdisciplinary applications are myriad and extend far beyond those ordinarily imagined. The future may even marry bioengineering and information processing by the use of bio-chips, which will be biological in nature but electronic in function.[4] Biotechnology applications already extend from agriculture to medicine and industrial factories and are creating new industries, products, and services.

This wave of change is so pronounced, and so different than the term industrial revolution often conveys that the need for new nomenclature, such as the Information Age, is deemed necessary by most observers. This Information Age involves, therefore, the convergence of many new technologies, some of which are dependent on previous discoveries while others were developed to meet current needs. An exhaustive list of the new individual information-based inventions and innovations would be beyond the purpose here. However, these technologies have resulted in today's new key industries, the names of which are recognizable.

Among the new key industries utilizing the new technologies of the Information Age, the most frequently cited include microelectronics, biotechnology, new materials, aviation, telecommunications, robotics, and computers, including software.[5] These high-technology industries are knowledge-based and, therefore, heavily dependent on individual intellect, organized research, and large expenditures in the fields of research and development. Expenditures in R&D as a percentage of sales for selected high-technology industries, when compared to American industry overall, are generally greater. Table 5.1 compares these percentages for the United States to 1991.

High-technology industries also require large investments in capital equipment in those areas in which processes rather than assembled products are keys to growth. For example, the cost of a modern fabrication facility for manufacturing computer chips today is $1 billion; it will produce about $1 billion of chips per year and be obsolete for its original purpose in less than four years.[6] Not only

Table 5.1
Research and Development as a Percentage of Sales, by Industry

U.S. Industry	1986	1989	1991
All Industries	3.5	3.4	3.6
Semiconductors (Microelectronics)	12.2	9.3	10.0
Computers	8.3	9.0	8.8
Computer Software/ Services	7.7	13.2	13.5
Telecommunications	5.1	4.7	4.0
Aerospace (including Aircraft)	4.5	4.1	3.8
Drugs and Research (including Biotechnology)	7.8	10.1	10.8

Sources: "Innovation 1990 Issue," *Business Week*, June 15, 1990; *Business Week*, June 22, 1987; *Business Week*, June 29, 1992.

Note: The percentages do not include federal government–funded R&D expenditure, which is substantial for a number of the industries shown (e.g., Aerospace).

is the absolute equipment-purchasing cost high, but the output per year as a ratio to capital facilities costs is very low. Although semiconductor electronics in terms of chip manufacturing is highly sophisticated and involves high technology, this fact does not guarantee high capital returns. In fact, the technological product trends are more likely to be predictable than the demand cycles that produce revenues, thereby resulting in erratic corporate financial performance involving large and risky investments.[7]

It is the importance of a nation's high-technology industries and their global competitiveness to its national infrastructure and economy that each nation proceeds to positively affect the three factors emphasized in this book—technology, globalization, and business-government relations.

The technological progress that a nation is able to achieve is strongly related to its R&D expenditures in high-technology industries. The ratios in Table 5.1 indicate that the high-tech industries in the United States in 1991 spent from 1.1 (aerospace) to 3.75 (computer software and services) times the average for all industries. If federal research funds provided to industry are added to the aerospace ratio, the ratio would rise to 4.2. The higher ratio for high-tech industries is necessary for technological progress. The major U.S. competitors—Japan and Germany—also have high-tech industry R&D proportions higher than their overall manufacturing industries.

With regard to globalization, the ratio of high-tech exports to overall exports indicates the forward thrust of trade being generated by a nation. A review of Table 5.2 indicates the changes in share of total world high-tech exports of the United States, Japan, and Germany. The U.S. share has been in decline since 1970, with Japan and the Asian NICs (Newly Industrialized Countries) being the primary beneficiaries. However, the EC has still been able to maintain an overall higher share than the United States, despite a similar decline. When analyzed, the results since 1989 may indicate an improvement for the United States due to relative economic conditions in Japan and Europe. However, the trend would also be likely to continue if economic trends reverse themselves again. If another view is taken (Table 5.3) as to the ratio of high-tech exports to all exports by country, then the United States has declined in four of the five industries, Germany has declined in an equal number, and Japan has declined in only one industry. The high-technology globalization race is still on, and going at an intense pace.[8]

Table 5.2

Share of World High-Technology Exports, Selected Countries, 1970–1989 (Percentages)

Country	1970-73	1988-89
United States	29.5	20.6
Japan	7.1	16.0
EC	46.4	37.4
Germany	16.6	12.5
Asian NICs	1.3	8.8

Source: Laura D'Andrea Tyson, *Who's Bashing Whom? Trade Conflict in High Technology Industries* (Washington, DC: Institute for International Economics, 1992), p. 23, Table 2.3. Copyright © 1993.

Note: High-technology industries are defined on page 20 of Tyson, *Who's Bashing Whom*, and include chemicals, pharmaceuticals, data processing, telecommunications, electronic components, aircraft, scientific instruments, power-generating machinery, electronic machinery, and electronic office machines.

However, the focus in this area thus far has solely been on technology and globalization. It is now essential to address the third element, that of business-government relationships. This is strongly related to business organizations—the associations.

ASSOCIATIONS AND HIGH-TECH GLOBAL COMPETITIVENESS

Part of the reason for the riskiness of the high-technology industries is that they are global enterprises with many large global competitors who are often assisted by their governments and whose firms tend to cooperate through their associations. The purpose of cooperation is to assist in the achievement of goals of the firms, the industry, and the nation. Trade associations, research associations, and other cooperative organizations are highly evident in all the high-technology industries and the leading nations, the United States, Japan, and Germany, and are therefore critical to this purpose.[9] However, to better demonstrate the degree of cooperative effort in industry trade associations in these three countries, Table 5.4 lists corresponding high-technology industrial associations of Japan, United States, and Germany by the specific industries. The sample of twenty-four specific industries and

Table 5.3
Revealed Comparative Advantage in Selected High-Technology Products, Japan, Germany, and United States, 1970–1989

Product Group	Japan '70	Japan '89	Germany '70	Germany '89	United States '70	United States '89
All High-technology Products	80	133	111	91	219	192
Chemicals and Drugs (including Biotechnology)	86	47	159	132	111	124
Electronics (including Computers and Semiconductors)	110	200	99	57	212	168
Aircraft and Parts	6	7	20	79	440	416
Mechanical Equipment	93	144	140	129	156	145
Scientific Instruments	86	100	138	135	217	208

Source: Laura D'Andrea Tyson, *Who's Bashing Whom? Trade Conflicts in High Technology Industries* (Washington, DC: Institute for International Economics, 1992), p. 24. Copyright © 1993.

Note: Tabular values are the ratio of a country or region's world export share in that product group to that country's share of total world exports and manufacturers, expressed as an index.

their associations (of which there may be more than one per industry) shows the degree of cooperative industry effort that is pervasive across each nation.

COMPARISON OF NATIONAL ASSOCIATION STRUCTURE: UNITED STATES, JAPAN, AND GERMANY

In order to achieve total cooperation between business and government, associations are formed that extend beyond the area of high-technology industries. Industries of all types have been described in this volume. However, after all the data has been compiled, there are eight types of associations existing in the United States, Japan, and Germany:

- Peak, Commercial
- Peak, Industry
- Broad Industry-Specific
- Segment-Specific Industry
- Research Associations
- Cartels
- Trade Promotion
- Employer Associations

These eight types and their designated, or sample, associations are shown for each country in Table 5.5. All these types and the examples have been described in this book, and therefore, a complete discussion of each type and example is unnecessary. However, a close examination of each one as part of the overall

Table 5.4

Selected High-Technology Industrial Associations of Japan, United States, and Germany

Industry	Japan	United States	Germany
Precision Instruments	Japan Precision Measuring Instruments Association	Precision Measurement Association	Precision Tools Association (within VDMA: see "Industrial Machinery")
Ceramics	The Ceramic Society of Japan	American Association of Ceramic Industries	Association of the German Ceramic Industry
		United States Advanced Ceramic Association	
		Technical Ceramic Manufacturers Association	
Telecommunications	The Telecommunications Associations	Telecommunication Industry Association	Federal Association of Telecommunications
	Japan Telecommunication Industries Federation		Telecommunication Manufacturers Association (within ZVEI; see "Electrical Goods")
Robotics	Japan Industrial Robot Association	Robotic Industry Association	Association of Assembling, Handling, Industrial Robots (within VDMA)
Information Industry	Japan Information Service Industry Association	Information Industry Association	German Information Technology Manufacturers' Association (within VDMA and ZVEI)

Table 5.4
Selected High-Technology Industrial Associations of Japan, United States, and Germany (Continued)

Industry	Japan	United States	Germany
Office Automation	Japan Institute of Office Automation	Office Automation Society International Computer and Business Equipment Manufacturers Association	German Information Technology Manufacturers Association (within VDMA and ZVEI)
Video	Japan Videotex Information Providers Association	Videotex Industry Association	German Video Association
Satellite Communications	International Satellite Communications Society, Inc.	International Association of Satellite Users and Suppliers	Telecommunication Manufacturers Association (within ZVEI)
Hydraulics	The Japan Hydraulic and Pneumatic Association	Hydraulic Tool Manufacturers Association	Fluid Power Systems and Components Association (within VDMA)
Communications	Japan Information and Communication Association	International Interactive Communications Society Computer and Communications Industry Association	Telecommunication Manufacturers' Association (within ZVEI)
Specialty Steel	Specialty Steel Association	Specialty Steel Industry of the United States	German Steelwork Association
Powder Metals	The Association of Powder Process Industry and Engineering Japan	Metal Powder Industries Federation	Powder Metallurgy Association

Table 5.4

Selected High-Technology Industrial Associations of Japan, United States, and Germany (Continued)

Industry	Japan	United States	Germany
Solar System	Solar System Development Association	Solar Energy Industries Association	German Solar Energy Specialists Association
Machine Tools	Advanced Machining Technology and Development Association	National Tooling and Machining Association	Machine Tools and Manufacturing Systems Association (within VDMA)
	The Japan Machinery Federation		
	Japan Machine Tool Builder's Association		
Industrial Machinery	Japan Industrial Technology Association	Association for Manufacturing Technology	German Machinery and Plant Manufacturers' Association (VDMA)
	The Japan Society of Industrial Machinery Manufacturers	American Supply and Machinery Manufacturers Association	
Motor Vehicle	Japan Automobile Manufacturers Association, Inc.	Motor Vehicle Manufacturers Association of the United States	Association of the German Motor Industry
Aerospace	The Society of Japanese Aerospace Companies, Inc.	Aerospace Industries Association of America	German Aerospace Industries Association
Electrical Goods	The Japan Electrical Manufacturers Association	National Electrical Manufacturers Association	German Electrical and Electronic Manufacturers' Association (ZVEI)

Table 5.4
Selected High-Technology Industrial Associations of Japan, United States, and Germany (Continued)

Industry	Japan	United States	Germany
Automatic Controls	Japan Automatic Controls Industrial Association	American Automatic Control Council	Association of Assembling, Handling, Industrial Robots (within VDMA)
	Japan Electric Measuring Instrument Manufacturers Association		Section Process Periphery (within VDMA)
Electronics	Japan Electric Measuring Instrument Manufacturers Association	American Electronics Association	Association of Test and Measurement Automation (within ZVEI)
	Radio Engineering and Electronics Association Electronic Industries Association of Japan	Electronic Industries Association	
Camera	Japan Camera Industry Association	National Association of Photographic Manufacturers	Federal Camera Association
Chemicals	Japan Chemical Industry Association	Chemical Manufacturers Association	Association of the German Chemical Industry

Table 5.4

Selected High-Technology Industrial Associations of Japan, United States, and Germany (Continued)

Industry	Japan	United States	Germany
Pharmaceuticals	The Federation of Pharmaceutical Manufacturers Association	Nonprescription Drug Manufacturers Association	Federal Association of the Pharmaceutical Industry
	Japan Pharmaceutical Manufacturers Association	National Association of Pharmaceutical Manufacturers	
	The Proprietary Association of Japan	Pharmaceutical Manufacturers Association	
Graphic Arts	Japan Association of Graphic Arts Technology	Graphic Communications Association	
		Graphic Arts Technical Foundation	

Sources: Zenkoku Kakushu Dantai Meikan, 1989 (Directory of all types of national associations), vols. 1, 2 (Tokyo: Shiba, 1989); Deborah M. Burek, ed. Encyclopedia of Associations, vols. 1–3 (Detroit: Gale Research, 1991); research by G. Rosler for German associations (1993).

Table 5.5
Comparison of Association Structure by Country

Association Type	Japan	Germany	United States
Peak, Commercial	*Chamber of Commerce and Industry*	*Chamber of Commerce and Industry*	*U.S. Chamber of Commerce*
	Voluntary membership; government regulated; publicly and privately funded. Includes most businesses; close cooperation with government.	Mandatory membership; government regulated; publicly and privately funded. Includes virtually all business; close dialogue with government.	Voluntary membership; totally private; 100,000s of members, but not all businesses. "Issue-by-issue" relationship with government.
Peak, Industry	*Keidanren*	*Bundesbund Duetsche Industries (B. D. I.)*	*National Association of Manufacturers*
	(Japan Federation of Economic Organizations)	(Federation of German Industries)	
	Strong organization comprised of large corporations and associations that generally speak for large businesses, industries. Almost universal membership, close cooperation with government.	Central organization of thirty-eight associations, no corporations allowed. Each association in turn has corporate and/or association members. Close ties to German government and parliament.	Primarily represents large corporations and associations. However, less than 10 percent of all corporations are represented. Relates to government on an issue-by-issue basis.

Table 5.5
Comparison of Association Structure by Country (Continued)

Association Type	Japan	Germany	United States
Broad Industry-Specific (Example used: Electronics. However industry organizations of this type exists for other industries)	*Electronic Industries Association of Japan (EIAJ)* Includes hundreds of corporations as well as thirteen other associations such as: -Japan Electronic Industry Development Association (JEIDA) (computers) -Communications Industries Association of Japan (CIAJ) (telephone, telegraph equipment) -Japan Business Machine Makers Association (JBMA)(business machines) Partially government funded; under jurisdiction of MITI; central data exchange between corporations	*Zentralverbund Elektotechniche und Elektronikindustrie ZVEI* (German Electrical and Electronics Manufacturers Association) Hundreds of corporations and twenty-nine product divisions including: electric devices, transformers, alternators and power supplies, power capacitors, switch gear and industrial central equipment plus twenty-three others. Partial government funds; data exchange between corporations.	*American Electronics Association (AEA)* Includes 3,500 companies; privately funded; Voluntary membership, little information interchanged. Association members as of 1994. AEA is organized by region. A parallel organization to the AEA, the Electronic Industries Association, is organized by industry but to a much lesser degree than the Electronics Industries Association of Japan (EIAJ) or the ZVEI.

113

Table 5.5
Comparison of Association Structure by Country (Continued)

Association Type	Japan	Germany	United States
Segment Specific Industry Associations	Segment specific associations are included in the related associations shown above and represent computers, business machines, communications, electronic measuring equipment, and similar industries.	Segment specific associations are included in the related associations shown above and represent electronic components, audio and video equipment, measurements and control, and similar industries.	Segment-specific associations are independent. See interrelated electronics association listed as Electronics Roundtable on previous pages as examples. All these associations are independent of each other and do not have a hierarchical superior.
Research Associations	Many research associations since earliest association history of this Meiji period. See Chapter 2 for list of present-day research associations in Japan.	Research associations have been part of Germany's association historical movements since the 19th century. See Fraunhofer Institutes in Table 4.3.	The National Cooperative Research Act (1983) allowed manufacturing firms to form research consortium without violating antitrust laws. See list of prominent U.S. consortia in Table 3.3.
Cartels	Cartels allowed by law, and often encouraged. Informal cartel behavior also exists within and between *keiretsus*. The Japan Fair Trade Commission that oversees this area is relatively weak.	Cartels allowed by law. Most cartels are vertical rather than horizontal, and the federal cartel office cooperates with domestic industries to reach agreements on cartel behavior. Cartel behavior is lessening since European Unions established.	Cartels are explicitly illegal, and their members may be punished by fine, imprisonment, or both.

114

Table 5.5
Comparison of Association Structure by Country (Continued)

Association Type	Japan	Germany	United States
Export Promotion Associations	Many examples with long historical standing. See Table 2.3 for example.	Export associations have existed since the nineteenth century and have at times acted as cartels.	The Webb Pomerene Act (1918) and the Export Trading Company Act (1982), which allowed export associations to be exempt from U.S. antitrust law, did not result in any significant export association developments.
Employee Associations	*Nikkeiren* Association of executives of corporations organized to negotiate with labor.	*Vereinigung der Dautschen Arbitgebervubande (VDA)* Association of employers which deals with labor matters. Employers and labor have developed closer bonds than in Japan or U.S.A since 1945.	*No organizational counterpart to either the Nikkeiren or the V. D. A.*
Summary	Associations, corporations, industries, and government agencies are closely and continuously intertwined with regard to business behavior and objectives. In summation: *collaborative capitalism.*	Associations, corporations, industries, and government tend to generally cooperate in an organized hierarchy such that government can generally rely on common industry positions being reached. In summation: *cooperative capitalism.*	Associations, corporations, industry, and government may cooperate but often take adversarial positions such that competition in all areas of private business as well as public policy is common. In summation: *competitive capitalism.*

structure and relating it to previous descriptions will provide an insight by nation that is unique, since this structure has apparently not been constructed elsewhere.

ASSOCIATIONS WITHIN THREE FORMS OF CAPITALISM

The method adopted in previous chapters was to link business history, political and social development, and the association movement so that the interrelationship of the three elements could be presented as an integrated picture.

The degree of central government control; the development of financial institutions; the place of the consumer, labor, and foreign interests; the extent of cooperation between all segments of the economy, both private and public; and the historical and cultural antecedents that formed the underlying basis of the national environment have been brought together so they could be added to the story of why associations in each nation have developed as they are presently. As each chapter was written, a summary of characteristics involving these factors was given in order to encapsulate the conditions of the periods, with emphasis on the influence of each segment of the political and economic structure, including associations, of each nation. In addition, at the end of the chapter on each country, the characteristics of these associations were given.

A clearer picture of the business-government relationships in each country would provide a better international comparison. To do so, it is best to specify the political-economic units that bring influence to bear on public policies related to global competitiveness. These political-economic units can be organized in five groups: government and its related institutions, including quasi-public and wholly funded organizations; business and its associations, consortia, and other formal groupings, as well as informal ties; labor, whether as individuals or as company unions or industry organizations of either skilled or unskilled worker members; the consumer, whose economic sovereignty must be highly regarded and whose influence has spread to social and environmental issues as well; and finally, foreign interests, which are each day becoming more important as the world's economy becomes increasingly globalized. These segments—government, business, labor, consumer, and foreign interests—are the major influential forces in each nation's quest for competitive industrial success on a global basis. In addition, each of these forces has organized itself into societies, agencies, unions, associations, consortia, or other association configurations in order to strengthen their positions and speak in as unified a manner as possible.

The organization of business into associations has been brought about in order to strengthen its position overall, whether the grouping is by specific industry, by industry life stages, or by international objectives. The relationship of organized business to the other forces or influences will be used here to label the forms of capitalism existing in the nations studied here.[10]

Examples of organized influences can be given for the United States, Japan, and Germany. The American experience, which occurred at a time when the fears of consumers were amplified by the cries of farmers and small businessmen, had great impact on the success of the antitrust movement and the later failure of the NRA in the 1930s.[11] An international comparison with regard to labor is illustrated by the period when American labor became legally able to organize. It became a greater force in its economy than the Japanese company unions but was less effective than the workers of Germany, who sit at the governance table with management in the larger German firms.[12] Foreign influence in the American economy is by far greater than that in Japan or in Germany, an issue that many American writers have addressed.[13] The degree of influence and the organization of that influence, including the use of associations, may be used to categorize a form of capitalism as it exists in Japan, the United States, and Germany.

In Table 5.5, the comparison of association activity in the three nations indicates the greatest degree of association activity in Japan, followed by Germany and then the United States. The relationship of business to government, as shown by the tie-ins of business associations to government actions and agencies, is also shown to have the same ranking by nation. In the case of Japan, the government and business tend to collaborate; in other words, they work in partnership and in a mutually reinforcing manner, with the consent of other social and economic groups such as labor and the consumer. Consequently, the term *collaborative capitalism* appears appropriate. In the case of Germany, new definitions of its forms of capitalism are not necessary. The term *cooperative capitalism* is milder than the older term, *organized capitalism*, and most researchers would agree, however, that today's German economy has more subtle means of close cooperation than the more explicit ones of a century ago. The close cooperative attitude of government and business is well entrenched there. Despite the realities of intense global competitiveness, the United States has attempted to maintain the ideals of free markets, free enterprise, and pure competition. It is only since 1970 that this model has been questioned as America's dominance in global markets has begun to drop dramatically and the standard of living of American citizens appears to have fallen markedly.[14]

However, in order to become more competitive globally, the United States may need to form a new American ideal. It may be necessary for this nation to place greater emphasis on a government-business partnership, which may, in turn, require extensive trade association activity. Moreover, for any nation, and not only America, to place greater emphasis on a business-government relationship, the relative influence of consumers, labor, and foreign interests on the nation's economy must diminish. Influential guidance of national economies by each of the various political-economic units can be considered in terms of the economic and political outcomes. The outcomes in terms of the benefit to every party will become the result of the decisions of those with the greatest power and influence.

One means of depicting the influence of national stakeholders in each country, and therefore the relative positions of Japan's collaborative capitalism, Germany's cooperative capitalism, and the U.S. competitive capitalism, is to draw them on a "spider web" graph. In Figure 5.2, each axis extending from the center depicts the degree of influence of each influencing force. The influence increases with the distance from the center. There are five axes, depicting the expanded definitions of government, business, labor, consumers, and foreign influences. Each of these are connected to provide a five-sided figure whose relative size and direction represents a graphic depiction of a form of capitalism. The full picture is shown in Figure 5.2.

The Japanese case indicates the strong collaborative influence of business and government at the expense of the other axes. The German depiction indicates a highly influential position for labor, with the government-business relationship less strong than in Japan but stronger than in the United States. The American case indicates, by its strong direction toward the high end of the consumer axis, the tendency for consumer sovereignty to have the greatest influence when compared to Japan and Germany.

SUMMARY

The preceding four chapters have dealt with associations from a historic perspective. The beginnings, development, and specialization into various types of associations have been described. The description of these past and present events by country also provides the background for understanding national differences between their associations. From these histories, then, the structure of associations for high-tech industries and for eight types of associations were shown, not only as data but also as the culmination of 150 years of business and economic history. These past events were also able to show how associations, in various ways and forms, were an essential part of business-government relations. Finally, the closeness of these relationships allows the categorizations of the specific forms of capitalism for the three nation-competitors. This last analysis (as a "spider web" diagram; see Figure 5.2) provides others with a framework for further study and analysis.

For Americans, the most important information from this part is that of the three competitors, the United States places the least emphasis on business-government relations and the functions and forms of American associations are not as formalized or directed to a purpose as those of Germany and Japan. The characteristics of each nation's associations, as described at the end of Chapters 2, 3, and 4, show a marked difference between the three nations.

The lessons to be learned from this historical perspective can only be validated by results in the global marketplace. The results in terms of high-tech exports and in world share in high-technology industries indicate that business-government relationships in Germany and Japan are assisting their industries in maintaining their competitive position in the world vis-à-vis the United States. When the relative sizes of each of these nations is considered in terms of population and resources, the maintenance of competitiveness by Japan and Germany, although not surprising, is certainly worthy of note. Moreover, since there are

Figure 5.2
**Relative Influence of Government, Business, Labor, Consumers,
and Foreign Interests in Japan, the United States, and Germany**

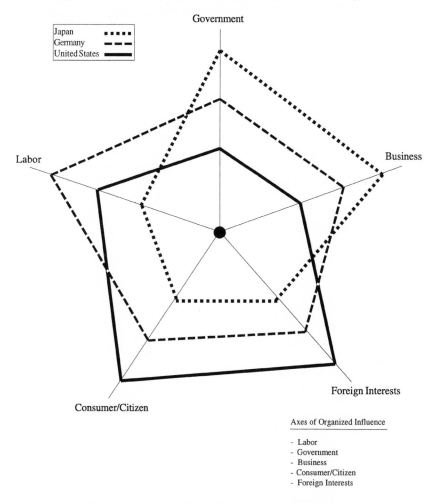

Note: Group influence increases as the distance from the center point increases.

major differences between the United States and the two foreign countries with regard to three factors—technology, globalization, and business-government relations—these elements are worthy of very close study. This study indicates that associations in all forms can play a crucial part in attaining global competitiveness through business-government partnerships. It also indicates that association leadership and cooperation in technology, and in increasing the rate of globalization by opening markets, are also crucial.

The lessons from our past and present legacies can now be used as a foundation on which to build the additional knowledge presented in this book to aid in designing associations for the coming era.

NOTES

1. American Electronics Association, *Call to Action: U.S. Technology Leadership Policy* (Washington, DC: American Electronics Association, 1992).

2. Robert U. Ayres, *The Next Industrial Revolution* (Cambridge, MA: Ballinger Publishing, 1984), 141–160.

3. John Markoff, "Building the Electronics Superhighway," *New York Times*, 24 January 1993.

4. Sheridan Tatsuno, *The Technopolis Strategy: Japan, High Technology and the Control of the 21st Century* (New York: Prentice Hall, 1986), 105, 161.

5. Lester C. Thurow, *Head to Head: The Coming Economic Battle among Japan, Europe and America* (New York: William Morrow, 1992), 45.

6. Lawrence M. Fisher, "Intel Raising Capacity of Chip Factory: A $1 Billion Investment in Future Market Share," *New York Times*, 2 April 1993.

7. Andrew A. Procassini, *The Volatility of Semiconductor Demand and Industry Performance*, DBA Diss., Nova University, 1987 (Ann Arbor, MI: University Microfilms International, 1987).

8. Laura d'Andrea Tyson, *Who's Bashing Whom? Trade Conflict in High-Technology Industries* (Washington, DC: Institute for International Economics, 1992), 23.

9. Warren Davis, Thomas R. Howell, and Brent L. Bartlett, *Creating Advantage* (San Jose, CA: Semiconductor Industry Association, 1992).

10. Jeffrey A. Hart, *Rival Capitalists: International Competitiveness in the United States, Japan, and Western Europe* (Ithaca, NY: Cornell University Press, 1992), 281.

11. Ellis W. Hawley, *The New Deal and the Problem of Monopoly* (Princeton, NJ: Princeton University Press, 1966), 81–84.

12. Hart, *Rival Capitalists*, 281.

13. Pat Choate, *Agents of Influence: How Japan's Lobbyists in the U.S. Manipulate America's Political and Economical Systems* (New York: Knopf, 1990), 257–280.

14. Thurow, *Head to Head*, 29, 164–166, 206.

III

HIGH-TECH INDUSTRIES AND THEIR TRADE ASSOCIATIONS

Chapter 6

Introduction to the High-Tech Sector

A number of industries have been singled out as representative of the global, high-technology environment in which the United States, Japan, and Germany are major players. From among these industries our attention has focused on microelectronics, computer systems, aerospace, and biotechnology. These industries, often called strategic industries by government officials, industry spokespersons, and academic experts, are believed to be essential to national economic growth and national security. There is some consensus that high-tech industries involve: (1) frequent infusion of new knowledge and discoveries; (2) economies of scale based on learning as well as other factors; (3) globally based product demand; and (4) major impacts on both upstream (supplier) and downstream (customer) industries. These high-tech industries have also been characterized by highly intense competition involving entrepreneurial start-ups as well as established corporations, high R&D expenditures, the need for large amounts of capital, rapid replacement of products by better, and generally less costly, generations, and a global competition that often involves government involvement. All these factors result in a high degree of business uncertainty and risk, which continues to encourage, as it has in the past, the organization of industry firms into trade associations of various types.

The trade associations of today that represent the interests of high-tech firms provide internal industry services as well as external activities in reaction to other groups with which they interact. The internal services, which are often similar to those of many other older trade associations, are traditional and government relations activities. The external forces that today's high-tech associations face, however, are more highly organized than those of decades ago. High-tech industries face organizations that represent (1) government, including its agencies and its quasi-public organizations; (2) labor, in all its organized forms; (3) consumer and citizen interests; (4) foreign entities, including foreign governments, industries and firms; and, finally, (5) other businesses, particularly the upstream suppliers and downstream customer industries. All these forces, taken together, form the high-tech industries' business environment.

With regard to the specific interactions of high-tech industries with these other forces, or influences, a few can be listed rather quickly. Government and quasi-public institutions attempt to focus on industry-related issues such as technology, trade, taxes, employment, and competition. Upstream and downstream industries attempt to influence technology, prices, quality, and supply. Consumer and citizen groups, although often accepting new and spectacular products quickly, may also in time set up opposition to the producing firms in attempts to influence various related environmental, safety, and health issues. Labor—organized labor unions as well as individuals who are skilled, trained, and highly educated—also impact these knowledge-intensive industries, but in a different manner than they impacted the older, more physically labor-intensive industries. Foreign governments and industries may be allies or competitors, depending on the circumstances and issues. In all, high-technology industries face a more diverse and aggressive set of influences and interactions than the more mature industries, which came to grips with similar forces in their earlier stages and have since reached some level of accommodation.

In order to offset these external forces, today's emerging high-technology industries tend to become organized into associations relatively early in their existence. The firms, individually or through their industry trade associations, attempt to deal with internal problems and external forces while at the same time achieving specific, key measures of business success, namely, a desired growth, an increasing share of market, high levels of profit, and equitable returns for their stakeholders. Achievements of these key measures for domestic industries will affect, in turn, the level of national employment, the gross domestic product, the state of the environment, and many other national measures of well-being. It is this linkage of new, quickly emerging high-tech industry sectors with future national well-being that forms the basis of determining appropriate public policy that takes into account the changing industrial structure and its corresponding business organizations.

Since high-tech firms are a focal point of external forces, they tend to form or join business organizations that can better deal with these influences. The existing trade organizations, which can be joined by high-tech firms, are often too broad in a business sense (e.g., the U.S. Chamber of Commerce and National Association of Manufacturers). Alternately, an appropriate association may not yet exist because the firms have not come together to form it. When new associations are finally formed, they sometimes broaden in a relatively short time and, in turn, split again to form more narrowly focused trade associations. Sometimes the reverse occurs and narrower industry segments, which had formed separate associations, later join to form a larger organization. The progression in trade association formation may be a function of new technologies that give birth to new industries or of the coalescence of relatively new trade associations, which recognize broader issues requiring greater breadth and strength but less need for representation of a narrower segment. Often the formation of industry organizations is on an ad hoc basis and they are disbanded after the pertinent issue has been resolved. These ad hoc types of organizations are generally called projects, task forces, or similar terms, rather than associations.

Regardless of its phase of formation, a trade association is intended to contribute to the success of the industry it represents. The clearest measures of success (the consequences of an industry's capabilities and competitiveness) can be definitively measured by profits, market growth, share of market, and the benefits to industry stakeholders—management, employees, stock owners, suppliers, and customers. The determinants of an industry's capabilities and competitive advantage are represented by two factors: (1) the sources of advantage, namely, the industry skills and resources; and (2) the positional advantage achieved by management through lowering costs or providing superior value.[1] The combination of source advantages and positional advantages, as developed and implemented by management, results in the consequences of competitiveness, namely, profits, growth, increased share of market, and stakeholder returns.

Trade associations assist their industries in achieving success by contributing positively to the sources of advantage, namely, skills and resources, or by supporting positional advantage by lowering the cost of operation or raising the value of the product. For example, trade associations can provide (1) training for employees, thereby raising their skills; (2) market data for use by market researchers as a forecasting resource; (3) assistance in removing odious government regulations, thereby lowering costs; or (4) technology programs that raise the value of the industry's products. Associations can and do affect competitive advantage, and they should be evaluated in this light. In many cases the evaluation is limited or solely qualitative, making their value indeterminate.

The remainder of Part 3 will describe several high-tech trade associations to help explain how industries form associations, how the associations provide internal services and interact with external organizations, how their activities relate to industry competitiveness, and how they are evaluated. The organizations described include (1) a trade association formed by the high-technology firms of decades ago that still represents a high-technology industry today and has grown from its initial base (Aerospace Industries Association); (2) a trade association (Industrial Biotechnology Association) formed by new and old firms utilizing a new technology, biotechnology, which was recently combined with another, parallel trade association (Association of Biotechnology Companies) to form a broader one; (3) a trade association (Semiconductor Industry Association) formed by firms that had, to some degree, separated themselves from a broad, specific industry association, the American Electronics Association; and finally, (4) a combination of three groups that act to represent a single industry, the computer systems industry—the Computer and Business Equipment Manufacturers Association, the American Electronics Association, and the Computer Systems Policy Project (which claims not to be a trade association but rather a short-term collective effort).

These trade associations and their related industries have been the subject of a great deal of scrutiny in the last decade. They are all industries based on American inventions and technology and whose firms were founded by American entrepreneurs or corporations. These industries achieved global dominance and yet today face great challenges by foreign nations and firms. Further scrutiny here will provide greater insight into the roles of their trade associations. The final findings and recommendations will be described in the concluding chapters of this book.

NOTE

1. George Day and Robin Wensley, "Assessing Advantage: A Framework for Diagnosing Competitive Superiority," *Journal of Marketing* 52, no. 2 (April 1988): 1–20; Michael E. Porter, *Competitive Advantage: Creating and Sustaining Superior Performance* (New York: MacMillan, Inc., 1985), 1-16.

Chapter 7

The Aerospace Industries and Their Association

THE PRESIDENT VISITS BOEING

In February 1993, President Bill Clinton arrived at the Boeing Aircraft plant in Everett, Washington, to present his new national technology plan for raising America's competitiveness in global commercial markets. The president was to speak, not only to 5,000 assembled Boeing employees, but also to a dozen key airline and aerospace industry executives who were there for a private meeting as well as to listen to his public speech. On arrival, the president's plane, *Air Force One*, taxied past a billion dollars worth of Boeing 747-400 aircraft lined up for delivery to foreign international carriers. He knew that although these planes, which were destined for export, represented American jobs, Boeing planned to reduce its work force by 20 percent in the next eighteen months because of U.S. defense cutbacks and weak demand from ailing U.S. airline companies. The contrast could not be easily dismissed.

The president spoke to the crowd in the plant from a platform placed next to a 747 aircraft completing production and slated for delivery to Air France. His speech was primarily about the new technology program, which included the redirecting of research and development; the education and training of workers; increased cooperation among government, business, and labor; and better access by small business to innovative technology and financing for it. Specific proposals for the aerospace industry called for revitalizing the country's aeronautical research and development infrastructure, including the building of new wind tunnels, and increasing civil aviation research into the safety and noise aspects of advanced aircraft. These were future efforts and did not address the impending massive layoffs.[1]

Note: The author is appreciative of the work of Dr. Philip A. Mundo, whose research reports on the specific association entities were incorporated into Chapters 7, 8, and 10. Dr. Mundo also conducted the interviews noted for these chapters.

The president blamed Boeing's business slump on "the $26 billion that the U.S. sat by and let Europe plow into Airbus" and pledged to "[invest] to change the rules of the game."[2] The game, however, had been in play since 1968, with a number of former presidents at the helm as the score against the United States in terms of the market share of commercial aircraft became more unfavorable by the year. The Reagan "Strike Force" cited the Airbus for unfair practices but took no action against the involved nations of France, Germany, United Kingdom, and Spain.[3] It was not until July 1992 that the U.S.-EC Commercial Aircraft Subsidy Agreement was signed and the European subsidies were limited.

After the speech to the crowd, the president met privately with a group of invited executives representing aerospace manufacturers and airline operators. Among the manufacturers were airframe assemblers, such as the host, Boeing, as well as aircraft components manufacturers. The airline executives were concerned with unfair competition by Chapter 11 companies, the proposed fuel tax on carriers, foreign ownership of U.S. airlines, fare structures, and the difficulty of obtaining financing. The Airbus, the president's "whipping boy," was either not addressed or any mention reported, although the media had just announced that Germany's Deutsche Aerospace was rolling out its first A321 aircraft from a new Airbus facility in Hamburg.

The ability to reach consensus on the application of U.S. trade law to the foreign subsidization of aircraft is stymied by the opposing views of the U.S. participants in the issue. The aircraft manufacturers sell to the foreign firm Airbus, and the U.S. airlines buy Airbus planes at cheaper prices than domestic craft and have close relationships with foreign governments. The U.S. aircraft components companies sell to both the U.S. airframe companies and Airbus. In fact, the U.S. content across Airbus Industries' entire family of aircraft is between thirty and forty percent.[4]

Despite the falling market shares of U.S. aircraft-manufacturing companies, the layoff of thousands of workers, and the willingness of the president to move aggressively to fight the battle, no U.S. trade laws have been invoked.

The issue of foreign subsidies, and its part in the industrial targeting of the aircraft-manufacturing industry by foreign governments, are but two of thirty-nine issues described in a Aerospace Industries Association document of January 1993, titled "Industry Competitive Enhancement Initiative."[5] The AIA already has a great deal on its public policy plate, and these two portions will be the toughest to handle.

THE INDUSTRY

Today the core of the U.S. aerospace industry is the aircraft industry, which began with the Army Signal Corps order of the first plane from the Wright brothers in 1908. With the beginning of World War I, the government rushed to order 25,000 more planes, an action meant to bring America's air strength up to par with that of the other combatant nations. By 1918, the United States had purchased 14,000 aircraft, costing $350 million, from companies employing 175,000 people. At that time America was dominated by large oil, steel, chemical, and banking corporations while organizations producing innovative consumer products—autos, household durables, and entertainment products—were entering their early stage of growth.

The aircraft industry (as well as these newer industries) was populated by a variety of makers who were intensely competitive. As one aspect of this competition, the new aircraft industry faced the specter of bitter patent disputes which delayed national production requirements. The industry attempted to find ways of settling the disputes, diffusing its knowledge and techniques and promoting defense preparedness by establishing the Aircraft Manufacturers Association.

Simultaneously, the Air Mail Act kept the industry afloat in the 1920s, and this resulted in a greater demand for civil aircraft as opposed to military planes. Soon civil aircraft production exceeded military output and the industry's thoughts turned toward passenger aircraft. The major customer, however, continued to be the U.S. government, which, for example, accounted for 90 percent of Douglas Aircraft's income in 1933. Government policy resulted in a highly concentrated industry, whereby ten airframe companies received 90 percent of the military's business and two firms produced 100 percent of its engines.

World War II made the aircraft industry a national industrial leader. In 1944, a total of 96,000 aircraft were built and a number of firms became recipients of tens of millions of dollars of government investment. With the end of World War II the industry fell into recession, but with the oncoming Korean War and the ensuing Cold War, military production returned.[6]

The postwar period also eventually brought back a great demand for domestic and international passenger and freight air transport. By 1958, the industry employed nearly a million workers. By the 1960s the aerospace industry not only produced civilian aircraft, it also manufactured products for defense (military aircraft, helicopters, missiles, and sophisticated command-and-control electronics) and outer space (rockets, spacecraft, satellites, and all the related communication and computer electronics). By the late 1970s the output of the industry was diversified among all three areas—civil aircraft, defense, and space. In 1977, the total sales of the U.S. aerospace industry had reached $32 billion with approximately $6 billion of civil aircraft, $11 billion of military aircraft, $4 billion of missiles, $5 billion for outer space, and $6 billion of related products and services.[7]

In the prior decade, however, other nations had also begun to seriously pursue aerospace endeavors, with particular attention to civilian aircraft. In 1968, France and Germany began joint development of a 267-seat wide-body A-300 aircraft and its derivative, the A-310. The two nations poured $2.6 billion into the project. In 1970, Airbus Industrie was formed by a consortium of Aerospatiale (France), Deutsche Airbus (Germany), British Aerospace (Great Britain), and CASA (Spain), with its headquarters in Toulouse, France.[8] By 1991, Airbus had captured over 30 percent of the world market for larger commercial jets and had replaced McDonnell Douglas as the second largest producer in the world.[9]

The success of Airbus has had a great impact on America's major aircraft manufacturers; however, a look at the world aerospace market would also show the overall impact of international aerospace products. In 1985, the U.S. share of the world's aerospace market stood at 73 percent ($97 billion), but by 1990, it had fallen to less than 60 percent ($134 billion), while the world marketplace grew from about $130 billion in 1985 to about $220 billion in 1990. Although U.S. exports of aerospace products as a percentage of total U.S. aerospace sales rose from 19 percent ($20 billion) in 1986 to 30 percent ($30 billion) in 1990, the U.S. imports also rose from $8 billion in 1986 to $12 billion in 1990.[10]

An overall view of the world's major-country producers, their major companies, their overall share, and their civil/military breakdown will help to assess the U.S. position as it is viewed, based on 1990 data. The world's major-country producers are the United States, Great Britain, France, Germany, and Japan, with the European countries accounting for 90 percent of the EC totals.[11] The United States, the European Community, Japan, and Canada account for well over 90 percent of the free world's production. The U.S. production accounts for about 60 percent of this groups' total. A division into civil versus military and sales by country or region gives a view of the aerospace business in 1990 (Table 7.1).

Table 7.1
Application Breakdown and Sales by Country/Region for the Aerospace Industry, 1990

Country/Region	Percentage		Sales	
	Civil	Military	$ Millions	(%)
Europe (EC) (includes Germany)	35	65	$50	26
Germany	57	43	14	7
United States	29	71	134	70
Japan	20	80	8	4
TOTAL	30	70	$192	100

Sources: Compiled from H. Shulte, "Aerospace Germany Restrictions," *Interavia Aerospace Review* 45 (April 1990): 282; and Aeropace Industries Associations, *Aerospace Facts and Figures* (Washington, DC: Aerospace Industries Association, 1992–1993).

The European Community has a substantial share of the total free world sales, with Germany having a significant portion and, more important, a greater majority of its output in the civilian fields, including the Airbus products. Japan is a small competitor, but its efforts must not be ignored. The world's ten largest companies in the aerospace field in 1992, ranked from largest to the smallest, were:[12]

Boeing (U.S.A.)
McDonnell Douglas (U.S.A.)
General Electric (U.S.A.)
Rockwell (U.S.A.)
United Technologies (U.S.A.)
British Aerospace (U.K.)
General Dynamics (U.S.A.)
Lockheed (U.S.A.)
Deutsche Aerospace (Germany)
Airbus (France, Germany, U.K., Spain)

The sales of the companies range from approximately $8 billion to $30 billion. Boeing, Airbus, and McDonnell Douglas, in that order, are the largest producers of commercial wide-body aircraft.

American Challenges in the 1990s

The American aerospace industry faces a number of significant challenges in the next decade. They include a decreasing defense budget, intensive competition from foreign firms, need for a continuance of technological leadership, and the requirements involved in satisfying broader environmental and health regulations, assisting to the ailing airline industry, maintaining of a viable industrial base, and effectively supporting a broad-based space program. All these issues are reflected in the industry's performance, namely, declining employment and revenues, lower profits, and a lower share of market. The end of the Cold War has resulted in the cutting of U.S. defense spending by $5 billion, changing overall aerospace sales in 1992 to $134 billion down from $139 billion in 1991. Estimates for 1993 indicated that revenues would decline even further, to $126 billion. Employment declines since 1989 have resulted in a 20 percent reduction in the work force (268,000 jobs). Aerospace profits have been significantly reduced in recent years and are lower as an average percentage of sales than that of all manufacturing industries. Finally, the U.S. free world market share of the free world has fallen to 58 percent. Only in the area of foreign trade has aerospace growth set records. Exports climbed over $44 billion, however, imports also climbed to almost $14 billion, with a slight gain, for a net surplus of less than $1 billion. From an overall industry performance standpoint, 1993 was estimated to show even further declines.[13] These declines have been attributed primarily to a reduction in domestic military sales and increasing European aggressiveness in the market.[14]

The reduction in defense spending is difficult to overcome unless new military applications, such as "smart" antimissile missiles, or future areas of government uses, such as space-based applications or federal agency computer systems, can be found. The drop in federal spending is not likely to be overcome by such activity. Instead, new sources of revenues and profits must come from commercial applications.

The major commercial activity of the industry is civil aircraft, which is the area in which international trade is important, especially since European firms are the major competitors. The primary European competition is from Airbus Industries, which has attained a 30 percent world share of the market in commercial aircraft, and its successful entry is largely attributed to the $26 billion of subsidies (from 1968 through 1990) provided by the governments of France, the United Kingdom, Germany, and Spain.[15] The Airbus challenge was underestimated by the U.S. industry, and there has been no industry-government consensus regarding the use of American trade laws to counter it. The factors blocking this consensus were (1) the desire of American airlines to purchase cheaper, subsidized Airbus products, (2) U.S. government subordination of trade issues to foreign policy priorities, and (3) concern by the U.S. aircraft industry of jeopardizing relationships with European airline customers.[16]

Both defense and commercial aerospace successes are dependent in large degree on technology leadership. Technology is time dependent, and therefore it must be quickly applied to commercial products if it is to be useful in global competition. This combination of knowledge and commercialization to support a national industry has resulted in the cooperation of government, industry, and academia in order to maintain technology leadership. This is true in every aircraft-producing nation and is also the case in the United States.[17]

Falling revenues from defense products, international competition, and technology leadership appear to be the three major issues for the American aerospace industries. A number of prescriptions to these problems in aerospace have been published. Some have recommended improving manufacturing technology, overhauling information systems, and improving the R&D process.[18] Others addressed recommendations for U.S. government actions, including (1) greater use of trade law, (2) eliminating export controls, (3) barring foreign governments from assisting U.S. customers, (4) limiting foreign offset requirements, and (5) standardization of product liability laws.[19] Further proposals have included a national strategy and greater industry collaboration for world technological leadership,[20] alliances to improve corporate health,[21] restructuring the industry,[22] and eliminating costly airshow events.[23]

The International Challenge

Since the future of the industry lies in the commercial direction and foreign firms are successfully entering the field, the most critical international challenge is achieving and maintaining American success in the global market. The key product for success is commercial aircraft. Thus far, the Airbus subsidies have been the major issue, but a recent government agreement, the U.S.-EC Commercial Aircraft Subsidy Agreement to limit subsidies, seem to have mollified American critics.[24]

Foreign industry strategies beyond subsidies are also of importance in the global competition. The European approach, through the Airbus consortium, is to achieve a degree of autonomy (i.e., lessening dependence on Boeing and McDonnell Douglas), while strengthening the overall technology base, increasing employment including technical skills, and sharing extremely high entry costs. The approach is based on close government and corporate cooperation.[25] A good example of this strategy is the role of Germany in the Airbus and that nation's parallel actions in the aerospace industry generally.

Germany is a major partner in the Airbus consortium, while the nation is simultaneously restructuring its national aircraft production industry. In order to accomplish both goals, Germany has restructured Deutsch Aerospace. The Deutsch Airbus, part of the Deutsch Aerospace family, is a member of the Airbus consortium and now provides an A321 assembly line in Hamburg. The sales of Deutsch Airbus in 1991 amounted to about $2.6 billion, and its principal activities include development, production, and product support for all Airbus aircraft and the Fokker 100 aircraft, joint development of the Super Airbus, and studies for new aircraft and technologies.

Deutsche Aerospace AG was structured under the management of Daimler-Benz to include Messerschmidt-Bolker-Blohm GMBH, the Darnier Group, and MTU (Motorean und Turbinen Union GMBH).[26] Its sales in 1991 were about $8 billion.[27] The German aerospace industry produces a higher proportion of commercial products than defense products. It also appears that Germany is well on its way to equal the French performance and reputation. As partners in European cooperation, both nations contribute extensively to European success in the commercial aircraft industry.

A recent study, however, indicated that not only are Germany and other nations of Europe tough present-day competitors, but a fledgling aircraft industry in Japan is poised to offer further competition to the United States. The aircraft industry in Japan is preparing to develop its own wide-body commercial air transport within fifteen years.[28]

As with the development of most important industries in Japan, MITI has been the driving force in the Japanese pursuit of an aircraft industry. MITI believes that the capabilities derived from an aircraft industry will further benefit their nation through the newly developed technology base. The emphasis has been on the manufacture of large commercial transports with the cooperation of overseas aircraft manufacturers, chiefly Boeing and McDonnell Douglas. The Japan Aircraft Development Corporation (JADC), which was formed as a subsidiary of MITI, has been a subcontractor to these and other U.S. firms. Japan hopes thus to gain production technology and manufacturing expertise. Other skills that Japan is seeking from this cooperation are project management expertise, skills in integrating aircraft systems, and specialized marketing techniques.

In addition to cooperative commercial ventures, Japan has sought to improve its aircraft industry infrastructure by participating in the U.S. FSX military fighter project. From this work Japan may gain experience in systems integration and the capability to design and manufacture a technologically advanced aircraft. The project would also justify government expenditures for costly advanced test facilities. By combining the gains obtained through the JADC and the FSX, Japan hopes to define the elements of a successful formula for developing its aircraft industry.

A recent comparison of the competitive advantages of the United States, Europe, and Japan indicated that Europe has the best overall potential advantage because it is equal to the United States in technology and management and stronger financially. Japan is weaker than the United States and Europe in technology and management, but stronger than the United States and equally as strong as Europe in financing.[29]

THE AEROSPACE INDUSTRIES ASSOCIATION (AIA)

If an association truly represents an industry, it should reflect industry concerns and work toward their elimination. The major industry challenges of lowered defense expenditures and European competition are two of a number of concerns that the AIA addresses. However, in order to do so, the association has to have the appropriate means and must take the requisite actions. One way to judge the AIA's efforts is to take a close look at its history, background, and operation.

AIA Origins and History

It is possible to trace the roots of the modern AIA to the first efforts to create an organization for the U.S. aircraft manufacturing industry, in 1917. The Aircraft Manufacturers Association was the first formal organization created for this purpose.[30] Although not a predecessor to the AIA in strict terms, it was the first effort to provide an institution through which the U.S. aircraft industry could address common issues, coordinate activities, and plausibly deal with government. The central issue underlying the formation of the Aircraft Manufacturers Association was the management of patents in the burgeoning aircraft industry. In the view of Howard E. Coffin, one of the organization's proponents, "technological complexity should have been a source of business cooperation, not discord."[31] Coffin, along with Henry B. Mingle, president of Standard Aircraft Corporation, founded the Aircraft Manufacturers Association, with organizing and coordinating the distribution of patents (i.e., the dissemination of new technology) as its central purpose.

In spite of the efforts of its founders, the incipient association could not overcome the unwillingness to join of major companies in the industry. Wright-Martin and Curtiss, two of the main firms at the time, saw no advantage to joining the new organization; indeed, Wright-Martin held many of the patents that were critical to the new industry and was not inclined to encourage ways to make them available to competitors.[32] The association, however (with the help of government pressure and the eruption of World War I), was able to attract Wright-Martin and Curtiss to its membership. However, the success was short-lived; the

Aircraft Manufacturers Association failed to become a permanent organization. Collective action among U.S. aircraft manufacturers did eventually become a reality, but only after a full-scale military aircraft program had actually materialized. At that point, aircraft manufacturers supported the U.S. Aircraft Production Board, which was created essentially to prevent the military from exercising excessive control over the industry.[33]

The modern AIA was initially formed as the Aeronautical Chamber of Commerce of America (ACCA) in 1919. Its 100 charter members included nearly every important aircraft manufacturer at the time.[34] While it was successfully established for the long term, the first twenty years of its history were marked by uncertainty and constant impediments to maintaining membership and holding together the organization. The central problem was that it was difficult to attract and hold aircraft manufacturers to the association because potential or actual members did not always see the benefit in membership. The exception to this rule was the problems that federal procurement regulations and potential labor unrest created for aircraft manufacturers. Thus, "only when it seemed immediately possible that associationalist activity might result in procurement-law reform and during the late 1930s when the Department of Labor sought to impose wage increases upon the industry did manufacturers display genuine interest in the chamber."[35]

Even with federal procurement regulations continuously at stake, the ACCA experienced difficulty sustaining itself throughout the 1920s and most of the 1930s.[36] As an additional inducement for aircraft manufacturers to join the association, beginning in 1928, ACCA leaders presented their organization as a way for them to present a common voice against unions.[37] Finally, ACCA leaders thought of their organization as a good way to deal with welcomed federal spending under Franklin Roosevelt's New Deal.

In spite of what might seem otherwise reasonable inducements to join the ACCA, these factors did not result in a firmly established trade association for the U.S. aircraft industry in the 1930s. The central problem was one of collective action. Individual aircraft manufacturers weighed—implicitly or explicitly—the costs and benefits of joining the association, and frequently found the costs to outweigh the benefits. While some joined for a time, obstacles to sustaining the association remained unrelenting. Aircraft manufacturers found that their individual efforts to deal with the federal government—and particularly with Congress—were more beneficial than a collective effort through the ACCA. This underlying problem of collective action led one historian to conclude that

> after the NRA [National Recovery Act] failure, the [ACCA] had reassumed its basic role as a trade association in name only, despite its continued hopes, as old as the World War I associationalist dream for aeronautics, that it could coordinate technical change, market development, and business-government relations for the aircraft industry.[38]

The situation changed dramatically with the onset of World War II in 1938–1939 as many aircraft manufacturers joined the ACCA in the face of stepped-up military production. The problem of collective action had been overcome by the need, in the view of aircraft manufacturers, to establish a clearinghouse between government and the aircraft industry. However, this burst of collective action could not be sustained through World War II as the ACCA could not get a permanent membership commitment from aircraft manufacturers. Instead, three councils were formed—one each in the West, East, and Midwest—all of which were part of the new National Aircraft War Production Council, an organization designed to coordinate aircraft production for the U.S. war effort.[39]

Thus, during World War II, the ACCA had limited functions. It did, however, publish information on the industry, but in general the National Aircraft War Production Council eclipsed the ACCA as the central organization coordinating the activity—in this case, military production—of the U.S. aircraft industry.

After World War II, the industry sought to continue the coordination it had experienced during the war, and at the same time address the changing market for its products, through membership in the ACCA, which was renamed the Aircraft Industries Association in 1945. The new name corresponded to new life for the association as it took over many of the functions of the War Production Council and reorganized its efforts to focus on commercial aviation. In these respects, the Aircraft Industries Association became a genuine permanent trade association for the first time.[40]

In the years immediately after World War II, the Aircraft Industries Association began to address issues that had some relevance to all companies involved in the manufacture of aircraft. In 1947, for example, the Aircraft Industries Association called for a national air policy to ensure survival of the industry and fulfill its national defense mission. Through its Export Committee, the association pressed for declassification of military aircraft so that they could be sold more easily. During the Korean War (1950–1953), the association was the central organization representing the U.S. aircraft industry in the production of military aircraft.[41]

Recognizing rapid changes in the industry and aerospace technology, the Aircraft Industries Association was renamed the Aerospace Industries Association (AIA) in 1959. In subsequent years, the AIA represented member firms in interaction with government, focusing in particular on defense issues. In 1965, the AIA played a key role in the formation of the Council of Defense and Space Industry Associations (CODSIA), a coordinating organization drawing together a range of industries that manufacture products used for defense and outer space purposes.[42] During this time, the AIA did not limit its activities to defense. The association was involved in the Tokyo round of the General Agreement on Tariffs and Trade (GATT) negotiations, which produced a multinational civil aircraft agreement that significantly liberalized and promoted trade in civil aerospace.[43]

Through the 1960s and 1970s, the AIA became an established trade association that focused on the immediate business concerns of its members. This largely meant defense issues, as many of the aerospace industries manufactured products primarily for defense purposes. However, it would be a misunderstanding of the industries and of the AIA to assume that defense issues were the only concern. As indicated by the AIA's participation in the creation of the civil aircraft agreement in connection with the Tokyo round of GATT negotiations, the association was also concerned with the commercial aircraft market. The enormously competitive and risky commercial aircraft industry occupied, and continues to occupy, a significant amount of the AIA's attention.

The 1980s saw a change in the AIA in terms of its organization, the definition of its mission, and the strategies it used to benefit its members. The mid-1980s were marked by extensive criticism of AIA firms. The central complaint involved government procurement practices. Defense contractors—which include many AIA members—were accused of excessive charges for products sold to the U.S. Department of Defense (DoD). The merit of the accusations is not at issue here. Rather, the concern here is the AIA responses, the most important of which was the way in which the organization adjusted its structure and activities to deal with these accusations and a general atmosphere that was critical of defense contractors.

To counter the negative media coverage of the aerospace industries' defense activities, the AIA improved its communications capabilities. A new president, former U.S. Representative Don Fuqua, came on board to lead the AIA in its effort to present the viewpoints of the aerospace industries, not only on the controversial issue of government procurement, but on other issues relevant to AIA members as well.[44] Early in 1987, the AIA "launched a pro-active program of actions designed to upgrade the public perception and status of the aerospace industry."[45] The action was a result of public criticism surrounding the cost of spare parts in particular, and defense costs in general. AIA's board of governors constructed a plan with three objectives: (1) reconsider reforms that hurt the aerospace industries, (2) restore the industry's image as an ethical supplier of high-technology equipment, and (3) ensure the strength of the industries in the international market.[46]

By the 1990s, the AIA had changed its staffing and activities, giving it a higher profile in an effort to present the aerospace industries' perspective on controversial public policy issues. This sort of activity, along with other typical trade association tasks such as maintaining data on the industries, characterizes a modern trade association. The AIA's history traces a fairly predictable path in the development of a trade association in American politics. From shaky beginnings that focused on coordinating the distribution of patents and technology, through nearly two decades of uncertain existence owing to classic problems of collective action, to its post–World War II emergence as a stable representative of the U.S. aerospace industries, the evolution of the AIA reflects in a general way the development of high-technology industries in an evolving business-government environment.

Industries Represented by the AIA

The AIA was originally intended to represent U.S. aircraft manufacturers. As the Aeronautical Chamber of Commerce of America, the association included virtually all major aircraft manufacturers in the United States. As its 1959 name change, to Aerospace Industries Association, suggests, AIA membership includes firms involved in defense, outer space, and civil aviation.[47] Firms in the defense business make a wide range of products, for example, military aircraft (including helicopters), missiles, tanks, and sophisticated electronic command-and-control technology. Similarly, AIA members manufacture products used in the U.S. outer space program, such as satellites and electronics. Civil aviation is mainly concerned with the production of commercial aircraft—from large transport planes to corporate jets.[48]

While the products of AIA members are varied, it is possible to make several generalizations that are relevant to the AIA's activities. First, and obviously, AIA members are involved in high-technology products. Hardware made for purposes of defense, space exploration, and civil aviation necessarily involves state-of-the-art technology and knowledge in a variety of fields. This forces the AIA to deal with public policy issues that deal with high technology—for example, federal military and civilian R&D spending, tax credits for engaging in R&D, and intellectual property protection of technological developments. These and other, related, issues are at the forefront of the national debate on the competitiveness of U.S. industries in the international market and the proper role of government in promoting competitiveness.[49]

A second characteristic of the industries represented by the AIA is that, taken together, they manufacture products for both military and commercial purposes. The defense aspect of these industries directs the AIA's attention to the central question of government procurement regulations—a longstanding concern of the association. The commercial aspect compels the AIA to consider the sorts of policies with which other high-technology associations typically must deal—for example, antitrust, export controls, and trade policy. The combination of defense-related and commercially related public policy issues presents a serious challenge to the AIA in terms of policy analysis, objectives, and effectiveness.

The poor performance of the aerospace industries in recent years, the grim outlook for 1993, the likelihood of major defense cuts by the Clinton administration, and the slowdown of the global commercial aircraft industry have focused the AIA's concerns on the economic health of the industries it represents. In a speech delivered at the AIA's twenty-eighth annual Year-end Review and Forecast luncheon, on December 16, 1992, in Washington, D.C., association president Don Fuqua reviewed the bad news and outlined the directions the AIA planned to take in reaction to the economic changes. He cautioned the Clinton administration in regard to defense cuts, argued that the federal government has a role in the health of the aerospace industries, and judiciously supported the new president's activist attitude in using government to promote industrial development. Fuqua discussed three ways to counter the decline in defense spending on aerospace products: (1) increase exports, (2) reverse a trend of the federal government to maintain aircraft in lieu of awarding that task to the private sector,[50] and (3) diversify the aerospace industries into such fields as national communications, transportation, and the environment.[51]

Thus, the AIA confronts a gloomy economic picture for its members. In industries that enjoyed considerable growth and success until very recently, a novel set of problems confronts their major trade association. The AIA's response to this dramatic change in its political and economic environment will be central to the association's success. It will require new ideas, proposals, and attendant organizational flexibility to adjust to the new realities of the aerospace industries.

Organizational Characteristics

In general, the structure and dynamics of the AIA are not surprising. The association is organized to allow member input into all its critical activities. Indeed, representatives of member companies do much of the detailed work that is carried out by the AIA. The association is sufficiently small to allow such participation, and because of the close interaction between staff and member firms, there is little opportunity for staff to go in directions of which members would disapprove.

As AIA members are companies that make products in defense, space, and civil aviation, members frequently are involved in many aspects of the aerospace industries, and as is true for virtually all trade associations, they do not necessarily limit their association activity to the AIA. Membership has hovered between fifty and sixty firms over the last decade, and their dues are based on a formula that relates to the level of sales.[52] The AIA offers a package of benefits to attract new members. Among these benefits, for example, is access to a considerable range of AIA publications; information on congressional activity relevant to the aerospace industries; participation in AIA councils, committees, and task forces; and an opportunity to interact with top aerospace company executives on special task forces and at biannual three-day meetings.[53] A partial list of AIA's current members (as of January 1993) are shown in Table 7.2.

The AIA then, provides a considerable range of inducements to members to join the association. These inducements relate directly to member companies' business interests, particularly in regard to government and public policy. The key to the formation and maintenance of the contemporary AIA is size; maintaining a group of approximately sixty members is not difficult. Each member or potential member can readily see the advantages of joining. Some benefits are immediate and concrete: research studies, publications, statistics on the industries, and technical information on public policies relevant to the industries. Other benefits are less concrete but their importance is nonetheless immediately apparent to members: organized interaction with other firms in the aerospace industries, a mechanism to present the member companies' perspective on policy

Table 7.2
Partial List of AIA Member Companies, January 1993

Aerojet, A Segment of GenCorp

Allied Signal Aerospace

B.H. Aircraft Company, Inc.

The Boeing Company

Chrysler Technologies Corporation

Digital Equipment Corporation

Du Pont Company

E-Systems, Inc.

Edwards Aerospace, Inc.

FMC Corporation

GEC-Marconi Electronic Systems Corporation

General Dynamics Corporation

General Motors Corporation
  General Motors Hughes Electronics
  Delco Electronics
  Hughes Aircraft Company
  Allison Gas Turbine Division

The BF Goodrich Company

Grumman Corporation

Gulfstream Aerospace Corporation

Harris Corporation

Hercules Incorporated

Hexcel Corporation

Honeywell, Inc.

ITT Defense and Electronics, Inc.

Kaman Aerospace Corporation

Lucas Aerospace, Inc.

Martin Marietta Corporation

Northrop Corporation

Raytheon Company

Rockwell International Corporation

Sundstrand Corporation

Teledyne, Inc.

Texas Instruments, Inc.

Textron, Inc.

Thiokol Corporation

TRW, Inc.

United Technologies Corporation

Vought Aircraft Company

Westinghouse Electric Corporation

Source: Aerospace Industries Association, *AIA Member Companies* (Washington, DC: Aerospace Industries Association, 1993).

issues, and an opportunity to help develop a broader industry perspective on these issues. With government action and public policy vitally important to the aerospace industries historically, and with the strong likelihood that they will remain so, an opportunity to speak out through a recognized voice on public policy questions is a significant inducement to join the association. Thus, since the association is small—compared with large organizations such as the U.S. Chamber of Commerce—the connection between joining and receiving benefits is clear, which is another factor increasing the probability that companies in the aerospace industries will join the association.

The AIA Board of Governors exercises formal authority in the AIA. Consisting of thirty-two executives from member firms, the board has four officers, including the AIA president, and meets twice yearly. The board chooses an executive committee from its members which consists of six members in addition to the AIA president and the chair of the AIA Board. The executive committee is responsible for the routine governance of the association, and on matters warranting the board's attention it presents the board with its actions for ratification.[54]

Much of the association's business is conducted through its council system. Councils consist of representatives of member companies that have an interest in a particular council's jurisdiction and are organized along issues that are of principal concern to the association. They typically create committees, task forces, and work groups to deal with specific issues that fall within its jurisdiction. Like the councils themselves, these subunits are made up of member company representatives who do the actual work.[55] The AIA president reviews council and committee reports and "may act on the recommendations, authorize action, transmit the recommendations to the Board of Governors, or refer them back to the council or committee for further study."[56] The councils are described in Table 7.3.

The councils and their committees are important, not only for conducting studies into areas that members consider important but also to provide a key means through which member companies participate in the association's activities. This helps to ensure, though by no means to guarantee, that the association's goals are in line with those of its members and server to maintain a strong connection between members and the Washington-based staff.

With roughly forty professionals and an operating budget of $10 million a year, the association staff structure roughly parallels the organization of the councils.[57] Several staff units correspond directly to a council in terms of the issues with which it deals, and they report to the president and secretary-treasurer. In addition to an administrative unit corresponding to each council, the AIA maintains the following four units: the Aerospace Research Center, which prepares studies and analyses of the aerospace industries for AIA members; Legislative Affairs, which monitors relevant public policy issues and presents the industry's viewpoint to Congress; Policy and Planning, which "coordinates the key policy issues identified by the association's Board of Governors and establishes goals and strategies for achieving consensus and action"; and the general counsel, which provides legal advice to the AIA.[58]

Table 7.3
AIA Councils, 1993

Civil Aviation Council: works with domestic and international agencies, Congress, and others in the aviation community concerning manufacture of civil aircraft, including commercial aircraft, business jets, and rotorcraft

> *Committees:* Transport, Rotorcraft, Propulsion, Airplane Noise Control, Commercial Customer Support, Manufacturing Integrity, Industry and Regulatory Affairs

Communications Council: supports the public activities of AIA's president and staff and conveys industry goals and accomplishments to AIA members, the news media, and the public

Human Resources Council: is concerned with labor and employee relations, industrial security, employee compensation, occupational safety and health, and environmental issues relevant to the aerospace industry

> *Committees:* Industrial Security, Occupational Safety and Health, Compensation Practices, Environmental Affairs

International Council: addresses international issues affecting the ability of U.S. firms to compete and cooperate in a global marketplace

> *Committees:* Defense Trade, Export Controls, Legislative, Regional Trade and Industrial Cooperation

Procurement and Finance Council: monitors and coordinates legislative and regulatory changes and initiates actions for improvement in procurement and procurement-related issues, including patent and data rights

> *Committees:* Cost Principles, Legal, Finance, Procurement Techniques, Tax Matters, Economic Advisory, Facilities and Property, Intellectual Property, Washington Procurement

Technical & Operations Council: focuses on all aspects of technological, operations, and engineering efforts to advance all aspects of program management, industrial base, engineering, development, test, manufacturing, quality, materiel management, product support, and information to better address issues stemming from the production of aircraft, missiles, and space vehicles

> *Committees:* Key Technologies, Technical Management, Space, Electronic Systems, Embedded Computer Software, Materials and Structures, National Aerospace Standards, Manufacturing, Quality Assurance, Materiel Management, Product Support, Service Publications, Spare Parts, Industrial Modernization, Information Technology, and Manpower, Personnel, and Training

---

Source: Aerospace Industries Association, *AIA: The Aerospace Leadership Team; AIA Councils and Committees* (Washington, DC: AIA, 1993).

The AIA's staff organization is unsurprising in most respects, although two aspects stand out. First, the key point to keep in mind with respect to the relationship between the staff and members is that there is a constant interaction, mainly through the councils and their corresponding staff units. Second, the AIA maintains a separate unit for coordinating policy issues identified by the board of governors, turning these issues into the association's goals and strategies.

In summary, the AIA maintains a sizable, though not extraordinarily large, staff in its Washington headquarters, which formally serves the interests of AIA members. In addition to general functions that are common among trade associations—communications, for example—the AIA maintains staff units dedicated to specific issue areas. This reflects the range and complexity of the public policy issues with which the association is concerned. It also allows for constant interaction between staff and members through the council system, the main source of the product of the association. The board of governors remains as the principal decision-making body, working on routine governance of the association through its executive committee. The Policy and Planning staff unit, working with, and perhaps for, the board, develops the policy goals of the association while leaving the day-to-day work to the councils and association staff.

Public Policy Issues and Goals

The AIA deals with numerous issues covering a wide range of public policies, all of which have some relevance to AIA members. The association produces lengthy studies of some issues and shorter analyses and position papers in various formats on virtually all of them.

The topics described in the following paragraphs by no means exhaust the AIA's policy concerns, but they do summarize the issues that occupy most of the AIA's time and resources. Two themes emerge from these issues. First, the policy concerns that have made the AIA's "top ten" list over the last four years clearly reflect members' interests. Second, these issues demonstrate the association's response to the aerospace industries' economic concerns. The next paragraphs consider each major issue area in light of these two themes.

Federal procurement and acquisition regulations have long been a concern to the AIA. Aircraft production for military uses has been critical to the growth of the U.S. aircraft industry since its inception, and the AIA has monitored federal regulations at least since the 1930s. Since much of the business of AIA members is in defense and national security, federal procurement and acquisition regulations remain, predictably enough, high on their public policy agenda. The persistence of this issue is noteworthy for two reasons. First, the federal government, mainly through DoD and the National Aeronautics and Space Administration (NASA), has played a major role in the aerospace industries for more than a half century, and continues to do so. Second, it is somewhat remarkable that a trade association has been concerned with essentially the same issue for most of its comparatively long history. This demonstrates the unusually important and consistent relationship between government and business in the aerospace industries.

Arguments supporting the maintenance of the defense and aerospace industrial base also grow out of a concern for defense-related aspects of the U.S. aerospace industries. As defense cutbacks continue in the Clinton administration, defense contractors had to adjust to a more hostile economic environment. One characteristically political adjustment is to urge the federal government to maintain a strong industrial base in these areas by, for example, encouraging technological development. AIA member companies, especially those involved primarily in defense contracting, have a clear interest in pursuing this general policy, and the AIA position reflects this.

Although policies dealing directly or indirectly with defense spending and defense technology policies are critical to the AIA and its members, the association's top issues also include a range of topics that focus on the civilian side of the aerospace industries. For example, the AIA is concerned with the health of civil aviation and the U.S. commercial aircraft industry. In the face of intense foreign competition (much of it subsidized by foreign governments), the AIA has addressed the need to maintain a healthy civil aviation sector in the United States by supporting a strong Federal Aviation Administration (FAA) and by encouraging the United States to ensure fair trade practices in the international market. Moreover, AIA president Don Fuqua has argued publicly for an increased government role in promoting U.S. aerospace industries abroad, noting that the United States needs to support its aerospace industries as much as its European competitors are supported by their governments.[59]

The AIA also supports policies that encourage the creation of an educated work force, stressing the need for improvement in math and science education in the United States. In this sense, the AIA joins hands with many other high-technology interests, arguing that the decline of U.S. education will cause serious problems for the economic health of U.S. industries in the not-too-distant future.

The concerns for a healthy U.S. civil aviation and commercial aircraft industry and for a strong educational base, particularly in math and science, reflect the AIA's roots in high-technology industries and the goal of supporting the commercial use of aerospace products. Perhaps the AIA's most focused effort in this regard is its support of government policy that encourages vigorous technological development. The AIA has made technological development a centerpiece in its array of public policy positions. Recognizing the critical role of technology in economic growth (which has become increasingly apparent in high-technology industries), the association has urged the federal government to support technological development through a variety of means: improved math and science education and an aggressive R&D policy, to name two. Perhaps the AIA's most focused effort in this regard is its Key Technologies program, which was designed to identify key technologies to the U.S. aerospace industries and lay out a "road map" for their development.

The AIA has also placed environmental issues among its top ten issues over the last four years. Aerospace industries necessarily involve the use of materials and processes of which the by-products may be considered pollutants. Reducing the production of pollutants is a matter of law, of course, and the AIA has addressed regulatory restrictions by urging a cooperative effort between industry and government in developing ways to deal reasonably with the environmental consequences. At stake from the perspective of AIA firms is the cost of conforming to environmental regulations. In addition, the AIA has taken a similar position with respect to occupational safety and health issues,· again urging a cooperative effort between industry and government in light of the costs of conforming to government regulations.

This overview of the key issues identified by the AIA indicates how the association's choice of key public policy questions reflects members' economic interests. Companies in the aerospace industries, whether manufacturing products for defense or commercial use, are facing intense international competition in some areas and must deal with defense spending cutbacks while coping with stricter environmental and occupational safety and health regulations. Not every firm is confronted with the whole range of issues. Thus, the AIA has constructed an array of public policy concerns that cover the range of issues important to its members' economic interests. The sheer breadth of issues, not to mention the detailed position papers on many, reflect the broad purpose of the association. In keeping with its mission of presenting the aerospace industries' perspective on public policy questions, the AIA provides a considerable amount of information—reports, analyses, and opinions—that are designed to inform various stages of the public policy process.

General Activities

The AIA pursues the collective interests of its members primarily through the production and dissemination of information that presents the aerospace industries' perspective on a variety of issues. While the association maintains a legislative affairs unit in its Washington headquarters, the unit's main responsibility is to monitor developments in Congress on legislation that is of some interest to the AIA. The AIA does not spend much time lobbying; according to one official, less than 5 percent of the association's legislative activity is in the form of lobbying.[60] This conforms with the AIA tax status as a nonprofit association whose main purpose is to provide information (education) on the issues that concern its members. The 501(c)(3) nonprofit prohibits the association from engaging in a high degree of direct lobbying and partisan activities but does not prohibit it from providing information on public policy issues.[61] Finally, the AIA does not operate a political action committee.

The AIA maintains a research department and a communications unit in its Washington headquarters. The research department conducts studies of various matters of concern to the association. The department works with the board of governors and councils in the selection of research projects. The process is interactive, certainly, and the research department essentially works at the service of AIA members through these organizational mechanisms. It produces studies of such issues as international trade and procurement, along with an annual volume entitled *Facts and Figures*. This document, which has been published annually for forty years by the AIA, summarizes developments in the aerospace industries through statistical tables, which are updated yearly. Additionally, the research department supplies articles for the association's publications.

There is no shortage of information coming from the AIA. The communication unit, as an organization whose primary technical mission is providing information, produces numerous documents as its central objective. The information in various forms including newsletters, speech reprints, and .data reprints, is intended for association members, official Washington—including members of Congress, congressional staff, and the executive branch—as well as the news media and the public in general.

While the AIA does not lobby members of Congress on specific issues or programs, the association does maintain contact with government officials. With respect to Congress, CEOs and other top executives of AIA member companies testify before congressional committees. AIA representatives also work with executive branch agencies in the implementation of programs. For example, in 1990, the White House asked the AIA to work with the National Academy of Sciences to study ways to develop the U.S. manned space program.[62] As one would expect, one area in which there is considerable contact between the association and government involves government procurement and acquisition regulations. AIA representatives also work with other agencies as issues call for it. In a current example, AIA's Clean Air Task Group is working with the U.S. Environmental Protection Agency (EPA) concerning regulation of the production of volatile organic compounds (VOCs). The AIA group's goal is to work with EPA officials "to develop cost-effective approaches to reducing emissions of VOCs and toxic compounds while maintaining some flexibility."[63]

AIA's Technology Program

The association has developed an ongoing program to promote technological development. Originally called "Key Technologies for the 1990s" and now entitled "Key Technologies for the Year 2000," this program identifies technologies that will be, in the AIA's estimation, critical to the economic health of the U.S. aerospace industries in the beginning of the twenty-first century. Initiated in 1987, the Key Technologies program is a result of discussions among aerospace industry officials to develop a consensus "that certain technologies would be most important—key—to the next generation of aerospace systems because they would allow new system capabilities that would leapfrog those of global competitors."[64] In addition to identifying the technologies, the AIA began to construct technology development road maps for the next ten to twenty years. Beyond these road maps, the association proposed to create National Technology Development Plans for each technology. Working with government, industry, and academia, the goal is to build consensus on these technologies while drawing from as many different perspectives as possible.[65]

To guide the Key Technologies program, the Aerospace Technology Policy Forum was created. Consisting of representatives from government, industry, and academia, the forum "provides top-down guidance for the technology development process, reviewing its progress with the aim of addressing issues that form barriers to implementation of the national strategic plans," including legislation and regulation.[66] After the first year or two of the Key Technologies program, the AIA established a formal institutional base through which the program could be run: the National Center for Advanced Technologies (NCAT), which was given the responsibility of connecting the Key Technologies effort to the Aerospace Technology Policy Forum; coordinating the work of the various technology teams; linking government, industry, trade associations, and professional societies in the effort; conducting symposia; and stressing the need for a better educated work force.[67] Summarizing the institutional arrangement of the Key Technologies program, "1) the Policy Forum gives a top-down perspective on technology needs, 2) the technology teams supply a bottom-up view of required technology development, and 3) NCAT integrates these activities and provides education regarding the goals and progress of the [program]."[68]

The coordinated effort among the aerospace industries, trade associations, and government is a response to the competitive demands facing the U.S. aerospace industries at present. A joint effort to identify key technologies for future economic health calls attention to the need for cooperation in the view of the AIA and the federal government. NCAT, which is at the heart of the effort, should not be understood as a research consortium or a joint industry-government R&D program; it is in fact incorporated as a nonprofit educational foundation. The success of this effort, its output, and whether it serves as a model for other high-technology industries remains to be seen, but it certainly deserves watching.

Relationships with Other Organizations

As public policies that affect high-technology industries become more complex, trade associations for various industries may find common interests with other associations. It is likely that some public policies affect a considerable range of high-technology industries, and it makes sense, therefore, that their trade association representatives cooperate with one another and perhaps coordinate their activities to some extent on issues of common interest. Formal efforts in this vein are apparent in high-technology industries other than aerospace.[69]

The AIA works with other associations on an ad hoc basis when issues arise in which the associations share an interest. For example, in the Clean Air Task Group's work with the EPA to reduce VOCs the AIA is accompanied by several other trade associations: the Air Transport Association, the General Aviation Manufacturers Association, and the National Paint and Coatings Association.[70] Additionally, AIA joined with the Electronic Industries Association (EIA) and the National Security Industrial Association (NSIA) to produce analysis and

position papers on independent research and development and on bid and proposal efforts.[71]

The AIA is a member of only one formal organization, consisting of a number
of trade associations: the Council of Defense and Space Industry Associations
(CODSIA), which was created in 1964 by industries involved in federal government procurement, with the support of the DoD. The organization is neither
another trade association nor an umbrella organization of trade associations.
Each member works voluntarily with CODSIA, taking different policy positions
as it chooses. CODSIA does not lobby on its own or its members' behalf; it is
designed, instead, to be a coordinating mechanism for firms represented by its
members that deal routinely with federal government procurement regulations
and procedures. CODSIA is governed by a policy committee, which determines
the general positions of the organization, and an operating council, which deals
with routine issues. In short, it is intended to provide a connection between business and government in the complex matter of procurement and acquisition, and
it is explicitly limited to that purpose.

CONCLUSION

How is the AIA affecting the determinants of advantage? It attempts to do this
primarily through affecting public policy decisions. It has taken action to improve
technology, obtain regulatory relief, open markets, and improve the quality of the
work force. Each of these areas, as well as many others, has been articulated in an
AIA detailed document called the *AIA's Industry Competitive Enhancement Initiatives for the Aerospace Industries*, which covers thirty-nine subjects.[72]

If the AIA does achieve its goals, the industry will have been provided with
new and important skills and resources. Although those association contributions
alone will not guarantee favorable consequences for the industry, they can be
extremely important in their achievement.

At this point in time, the AIA's efforts either have not been fully applied to the
industry or they have not been sufficiently successful in effectively altering the
course of the industry's decline in profits, growth, and share of market.

NOTES

1. Paul Proctor, "Clinton Offers U.S. Technology Plan," *Aviation Week and Space
Technology*, 1 March 1993, 18–19.

2. [Editorial], *Aviation Week and Space Technology* 138, no. 10 (8 March 1993): 66.

3. Clyde V. Prestowitz, Jr., *Trading Places: How We Allowed Japan to Take the Lead*
(New York: Basic Books, 1988), 66.

4. [Editorial], 18–19.

5. Aerospace Industries Association, *Industry Competitive Enhancement (ICE) Initiative* (Washington, DC: Aerospace Industries Association, January 1993).

6. A. Markusen and J. Yudken, "The Birthing of Aerospace," Technology Review 95 (April 1992): 28–29.

7. Aerospace Industries Association, *Aerospace Facts and Figures* (Washington, DC: Aerospace Industries Association, 1992–1993), 15.

8. Laura D'Andrea Tyson, *Who's Bashing Whom? Trade Conflict in High-Technology Industries* (Washington, DC: Institute for International Economics, 1992), 155.

9. Ibid., 156.

10. *Global Perspectives* (Washington, DC: Aerospace Industries Association), 24.

11. Ibid., 36.

12. Gunter G. Endres, "The World's Leading Aerospace Companies: Part One," *Interavia Aerospace Review* 47, no. 4 (April 1992): 13.

13. Aerospace Industries Association, *1992 Yearend Review and Forecast—An Analysis* (Washington, DC, January 1993).

14. Aerospace Industries Association, "Profile . . . Aerospace" (Washington, DC: Aerospace Industries Association, January 1993).

15. G. Klepper, "Entry into the Market for Large Transport Aircraft," *European Economic Review* 34 (June 1990): 775–798; Keith Hayward, "Airbus: Twenty Years of European Collaboration," *International Affairs* 64, no. 1 (Winter 1987–88): 19.

16. *Roadmap for Results: Trade Policy, Technology, and American Competition* (Washington, DC: Council on Competitiveness, June 1993), 36–37.

17. *Key Technologies for the Year 2000: The NCAT Strategy, National Center for Advanced Technologies* [Booklet] (Washington, DC: Aerospace Industries Association, 1991).

18. Reed S. Gardiner and Saul J. Bergman, "U.S. Aerospace Industry Dominance under Siege," *Aviation Week and Space Technology* 137, no. 16 (19 October 1992): 84–85.

19. Don Fuqua, "U.S. Aerospace Needs Higher Profile Government Role to Flourish Globally," *Aviation Week and Space Technology* 136, no. 19 (11 May 1992): 60–61.

20. "AIA Proposes National Strategy for World Technology Leadership," *Electronic News* 37, no. 9 (September 1991): 20.

21. Anthony L. Velocci, Jr., "Douglas Eyes MD-12X Alliance as Financial Health Improves," *Aviation Week and Space Technology* 135, no. 12 (23 September 1991): 42–45.

22. Jon B. Kutler, "Aerospace Industry Must Restructure to Remain Competitive in World Market," *Aviation Week and Space Technology* 132, no. 2 (8 January 1990): 67–68.

23. Anthony L. Velocci, Jr., "U.S. Firms Slashing Foreign Air Show Participation," *Aviation Week and Space Technology* 137, no. 3 (20 July 1992): 20–21.

24. Counsel on Competitiveness, *Roadmap for Results*, 37.

25. D. W. Cravens, H. Kirk Downey and Paul Lauritano, "Global Competition in the Commercial Aircraft Industry: Positioning for Advantage by the Triad Nations," *Columbia Journal of World Business* 26, no. 4 (Winter 1992): 46–58.

26. H. Schulte, "Aerospace Germany Restrictions," *Interavia Aerospace Review* 45 (April 1990): 282.

27. Endres, "World's Leading Aerospace Companies," 12–27.

28. Anthony L. Velocci, Jr., "Study Says Japan, Europe Threaten U.S. Leadership in Air Transports," *Aviation Week and Space Technology* 136, no. 12 (23 March 1992): 23.

29. Cravens, Downey, and Lauritano, "Global Competition," 52.

30. Aerospace Industries Association (AIA), *AIA Newsletter* (Washington, DC: AIA, January–February 1989): 9.

31. Jacob A. Vander Meulen, *The Politics of Aircraft: Building an American Military Industry* (Lawrence: University Press of Kansas, 1991), 21.

32. Ibid., 21.

33. Ibid., 22.

34. Aerospace Industries Association, *AIA Newsletter*, 9.

35. Vander Meulen, *Politics of Aircraft*, 64.

36. Ibid., 90, 102–10.

37. Ibid., 158.

38. Ibid., 199.

39. Ibid., 200.

40. Aerospace Industries Association, *AIA Newsletter*.

41. Ibid.

42. CODSIA is discussed in more detail later in the chapter.

43. Aerospace Industries Association, *AIA Newsletter*.

44. Interview with AIA official, 28 January 1993.

45. Don Fuqua, "Washington Pipeline: AIA Leads Industry Recovery Effort," *AIA Newsletter*, June 1988, 3.

46. Ibid., 3.

47. A Board of Governors resolution enacted on 17 November 1990 defined business activity required for AIA membership as the production of aerospace systems, which means:

the manufacture of manned and unmanned aircraft, missiles, aeronautical vehicles[,]. . . propulsion units or control equipment for such products, materials or structural components for such products, avionic, electronic or ground equipment necessary to the operation and functioning of such products, including subsystems, components, software or associated equipment and providing services unique to the production or operation of aerospace systems, such as systems engineering and/or integration. (Aerospace Industries Association, *Membership Benefits*, Washington, DC, 1993).

48. Aerospace Industries Association, *1991 Annual Report* (Washington, DC: Aerospace Industries Association, 1992), 10–29.

49. While this would be true in any administration, the Bill Clinton administration indicated that it would be active in promoting the international competitiveness of U.S. industries through a variety of policies. Indeed, during the presidential campaign, Clinton had planned to give Vice President Al Gore the task of leading the executive branch effort in this regard.

50. The AIA argued that maintenance also includes modifications, conversions, systems upgrades, and service life extension programs, all of which go beyond simple aircraft maintenance. See Don Fuqua, "Year-end Review and Forecast" (Talk delivered at the AIA's 28th annual Year-end Review and Forecast Luncheon, 16 December 1992, Washington, DC; reprinted in *Key Speeches* [December 1992]: 1).

51. Concerning diversification, see ibid., 1–4.

52. "The current dues formula works out to $27,500 for every $100 million in aerospace sales up to $500 million with an additional $4,400 for every $100 million over that. . . . Maximum dues are $200,000 and minimum dues are $6,875" (Aerospace Industries Association, *Membership Benefits*).

53. Ibid.

54. Aerospace Industries Association, *1991 Annual Report*, 6; interview with AIA officials, 27 January 1993 and 28 January 1993.

55. Author's interview with AIA official, 28 January 1993.

56. Aerospace Industries Association, *AIA Councils and Committees*, 1993.

57. Concerning staff size, see "AIA Staff Directory," *AIA Newsletter*, April 1990, 12. Concerning the operating budget, see Deborah M. Burek, ed., *Encyclopedia of Associations*, vol. 1, part 1 (Detroit: Gale Research, 1991), 120.

58. Aerospace Industries Association, *The Aerospace Leadership Team* (Washington, DC: Aerospace Industries Association).

59. Don Fuqua, "U.S. Aerospace Needs Higher Profile Government Role to Flourish Globally," *Aviation Week and Space Technology* 136, no. 19 (11 May 1992): 60.

60. Author's interview with AIA official, 28 January 1993.

61. Ronald G. Shaiko, "More Bang for the Buck: The New Era of Full-Service Public Interest Organizations," in *Interest Group Politics*, 3 ed., Allan J. Cigler and Burdett A. Loomis, 3rd ed. (Washington, DC: CQ Press, 1991): 117–126.

62. William J. Broad, "NASA Losing 30-Year Monopoly in Planning for Moon and Mars," *New York Times*, 15 January 1990, A1.

63. "Environmental Outlook for 1993," *AIA Newsletter,* January-February 1993, 1.

64. "Key Technologies for the 1990s: A Model for National Technology Development," *AIA Newsletter*, January-February 1990, 10.

65. "Key Technologies for the 1990s," 10.

66. Aerospace Industries Association, *Key Technologies for the Year 2000*, 6.

67. Ibid., 7.

68. Ibid., 7.

69. Note, for example, the Electronics Roundtable, a group of electronic industries trade associations. For a discussion of the Electronics Roundtable, see Philip A. Mundo, "Political Representation of the U.S. Electronics Industries" (Paper presented at the annual meeting of the American Political Science Association, Washington, DC, September 1991).

70. "Environmental Outlook for 1993," 1.

71. Aerospace Industries Association, *Maintaining Technological Leadership: The Critical Role of IR&D/B&P* (Washington, DC: Aerospace Industries Association, September 1989).

72. *Industry Competitive Enhancement (ICE) Initiatives*, [Booklet] (Washington, DC: Aerospace Industries Association, 1993).

Chapter 8

The Biotechnology Industry and Its Trade Organizations

THE PRESIDENT SPEAKS ON HEALTH CARE

Bill Clinton as a candidate for president often spoke on the necessity of reforming the health care system. The possible reforms mentioned by him and others were included for discussion in the final economic report of the George Bush administration. Among them were managed competition, national health insurance, rate setting, and global budgets—all of which envision a larger government role.[1] The eventual election of President Clinton, with his focus on health care as part of his program; the role of his wife, Hillary Rodham Clinton, in formulating health care policy; and the general debate on health care issues; coupled with several highly profiled technical setbacks at a number of prominent biotechnology (biotech) firms, had a frightening effect on investors. The average value of selected health care stocks dropped from $390 to $300 in February 1993, and eventually to about $280 in April of that year. The drop, of 28 percent in less than three months, was without a doubt rather sobering.[2]

Whether because of this financial impact, the prior long period of campaign rhetoric on restrictive health care legislation, or officials of the Industrial Biotechnology Association (IBA) and Association of Biotechnology Companies (ABC) publicly stating that merger discussions had been underway for a long period, these two organizations, the IBA and the ABC, finally decided, in February 1993, to merge by July 1, 1993. The merged groups would be called the Biotechnology Industry Organization (BIO). The background of this merger and a brief description of the ABC are an appropriate prelude to a detailed discussion of the IBA, which will be the association of concern in this chapter.

The ABC was formed by Bruce Mackler, an attorney with a U.S. Food and Drug Administration (FDA) practice, who assisted firms in dealing with the FDA. In essence, the ABC grew out of his law practice. It was formed as a nonprofit association for biotechnology companies and related services. Initially, the ABC operated out of Mackler's office, but within a couple of years, the ABC board of directors divorced the association from the law firm entirely, although Mackler remained in the picture as general counsel to the ABC. The ABC then hired an executive director and the association became distinct, taking on its own character as it matured.[3]

While the IBA focused on legislation and regulation for relatively large companies, the ABC served smaller companies that lack the resources to follow government activities. Typically, these are small operations with a handful of employees who focus all their energies on developing the business. The ABC also represented research laboratories, universities, foreign entities, and service organizations. There was little overlapping of memberships between the IBA and the ABC. In 1992, 26 ABC members out of 329 listed were IBA members, while 18 IBA members out of 135 were listed as members of the ABC.[4] Thus, the ABC filled a niche not covered by the IBA, and vice versa.

The ABC provided a variety of services to its members: networking opportunities for executives at various meetings, a forum in which company executives could discuss common problems, and legal services. The ABC eventually developed a large, international meeting that included these services along with providing trade shows on equipment and technology. These meetings also featured seminars on issues such as politics and government, law, sales abroad, and patents. These activities might be classified as typical trade association services.

The chief reason for the merger of the two biotechnology associations was to provide the industry with a unified voice. Combining different parts of the industry—producing firms, start-up firms, research organizations, and service companies—in theory should help the industry to present government with a single position on public policy issues affecting the biotech industry, hopefully making the industry more effective in influencing government decision making. Presumably, the merger will also achieve new organizational economies, as the strengths of the two former associations will be combined into one. Prior to the merger, the two associations worked together, delivering a joint letter, for example, to President-elect Clinton in December 1992 that outlined the industry's main short-term policy considerations: capital formation, intellectual property protection, and supplemental appropriations for the 1992 Prescription Drug User Fee Act.[5]

By February 1993, the first executive director of the new association had been selected—Carl B. Feldbaum, formerly chief of staff to Senator Arlen Specter (R-Pa.)—who set out to work with the two existing associations to achieve a successful merger, both administratively and with respect to public policy objectives. The policy agendas of both organizations overlapped, and it appears that the new association would seize on common interests in shaping its policy goals, including capital gains reform, R&D tax credit reform, use fees, and health care reform.[6]

In its initial publication, BIO articulated the basic structure and goals of the new association. Emphasizing the contributions of the IBA and the ABC, BIO will be the "leading voice" for the biotechnology industry, representing companies of all sizes involved in the range of activities encompassed by biotechnology. BIO lists in general terms its basic purposes: build an industry consensus on public policy issues affecting health care, communicate with government officials, inform the public about biotechnology, maintain good relations with the news media; keep members updated on significant public policy developments, and provide a forum for sharing expertise. BIO reiterated support for the Congressional Biotechnology Caucus, suggesting that the caucus would be a permanent vehicle through which the industry can influence public policy development.[7]

The structure of the new association reflects the structure of the industry it represents. In addition to roughly thirty committees assigned to issues ranging from regulatory affairs to education to biopesticides, the association will have two sections. The Emerging Companies Section is designed to attend to the interests of start-up firms, while the Food and Agriculture Section will accommodate the needs of a fast-growing application of biotechnology. Finally, BIO will maintain relationships with state affiliates, presumably drawing on state organizations affiliated with either the IBA, the ABC, or both.[8]

It is possible to discern some basic implications of the creation of BIO out of the IBA and ABC. First, it may be the case that as far as members are concerned, it makes more economic sense to have one organization represent the industry than two. Second, a unified voice on issues and a mechanism through which such agreement can be achieved will undoubtedly enhance the industry's ability to influence public policy. Third, the fact that one organization will now encompass the whole range of biotechnology companies suggests changes in the industry; small start-up firms will now be able to speak with the same voice—and clout— as the larger, more established biotechnology firms (bearing in mind the limited meaning of "established" in this still new industry).

At this point, of course, one can only speculate about what the merger of the IBA and ABC means for the political organization and representation of the biotechnology industry. It is likely that a single group will indeed provide one voice for the industry, but whether it is in fact unified, representing widespread agreement among participants in the industry, depends on the inclusiveness of the membership and the extent to which the new organization's decision-making process promotes agreement. Moreover, if the creation of a new association through this merger signifies an agreement among members of both associations that the industry is ready to be unified, then this suggests changes and, perhaps, a new maturity of the biotechnology industry. On the other hand, it may also be the case that the merger was spawned out of economic necessity as operating two associations costs more than operating one, and that not all participants in the biotechnology industry will be adequately represented by one, encompassing association. If this is so, then it would be reasonable to expect the formation of still another group in the future to offer an alternative to the single biotechnology association.

BIOTECHNOLOGY—THE U.S. INDUSTRY GENE POOL?

Among the most exciting of the modern industries, in terms of its future impact on human health, agricultural production, environmental remediation, and industrial application, is the biotechnology industry. The modern origin of the industry began with the scientific discoveries uncovered since 1943, when evidence that DNA (deoxyribonucleic acid), a complex molecule, contained hereditary information that is passed from parent to offspring. It was realized that the character, or signature, of the DNA molecule could be read to determine its characteristics; that this molecule, in any living organism, could be manipulated and changed; and that the result could be used to produce drugs or agents that acted in ways that chemically produced substances could not. The applications appeared most promising in the fields of health care and agriculture, but also held spectacular promise in environmental remediation and bioremediation.

Consequently, biotechnology is becoming a major source of innovation in research and product development in the pharmaceutical industry. Although slow in developing, the application of biotechnology is now flourishing in this industry. By 1993, over 600 approved biotechnology drugs and vaccines were on the market.[9] Products such as Activase (for acute myocardial infarction) and Interferon Alfa-2a (for AIDS-related cases of Kaposi's sarcoma) show great promise medically, as well as financially, for this high-technology, global industry.[10] The number of U.S. firms involved in biotechnology has exploded, with "more than 400 start-up firms, more than 200 established firms that have diversified into biotechnology, and more than 200 supply firms" in operation by 1991, and with products worth nearly $2 billion.[11]

Agricultural applications of biotechnology have the potential of creating further advances in the industry with respect to production, yield, and cost. However, of even greater impact, applications of biotechnology in agriculture "include health products, hormones, transgenic animals, biopesticides, and transgenic plants."[12] While exact comparisons are difficult, the U.S. firms lead in the area of transgenic plants, followed by the European Community and Canada.[13] Transgenic animals and plants have genes from other animals and plants, which are transferred to them by biotechnological means, resulting in new types of animals and plants.[14] Major public policy questions continue to arise in this area because of attitudes about cloning and the creation of new organisms.

The chemical industry is also using biotechnology applications, although they will likely go unnoticed by the general public. Most biotechnology applications in this industry "will be developed to improve production processes used by major chemical companies."[15] The Congressional Office of Technology Assessment has argued that biotechnology applications in the chemical industry will be most beneficial as the industry develops products in the high-value-added pharmaceutical and pesticide industries.[16]

Biotechnology applications in these areas all offer the promise of high profits, but firms engaged in these activities typically take six to twelve years to make a profit on their products. Biotechnology research and production in countries other than the United States are carried out by large, multipurpose firms, which have the necessary financial resources to sustain as many as ten years of R&D before a product can bring in revenue. Firms solely dedicated to the development of biotechnology products are a uniquely American phenomenon.[17] These "dedicated biotechnology companies" typically start out as small firms, sometimes consisting only of one or two research scientists.[18] Beginning in the late 1970s, dozens of these firms sprung up in the United States, seeking vast amounts of capital to sustain unusually long periods of R&D. As these firms found the financial going difficult, they sought partners to support the business end of their activities. Small dedicated biotechnology companies needed the financial resources of large firms to complete the R&D process and their substantial marketing and distribution capabilities to sell the product. For example, Genentech, one of the first publically traded biotechnology companies, was purchased, in part, by Hoffman-LaRoche, a large Swiss chemical and pharmaceutical concern. Genentech benefited from the pharmaceutical giant's financial and distribution resources, and Hoffman-LaRoche benefited from Genentech's research technology. This pattern is being repeated throughout the industry as large pharmaceutical companies (U.S. as well as foreign) offer their resources in exchange for the technology developed by the small dedicated biotechnology companies (DBCs).[19] Some opinions state that these exchanges are short term only and that the DBCs will attempt to become fully integrated, virtually independent, and strong in downstream markets now served by the pharmaceutical firms.[20] A very comprehensive listing and analysis of various forms of alliances in the biotechnology industry have been published.[21]

Biotechnology companies are concentrated in nine geographic regions of the United States, with the largest number located in the San Francisco Bay area, New York, Boston, and Washington, D.C. Seventy-five percent of these firms are small—from 1 to 50 employees, with 15 percent employing 51–135 people. Only 9 percent of the firms have more than 135 employees. Currently, 79,000 people work in the biotechnology industry, with 200,000 anticipated in the industry by the year 2000.[22] The biotechnology industry is an intensive research and development industry. In 1990, total biotechnology industry R&D spending amounted to $4 billion, with R&D spending at about 60 percent of revenue and 30 percent of total expenditures. The total federal R&D expenditures for biotechnology equaled $3.8 billion.[23]

Among the unique aspects of the industry that have been touched upon, several will now be expanded upon further. These aspects are: financial, regulatory, intellectual property with emphasis on patents, and international competition.

Although the long-term competitiveness of U.S. developed products and processes may depend on the regulatory climate, the patent protection mechanisms, and international fair trade practices, R&D and innovative competitiveness are determined by the amount of investment funds required for survival. Therefore, the financial requirements of the biotechnology industry, especially with regard to DBCs, are substantial, and access to inexpensive capital is crucial. From 1985 to 1989 the venture capital industry invested about $1.1 billion in biotechnology companies. The number of companies invested in per year ranged from 65 in 1985 to 118 in 1989 and 97 in 1990, with the dollar amount invested per company ranging from about $1.5 million to $2.8 million per venture capital fund.

Venture capital has been available in the founding stages, but secondary financing has become difficult and more costly to obtain. Initial public offerings have been less successful since the 1987 stock market crash, and public equity financing has become less favorable, while financing through alliances with domestic and foreign firms have become more favorable.[24] Capital needs, while paramount, are not the only reason for alliances. Two other major reasons are marketing capabilities and regulatory expertise. As of 1989, forty-six American firms had made 160 agreements with European and Asian firms.[25] Also in 1989–1990, thirty-eight outright mergers and acquisitions occurred between firms of different nations, including the United States, Japan, and the European Community countries.[26]

Although funding has proved difficult to obtain and various means are used (venture capital funding, initial public offerings [IPOs], alliances, mergers and acquisitions), companies already listed on the stock exchanges can do well. From 1989 to 1990, medical and agricultural biotech stock values grew by about 37 percent, compared to the growth of the Standard and Poors 500 company, of 13 percent for the same period.[27] Some stocks of the more successful companies grew at an even greater rate: for example, Genentech, up 55 percent; Chiron, up 128 percent; and Amgen, up 80 percent. Despite the overall growth of biotech stocks, only a few firms by that time had generated annual revenues of more that $100 million, and even fewer (perhaps three) had generated any profits.[28] Overcoming their lack of overall financial success, biotech companies sold $17.7 billion of new stocks, the highest five-month amount in history, in 1991.[29] In October of the same year, it was reported that the industry had received sales of $4.0 billion and record revenues of $5.8 billion for the fiscal year 1990–1991.[30]

The basic reason for the great need for funds is the rate at which R&D progresses relative to the revenues obtained from the products introduced. The precommercialization period, which starts with the initial R&D (a long process in itself), moves to the patent application and issuance phase, requiring overall as many as six to ten years. If patent application begins at the initial R&D stages and the entire approval process, including FDA approval, takes ten years, then as little as seven years will remain on the patent. The patent registration of products and the entire issue of intellectual property protection are, therefore, key to the success of biotech firms. In 1989 alone, 3,135 patents were issued, which required an average of three years of waiting time from application to issuance. By 1990, the backlog of patents to be examined had reached 8,200 in number.[31] In addition, the various kinds of intellectual property protection and the differences in the laws of various countries place tremendous pressure on the legal and research resources of any one company.

Once a product has been developed and a patent applied for, it must then be approved by a number of government agencies prior to its market introduction. The U.S. regulatory agencies include the Food and Drug Administration (FDA), the Environmental Protection Agency (EPA), and the U.S. Department of Agriculture (USDA). New regulations, laws, coordinating committees, and federal laboratories all come into play. From an international perspective, the degree of regulatory controls for sales in foreign countries range from relatively loose in the growth-oriented nations in the Pacific Rim and limited restrictions of the United States, Japan, and most European countries to the stringent regulations in countries with a high degree of concern, namely, Denmark and Germany.[32]

Finally, the one aspect of the industry that will be of greater concern in the future is that of international trade and global competition. It is possible to assess the present strengths and weaknesses of many countries' industry and, in fact, one analysis did cover fifteen countries, but for the purpose here, an assessment of Japan and Germany is the most important. The same analysis of fifteen countries stated that Japan must be considered among the main competitors in the global industry.[33] The Japanese biotech industry, as with many other industries in that country, focuses initially on applied research primarily performed by large companies, either alone or in joint efforts such as associations rather than in government laboratories or universities. Most government funding is channeled into the firms and government-led initiatives which include the research associations. The approach is essentially different from that in the United States, where government and academia are the driving force for R&D and basic research receives a larger share of public R&D funds than does applied research. The government of Japan funds about 20 percent of biotech-related R&D, while the U.S. federal government's share is 50 percent. About $700 million (compared to $3.4 billion in the United States in 1990), was budgeted by Japan, with 40 percent going to the Ministry of Health and Welfare and another 40 percent split between the Science and Technology agency and the Ministry of Education. MITI, which receives less than 10 percent of the total government funds, sponsors two important associations for collaborative research. They are the Japanese Bioindustry Association (JBA), a nonprofit organization of 320 companies from diverse industrial sectors, and the Research Association for Biotechnology, which includes a number of large firms. MITI also provides biotechnology funding to specific industries such as chemicals, pharmaceuticals, food, and an alcohol fuel program.[34] In 1981, MITI designated biotechnology as a targeted industry, which is similar to other industrial targeting. Alliances with foreign firms, where Japanese market availability is offered in return for technology, investment in foreign firms and research associations, and an entire range of industry variables, is guided by MITI. As reported recently, MITI guidance still continues today.[35]

With regard to regulation, the Japanese approach is similar for most industries, including biotechnology. The major determinants and influences are government bureaucracies, which involve industries, usually through associations. By comparison, in the United States various interest groups appear to be the major influence. Overall, though, the effective regulations are not much different in the United States and Japan.[36]

The differences in patents and intellectual property laws between Japan and the United States do pose some problems for American firms.[37] Because of these problems, U.S. firms often end up licensing technology to Japanese firms in order to avoid the long and involved process for a foreigner to obtain intellectual property protection or to get products approved by various regulatory authorities in that country.

Japan must be viewed as a significant global competitor based on its strong fermentation and bioprocess industries, its large domestic market for pharmaceuticals, and its targeted government-supported applied research base. Its weaknesses have been noted as a lack of strong discovery research capabilities, lack of entrepreneurial and venture capital activity, and interagency rivalry.[38] The Japanese Bioindustry Association, in a recent report, ranked Japan's technology levels comparatively with the United States and Europe in thirty-two technologies and eleven applied fields. Japan ranked first in four areas, the United States in thirty-seven, and the European nations in two. The report also stated that the Japanese market was about $5.5 billion in 1992 and had grown at a 40 percent rate every year since 1987. By the year 2000, the Japanese market could grow to over $25 billion. The Japanese governmental budget for bio-related R&D for 1993–1994 is slightly over $1 billion.

With regard to Japan, the question relevant to biotechnology, as it is to any emerging industry in global competition, is, "How can American firms take advantage of alliances with Japanese industry without eventually suffering losses in global markets because of the ramifications of these same alliances?" There are several recently published studies in this area. One view is that the United States is at risk of losing its lead by the year 2000 unless technology exchanges between the United States and Japan become reciprocal, intellectual property regulations are made equivalent, and the U.S. develops a technology strategy.[39] The findings of another study focusing on biotechnology further stated:

> While the United States seems to lack policies that coordinate private firms in international competition, Japan appears to have perfected such policies designed to "acquire" competitive advantages in high technology industries. Together with governmental support and coordination and transfer of technology are an integral part of its high technology development strategies.[40]

The other nation successfully competing with the United States in biotechnology is Germany. The public and private sectors of biotechnology activity in Germany have made greater strides than those of any other European counterpart, despite some of the most stringent regulatory activities. The fundamental basis of Germany's strength in biotechnology includes the very strong pharmaceutical and chemical industries, which are the most concentrated in Europe; the high-quality discovery research and scientific training base; strong industry-university relationships; and, finally, its head-start in being the first nation to establish a biotech program and institute.[41] The Fraunhofer Institute, described in Chapter 4, is among the most prominent.

Germany's major firms, BASF, Hoechst, Bayer, and others, are funding R&D at dollar rates equivalent to the corresponding U.S. firms. Licensing, alliances, and acquisitions involving U.S. firms are also contributing to their overall capabilities.[42] Their financing comes primarily from internal funds, large banks, and government, similar in nature to that of other large and growing industries in Germany. The regulatory environment in Germany is very complex and at times difficult to interpret. In 1989, for example, the German state court blocked Hoechst from completing a plant to produce genetically engineered insulin. A law was later passed to provide a legal basis for permitting genetic engineering. The long-term European Community plans to harmonize all regulations may, however, blunt the attempts by many German public interest groups to shut down biotechnology research and manufacturing in Germany. In the meantime, short-term discord continues to exist, and the public opposition to biotechnology may be Germany's greatest weakness. In terms of intellectual property laws, however, American firms find little difficulty in obtaining national treatment in Germany.

In summary, the biotechnology industry, is a rapidly growing high-technology industry encompassing every characteristic of a national "strategic industry" and promising to provide tremendous financial rewards.[43]

THE IBA IS FORMED

With the establishment of any new industry, the likelihood of a representative trade association being formed is quite high. This was the case with the biotechnology industry and the IBA. The formation of the Industrial Biotechnology Association, therefore, in part follows the general pattern of trade association formation in the United States. The importance of a political entrepreneur, so frequently observed in other political organizations, is also apparent in the IBA case. However, the immediate impetus or events causing the formation of the association are not altogether clear, making the IBA an unusual case.

The IBA was formed in 1981 by seven dedicated biotechnology companies, which were brought together by Harvey S. Price, an attorney with the Atomic Industrial Forum, an association for the nuclear power industry. Price, who was an experienced Washingtonian, saw the potential need for a trade association to address the policy issues that would likely affect the emerging biotechnology industry (or bio- or genetic engineering, as it was commonly referred to at the time). Price approached Harold Green, the legal counsel for Genex, to discuss a new trade association for the industry. Leslie Glick of Genex, later the first president of the IBA, met Glick through Green to consider a new association.[44] Thus, only a few individuals were involved in conceiving the idea of a trade association for the biotechnology industry. Price spelled out his view of the industry and trade associations in a brief, which was made available to industry leaders.[45] In this document, Price reviewed different organizational forms that various industries had adopted to give them a voice in policy-making in Washington, settling upon a trade association that lobbies government officials and provides information on the industry it represents. Price anticipated the problems that the industry would likely face including, for example, safety, the relationship between science and industry concerning pure and applied research, misleading and exaggerated accomplishments for financial purposes, and intellectual property rights.[46] Although at the time the industry was not facing problems created by, or solvable by, government, Price believed that such issues would arise soon enough, and a trade association would be the best way for the industry to address them. Price argued: "Many of these issues, challenges, and problems now coming over the horizon appear susceptible to amelioration by cooperative, industrial efforts in the best tradition of our nation's governmental and economic systems. Thus, creation of an association now, a genetic engineering services institute, seems like a very good idea."[47]

The themes first articulated by Price were picked up in comments by U.S. Representative George E. Brown, Jr. (D-Calif.). In a published speech, Brown cited the need for the emerging industry of genetic engineering to create a trade association to meet inevitable legal and governmental problems.[48] Although Brown acknowledged that such problems for the industry in 1981 were few, they would likely arise in the near future. The industry needed to deal with regulatory activity and new legislation, and the industry needed to educate the public about biotechnology to correct public misperceptions about genetic engineering.[49] Finally, Brown called for the creation of something like a blue-ribbon panel to set standards of behavior for the industry.[50]

With the rhetorical groundwork laid, Price set out to make his idea of a trade association for genetic engineering a reality. On June 2, 1981, he organized a meeting in Washington, D.C., of top executives from leading dedicated biotechnology companies in the United States. The participants at the meeting included Price (serving as counsel), Sam Dryden (Agrigenetics), Joseph Rubinfeld (Applied Molecular Genetics), Robert Fildes (Biogen), Ron Cape (Cetus), Orrie Friedman (Collaborative Research), Sandy Ronspies (Genentech), Gabriel Schmergel (Genetics Institute), Leslie Glick (Genex), and Franklin Pass (Molecular Genetics).[51] The group determined that the new trade association would be open to all industrial participants in biotechnology but that the initial action to form the group should be taken by specialized firms (dedicated biotechnology companies).[52]

The group also set forth the new association's principal objectives. The executives identified four areas in which the new trade association should work. First, the association would be involved in government relations, monitoring government activities in both the executive and the legislature. The association would develop the industry's positions on public policy along with creating industry codes of desirable practice. Second, the association would build goodwill in the general public. Acknowledging the public's ignorance and fear of genetic engineering, the group determined that the new association should launch a major educational effort aimed at the public as well as government leaders. Third, the association should collect and disseminate information on the industry. Finally, the association should address the problem of product liability insurance, making it easier for the industry to obtain such insurance at reasonable cost.[53]

The association's initial staff would consist of two or three professionals. The executives set the initial fee for joining the association at $10,000 for the first year, with annual dues adjusted subsequently according to a sliding scale.[54] The original seven members of the association handled the administrative tasks related to forming a new association, including, for example, drafting its bylaws. The original seven also became officers in their new organization as follows: Leslie Glick, president (Genex); Robert Fildes, vice president (Biogen); Gabriel Schmergel, secretary (Genetics Institute); Sam Dryden, treasurer (Agrigenetics); Ron Cape, director (Cetus); Franklin Pass, director (Molecular Genetics); and Joseph Rubinfeld, director (Applied Molecular Genetics). Of the nine companies represented in the original organizing group, Genentech and Collaborative Research delayed the decision to join the Industrial Biotechnology Association.[55]

The founding firms determined that the association needed to recruit twenty-five members by October 1, 1981, to be successful.[56] Toward this end, Glick, who was serving as the IBA's first president, sent letters to biotechnology executives to invite them to join the IBA. The letter (along with subsequent correspondence) stressed the importance of government relations and education. Glick argued that monitoring executive and legislative activity would be crucial to the industry and that the public and government officials were in need of clear, correct information about genetic engineering.[57]

On June 16, 1981, the newly formed executive committee met at National Airport in Washington, D.C., to solidify the foundation of the Industrial Biotechnology Association. The committee approved the articles of incorporation, settled on the location of the association (in Rockville, Maryland), analyzed and revised the bylaws, and developed strategies to recruit members.[58] A month later, on July 13, 1981, the IBA's board of directors met for the first time. The seven-member board took the next series of steps to turn the idea of a trade association into a concrete organization. The directors voted on officers, elected and described the responsibilities of the board's executive committee, selected auditors, discussed media relations, defined membership, considered insurance and legal needs, and began a search for an executive director for the association. As was perhaps expected, Harvey Price became the association's first executive director.[59]

By late 1981, the IBA had become a formal trade association representing the biotechnology industry, albeit a new organization with only seven members. Its formation is typical in some ways of interest group formation in the United States. For example, Harvey Price is an excellent example of the political entrepreneur. Donating his time, experience, and expertise, he provided the starting point for the formation of the new association. Virtually all interest groups have the equivalent of Price, either in an individual or a group of like-minded individuals. Moreover, the industry at the time was made up of very few firms. The top executive of each company—the potential member—could readily see the benefit of cooperative action with respect to influencing public policy, educating the public, and in general promoting the biotechnology industry in the United States. Knowing other potential members—top executives of other companies in the business—and informing them of the need to join the group for it to be viable are effective incentives for would-be association members to join.

What is striking about the formation of the IBA in 1981 is the absence of a major perceived threat to the industry. Trade associations typically form because the potential members perceive a common problem to their industry and the need for collective action to address it. In the past in the United States, this common problem has often come in the form of rising unionism (early twentieth century) and foreign competition (mid- to late twentieth century). These examples do not limit the possibilities, of course; government regulation, rapid and dramatic changes in the economic environment, and shifts in public policy could all conceivably be perceived by members of an industry as a threat to their economic well-being.

In the case of the IBA, there was no clear or definite threat to the emerging biotechnology (or genetic engineering) industry. Indeed, firms engaged in biotechnology had been in existence for only a few years, and none had yet delivered a product to market. Thus, the issues cited by the association's founders were anticipated to be a problem in the future; since there were no biotechnology products, for example, government regulation had not yet become directly relevant to the industry.

The absence of a clear threat suggests that the persistence of Price and the other founders of the association was rather remarkable. They were able to start an organization based on anticipated threats: regulation, intellectual property protection, and public perception of genetic engineering. At the same time, the absence of a clear threat may have stunted the early growth of the IBA. The association's founders and charter members had envisioned a burgeoning trade association with membership growing at a rapid pace. That did not happen in the first few years of the association's existence. After five years, some in the association suggested that the fee structure was too high to attract new members.[60] Another possible explanation is that executives in the industry did not yet perceive a need for an association and that only later, as they produced marketable products and government action became more relevant, did they find the benefits of association membership worth the price of membership.

In sum, the formation of the Industrial Biotechnology Association represented that of many trade associations. A political entrepreneur proposed the idea of a trade association for the industry and was crucial in organizing the founding members into a viable organization and recruiting firms into it. On the other hand, the creation of the IBA is a somewhat unusual case of trade association formation in the sense that there was no immediate perceived threat to the industry that caused its members to seek some form of collective action. The issue—mainly, government regulation—lay in the future, when genetically engineered products would become available. The absence of a pressing issue is probably one reason why the IBA did not grow as expected in the first five years of its existence.

The Development of the IBA

The IBA's development reflected that of the industry. The major change in the industry that affected the IBA was that in the 1980s, biotechnology products were becoming available. The manufacturing process and the products themselves became subject to considerable government regulation—mainly at the federal level, although state governments engaged in significant activity as well.

Over its twelve-year history, IBA membership grew to approximately 150 firms. Initially, membership consisted exclusively of dedicated biotechnology companies, but as the industry changed, so did IBA membership. Because of the long product development period—which may be as long as ten or twelve years—biotechnology companies need infusions of capital. Moreover, as they actually moved a product to market, these firms found their shortcomings in marketing and distribution limiting to their success. Thus, small, dedicated biotechnology companies turned to large pharmaceutical firms for capital, marketing, and distribution, while the large firms invested in the biotechnology firms for the technology. As the large firms—for example, Hoffman-LaRoche and Schering-Plough—entered the biotechnology industry, they joined the IBA. In spite of their size, the major pharmaceutical manufacturers failed to gain a dominant position in the IBA. The association maintained a balance between large, multipurpose firms and small, dedicated biotechnology firms on its board of directors.[61]

Upon celebrating its fifth anniversary in 1986, the IBA had become an established trade association. Seven full-time employees staffed the association at its Rockville, Maryland, headquarters, and the number of committees—consisting of company representatives working on issues important to association members—had grown from the original one to fourteen. Further reflecting its goal of becoming a player in policy-making in the capital, the IBA headquarters was scheduled to be moved to downtown Washington, D.C., on January 1, 1987. The association also showed signs of developing beyond its original entrepreneurial character as the second executive director, Richard D. Godown, who had originally joined the IBA staff in 1985, took office.[62]

In terms of political activity, by 1986, the IBA had become more involved in representing its members' interests and attempting to influence public policy outcomes. The association won a major victory for its members in Congress, pushing through a piece of legislation in 1986.[63] Additionally, the IBA had become fully involved in monitoring regulations coming from the executive branch.[64]

The IBA Structure and Decision-Making Process

The IBA is typical among trade associations in its structure and decision-making process. Committees comprised of member company representatives undertake most of the routine work. A board of directors sets the general policy for the association, and a small staff in the IBA's Washington headquarters carries out the association's daily operations. In addition to these structural units, the IBA maintains relationships with eight state affiliates.

As is the case with most trade associations, the principal governing body of the Industrial Biotechnology Association was the board of directors, consisting of thirty members elected for one-year terms. Candidates for the board were chosen by a nominating committee, which consisted of seven individuals including the board chairman and the IBA president. The nominating committee chose nominees from a list of member company chief executive officers or otherwise designated executives. The list was then presented before the general membership at the IBA's annual meeting where nominees were elected to the board by a majority vote.[65]

By convention, the board of directors was evenly balanced with representatives from large and small firms. The association followed this practice to prevent large firms from dominating the group. Additionally, board membership was balanced between companies in health care and those in agriculture, reflecting the two principal industrial applications of biotechnology.[66] The IBA created this balance presumably to sustain the dual perspective of the association with respect to public policy.

The board of directors created the IBA's standing committees, each consisting of members of the board with a board-approved chairperson.[67] In addition, each IBA member company named a representative to each committee. The association maintained sixteen committees dealing with a range of issues of some concern to members (Table 8.1).[68]

Table 8.1
IBA Committees–1992

Biopesticides

EPA Relations

FDA Regulatory

Food and Agriculture Communications

Food and Agriculture Division

Government Relations

Health Care Reform/Reimbursement

Health Communications

Human Resources

Insurance

International Affairs

Law

Patent

Plant Biotechnology

State Government Relations

Tax and Finance Ad Hoc

Source: "Description of IBA Committee Activity" (IBA document), Washington, DC: Industrial Biotechnology Association, 1992.

The IBA maintained working relationships with state affiliates including California, New York, Massachusetts, and six others. The state affiliates were independent organizations and not subunits of the IBA. Membership in the national organization was separate from membership in the state organization. The IBA referred its members to a state affiliate in the member company's state, at which point the company could chose to join the state organization (in addition to IBA membership). Similarly, state affiliates referred their members to the IBA for possible membership. Initially, state organizations in Massachusetts and California approached the IBA to establish a working relationship, and finding the relationship useful, the IBA thereafter approached state organizations to establish a connection. Since the IBA was at least partially concerned with state legislation and regulation, maintaining links to state biotechnology organizations was an asset to the organization.[69]

The board of directors determined the IBA's policies. Like other trade associations, the IBA sought consensus as much as possible; a united front on issues is more effective with respect to influencing public policy than half-hearted support of a particular position. Although major rifts within the association were rare, one did take place in 1990 that caused two major IBA members to resign from the association. Positions taken by the association on two issues, along with the way these positions benefited some IBA members at the expense of others, led to a public dispute between members and the association. Contending that the association took legislative positions that would benefit Genentech and Amgen, two of the major firms in the industry and the association, Cetus Corporation and Genetics Institute resigned from the IBA. The two issues at stake were proposed modifications of the Orphan Drug Act, which would have loosened patent protection on drugs developed for rare diseases, and a bill "that would extend patent protection to processes employing biologically engineered organisms that are not now eligible for patents."[70] The IBA, along with Amgen and Genentech, opposed changes to the Orphan Drug Act and supported the extension of patent protection to biologically engineered organisms. Cetus and Genetics Institute contended that these positions reflected a takeover of the association by Amgen and Genentech, while the association denied the claim.[71]

The internal dispute in the IBA is a reminder of the fact that trade associations—whether the IBA or virtually any other—consist of companies that have chosen to collaborate on a well-defined set of issues. In other respects, these firms usually are fiercely competitive with one another. In the field of biotechnology, given the excessive costs of developing a product, patent protection is extremely important to firms, both for obtaining a profit on products they develop and for gaining access to technology developed by their competitors. Thus, agreement among association members on this clearly limited issue is possible, but because of the highly competitive nature of the industry, it is by no means guaranteed. The task of the association is to find common ground on issues to the extent possible, and frequently to table or otherwise sidestep matters on which widespread agreement cannot be reached. In this case, the IBA was unable to find that common ground which resulted in a dramatic dispute within the association with implications for the industry as a whole.

Political Activities

The IBA was created primarily to provide a political voice for the industrial biotechnology industry. The main concern was government regulation, which was soon accompanied by legislative issues. Thus, the IBA monitored both the executive and legislative branches and sought to influence policy in both areas. The IBA did not maintain a political action committee (PAC), but it lobbied Congress actively.

With respect to regulation, the IBA concentrated its efforts on three federal agencies: the Food and Drug Administration (FDA), the U.S. Department of Agriculture (USDA) and the Environmental Protection Agency (EPA). Each of these agencies has some measure of regulatory control over the industry's products. The FDA is responsible for approving new drugs in the United States, and its importance to industrial biotechnology is obvious. The USDA regulates agricultural applications of biotechnology and is a major source of rules and procedures governing the development of these products. The EPA deals with releases of genetically engineered products into the environment and the development of biotechnology products.

In addition to monitoring and providing input into federal regulatory activities, the IBA was active in Congress. The association monitors legislative developments in Congress, highlighting bills that have some effect on industrial biotechnology. Summarizing the legislation, reviewing its status, and taking positions (although not always) on specific bills, the IBA publishes a document for its members to keep them apprised of relevant congressional activity.[72]

In 1990, the IBA took a major step in enhancing its influence in Congress. Led by its government relations office, the IBA encouraged members of Congress to form the Biotechnology Caucus.[73] As of November 1, 1992, twenty-two Senators (twelve Democrats and ten Republicans) and sixty-nine Representatives (forty Democrats and twenty-nine Republicans) were members of the Congressional Biotechnology Caucus.[74] The IBA recruited legislators to the caucus based on several factors: the legislator's policy interest, a constituency interest, moderate positions on issues, and the desire to keep a balance between Republicans and Democrats.[75] In sponsoring various activities designed to promote interaction between legislators and industry and to educate public officials about biotechnology, a major goal of the caucus has been to raise the visibility of biotechnology and public policies relevant to it. The creation of the caucus should be considered a major political success for the IBA; it gave the industry a group of legislators favorably inclined to the industry's needs in Congress.

While most of the IBA's political activity was at the federal level, the association monitored the activities of state governments as well.[76] Many states have passed legislation dealing with biotechnology with respect to such matters as genetic screening, environmental release of bioengineered substances, and animal research.[77] State legislatures introduced nearly 160,000 bills and passed over 20,000 pieces of legislation affecting biotechnology in their 1991–1992 sessions.[78] One of the IBA's main concerns with regard to state government activity was the possibility that states will enact legislation or create regulations that supersede those of the national government, thereby complicating the task of complying with laws and regulations for its member companies. In connection with this effort, the IBA published a review of major state legislation relevant to biotechnology in 1992, which summarized state government activity by state and issue area.[79]

In sum, the IBA's main goal was to provide a means through which its members can influence public policy on issues relevant to industrial biotechnology. Concentrating the bulk of its effort at the federal level, the IBA created an effective capacity to monitor and influence the development of legislation and regulation. Though less important, the IBA also followed state legislation, keeping members informed of potentially important legislation at the state level.

Industry Issues and the IBA

The IBA was concerned with a considerable range of issues that affect biotechnology. However, given the limits of its resources, it focused on policies that affect the major applications of biotechnology: health care and agriculture. This was no mean task as these two areas encompass an impressive number of complicated, nettlesome, and frequently contentious issues (recall the conflict among IBA member companies on patent law).

Writing in 1990, Richard D. Godown, executive director of the IBA, identified ten policy areas in which improvement was needed from the industry's perspective. Two of these deal directly with intellectual property protection: maintaining patent protection for animal biotechnology and reducing the patent backlog. Two general goals were, first, to increase regulatory certainty and agency resources and, second, to address health care costs and reimbursement. Three policy areas involved improving public perceptions of biotechnology in general, and particularly focused on food safety. The other three concerned state government activity, liability insurance, and opening European markets to U.S. biotechnology products.[80] These policy priorities reflect the two central concerns that underlie the IBA's routine political activity: regulation and intellectual property protection. Foreign competition did not absorb as much of the association's political energies as these two issue areas. State government activity constituted a small part of the association's political activity, and public relations and education, while important to the long-term health of the industry, was not central to its political activity.

The FDA, USDA, and EPA all regulate biotechnology products. While regulation is frequently cumbersome from the companies' point of view, scientific consensus at this point suggests that genetically engineered organisms pose no dramatically unusual threat to the population. A U.S. Office of Technology Assessment (OTA) report concluded that such organisms are similar to nonengineered "organisms or organisms genetically modified by traditional methods, and that they may be assessed in the same way. Where similar technologies have been used extensively, past experience can be an important guide for risk assessment."[81] The three regulatory agencies have made considerable progress in approving products. OTA noted:

> Under the existing Framework for Regulation of Biotechnology, FDA has approved hundreds of diagnostic kits, 15 drugs and biologics, and 1 food additive; the Department of Agriculture (USDA) and the Environmental Protection Agency (EPA) have established procedures for reviewing field tests of modified plants and micro-organisms, and have approved 236 field tests as of May 1991.[82]

Problems, delays, and inconsistency still plague the federal regulatory process, however. These difficulties form the basis for many of the complaints the IBA had about regulation and the solutions it suggested to rectify them.

The IBA's response to problems with federal regulation of biotechnology was a major part of its political activity and comprised an equally significant part of its policy objectives. During the 102nd Congress, the IBA focused on three pieces of drug regulatory legislation and six agricultural regulatory bills. The IBA opposed legislation that would have amended the Orphan Drug law "to eliminate market exclusivity for a drug when cumulative sales reach $200 million."[83] The association also opposed legislation that would have given the FDA new enforcement powers, "including subpoena authority, expanded inspection authority, recall authority, and civil money penalties."[84] On the other hand, the IBA supported legislation that would have accelerated the FDA drug approval process for drugs and biologics that would treat life-threatening and debilitating diseases.[85] With respect to agriculture regulatory activity, the IBA opposed three pieces of legislation: (1) an amendment to the FIFRA that would "prohibit export, and restricts foreign research, of pesticides that have not been approved by EPA for sale in the U.S."; (2) a proposal that would prohibit "USDA from funding research on herbicide resistant plants and transfer these federal funds to develop nonchemical weed control systems"; and (3) a bill that would amend the Federal Food, Drug, and Cosmetic Act "to require that foods derived from plant varieties developed by methods of genetic modification be labeled to identify their derivation."[86] The association supported legislation that would prevent state and local governments from regulating pesticides and took no position on two other relevant bills: one that would amend "FFDCA to require premarket approval of food derived from genetically modified plants" and another that would "tighten registration requirements for pesticides." Finally, the IBA supported a bill, enacted by Congress, that "establishes an FDA user fee program to fund faster review and approval of new drugs and biologics, as well as new indications for approved drugs and biologics."[87]

Intellectual property protection is another major issue area affecting the biotechnology industry and was therefore an important policy concern to the IBA. Although patent protection exists in the U.S. for all types of biotechnology-related inventions, difficulties persist with gaining patent protection and with intellectual property protection worldwide. One stumbling block for obtaining adequate protection of biotechnology inventions is the length of time required to get a patent from the U.S. Patent and Trademark Office (PTO). Biotechnology inventions require more time to get a patent than any other type of technology, and although the PTO has made efforts to address this difficulty, the problem continues. Process patents are particularly critical to biotechnology companies. Although Congress passed legislation in 1988 dealing with process patents, considerable debate over its adequacy continues.[88]

The IBA gave considerable attention to these issues. In the 102nd Congress, it supported legislation that would have strengthened process patents. The legislation did not pass, but some version of it was to be considered in the 103rd Congress. The IBA opposed two other pieces of patent legislation, one that would impose "a five year moratorium on the patenting of genetically engineered animals in order to provide time for Congress to assess the economic, environmental, and ethical issues," and a bill that would prohibit the PTO "from issuing patents on a wide range of genetic engineering inventions for a three-year period that is renewable for successive three-year periods." Finally, the IBA supported legislation that was passed by the 102nd Congress that made clear "Congress' intent that state governments and state government entities are not immune from infringement suits under the Patent Code and the Plant Variety Protection Act."[89]

In all these cases, it is virtually impossible to measure precisely IBA's influence. Certainly the association had allies among other groups on its positions on various pieces of legislation. Of the legislation considered in these areas, the IBA had emphasized several victories: the establishment of an FDA user fee program that will speed up the agency's review process; enactment of a state sovereign immunity bill closing a loophole "that enables state governments to legally infringe patents and plant variety protection certificates"; and the close failures of bills dealing with patent protection and expedited drug approval.[90]

Success can also be measured as victory in stopping undesirable legislation. The IBA noted several instances in which legislation deemed harmful to its members was successfully opposed. For example, it opposed legislation that would have imposed a three-year moratorium on the patenting of a wide range of genetic engineering inventions.[91] The association mobilized its political forces using such techniques as contacting the White House and the PTO and using the Congressional Biotechnology Caucus to contact Senators to urge opposition to the legislation.[92] The political tactics—which were ordinary but effective—demonstrated the association's political agility and acumen, in addition to its effectiveness. Moreover, the IBA boasted of its success in keeping the orphan drug bill from being voted on.[93]

In addition to legislation in the areas of regulation and intellectual property protection, the IBA targeted health care policy, which would clearly affect the biotechnology industry. With the Clinton administration likely to propose sweeping changes in health care, this issue became particularly important to the association. During the 102nd Congress, the IBA highlighted fourteen bills in the categories of health care reform and drug price control as being of particular significance to its members. The various bills covered the following topics: prices of drugs purchased by the Veterans Administration and Public Health Service, employer-provided health insurance, nationalized health insurance, health insurance tax credits, health insurance market reform, health care cost containment, managed competition, Medicaid reimbursement for drugs, prescription drug cost containment, drug price review board, drug purchasing assistance, and a windfall profits tax on orphan drug earnings.[94] The central issue for the member companies is preserving or creating conditions under which they can make a reasonable profit. With this in mind, the association opposed legislation that reduces the ability of biotechnology companies to do so. Thus, the IBA opposed legislation that would have attached a windfall profits tax on orphan drugs, legislation cutting tax credit to drug manufacturers whose prices rise faster than inflation, and a bill that would have, among other things, considered the establishment of a pharmaceutical products price review board.[95]

Finally, the IBA concerned itself with tax policy and technology policy. The IBA supported legislation in the 102nd Congress that provided for a capital gains tax cut, created an investment tax credit, and extended the Research and Development tax credit.[96] With respect to technology policy, the association highlighted legislation to its members concerning tax and investment incentives for small businesses in critical technologies, and brought to its members' attention the National Competitiveness Act of 1992.[97] These technology issues did not constitute a major portion of the IBA's legislative agenda, however.

In sum, at the federal level, the IBA focused on issues that were most important to its members' biotechnology applications: health care and agriculture. With this in mind, the association worked to promote policies that strengthen intellectual property protection, foster the development of a health care program that secures a reasonable profit for its members, and influence regulatory action that affects product development in biotechnology. Like trade associations representing other industries, the IBA concerned itself with tax policy, though it placed less emphasis on technology policy than other high-technology associations. The IBA enjoyed some success in these areas. Featuring the operation of the IBA-sponsored Congressional Biotechnology Caucus, the IBA succeeded in blocking unfavorable legislation, and supported legislation that is beneficial to its members.

The IBA was also active at the state level, though it spent much less time on state issues than on federal ones. Three issues account for more than half the state legislation dealing with biotechnology: animal research, environmental release of genetically engineered organisms, and DNA fingerprinting. Several issues at the state level are of particular significance to the association. The IBA wanted to prevent state governments from undermining federal patent protection, and toward this end, it supported closing a loophole in federal law that would allow state governments to do so. The association also concerned itself with Medicaid payments. As states are involved in determining payment, the IBA wanted to make certain that biotechnology products are included in routine pay schedules by states for Medicaid. Several other state-level issues attracted the IBA's attention, such as food labeling requirements that mandate that genetically engineered products be listed on food packages.[98] To keep its members informed of state issues, the IBA published a summary of state legislation for distribution to its membership.[99] The IBA's considerable activity at the national level, along with its concern for state legislation, reflected its main purpose, which was to deal with public policy on behalf of the biotechnology industry.

MEASURING SUCCESS

How do we measure the success of the biotechnology industry associations? It is much too early to tell with regard to BIO, which is focused on a very broad constituency, and is, therefore, difficult to assess in regard to member satisfaction with the organization. The IBA, however, did represent a limited number of producing firms operating for profit. Did the IBA contribute favorably to the profits, market growth, and share of market of the member firms? Did it reduce the costs of regulation, patent protection and R&D? Have foreign markets been opened and intellectual property protected? These questions are not quantitatively, and in some ways not even qualitatively, answered by any of the association's public documents. Only successes in terms of specific legislation and regulation have been singled out for praise. However, have other associations, such as the Pharmaceuticals Manufacturers Association, played an essential role in areas in which the IBA claimed success, such as orphan drugs, product pricing and tax concessions, to name a few? The overall value of the IBA, the ABC, and now the new joint organization, the BIO, is yet to be clearly judged.

NOTES

1. Office of the President of the United States, *Economic Report of the President* (Washington, DC: U.S. Government Printing Office, January 1993), 154–165.

2. "Clinton's Economic Policy Will Pound Stocks, Some Say," *Wall Street Journal*, 6 July 1993, Sec. C-1.

3. Interview with industry member, 13 July 1993.

4. The Associations, "Association of Biotechnology Companies Membership List" (1992); The Associations, "Industrial Biotechnology Association Membership List" (April 1993).

5. "ABC, IBA Send Joint Letter to President Clinton," *Details: News of Interest to Members of the Association of Biotechnology Companies*, January-February 1993, 1.

6. "ABC, IBA Send Joint Letter to President Clinton," 1.

7. Biotechnology Industry Organization, *Bio: The Voice and Vanguard of the Biotechnology Industry* (Washington, DC: BIO, 1992).

8. Ibid.

9. Interview with IBA official, 23 April 1993. See also Industrial Biotechnology Association (IBA), "Backgrounder Series: U.S. Biotechnology Industry Fact Sheet" (January 1993), 1.

10. U.S. Congress, Office of Technology Assessment, *Biotechnology in a Global Economy*, OTA-BA-494 (Washington, DC: U.S. Congress, Office of Technology Assessment, 1991), 73–94.

11. President's Council on Competitiveness, *Report on National Biotechnology Policy* (Washington, DC: U.S. Department of Commerce, 1991), 4–5.

12. U.S. Congress, *Biotechnology in a Global Economy*, 113.

13. Ibid., 112.

14. Alex Barnum, "Making Medicines in Biotech Barns: Gene Splicing Turns Plants, Animals into Drug Factories," *San Francisco Chronicle*, 6 July 1993, E1.

15. U.S. Congress, *Biotechnology in a Global Economy*, 120.

16. Ibid., 124.

17. Ibid., 1–6.

18. Interview with IBA official.

19. U.S. Congress, *Biotechnology in a Global Economy*, 6. "Whittling Down in Biotech," *Chemical Week*, 7 August 1991, 31.

20. W. F. Hamilton and H. Singh, "The Evolution of Corporate Capabilities in Emerging Technologies," *Interfaces* 22 (July-August 1992): 13–23. Scott Cahill, Richard Caligaris, and David Williams, "Have Pharmaceutical Companies Missed the Boat on Biotechnology?" *Medical Marketing and Media* 27, no. 1 (January 1992): 28–38.

21. Janet E. Forrest and M. J. C. Martin, "Strategic Alliance between Large and Small Research Intensive Organizations: Experiences in the Biotechnology Industry," *R&D Management* 22, no. 1 (January 1992): 41–53.

22. IBA, *U.S. Biotechnology Industry Fact Sheet*, 1–2.

23. Ibid., 2.

24. U.S. Congress, *Biotechnology in a Global Economy*, 51.

25. Ibid., 59.

26. Ibid., 55.

27. Ibid., 49.

28. Gene Bylinsky, "Biotech Firms Tackle the Giants," *Fortune*, no. 4 (12 August 1991): 78–82.

29. U.S. Congress, *Biotechnology in a Global Economy*, 30.

30. "Biotechnology Industry Posts Record Revenue," *Chemical and Engineering News*, 7 October 1991, 12.

31. U.S. Congress, *Biotechnology in Global Economy*, 212–213.

32. Ibid., 196.

33. The analysis is in ibid., 229–248.

34. Ibid., App. B, 243–244.

35. Norris Kageki, "MITI Promoting Biotech Industry Growth: Report Calls for Big Increase in R&D Projects," *Nikkei Weekly* 31, no. 1575 (28 June 1993): 1.

36. U.S. Congress, *Biotechnology in a Global Economy*, 247.

37. Margaret Ryan, "Japan-U.S. Patent War?" *Electronic Engineering Times*, 5 July 1993, 28.

38. U.S. Congress, *Biotechnology in a Global Economy,* App. B, 243.

39. "U.S. Biotech Lead Dependent on Links with Japan," *Chemical and Engineering News,* 25 May 1992, 11.

40. Weijian Shan and William Hamilton, "Country-Specific Advantage and International Cooperation," *Strategic Management Journal* 12, no. 6 (September 1991): 419–432.

41. U.S. Congress, *Biotechnology in a Global Economy,* 233.

42. Ibid., 233–234.

43. "Biotech: America's Dream Machine," *Business Week,* 2 March 1992, 66–97; "Mutating into a Second Era: Nonmedical Biotech Will See a High Growth," *Business Week/Reinventing America, 1992,* 23 October 1992, 175.

44. "IBA: The Visionary Association for a Visionary Industry," *IBA Reports,* October 1986, 2.

45. Harvey S. Price, "Thoughts Concerning a Genetic Engineering Service Association" (unpublished ms., 30 March 1981).

46. Ibid.

47. Ibid.

48. George E. Brown, Jr., "News and Comment: The Policymaking Challenge of the Bioengineering Industry" [speech delivered at Battelle Memorial Institute], In *Genetic Engineering: the 1981 International Conference* [10 April 1981], 121.

49. Ibid., 122.

50. Ibid., 123.

51. Industrial Biotechnology Association, "Meeting to Organize the Industrial Biotechnology Association" (unpublished document, IBA, 2 June 1981).

52. Ibid.

53. Ibid.

54. Ibid.

55. Ibid.

56. Ibid.

57. Letter, Leslie Glick to potential member, 1981.

58. "IBA: The Visionary Association for a Visionary Industry," 2.

59. Ibid.

60. Ibid., 9

61. Ibid.

62. Ibid.

63. "IBA: 'I Think I Can, I Think I Can,'" *IBA Reports,* November-December 1986, 1.

64. Interview with IBA official.

65. Industrial Biotechnology Association (IBA), *Bylaws of the Industrial Biotechnology Association* (IBA, 17 February 1992), 3.

66. Interview with IBA official.

67. IBA, *Bylaws of the Industrial Biotechnology Association,* 4–5.

68. Industrial Biotechnology Association, "Description of IBA Committee Activity" (unpublished document, IBA, 1992).

69. Interview with IBA official.

70. Andrew Pollack, "Group Split over Law on Drugs," *New York Times,* 28 March 1990, D3.

71. Ibid. See also Stephen Kreider Yoder, "Trade Association for Biotechnology Becomes Unspliced," *Wall Street Journal,* 28 March 1990, B8.

72. Industrial Biotechnology Association (IBA), "Biotechnology Legislation Enacted or Considered by the 102nd Congress: Current Status and Future Prospects" (IBA, n.d. [issued in 1993]).

73. Congressional caucuses generally consist of senators and representatives of both parties who have some interest in the central focus of the caucus. For example, a member might be interested in the caucus policies, he or she may represent a district or state in which there is a concentration of people concerned with the caucus' s main goals, or he or she may have related interests that are linked to the main goals. Congressional caucuses give like-minded representatives and senators an organizational basis for discussing issues of common interest, developing legislation, and constructing strategies to enact legislation. Examples of congressional caucuses include the Congressional Black Caucus,which was intended to promote the interests of African-Americans, and the Northeast-Midwest Caucus, which was created to promote policies that benefit the old Industrial Belt in the United States.

74. IBA, "Biotechnology Legislation Enacted or Considered by the 102nd Congress," 68.

75. Interview with IBA official.

76. One former IBA staff member estimated that between 66 and 90 percent of the association's political activity is at the federal level. Interview with IBA official.

77. Industrial Biotechnology Association (IBA), "Year-End Survey of State Government Legislation on Biotechnology 1992" (unpublished document, IBA, 1993), ii.

78. Ibid., i.

79. Ibid.

80. Richard G. Godown, "The Industrial Biotechnology Association," *Chemtech*, October 1990, 612–614.

81. U.S. Congress, *Biotechnology in a Global Economy*, 14.

82. Ibid., 15–16.

83. IBA, "Biotechnology Legislation Enacted or Considered by the 102nd Congress," 38.

84. Ibid., 40.

85. Ibid., 39.

86. Ibid., 42–44, 47.

87. Ibid., 12, 45, 48–49.

88. U.S. Congress, *Biotechnology in a Global Economy*, 16–19.

89. IBA, *Biotechnology Legislation Enacted or Considered by the 102nd Congress*, 14, 57–59.

90. Ibid., 4–5.

91. Ibid., 5.

92. Ibid., 5–6.

93. Ibid., 6.

94. Ibid., i-ii.

95. Ibid., 33–34, 36.

96. Ibid., 52–54.

97. Ibid., 61–62.

98. Interview with IBA official.

99. IBA, "Year-End Survey of State Government Legislation on Biotechnology 1992," 1993.

Chapter 9

The Semiconductor Industry and Its Association

THE PRESIDENT ATTACKS, SURPRISINGLY

In 1985, President Ronald Reagan was on a first-name basis with Prime Minister Yasuhiro Nakasone of Japan. The "Ron-Yasu" relationship appeared to be a warm, personal one as opposed to the correct, diplomatic bond that often exists between leaders of countries. At the time, Japan was still the "unsinkable aircraft carrier," America's staunch ally in the Pacific, positioned strategically in relation to the former USSR, the enemy. On one of my visits to the U.S. embassy in Tokyo, the ambassador to Japan, Mike Mansfield, reminded me of the importance of Japan to the U.S. Sixth Fleet. Discussing with the ambassador the fact that Japan's government policies were restricting U.S. semiconductor firms from penetrating the Japanese market appeared to be of minor interest to him. In addition, not only the State Department, which maintained the embassy, but also many other agencies of the U.S. Government (USG) were much less concerned about U.S.-Japan trade than other subjects, such as Pacific defense and the sale of U.S. treasury bonds to Japan.

In 1985, the possibility that the administration would seek an abrupt change in America's relatively benign trade policy toward Japan seemed remote, despite cries from Congress that Japan was a difficult and rapacious trade adversary as well as complaints from several industries that Japan was an unfair trader which dumped products (sold them at below cost) in world markets. Japan also protected its home markets, and did so with disdain for complaints from foreigners. Japan and its economic miracle also had many admirers in America, including a full complement of former U.S. government officials who acted as lobbyists for Japan and Japanese firms.[1]

Note: The sections of Chapter 9 describing the SIA have been adapted from Philip A. Mundo, "Interest Groups; Cases and Circumstances" (Chicago: Nelson-Hall Publishing Company, 1992).

Despite numerous attempts to obtain a negotiated informal agreement with Japan with regard to the American semiconductor maker's complaints, little progress was made in 1985. Finally, the Semiconductor Industry Association filed a Section 301 complaint requesting that the U.S. government take action against Japan for failing to provide foreign firms with access to its markets, especially American firms. At nearly the same time, three American chip makers— Advanced Micro Devices, Intel, and National Semiconductor—brought "dumping" suits against several Japanese makers in the case of erasable programmable read-only memory chips (EPROMs) and, finally, the U.S. Department of Commerce, under the leadership of Secretary Malcolm Baldridge, self-initiated a dumping suit against Japan in the case of Dynamic Random Access Memory (DRAMs) with densities of 256 kilobits (K) or more.[2] These three actions, all strongly supported by the SIA, culminated in Japan facing a three-front semiconductor trade battle: opposing the SIA on access, three major U.S. firms for EPROM dumping, and the U.S. government for DRAM dumping. As a result, MITI arranged to have all three actions swept up as part of one negotiated settlement with the U.S. government. In turn, the government, combining the efforts of the U.S. Department of Commerce and the chip industry and represented by the U.S. Trade Representative's office, led by Clayton Yuetter, was able to have an agreement finally initialed in July 1986. The agreement that was formally signed in September 1986 was called the U.S.-Japan Semiconductor Trade Agreement.[3] The main tenets were that the Japanese chip suppliers would no longer dump in world markets and that the Japanese electronics equipment and systems producers would open their market to American and other foreign semiconductor manufacturers. An interesting aspect of the agreement was that Japan agreed (in a separate, secret side letter) that an expectation of a 20 percent share of the Japanese market could be achieved within five years by foreign chip makers. The U.S. makers were well known to be the dominant foreigners. This expectation was attainable because foreign firms (primarily U.S. manufacturers) held 50 to 80 percent in each of the major semiconductor markets outside Japan. Japan had managed trade in semiconductors for years, holding the foreign penetration to an average of 10 percent, and its chip imports were of types that Japan could not or chose not to make.[4] In return for the Japanese agreements, the United States agreed to suspend dumping duties and the Section 301 action. All appeared to have been settled and in order.

Unfortunately, however, for six months, Japan failed to meet the terms of the agreement. The dumping continued, and its home market was as closed as ever. It appeared as if the agreement had been forgotten the moment after it was signed. The American lobbyists for Japan may have been able to assure their clients that the "free traders" in the Reagan administration would prevent any drastic enforcement or penalties for Japan's lack of compliance. Perhaps, they may have reasoned that this would be one more case of loud American complaints with no resultant actions—another "paper tiger"—because of the U.S. administration's desire to maintain excellent diplomatic, financial, and security relations with

Japan, even at the expense of the U.S. trade interests.

However, surprising his friend, the Prime Minister of Japan; MITI; the "free traders"; the Washington lobbyists for Japan; and even some American systems makers who purchased Japanese chips, President Reagan, on March 27, 1987, imposed immediate duties of $320 million on Japanese products imported into the United States. This was his reponse to Japanese noncompliance with the U.S.-Japan Semiconductor Trade Agreement.[5] An even greater surprise was that the duties were imposed, not on Japanese semiconductor chips, which were purchased by American computer makers (which would hurt the U.S. industry), but on many consumer-type products made by kieretsu chip-related Japanese firms and for which American consumers could obtain many low-cost substitutes from Korea, Taiwan, Hong Kong, and other foreign countries.

The date, March 27, 1987, should be flagged as the date of a U.S. surprise attack on Japan (in economic rather than military terms) and the first shot in the U.S.-Japan trade war in the U.S. defense of its industrial forces. The imposition of duties by Commander-in-Chief Reagan was the first trade torpedo to damage, though it did not disable, the "unsinkable aircraft carrier," Japan. The torpedoes have continued, the most recent being fired by President Bill Clinton at the trade talks with Japan in Tokyo during the first week of July 1993.[6] The trade counterattack on Japan by the United States, which was started by President Reagan in 1987 and carried on by President George Bush, was to continue in 1993 under a new commander-in-chief, President Clinton.

THE CHIP BUSINESS (SILICON, NOT POTATO)

The invention of the transistor at Bell Telephone Laboratories (BTL) in 1948 by W. Shockley, W. Brattain, and J. Bardeen signaled the beginning of a world revolution in microelectronics. That revolution is still in progress and is transforming all facets of life so profoundly that the period that began with this event over 40 years ago is increasingly called, the Information Age, referring to the mass phenomena to which it has given birth. This phenomenom—the widespread use of information age technology—has been made possible by the electronic capability enabled by tiny silicon semiconductor devices no larger than a fingernail. This new enabling technology and its products provide the electronics capability to detect, measure, record, process, and communicate information at real-time speeds or for long-term electronic storage—information that may be in the form of audio, video, data, text, graphics, or images and may be transmitted and received across distances as short as house to house or as distant as from the earth to the moon. These tiny silicon products have come to be called chips. Sometimes they are called computer chips because of their great usage in computers.

The 1948 invention of the transistor was followed in ten years by the invention of the integrated circuit (IC), which allowed the production and connection of many transistors on the same chip. From one transistor per chip in 1948 and several transistors per chip a decade later, the industry has progressed to the point where, today, integrated circuits are produced with 16 million transistors on a chip no larger than a thumbnail. This technological progression began when two men, the late Robert Noyce, at Fairchild Camera and Instrument, and Jack Kilby, at Texas Instruments, invented the integrated circuit in 1958. During the years from 1948 to 1958, from the discovery of the transistor to the invention of the IC, two major forces directly affected the emergence and growth of semiconductor technology and the production of semiconductor chips. These forces were the U.S. government, through the Department of Defense, and American Telephone and Telegraph (AT&T), through BTL and Western Electric, its manufacturing arm. The Defense Department during these years provided tens of millions of dollars to the industry for the development of devices for use in military and space applications, while at the same time, in the field of semiconductor research and development, BTL was paramount in America. The BTL sister operation at AT&T, Western Electric, was also developing and putting into place manufacturing technology and processes. Eventually, knowledge was diffused from these organizations based on discoveries that are now in the public domain. Large numbers of scientists and engineers left the AT&T operations to join commercial enterprises with no threat of legal suits against them for the theft of trade secrets.[7]

These two bodies—the U.S. Defense Department and AT&T—were unquestionably responsible for the emergence of the semiconductor industry in America. By the end of the 1950s, about $300 million of semiconductor products were manufactured annually and the establishment of some of the premier and highly influential firms of the next three decades had occurred. Despite the fact that older, larger firms—General Electric, RCA, Sylvania, and Westinghouse—that had produced electronic components such as vacuum receiving tubes, had entered the transistor and integrated circuit fields early, they were soon to be overtaken, and eventually eliminated from leadership positions in the industry, by smaller and more agile firms. The industry's new and emerging commercial merchant producers—Texas Instruments, Motorola, and Fairchild—were to make large strides that were to maintain them in leadership positions through the 1960s and into the next decade. Fairchild especially was to gain a great reputation as the hotbed of new technologies, home of the brightest scientists and engineers, and main source of flocks of aggressive California entrepreneurs, and it was located in an area that was to be dubbed Silicon Valley.

By the late 1960s and early 1970s, other present-day leaders began to emerge—Intel, Advanced Micro Devices, and National Semiconductor, among others. In a parallel course to the merchant producers, semiconductor R&D and manufacture for internal use flourished in the major computer and telecommunications firms, including International Business Machines, Hewlett-Packard, and Digital Equipment Corporation, as well as the pioneer, AT&T. The internal semiconductor operations of these large producers of electronic equipment were called "captive" producers, in contrast to the open market "merchant" producers. Their output, however, was significant and estimated to be as high as 20 to 25 percent of the total U.S. production by all firms.

In 1970, the United States led the world in R&D as well as in consumption and production, and the 1970s were to be a continuation of the 1960s American dominance in the global semiconductor market. Of the top five companies in the world, three were American, one Japanese, and one European. At the same time that the U.S. market was growing, from $500 million in 1960 to over $1 billion in 1970,[8] the costs and prices per unit of integrated circuits continued to drop, primarily because of the economics of scale, scope, and learning, at a rate of about 30 percent per year.[9] Another characteristic of the market was its changing composition. While in 1962, 100 percent of the U.S.-produced ICs went to government uses, only 36 percent were so used by 1969.[10] Commercial computers consumed 44 percent of the total semiconductor consumption, and the computer systems industry became the largest user by 1969. In 1970, the European industry leadership was held by Philips (Netherlands), followed by Siemens (Germany), S-G-S (Italy), and Plessey (United Kingdom), while among the leading firms in Japan were Hitachi, NEC, and Toshiba.[11] The European firms focused on the industrial and consumer equipment manufacturers applications, while Japan focused on these markets as well as also accelerating their major thrust into the computer systems marketplace.

After 1970, however, the state of play in the chip business began to change. Japan, as part of its industrial policy orientation, had designated electronics as a targeted industry when it passed its Electronics Industry Promotion Act in 1958.[12] Consequently, foreigners were not allowed to directly sell their products in Japan, and it was not until 1975 that foreign investment in chip factories in Japan was even allowed. In 1976, the well-publicized VLSI Project to develop the manufacturing of very large-scale integration (VSLI) chips (i.e., ICs with a high density of active elements) brought together a number of giant Japanese electronics companies to cooperate in an industry/government-sponsored effort to raise the level of Japanese capability in integrated circuits. While sponsoring collaborative R&D, MITI also rationalized the semiconductor production of the major Japanese producers; closely watched new foreign technology developments and only allowed joint ventures where technology transfer into the nation's firms was mandated; slowed the issuance of foreign patents such that even TI's IC patent, which was accepted throughout the world, was only issued by Japan in 1985, over twenty-seven years after the invention by Jack Kilby; encouraged massive investment by Japanese firms in production facilities; and, overall, openly managed the semiconductor industry and foreign trade with impunity. Industry/government collaboration in a virtual cartel-like setting, where home market protection and penetration of foreign markets were the "marching orders," was the essence of Japan's semiconductor industry activity.

The Europeans, on the other hand, led by Philips and Siemens, allowed American firms to enter the European market as exporters under a heavy 17 percent import duty and to set up factories in Europe for local production free of duties. The direct result of this policy was that major American firms—Texas Instruments, Motorola, National, and others—set up factories for production in Europe but, as did many others, they also exported to Europe from their factories throughout the United States, Asia, and other regions. The effect was that by the end of the 1970s, American firms had achieved a dominant position of about 50 percent of the European chip market. However, by 1980, this was not the only global change: Japan had captured 25 percent of the semiconductor world market share. The stage was set for intense U.S.-Japan rivalry that was to dominate global competition in chips to the present day.[13]

By the beginning of the 1980s, Japan had established its technology, capacity, and reputation in the production of VLSI, and specifically in dynamic random access memories (DRAMs) for computer systems. The Europeans had become minority suppliers within their own market and were concentrating on bringing about cooperative efforts to restore themselves to a dominant position in Europe. The U.S. firms were put into a position of defending the market for their computer memory device (the DRAM) against Japanese firms; continuing to invest in Europe as well as in the U.S. in order to avoid paying high tariffs; and at home, facing high costs of capital, the need to improve their factory quality and productivity, and increased R&D expense in the development of advanced value-added products such as microprocessors. In addition, other Pacific Rim countries (mainly Korea and Taiwan) although not yet global factors were pouring significant amounts of industry and government funds and resources into building major semiconductor operations. The year 1980 was the beginning of the toughest decade to date for American chip makers.

The decade began ominously with the acquisition of Fairchild by a French firm, Schlumberger, after an attempt by Fujitsu to purchase the company had been thwarted by the U.S. government.[14] Then, in 1984, the highest year-to-year growth rate of 50 percent was followed by the worst decline ever, with a 30 percent drop in sales from 1984 to 1985. It was estimated that between 1985 and 1987, American firms lost a total of $2 billion and the Japanese industry lost over $4 billion.[15] Worst of all, 1984 ended with Japan garnering over 50 percent—the major share—of the world memory market.[16] By 1987, of the top ten chip makers in the world, six were Japanese, one was European, and only three were American.[17] The Japanese semiconductor industry producers had overtaken the United States as the dominant global producer through the sales of high-quality, large-scale ICs at low prices; they had achieved the world's largest semiconductor global share of market (45 percent), and managed imports to protect its home market by continuing to hold over 90 percent of what was now the largest semiconductor market in the world.[18] Japan had become, not only the largest producer, but also the largest consumer of semiconductor devices in the world.

With intense competition in 1985 due to falling demand and excess capacity, the poor financial performance of American firms was not unexpected, but the new dominant market position of the Japanese was the real shock. The American semiconductor industry, as with many industries with trade problems, turned to U.S. government action to correct the major causes of their loss of market position and their subsequent poor financial performance: Japanese dumping (i.e., selling below cost) and a closed Japanese market. The Japanese market share had been maintained at a low 10 percent for foreigners for at least the prior fifteen years.

The eventual outcome of the combined U.S. industry/government action was the U.S.-Japan Semiconductor Agreement, described in the opening section of this chapter. The actions of the Semiconductor Industry Association (SIA), which was formed in 1977, played a significant part in the negotiation and finalization of that agreement.

To further bolster its falling fortunes, the semiconductor industry, as represented by the major companies, believed that U.S. manufacturing technology required an uplift. In order to accomplish this improvement, the SIA successfully convinced the U.S. government to become an equal partner with industry in the establishment of a manufacturing development consortium called SEMATECH (for SEmiconductor MAnufacturing TECHnology) and funded by industry and government equally at a level of $100 million each year for five years. SEMATECH was eventually based in Austin, Texas. The consortium, which was initially headed by the late Bob Noyce, has continued to operate to this day, with funding still forthcoming from industry and government. An older consortium, the Semiconductor Research Corporation (SRC), was initiated by the SIA in 1983 and has been totally funded by industry. The SRC celebrated its tenth anniversary in 1993 with a budget of $30 million, and with this money, it focuses on supporting basic semiconductor research in the nation's universities. Through this effort, hundreds of trained engineers and scientists have been employed by the semiconductor industry. By comparison, the efforts of SEMATECH were utilized in the development of equipment, processes, and procedures to increase the manufacturing capability and productivity of the U.S. industry overall.

By 1988, as a result of the U.S.-Japan Semiconductor Agreement, dumping by Japanese firms in DRAMs was in remission and the Japanese market was beginning to open up slightly. The Koreans had entered the world market for DRAMs and the Europeans were holding fast to a high-tariff philosophy while attempting to implement joint research and development plans. By 1991, the first U.S.-Japan Semiconductor Trade Agreement had ended and a second agreement, called the New Semiconductor Agreement (NSA), was put in place for an additional five years. The foreign chip makers, which were mostly American, had achieved 15 percent of the Japanese market—not the expected 20 percent—by December 1991.[19] Progress had been made, but signs that the Japanese market was open as required by the first agreement had not been observed.

The NSA had been obtained by the chip industry with the help of the other electronic industry groups represented by the American Electronics Association (AEA) and the Computer Systems Policy Project (CSPP), a group of eleven computer company CEOs that was formed expressly to affect trade and technology policy. The roles of the AEA and CSPP, along with the Computer and Business Equipment Manufacturers Association (CBEMA), will be covered in greater detail in the next chapter, which concerns the computer systems industry.

The early 1990s have shown that, due to a number of reasons (among them, the trade agreement, new value-added products, the consortia activity, and quality and production improvements), the U.S. semiconductor industry has been able to regain its leading position after having lost it to Japan. This industry may be the only one to have reversed its fortunes vis-à-vis Japan thus far. The comparison of world market shares of integrated circuits from 1985 to 1992 is shown in Figure 9.1.

Also by December 1992, foreign firms had achieved a 20.2 percent share of the Japanese semiconductor market.[20] At the same time that this marketplace change has been taking place, the price-to-performance ratio is still highly favorable to the industry's customers. For example, the 1992 price of one-megabit DRAMs were approximately only one-sixth of the 1988 price. Along with various impacts over the years, such as advances in technology, the price changes resulting from dumping or antidumping actions, and the changes in investment level, the price-performance ratio continues to improve. These price-performance ratio advances show that regardless of the state of the global industry and the positions of the leading firms, the consuming industries and the public have continued to benefit from this high-tech industry.

The role of this industry's trade association, the Semiconductor Industry Association, in the global competitive marketplace has been well noted in the general press as well as in the business and academic presses. The origins, structure, and activities of this association will be described in the following sections of this chapter.

THE SEMICONDUCTOR INDUSTRY ASSOCIATION—ITS ORIGINS AND MEMBERSHIP

In March 1977, five semiconductor company executives met at Ming's Restaurant in Palo Alto, a geographical and academic part of Silicon Valley, California, and the home of Stanford University. The five included the late Robert Noyce, vice chairman of the board, Intel Corporation; Wilfred Corrigan, chair of the board and CEO of Fairchild Camera and Instrument; Charles Sporck, CEO, National Semiconductor Corporation; W. J. (Jerry) Sanders III, chair of the board and CEO of Advanced Micro Devices; and finally, John Welty, president, Motorola Semiconductor Products Division, Motorola Incorporated. The purpose of the meeting, as reported in the San Jose Mercury on the following day, was to form the Semiconductor Industry Association.[21] All five men had been watching the Japanese threat as it formed, and in anticipation that it would include predatory practices, maintenance of a protected home market, cooperative research and development, and other Japanese industrial policy practices, they believed that the ultimate solution lay in the formation of a focused trade association that could, with U.S. government help, blunt the Japanese thrust. All these companies were members of the American Electronics Association (AEA), which is the largest existing electronics industry association, and they maintained their membership in that organization. The objective was for the SIA

Figure 9.1
Total Worldwide Integrated Circuit Market Share

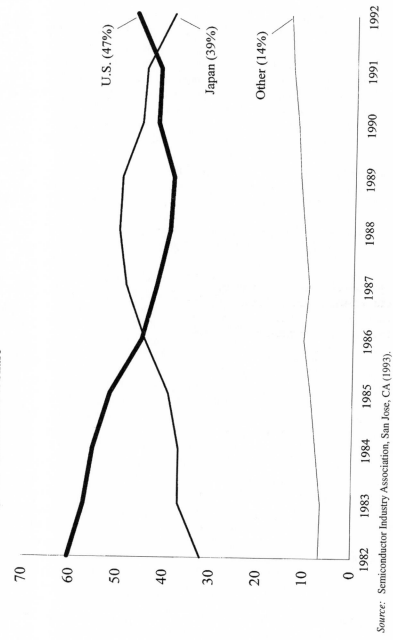

Source: Semiconductor Industry Association, San Jose, CA (1993).

to be able to act independently as a chip makers' association in the area of trade and other industry needs while continuing to take advantage of the traditional offerings of the AEA.

The companies forming the new association leadership included five of the top six in the country, the exception being Texas Instruments (TI), which did not join for several years. Its reasons may have been related to the fact that it had invested in plants in Japan and may have been construed to have an interest in that country's situation. Alternately, perhaps, being the leading firm in the industry, it may have felt that membership in SIA would be to the greater benefit of its most aggressive competitors. Whatever the reason, TI waited. It joined later, took an SIA board of directors' seat, and therafter soon became a staunch supporter of the new association.

In the SIA's short (seventeen-year) history, its membership has not changed dramatically. It grew from its five member beginnings to a modest size, ranging up to thirty regular members. While these members account for 90 percent of semiconductor production in the United States, approximately 150 other U.S.-based semiconductor firms, accounting for the remaining 10 percent, do not belong to the SIA.[22] The regular, or voting, members are American-owned firms and do not include foreign subsidiaries operating in the United States.

Two aspects of the SIA's membership reflect the group's orientation in the industry. First, most SIA members are merchant firms, which manufacture semiconductors for sale to outside customers, but the SIA has also made a deliberate effort to include captive firms: companies that produce semiconductors for their own use. Thus, in 1982, such captives as Hewlett-Packard Company (HP), International Business Machine Corporation (IBM), Digital Equipment Corporation (DEC), and American Telephone and Telegraph (AT&T) (all large firms) joined the SIA. All four are represented on the SIA's board of directors.[23] From the perspective of the general health of the U.S. semiconductor industry, it is critical to include such large firms in its principal trade association since their dual role (as consumers as well as producers) is critical to the position of the U.S. semiconductor industry in the international market.

Second, since roughly 150 semiconductor firms do not belong to the SIA, the association does not even approach the entire universe of semiconductor suppliers in the United States. Companies that are not SIA members are typically small start-up or specialty firms often without internal manufacturing capability, that do not have even a fraction of the market share of the typical merchant companies that make up the bulk of the SIA's membership. The small chip makers apparently have the opportunity to join the SIA, and the SIA officially would welcome them. Several reasons might explain why these firms have not joined. First, they may simply disagree with the association's policy objectives. This explanation is not compelling, however, since only a few small firms have stated opposing views. Second, these small firms may not be able to afford the cost of joining the SIA. They are small, after all, and therefore not likely to have surplus funds to spend on trade association membership. Third, these firms may be enjoying a free ride, compliments of SIA. Since the SIA will fight the same political battles either with or without their membership, it makes sense to remain outside the SIA, thus enjoying the benefits while avoiding the cost of membership.

Organizational Characteristics

The SIA's organizational character sets it apart from other trade associations. Its location away from Washington, D.C., is unusual among American interest groups, and its consensus-based decision-making style reflects the industry that the association represents. The SIA is unorthodox in its approach to politics, which is precisely what one would expect, given the people who formed it.

Reflecting their disinclination to "play the political game" in the usual way, the founders of the SIA located their new trade association in Silicon Valley rather than in Washington. Since the industry is based in large part in California, its trade association is there as well.[24] In this way, the SIA is close to the companies it represents and is better able to understand their concerns as well as the problems of the industry as a whole.

Its insulation from Washington was reinforced by the extent to which members of the industry knew each other. Many semiconductor industry executives had worked together for years in the development of new technology and products. Frequently, new companies were started by former employees of established companies (bearing in mind the limited meaning of "established" in the semiconductor industry). Thus, members of the industry knew each other well and tended to agree on the economic and, now, political issues with which the industry must deal.

The tight network that defined U.S. semiconductor manufacturers carried over into the original design for decision making in the SIA. Decisions would be made on the basis of consensus. Such commonplaces as binding votes and majority rule would be avoided in determining the SIA's political goals and strategies. To the experienced political or organizational practitioner, such a plan sounds like the idealism of the political novice, which doubtless will be quickly replaced by the pragmatic style of decision by vote. However, this has not happened in the SIA, and its unusual organizational character persists.

Staff

The SIA prides itself on being a small organization that is at the leading edge of technology, innovative in political strategy and tactics, and has consensus underlying decisions. SIA staff members reflect the character of the organization in style and goals. The founders of the organization did not want to contend with a growing staff with bureaucratic tendencies. Rather, the staff would remain small to serve the needs of the industry, not to serve the needs of the individual staff members.

The staff currently consists of twelve people at SIA headquarters in San Jose, California (in Silicon Valley), and one person in Japan. Staff size has not increased much in the SIA's history, although the budget has risen significantly. Thus, while there is enough money to pay for more staff members, the SIA refrains from creating new positions, reflecting its commitment to remain small. Staff members are generally hired from the semiconductor or a related industry. They know the industry and have a good understanding of its problems, goals, and culture. The SIA tries to avoid recruiting from outside the industry; for example, it has not hired career trade-association executives.

Major organizational responsibilities are assigned to a few key SIA staff members. Currently, the main positions include the president, who is responsible for the entire operation; a vice president of international trade and government affairs; a vice president, who provides support to technology policy programs; the executive director in the Japan office, who provides a liaison between U.S. member firms based in the United States and their operations in Japan within the SIA framework; a director of occupational health, safety, and environmental programs; a director of communications; and a director of industry statistics. These positions reflect the scope of the SIA's economic and political activities. Each person on the staff has little additional support which, for better of worse, keeps the SIA "lean."

The SIA's decision not to maintain a staff in Washington, D.C., has possible disadvantages. The principal problem is that the absence of a continuous staff presence in Washington could reduce the SIA's, and the U.S. semiconductor industry's, ability to influence top government officials. Clearly, semiconductor executives do not believe that this is a problem. Quite the contrary; SIA officials and semiconductor industry executives argue that the SIA has an advantage in being located outside Washington, which allows it to approach policy and politics free of the "inside-the-Beltway" mind-set which, from the perspective of the U.S. semiconductor industry, produces policy as usual and not policy innovations. The absence of staff in Washington, however, does not mean that a Washington presence does not exist. On the contrary, it is accomplished in a different manner, which SIA believes is most effective.

Equally curious is the presence of an SIA staff member in Japan, meaning that the SIA staff maintains a continuous presence in Japan but not in Washington. This might suggest something about the SIA's orientation toward government and politics, but one should not draw too stark a conclusion. The importance of the location of the SIA for its political strategy and effectiveness is taken up later in this chapter.

Contracting Out

One way in which the staff has been kept small has been by contracting our major tasks and responsibilities. The SIA retains outside assistance for legal, political, economic, and health and safety matters. For example, in 1986 the SIA gave a grant to the University of California at Davis to evaluate a specific issue of occupational health and safety in the workplace. The results of the study form the basis of SIA policy on that issue.

The SIA retains the services of several law firms for legal and political work. The SIA's most important relationship in this regard is its long-term use of the law firm of Dewey Ballantine as its lobbyist in Washington. The association entrusts its political strategy to the firm, relying on the expertise of Dewey Ballantine lawyer Alan W. Wolff in international trade, and that of his colleague Clark McFadden in technology and consortia issues.[25]

SIA officials argue that contracting out these tasks makes the interest group more effective as well as more efficient. The SIA can use the skills of these experts as it needs them, avoiding the cost of maintaining such expertise in-house on a full-time basis, on the one hand, or relying on less effective generalists to perform these tasks, on the other. In any event, the staff can remain small as a result.

In addition to contracting out for health and safety research and for legal, economic, and political matters, the SIA has shown a marked reluctance to assume operating responsibilities for its two principal spin-offs: the Semiconductor Research Consortium (SRC) and SEMATECH, the Semiconductor Manufacturing Technology initiative. The SIA created these two organizations to help the U.S. semiconductor industry retain its competitive edge, and to regain it where it had been lost to the Japanese.[26] In recent years, however, the SIA, through its Technology Strategy Committee, has taken a greater role in determining technology policy for the SIA, and therefore, although the independent day-to-day operation of these spin-off consortia continues, their overall plans and objectives are subject to greater oversight by the SIA board.

Staff and Bureaucracy

Interest groups frequently develop large staffs. As membership grows, responsibilities assumed by the group increase, and political activities grow to meet new demands, interest groups tend to create new positions and hire professionals to fill them. Although staff growth may be useful as well as inevitable, it can create problems for the interest group.

First, the distinction between a large staff and an unwieldy bureaucracy is subtle. As tasks are carved up into smaller pieces, the organization is increasingly dominated by specialists—primarily policy experts and administrators. These experts, while loyal to the interest group and its goals, are also subject to the norms and standards of their professions. Thus, administrators are concerned with the operation of the interest group—revenue, expenditures, purchases, personnel, and budgets—but their behavior may be determined more by their professions than by the nature of the group. This creates some distance between the staff, on the one hand, and the central purpose of the group and its membership, on the other. This can easily be interpreted as a lack of responsiveness by the staff to the group membership.

Second, staff tends to beget more staff. Positions may be created for no clear purpose, at least from the perspective of the group's membership. The administrative unit then becomes large and lumbering, with a life of its own and vulnerable to the accusation of being unresponsive to the membership. The SIA deliberately avoided these problems by keeping the staff small. Additionally, the staff maintains a close relationship with the board of directors. Since the SIA is located in Silicon Valley, where many of its members are located as well, it is easy for staff members and company executives and other personnel to remain in close contact. The constant interaction—once again occurring by design—helps to keep the staff's goals and activities in line with member preferences. Finally, the relatively few members of the SIA—thirty full members—make it somewhat easier than in a larger organization for staff to know what the members want.

The Board of Directors

The board of directors makes the important decisions in the SIA. Notably absent from the SIA are an elaborate decision-making structure and procedures. Moreover, since the organization is small, there are no subunits (except board-approved committees).

Size is certainly one reason for the SIA's organizational simplicity, but it is not the only one. A common perspective among members has allowed for highly centralized decision making based on consensus. As long as the underlying agreement continues, simple structure and procedures will suffice. Disagreement forces organizations to develop structures and procedures to accommodate it, lest the organization fall apart. This has not yet been required at the SIA.

The board of directors consists of fourteen company executives representing both merchant and captive firms, with ten merchant firms and four captive firms represented on the board.[27] Board members invite new members to join, and they are elected as a slate each year. The relative informality of selection to the board reflects the comity among executives of the U.S. semiconductor industry. Moreover, it probably encourages consensus and preference for common ground over disputes and intransigence. On the other hand, the "inner club" of the industry, as indicated by membership in the SIA and, especially, on the association's board of directors, may cause executives from other U.S. semiconductor manufacturers to feel excluded and therefore less inclined to support the member companies' policy preferences.

Meeting four to six times a year, the SIA board makes most fundamental policy decisions on the basis of consensus. If agreement cannot be reached or if dissenters cannot be persuaded to refrain from an open break with other board members, the board generally postpones action until an accommodation can be reached. There have been a few cases where fundamental issues have required a decision vote. This is a uniformly understood feature of the board's decision-making style: members deliberately work with each other to build consensus.

Two factors explain the importance of consensus on the SIA board. First, the founders of the SIA were all members of a small, dynamic industry. They knew each other well and they agreed on the main concerns of their industry. With this much basic agreement to start with, it made sense that the principals in the SIA would continue to seek agreement in their collective action. Second, company executives believe that it is necessary to reach agreement on policies before presenting their preferences to government officials. A united front is likely to make the SIA more effective, while open rifts within the SIA would weaken its position. Thus, the board seeks to reach a position that members can support (or not disagree with openly) before taking it to Washington.

Consensus has possibly increased the SIA's political effectiveness and perhaps enhanced the cohesion of the U.S. semiconductor industry as a whole, but it can have negative effects as well. The need to reach consensus on a policy position may prevent the SIA from reacting quickly to a problem. Moreover, consensus may be one factor that forces the SIA to keep its membership limited to mainstream semiconductor companies, excluding the numerous small specialty and start-up companies that appear throughout the U.S. semiconductor and computer industries. The test will be the SIA's ability to maintain its consensus decision-making style as it confronts future demanding problems.

SIA Committees

The SIA has several standing committees with functional responsibilities. Additionally, it forms ad hoc committees for specific issues or problems. Committees consist of member company executives and, because of the close relationship between the committees, the board, and the SIA staff, committees do not necessarily have to wait for a quarterly meeting of the board before they act. Of the several standing committees, the most visible and most important for the SIA's political activities are the public policy committee, the technology strategy committee, and the communications committee, while other committees are essential in other areas (see Table 9.1).

The Public Policy Committee deals with government at the national level. The major issue for this committee is, of course, foreign competition—mainly from Japan, though South Korean firms are also significant competitors in the international DRAM market and the Europeans may become more competitive as a result of the economic unification of the European Community. The Public Policy Committee develops the SIA's positions on these issues and is the source of options in the overall strategy and activity of the association.

An extremely important facet of the Public Policy Committee is that its Washington-based, government-relations company executive participants form a Washington Representatives Group within the Public Policy Committee. This group is essential in the achievement of specific tasks such as lobbying, communication, and assistance to the administration, the Congress, and the various government agencies, with the end objective to accomplish SIA's goals. Its charter allows the

Table 9.1
Standing Committees of the SIA, 1993

Public Policy
Recommends public policy objectives to the board of directors that are primarily related to international trade and competitiveness.

Technology Strategy
Recommends technology policy for the industry to the board of directors and oversees implementation of the industry's technology roadmap.

Communications
Provides information on the semiconductor industry, companies, activities and issues. The committee works with other SIA committees as the main source of media relations.

Japan Chapter
Provides the SIA with information about Japanese markets, technology, and government policies. Its members are executives of Japanese subsidiaries of American chip manufacturers.

Industry Statistics
Works with foreign associations in making policy for the World Semiconductor Trade Statistics (WSTS) program. Also initiates new programs.

Government Procurement
Has responsibility for improving the government and industry procedures for the procurement of semiconductors.

Occupational Health
Provides a forum for industry discussions and studies on health and safety.

Facilities and Building Standards
Works with local officials in connection with the design and construction of new semiconductor fabrication plants.

Environmental
Monitors proposed environmental regulation relevant to the industry and provides technical data to companies regarding solutions to environmental problems.

Law
Advises the board on legislation and legal matters related to the industry. The committee files amicus curiae briefs and retains private law firms to assure compliance with U.S. laws governing trade associations.

implementation in specific terms of the means for achieving the broader goals shaped by the Public Policy Committee in total. It is this group and its functioning that allows the SIA staff to work at a location remote from Washington, D.C.

The Technology Strategy Committee, which is made up of seven members (either directors or alternates), is responsible for setting policy for the SIA technology goals. In November 1992, the SIA brought together 170 engineers and scientists from chip firms, universities, government laboratories, and industry consortia in order to shape a roadmap for critical semiconductor process technology for fifteen years into the future. The Technology Strategy Committee will be the policy-making and oversight organization responsible for implementation of the industry roadmap. It plans to operate in such a way that industry, government, and academia are an integrated part of achieving the objectives.

The Communications Committee's main purpose is to project the association's perspective on various issues as broadly and clearly as possible. It tries to convince government officials, members of the news media, executives from other industries, policy analysts, and academicians of the strength of the SIA's positions on issues—international trade and foreign competition, for example.

Since the SIA staff is small, company executives involved in the SIA committees do much of the work that is traditionally reserved for staff in other associations. This arrangement requires frequent meetings between company officials and SIA staff members.

Goals

The SIA keeps its goals narrow, reflecting the view of key members that it should focus solely on issues directly affecting the U.S. semiconductor industry and avoid broader economic issues. This prevents the SIA from becoming concerned with so many issues that it cannot be effective with respect to any single one, and it makes it easier to achieve consensus in the board of directors.

In general, SIA has two major sets of goals: international trade and technology policy. These issues, trade and technology are of equal import and require most of the SIA's time and resources. The association would like to open foreign markets that are closed because of government protectionist policies (a case in point is Japan). The SIA also sees a problem for the U.S. semiconductor industry in the international market in connection with the economic unification of the European Community (EC). The EC currently maintains a 14 percent duty on semiconductor imports, while the United States, Canada, and Japan impose no import duties. Moreover, the EC plans to, in effect, place local content limits on semiconductor chips sold within its borders. Chips must be manufactured within the EC—not merely assembled, but substantively fabricated. Some U.S. semiconductor firms, such as Intel, have responded by constructing new fabrication facilities in the EC, but others have been slow or unable to respond. This could place these companies at a serious disadvantage with respect to selling products in Europe.

With international competitiveness of the U.S. semiconductor industry as its goal, the SIA has also pursued policy objectives involving U.S. domestic economic policy. A significant part of this area is known as technology policy. Since the Cold War ended and global competition intensified, one option for America has been to use the research and development resources formerly used for war and apply them to a peaceful economy. In addition, it has become evident that the success of high-technology industry in global trade, as well as in creating jobs at home, is dependent on investments in technology and the resulting manufactured products. Since the manufacture of semiconductors is a high-technology industry and the government, as well as industry, is spending billions of dollars in research, it appears that a national technology policy is required. The SIA, through the Technology Strategy Committee and its affiliates, the Semiconductor Research Corporation and SEMATECH, is uniquely positioned to contribute to, and even take advantage of, this shift in national economic policy. Technology streaming forth from government laboratories, university research, industry consortia, and the chip firms themselves can be guided to achieve the maximum results in the shortest time possible and with a minimum of duplication of resources. SIA positioned itself well to be among the first to take advantage of the Clinton administration's emphasis on technology, including such downstream efforts as the National Information Infrastructure.

The association has also emphasized activities in the areas of capital formation, environment, health and safety, and industry statistics. Although not pursued at the same level as the major areas described above, these activities do require significant resources and have achieved notable success.

Political Success

The SIA has had to overcome two disadvantages to achieve political success. First, the U.S. semiconductor industry alone is comparatively small: it is worth about $40 billion, while IBM alone has sales of about $60 billion. Second, the industry is concentrated in the Sun Belt, the Pacific Northwest, and several eastern states and therefore cannot easily attract sympathy from legislators in the large number of states that do not have semiconductor firms.[28] Thus, that the strategy of basing the SIA in California, keeping it small, not hiring a full-time lobbyist, and using company executives to lobby government officials has resulted in considerable success for the SIA is all the more remarkable (see Table 9.2).

While the list of successes is impressive, it is not likely that the SIA is solely responsible for all of them. The SIA capitalized on a growing wave of support for international trade agreements that would curb the aggressiveness of Japanese firms, especially in U.S. markets—thus, the 1986 chip agreement with Japan. The SIA also took advantage of unenthusiastic enforcement of antitrust laws in the Reagan administration to promote the creation of SEMATECH and benefited from the administration's emphasis on defense technology. In the more recent months of 1993, SIA has been able to take advantage of the Clinton administration's emphasis on technology policy to put in place an SIA technology roadmap, which involves more cooperation, and possibly even greater joint industry-government research and development efforts, than have been the case in the past. This is not to say that the SIA was unsuccessful; indeed, it took full advantage of the prevailing political winds. The SIA's strategy has worked well so far: indeed, it has been singled out as the greatest political success story of the American electronics industry.

Table 9.2
SIA Industry/Political Successes

1982

– The Semiconductor Research Corporation (SRC) is founded by SIA to provide funding and direction for basic semiconductor research at American universities. The SRC becomes an independent affiliate of the SIA.

1983

– SIA efforts lead to the creation of the U.S.- Japan Working Group on High Technology, a bilateral government effort to address semiconductor trade conflicts.

1984

– The National Cooperative Research Act is signed into law by President Reagan. The SIA-supported measure encourages joint R&D consortia by reforming U.S. antitrust law.

– The Trade and Tariff Act of 1984 becomes law, authorizing negotiation of high-tech trade issues and tariff elimination.

– President Reagan signs the Semiconductor Chip Protection Act, creating the first new form of intellectual property protection in the U.S. since the nineteenth century.

1985

– At the urging of the SIA, the United States and Japanese governments completely eliminate tariffs on imported semiconductors. European manufacturers refuse to join the United States and Japan, and to this date still maintain high chip tariffs.

– SIA files a Section 301 Petition with the U.S. government citing unfair Japanese market barriers. The U.S. share of the Japanese market at the time is just 8.5 percent versus a U.S. worldwide market share outside Japan of more than 70 percent.

1986

– The U.S. Department of Commerce conclusively finds that Japanese semiconductor firms are selling far below the cost of production, dumping memory chips in the U.S. market at margins of up to 188 percent.

– The U.S. and Japan sign a historic bilateral Semiconductor Trade Agreement to eliminate dumping and open the Japanese market to foreign semiconductors.

1987

– The industry consortium SEMATECH is founded by fourteen U.S. semiconductor manufacturers. Its mission is to sponsor and conduct research in semiconductor manufacturing technology for the U.S. industry.

– President Reagan imposes 100 percent duties on $300 million worth of goods exported by Japan for its failure to comply with the terms of the 1986 trade agreement.

1988

– Congress approves formation of the National Advisory Committee on Semiconductors (NACS), made up of top-level officials from government and industry, to report on proposals for a "national semiconductor strategy."

Table 9.2
SIA Industry/Political Successes (Continued)

1989

– The SIA signs a three-year, $3.5 million research agreement with the University of California, Davis, to conduct an industry-wide health study.

1990

– SIA joins with the computer systems industry to support a new semiconductor trade agreement with Japan. The new agreement is necessary to ensure Japan fulfills its commitments under the 1986 trade accord.

1991

– The United States and Japan sign a new semiconductor trade agreement committing Japan to open its market to foreign semiconductors and providing a strong deterrent to dumping. Two significant improvements over the 1986 trade agreement are Japan's public recognition of a 20 percent foreign market share commitment and the inclusion of a "fast-track" approach to resolving dumping allegations.

– The U.S. Department of Commerce presents SIA with its prestigious "E Award" for the association's efforts to increase American exports.

1992

– SRC commemorates its tenth anniversary and provides figures indicating the number of Ph.D.s granted in electrical engineering from U.S. universities over the last ten years has more than doubled. This increase occurs after a decline in Ph.D. graduates in electrical engineering from 1970 to 1982.

– More than 150 technologists from industry, government, and academia gather in Dallas for a semiconductor industry technology workshop designed to produce a roadmap for the nation's semiconductor research needs for the next fifteen years.

– SIA's $3.7 million epidemiologic study of worker health in the semiconductor industry is completed. Based on the study results, the industry announces a four-part action plan to ensure a safe workplace for industry employees.

1993

– SEMATECH announces achievement of one of its primary technical goals: demonstrating 0.35 micron manufacturing capability on all-American made equipment.

– Japan and the United States announce that foreign semiconductor manufacturers achieved a 20.2 percent share of Japan's chip market in the fourth quarter of 1992, in accordance with the U.S.-Japan semiconductor trade pact.

– Final figures for 1992 confirm U.S. companies have surpassed Japan in worldwide market share for integrated circuits, 45.5 percent to 41.6 percent. Estimates indicate the United States will surpass Japan in worldwide market share for total semiconductors in 1993.

Factors Contributing to the SIA's Success

Several articles have heralded the SIA's success in influencing public policy.[29] Of course, the SIA's size, location, goals, and political strategy have been credited for the success. Not least among these in contributing to the association's success is the SIA's strategy of delivering to government officials a clear message that stresses the importance of maintaining a U.S. industry that manufactures a product critical to the computer industry, defense, and the electronics industry as a whole. While these factors have played an important role, developments outside the association, and beyond its control, have contributed to its success as well.

The federal government has been somewhat receptive to problems of U.S. competitiveness in the international market. Congress and the executive branch have carried out numerous studies evaluating the U.S. position in various industries.[30] The United States has avoided blatantly protectionist policies, but it has engaged in efforts to establish a "level playing field," using punitive measures allowed in federal trade law.[31] At the same time, the United States has avoided the use of policies designed explicitly to help specific industries, especially those with the potential to become "winners." More recently, under the Clinton administration, technology policy heavily weighted toward information-age technology has provided even greater impetus to government support.

Noting the importance of the semiconductor industry to the electronics industry in general and to national security (new weapons requiring sophisticated electronics), the federal government has responded to the requests of the U.S. semiconductor industry. The SIA has taken advantage of the receptiveness to the U.S. semiconductor industry's concerns to date, though it is not clear that the federal government will continue to be so responsive.

Relationships with Other Groups

The SIA is one of several associations representing various aspects of the electronics industry in the United States. Among the more prominent of these groups are the Computer and Business Equipment Manufacturers Association, the Semiconductor Equipment and Materials International, and the Electronic Industries Association.[32] Perhaps the most important of these groups is the American Electronics Association (AEA), jointly headquartered in Washington, D.C., and San Jose, California (Silicon Valley), which is the major trade association for U.S. electronics manufacturers.

The SIA is, in part, a spin-off of the AEA, although nearly all SIA members belong to AEA as well. The SIA formed partly because U.S. semiconductor companies that were members of the AEA's predecessor (Western Electronics Manufacturing Association) found that organization insufficiently responsive to the specific needs of their industry. While they formed the SIA, however, they did not leave the AEA.

The relationship between the SIA and the AEA reflect the business and political connection between the U.S. semiconductor and computer industries. The business relationship between the two industries is the basis of the political one, and because of its crucial importance to the U.S. semiconductor industry, finding common ground with the AEA is critical to the SIA. Despite the efforts of the

AEA to work with the SIA in terms of representing the computer industry, a number of computer industry executives held a press conference on 14 May 1990 to announce the formation of the Computer Systems Policy Project (CSPP) and the group's policy position on international trade and technology.

Growing out of the AEA, the CSPP consists of the chief executive officers of a dozen major U.S. computer manufacturers. Like the SIA, CSPP companies remain members of the AEA. The charter members include the CEOs of some of the major firms in the U.S. computer industry: IBM, Hewlett-Packard, and Compaq among others.

CSPP members are doing now what SIA members did in 1977: pursuing public policies most important to their sector-specific industry. Designed to articulate the interests of U.S. computer manufacturers clearly and quickly, the CSPP began meeting in the fall of 1989 to construct policy positions. Since then, the SIA has discussed issues with the CSPP. In an effort to make its economic problems and policy positions clear to the CSPP, the SIA attempts to show computer company executives the logic of its positions in trade and technology.

At this time, it appears that the same issues that have separated the AEA and the SIA may plague the relationship between the semiconductor trade association and the CSPP. For example, CSPP member companies would like U.S. antidumping laws to be relaxed with regard to certain aspects. One of the remedies to dumping is the application of duties on imported products to compensate for the below-fair-value price, making domestic products more competitive. CSPP companies claim that the result of this is to raise import prices, something computer companies want to avoid. The CSPP has suggested that these duties not be applied in cases where domestic manufacturers cannot meet the current demand. This suggestion has not met with enthusiastic approval by the SIA.

Although the CSPP and the SIA are likely to come into conflict over specific policy proposals, there is still room for agreement and cooperation. The key will be the acceptance by the computer companies of the argument that their success depends in part on a healthy U.S. semiconductor industry.[33]

SUMMARY

The SIA is a new, remarkably influential business group. It represents a leading-edge high-technology industry that is central to the whole American electronics industry, as well as to national security. As an interest group, the SIA has capitalized on an unusual history, structure, location, and decision-making style to create a unique political strategy that has worked well. It is unburdened by a bureaucratic, self-interested staff; its goals are sharply focused; and it is relatively new.

In another sense, however, the SIA grows out of a long tradition in business-government relations in the United States. Business wants to be left alone, for the most part, until it needs help from the government. This has been the pattern in one industry after another in the United States, and so it is with the SIA. As the U.S. semiconductor industry began to feel the pinch of foreign competition, it organized itself into a trade association for the purpose of seeking help from the government. Moreover, its formation is consistent with the main theories of interest group formation in the American political system.

The SIA will undoubtedly have to adapt to new economic and political developments. Only seventeen years old, it has not had to transform itself in its short history. Its adaptiveness will be key to its success.

NOTES

1. Pat Choate, *Agents of Influence: How Japan's Lobbyists in the U.S. Manipulate America's Political and Economic Systems* (New York: Knopf, 1990), 207, Apps. A, B.

2. Michael G. Borrus, *Competing for Control: America's Stake in Microelectronics* (Cambridge, MA: Ballinger Publishing, 1988), 185–189.

3. Laura D'Andrea Tyson, *Who's Bashing Whom? Trade Conflict in High-Technology Industries* (Washington, DC: Institute for International Economics, 1992), 106–124.

4. Clyde V. Prestowitz, Jr., *Trading Places: How We Allowed Japan to Take the Lead* (New York: Basic Books, 1988), 63.

5. White House Announcement on Semiconductor Sanctions, 27 March 1987.

6. "Clinton Presses Japan on Trade," *San Jose Mercury News*, 7 July 1993, 8A.

7. Semiconductor industry's historical information on the following pages is based primarily on Thomas Howell, William A. Noelert, Janet H. MacLaughlin, Alan W. Wolff, *The Microelectronics Race: The Impact of Government Policy on International Competition* (Boulder, CO: Westview Press, 1988).

8. Concerning the growth of the U.S. market, see Semiconductor Industry Association (SIA), *SIA Yearbook and Directory, 1986* (San Jose, CA: Semiconductor Industry Association, 1986), 27; and Semiconductor Industry Association (SIA), *Semiconductor Statistical Review* (San Jose, CA: Semiconductor Industry Association, May 1986).

9. Concerning the declining costs and prices, see Howell et al., 72.

10. Ibid., 73.

11. Ibid., 108, 196.

12. Prestowitz, *Trading Places*, 33.

13. Howell et al., 8, 35–42; Tyson, *Who's Bashing Whom?* 93–100.

14. Prestowitz, *Trading Places*, 38.

15. Based on author's correspondence with William Finan, President, Technecon Analytic Research, Washington, DC: 15 October 1993.

16. Howell et al., 56.

17. "Components Division Newsletter," *Dataquest*, January 1989.

18. Concerning market share, see Howell, 18.

19. "Japan Admits Foreign Companies' Shares of Chip Market Stagnated in 4th Quarter," *Wall Street Journal*, 31 March 1992, B6.

20. "Japan's Imports Hit Chip Target: Foreigners Capture 20.2% Share of the Market, Fulfilling a Key Goal of Trade Agreement," *San Jose Mercury News*, 20 March 1993, 1A.

21. "Top Semiconductor Execs Form Trade Association," *San Jose Mercury*, 5 April 1977, 71.

22. In March 1990, thirty-three firms belonged to the SIA. See Andrew Procassini, "An Overview of the U.S. Semiconductor Industry" (report presented at the SIA Symposium on Trade and Competitiveness, Woodrow Wilson School, Princeton University, 2 March 1990), 4.

23. Semiconductor Industry Association, *Semiconductor Industry Association Yearbook and Directors, 1991–1992*, San Jose, 1991, 10–11.

24. Contrary to popular belief, the U.S. semiconductor industry is not entirely located in northern California's "Silicon Valley." Some firms have facilities located in other states such as Texas, New York, Florida, Massachusetts, Idaho, Arizona, Oregon, and New Mexico.

25. Wolff served on the staff of the U.S. Trade Representative during the Jimmy Carter administration and is acknowledged to be one of the foremost experts on trade issues, law, and politics in Washington.

26. U.S. Memories was created in 1989 to be a profit-making semiconductor manufacturer in the industry's effort to recapture the DRAM (Dynamic Random Access Memory) business from Japanese companies. A CEO was hired—Sandy Kane of IBM—and the organization was intended to be an independent company (in particular, operating without interference from the SIA). Early in 1990, U.S. Memories collapsed (before it got started), apparently because of lack of support from key executives and companies in the U.S. computer industry.

27. Semiconductor Industry Association, *SIA Directory and Yearbook, 1992–1993*, San Jose, 1992.

28. Carolyn Sherwood-Call, "Changing Geographical Patterns of Electronic Components Activity," *Federal Reserve Bank of San Francisco Economic Review*, no. 2 (1992): 25–35.

29. Carol Matlack, "Shoestring Success," *National Journal* 21 (20 May 1989): 1239–1241; Christopher H. Schmitt, "Chip Clout," *San Jose Mercury News*, 20 April 1987, D1; David B. Yoffie, "How an Industry Builds Political Advantage: Silicon Valley Goes to Capital Hill," *Harvard Business Review* 66 (May-June 1988): 82–89; SIA, *SIA Yearbook and Directory, 1991–1992*.

30. See, for example, U.S. Congress, Office of Technology Assessment, *International Competition in Services*, OTA-ITE-328 (Washington, DC: U.S. Government Printing Office, 1987); Office of Technology Assessment, *International Competitiveness in Electronics*, OTA-ISC-200 (Washington, DC: U.S. Government Printing Office, 1983); and U.S. Department of Commerce, International Trade Administration, *The Competitive Status of the U.S. Electronics Sector from Material to Systems* (Washington, DC: U.S. Government Printing Office, 1990).

31. For a useful summary of U.S. trade laws, see David B. Yoffie, "American Trade Policy: An Obsolete Bargain?" in John E. Chubb and Paul E. Peterson, eds., *Can the Government Govern?* (Washington, DC: Brookings Institution, 1989), 100–138.

32. Note members of the Electronics Roundtable listed in Chapter 5 of this book.

33. Evelyn Richards and John Burgess, "Computer Makers Propose New Trade Policies," *Washington Post*, 15 May 1990, D2.

Chapter 10

The Computer Systems Industry and Its Associations

THE FIRST LADY'S ESCORT

Every year in January, the president of the United States gives his State of the Union address to the joint Houses of Congress. It is an occasion of great interest because of the broad scope of national policy that is presented by the president. Thus, in 1993 President Clinton addressed the gathered legislators for the first time as tens of millions of viewers watched the nationally televised event.

In addition to the Congress, members of the Supreme Court, cabinet members, members of the Joint Chiefs of Staff, important invited guests, and members of the president's family were also present, including Hillary Rodham Clinton, who was seated front row center in the balcony. To the surprise of many, the first lady's escort, seated to her left, was John Scully, chief executive officer and chair of the board of Apple Computer Company of Cupertino, located in Silicon Valley, California. However, the presence of John Scully was not totally surprising to those who knew the relationship of Scully to the Clinton campaign.

Scully, along with John Young, then CEO of Hewlett-Packard (one of the largest electronics and computer systems companies in America), were public supporters of candidate Clinton. The rationale during the campaign appeared to be that Silicon Valley would go as Scully and Young had gone, and that California as a state would follow Silicon Valley into the Clinton column come election day. Candidate Clinton did win, and in the minds of many in the high-technology industries of America, he would be a sympathetic listener who understood their concerns.

The story of the Clinton–Silicon Valley relationship began many months before the State of the Union address, but one event signified it better than any other. On a visit to the San Francisco Bay Area in the fall of the campaign, Clinton dined, in Los Gatos, California, with a small group of Silicon Valley's high-tech executives. Part of the discussion centered on the needs and concerns of the companies present, and it was evident that Clinton and his party listened to each other carefully. Closer relationships were then developed than had existed between high-tech executives and George Bush and his appointed officials. From these Los Gatos discussions came an explicit technology policy, the assignment of the vice president to oversee the policy, and a mutual feeling that ideas were being exchanged freely. A new era began, although more in terms of attitudes embracing a new government-industry cooperation than in terms of promised substantive changes.

Those in high-tech manufacturing now had sympathetic friends in Washington and a particular friend in the White House, the president of the United States. One indication—a very visible one—of the degree of presidential friendliness to high-tech industries was the selection of John Scully, who personified high technology and Silicon Valley, to escort the second most powerful person in Washington, Hillary Rodham Clinton, to the premier event of a brand new "presidency"—the State of the Union Address.

THE COMPUTER SYSTEMS INDUSTRY

Although industry writers are tempted to start with the abacus in writing a history of computers, the true age of electronic computing devices dawned in Europe in the 1930s and early 1940s, and the actual beginning of a computer industry began in America during World War II. The first truly electronic computer was built at the University of Pennsylvania by J. P. Eckert and J. W. Mauchly, between 1943 and 1946, for the U.S. Army. It was called ENIAC (Electronic Numerical Integrator And Computer) and consisted of 18,000 vacuum tubes, measured 8 feet by 100 feet in size, weighed 80 tons, and could perform 5,000 additions and 360 multiplications per second. It had no high-speed memory, nor did it have stored program capacity.[1] It was not until Jay Forrester and Ken Olsen (the future founder of Digital Equipment Corporation) invented the MIT-Whirlwind computer and utilized ferrite cores for memory that the technology advanced. In the meantime, Eckert and Mauchly founded UNIAC, a private firm, to exploit the technology and build machines for government agencies. By 1954, several machines went to the government, but because of the company's financial difficulties it was sold to Remington-Rand. By this time, IBM had also entered the market and the American computer industry began to develop.

Between 1950 and 1970 a number of new American computer manufacturing organizations were established in addition to Remington-Rand and IBM. Among them were Wang Laboratories (1951), Control Data (1957), and Digital Equipment Corporation (1957). Older business machine firms established computer manufacturing divisions as well—Honeywell, Burroughs, General Electric, RCA, and Philco, among others. Overseas, Nixdorf and Siemens in Germany, Bull in France, Olivetti in Italy, and the keiretsu firms of Fujitsu, Nippon Electric Corporation, and Hitachi in Japan began production.

The computer systems of the 1960s and their successful commercialization depended to a large degree on the new microelectronics of the transistor and, later, the integrated circuit. The story of microelectronics has already been told; however, with respect to computer technology, microelectronics became the basis of computers that span the range from scientific calculators weighing a few ounces to supercomputers weighing tons. By 1970, the world revenues of U.S. computer makers had approached $11 billion, and with the addition of sales of all business equipment, including software, services, and forms, the total computer and business equipment sales exceeded $20 billion. The early 1970s, however, spawned more innovation when several new microelectronic devices were introduced, namely, four-bit and eight-bit microprocessors and dynamic random access memories (DRAMs). Other computer-related devices, such as floppy disks and Winchester disc drives, were also introduced. By 1975, the first personal computer, Altair, was introduced by a very small firm named MITS. Also in 1975, Bill Gates and Paul Allen founded the Microsoft Company and developed the BASIC computer language for the Altair personal computer (PC). The 1970s began a veritable revolution in the electronics of computers and through the combination of a number of these events, the personal computer had arrived on the scene.

By 1979, new product introductions in the computer field had included Cray's supercomputer (1975); the Altair personal computer (1975); Microsoft's BASIC language (1975); Tandem's fault-tolerant computers (1976); super minicomputers by SEL (1976); the Apple MacIntosh computer (1977); DEC's 32-bit super minicomputer (1977); Texas Instruments' Speak and Spell, (1978); the first spreadsheet software, Visicalc (1979); and the popular word-processing package, Wordstar (1979). The developments came quickly, and both the technology and the economics of the computer industry continued to change rapidly.

In 1975, before many of the technologies for personal computers had been applied, worldwide, the top fifteen major companies manufacturing data-processing equipment were still those manufacturing medium- and large-scale computers. However, by 1989, the list had changed greatly, with almost half the firms not on the 1975 list. The changes in rankings for 1975, 1989, and 1992, are shown in Table 10.1.

In 1975, the computer industry revenues, consisting of sales of hardware, software, and services, amounted to $30 billion. The major hardware products were still medium- and large-scale systems. Of the top fifteen world companies in 1975, ten were American, four were European, and one was Japanese. By 1989, American firms were down to seven, five were Japanese and three were European firms.

During that period, 1975 to 1989, the character of the computer system market changed significantly. Personal computers in 1984 now comprised 26 percent of the world market, with the leaders in the market being IBM, at 36 percent share of the personal computer (PC) market; Apple (14 percent); Commodore (7 percent); Tandy (5 percent); and Hewlett Packard (4 percent), the top five in the PC field. By 1989, 39 percent of the world market would be in PCs, and two compa-

Table 10.1
Ranking of World Computer System Manufacturers, 1975, 1989,
and 1992

	1975	1989	1992
1.	IBM	IBM	IBM
2.	Borroughs	DEC	Fujitsu
3.	Honeywell	Fujitsu	NEC
4.	Sperry	NEC	DEC
5.	Control Data	Unisys	Hewlett-Packard
6.	NCR	Hitachi	Hitachi
7.	Groupe Bull	Hewlett-Packard	AT&T
8.	DEC	Groupe Bull	Siemens/NIXDORF
9.	ICL (U.K.)	Apple	Unisys
10.	NIXDORF	NCR	Toshiba
11.	NEC	Olivetti	Apple
12.	Memorex	Siemens	Olivetti
13.	Hewlett-Packard	Toshiba	Groupe Bull
14.	TRW	Compaq	Matsushita
15.	Olivetti	Matsushita	Compaq

Sources: McKinsey and Company, Inc., *The 1990 Report on the Computer Industry* (New York:
         McKinsey and Co., 1990); *Datamation* (New York: Cahners Publishing Co., 15 June 1993).

nies based solely on the personal computer equipment and related products were
now in the top fifteen worldwide firms.

Also in 1985, the North America market provided 55 percent of the world's
demand, while the region's producers provided 75 percent of the world's supply.
The United States was the world's largest market and the world's largest supplier.
However, by the end of the decade, in 1989, North America (primarily the United
States) was at 39 percent of the world demand and at 62 percent of the world's
supply. The United States was losing share in both areas. At the same time the
Asia-Pacific region had doubled its share of supply, from 12 percent to 22 percent. The phenomenon of falling market share, which was also evident in micro-
electronics, was now present in the computer systems industry.[2]

By 1991, the U.S. share of world production appeared to stabilize at about 60
percent, while Japan was now a significant world producer (29.8 percent) and

consumer (30.9 percent) of computer systems. Europe was a large regional consumer, but European companies supplied only 9.9 percent of the world's demand. The absolute data and percentages are shown in Table 10.2.

Table 10.2
Data-Processing Equipment Industry

		Sales ($ Billions) Share of World Market (%) (1991)			
		Major Consuming Market			
		United States	Japan	Europe	Total
Production Firms by Primary Country of Capitalization	United States	72 (37.7)	11 (5.8)	32 (16.7)	115 (60.2)
	Japan	4 (2.1)	48 (25.1)	5 (2.6)	57 (29.8)
	Europe	2 (1.0)	0 (0.0)	17 (8.9)	19 (9.9)
	Total	78 (40.8)	59 (30.9)	54 (28.2)	191 (100)

Source: Electronics International Corporation, *Electronics in the World Markets, Manufacturing, Trade* (New York, 1992).

Note: Horizontal and vertical sums may not add due to roundship; 135 yen=$1;0.81 ECU=$1.

Despite the seeming preeminence of the United States in the computer systems industry there is one troubling aspect of this industry. The American computer systems industry—mainframe, personal computer, portables, and so forth—continues to purchase a great deal of its components and subsystems from foreign sources. Although foreign suppliers may be less costly, another possible reason is that the United States has been falling behind technologically. If the critical technologies list of the CSPP were used as the basis, the following table (Table 10.3) would indicate the U.S. position vis-à-vis foreign sources from the listed technologies.[3]

The indication here, which is applicable to every high-tech industry discussed in this book, is that many, if not most, critical component materials and parts are purchased from foreign sources. This is true in microelectronics and aircraft as well as in computer systems. In addition, an appropriate study of high-technology industries would include not only foreign technology dependency but also an assessment of the sources of value-added rather than the source of supply alone.

The information technologies industry, of which the computer systems industry is the most significant component, continues to grow, and data based on the top 100 world firms indicates that information technologies will have achieved a sales

Table 10.3
Competitive Position of the U.S. Computer Systems Industry with Regard to Critical Technologies

Critical Technologies	U.S. Status in 1990 (Ahead, Diminishing Lead, Behind, or Losing)
1. Database Systems	Ahead
2. Processor Architecture	Ahead
3. Networks & Communications	Diminishing Lead
4. Human Interface	Ahead
5. Visualization	Ahead
6. Operating Systems	Ahead
7. Software Engineering	Ahead
8. Application Technology	Ahead
9. Display	Behind
10. Hard Copy Technology	Behind
11. Storage	Diminishing Lead
12. Manufacturing Technology	Behind
13. IC Fabrication Equipment	Behind
14. Microelectronics	Diminishing Lead
15. Optoelectronics	Diminishing Lead
16. Electronic Packaging	Behind

Source: Computer Systems Policy Project, *Perspectives: Success Factors in Critical Technologies* (Washington, DC: Computer Systems Policy Project, July 1990).

level of $318 billion in 1992, with a revenue growth of 10 percent. The average growth rate for these largest firms has been over 10 percent per year for the 1987-to-1992 period as well (Table 10.4). Based on an estimate that the top 100 firms constitute 85 percent of all firms, the total market for computer systems and their related products of hardware, application software, operating software, services, and field maintenance was approximately $375 billion worldwide in 1992.

Finally, one researcher has provided an indication of how associations are related to the industry. In 1988, the number of organizations and agencies related to the computer industry were as shown in Table 10.5. The same source listed 389 computer industry–related associations, U.S. government agencies, groups, consortia, and major worldwide standards organizations for 1992.[4] The breadth of industry interest groups is phenomenal. The number of key U.S. computer-related trade associations, however, is probably limited to no more than twenty, including most of the members of the Electronics Roundtable. The most prominent groups representing the computer industry are the AEA, CBEMA, and CSPP. Their description concludes this chapter.

Table 10.4

Information Technologies, Top 100 World Firms, Revenue and Growth, 1987–1992

Revenues, $ Billions Revenue Growth, %						
Year	1987	1988	1989	1990	1991	1992
Top 100 World Firms ($B)	209	243	256	279	290	318
Revenue Growth %	18	16	5	8	4	10

Source: Datamation (New York: Cahners Publishing Co., 15 June 1993).

Table 10.5

Computer System Industry–Related Organizations, 1988

Types of Organizations/Agencies	Number of Organizations
Professional and Trade Associations	61
Standards Organizations (Worldwide)	15
Government Agencies	13
Users Groups	42

Note: All Organizations are U.S. except standards.

Source: Egil Juliussen and Karen Juliussen, *The Computer Industry Almanac, 1989* (New York: Simon and Schuster), 13.1–13.54.

THE TRADE ASSOCIATIONS: CBEMA, AEA, AND CSPP

CBEMA—The Oldest Association

Origins and History

Founded in 1916, the Computer and Business Equipment Manufacturers Association is the oldest of the three groups considered here. The companies that met to form the new association—the National Association of Office Appliance Manufacturers (NAOAM)—produced various types of office equipment designed to "enhance the performance of office workers."[5] The association was comprised of fifteen firms, and it focused on improving sales and the sales force. Thus, the association studied ways to improve the productivity of the members' salespeople.

This early predecessor of CBEMA became involved with government activity in 1918 in connection with restrictions placed on the use of raw materials resulting from World War I. In 1923, NAOAM began working with the federal government in the development of "the prototype for the Standard Industrial Classification Codes (SICs) covering the industry."[6]

In 1929, the association changed its name to the Office Equipment Manufacturers Institute (OEMI) and took another step in its involvement in public policy by forming a committee on state tax matters. In spite of these initial forays into public policy, the association remained focused on sales issues throughout the 1920s and 1930s. Eighteen years after its creation, the association established its headquarters in New York City, signaling a commitment to a permanent association by its members.[7]

During World War II, OEMI took measures to deal with the wartime economic situation and began to prepare for the postwar era. The central issues involved the ways in which member firms would convert their production to meet the demands and challenges of a civilian, postwar economy.[8] Following World War II, OEMI admitted thirteen new members from the former Steel Office Furniture Institute. Suddenly larger and covering more than one industry, the association became more involved in its interaction with the executive branch and Congress. In keeping with this new policy orientation, the association chose, in 1946, to move its headquarters from New York to Washington, D.C.[9]

In the 1950s and 1960s, OEMI acknowledged the inevitable advent of "automation," emphasizing the benefits of new, labor-saving devices for the individual, the firm, and the economy as a whole. The association organized itself into three groups: data processing, office furniture and equipment, and office machines. The distinctions characterized the different interests of member firms. At the same time, OEMI maintained its historical interest in sales—mainly through the establishment of trade shows—and formed issue-based councils to deal with standards.[10] The association's voluntary efforts to establish industrial standards became more formalized in 1960 when "it became the secretariat for the newly formed American National Standards Institute committees on computers (X3) and office equipment (X4)."[11] Responding to changes in the industry it represented, the association changed it name to the Business Equipment Manufacturers Association (BEMA) in 1960. In sum, by its fiftieth anniversary in 1966, the association had developed into an organization providing considerable services to its members, such as public relations, councils that dealt with industry issues, and its major trade show, the Business Equipment Exposition.[12]

By the 1970s, the computer had become a mainstay in the American economy. Recognizing the importance of computers and information technology in the workplace, BEMA became the Computer and Business Equipment Manufacturers Association (CBEMA) in 1973. With the name change, CBEMA membership became more homogeneous: furniture manufacturers left to form their own association and other firms restructured or merged, concentrating their business on computers and information technology.[13]

The current association is a clear product of the changes instituted in the 1970s. Its focus is primarily on computers and information technology. Since these industries have become a part of virtually every organization, and since CBEMA's members have become increasingly involved in these technologies, CBEMA has responded by making them the focus of its work.[14]

Membership

The Computer and Business Equipment Manufacturers Association consists of twenty-eight large corporations in the computer and information technology industries (Table 10.6). Until recently, membership was equally open to U.S. and foreign firms. In May 1990, however, members voted to limit the number of foreign companies in the association to 30 percent of the entire membership. The reason for doing so was to concentrate the association's efforts on the problems of U.S. firms, particularly in regard to international trade issues.[15]

Table 10.6
CBEMA Members, 1992

3M
Amdahl Corporation
AMP Incorporated
Apple Computer, Inc.
AT&T
Bell & Howell
Bull HN Information Systems, Inc.
Compaq Computer Corporation
Dictaphone Corporation
Eastman Kodak Company
Fujitsu America, Inc.
Hewlett-Packard Company
Hitachi Computer Products (America), Inc.
Honeywell Keyboard Division
IBM Corporation
ICL, Inc.
Information Handling Services
Lexmark International, Inc.
Multigraphics, A Division of AM International, Inc.
NCR Corporation
Panasonic Communications & System Company
Smith Corona Corporation
Tandem Computers Incorporated
Tektronix, Inc.
Texas Instruments Incorporated
Xerox Corporation

Source: Computer and Business Equipment Manufacturers Association, *Annual Report 1992* (Washington, DC: 1992), p. 1.

All CBEMA members are large firms with business in the computer and information technology industries. The current membership list bears little resemblance to the association's charter members. Members deal in leading-edge information technologies, are mostly U.S. firms, and produce a considerable variety of products.

Structure and Decision Making

The Computer and Business Equipment Manufacturers Association's organization is typical of American trade associations. Consisting of company executives (usually below the CEO level), the board of directors makes CBEMA's major decisions and sets its general goals. The board maintains an executive committee in addition to committees assigned responsibilities corresponding to the issues with which CBEMA deals (Table 10.7). CBEMA efforts are supported by a staff based in Washington, D.C., and organized to correspond to board functions.

Political Strategy

CBEMA relies on direct lobbying of Congress and the executive branch to achieve its policy objectives. The association does not have a political action committee, nor does it use traditional grassroots tactics. CBEMA has approximately eight to ten lobbyists on its staff, who account for much of the association's lobbying effort. In addition to these staff members, the Washington representatives of CBEMA members, which are large corporations with the necessary resources to maintain Washington offices, work closely with CBEMA in determining how to deliver the industry's message to government officials. Thus, CBEMA coordinates the political activities of the industry, and in doing so, leverages its political influence.[16]

Along with working on policy concerns alone, CBEMA has led efforts to form ad hoc coalitions of trade associations to take a position on a piece of legislation. For example, CBEMA has organized coalitions on such issues as the recent legislation on the role of National Institute of Standards and Technology and the definition of a U.S. company.[17] This activity represents another aspect of CBEMA's coordinating role in terms of presenting industry positions to government officials.[18]

In sum, while CBEMA is a small association as measured by the number of its members, it can achieve a considerable political impact. Because its members have the resources to maintain their own Washington presence, they are available to CBEMA when the association needs to address important policy issues. The association has also developed a working relationship with other associations, adding to its political clout.

Central Mission and Policy Goals

CBEMA has refocused its central mission in recent years. Recognizing changes in U.S. industry, the association now places computer and information technology at the center of its main purpose. From CBEMA's perspective, computers and information technology are integrally connected; it is difficult to think about computers apart from the broader context of information technology. Thus, CBEMA's central mission connects the two industries in terms of public policy objectives. Nevertheless, it is still possible to separate them with respect to specific legislation (e.g., export controls on computers).[19]

With increasing pressure on U.S. firms from foreign competition, CBEMA limited foreign membership to 30 percent and rewrote its mission statement to account for the new economic reality facing U.S. industry. The new mission statement reads as follows: "The Computer and Business Equipment Manufacturers Association represents the interests of leading companies providing computer, business equipment and telecommunications hardware, software and services, so as to strengthen the industry in the United States with emphasis on improving the global competitiveness of U.S.-owned industry."[20] The invigorated international focus suggests member firms' recognition of the importance of global competitiveness of U.S. firms; companies that cannot compete internationally are not sustainable.

The association's policy goals reflect the international aspects of the computer and information technology industries, but still incorporate some of CBEMA's long-term objectives and concerns (Table 10.8).

CBEMA's policy objectives cover a range of issues relevant to association members. The concern for standards, intellectual property rights, antitrust, and tax policies has been a mainstay for the association for years. What is most striking about the goals articulated in 1992 and 1993 is the addition of international trade in itself and the inclusion of global concerns into other issues (e.g., intellectual property protection). Missing from CBEMA's array of policy objectives is an outline of technology development directions. CBEMA focuses on standards with respect to technology development and has been involved with this issue for years, but the association does not attempt to indicate where the industries it represents ought to be technologically in the future.

A central theme of caution about government activity runs throughout many of CBEMA's policy objectives. In many instances, the association wants to limit government activity as much as possible, relying instead on voluntary industry action to address problems. This has been the case certainly with respect to standards; CBEMA has historically been a lead player in setting industry standards. It is also true for energy efficiency and environmental regulation. The association does call for limited government actions; for example, CBEMA argues for the need for government involvement in intellectual property protection and international trade issues. It seeks to avoid government intervention that may damage the industry in some way—for example, a government-imposed encryption standard.

Table 10.7
CBEMA Board Committees

Executive Committee
    Nominating Committee
    Performance & Compensation Review Committee

Program & Budget Committee

Plans & Programs Committee

Public Policy Committee

Government Relations Committee
    Government Procurement
    International Property Rights
    Taxation
    Telecommunications

Technology Policy Management Committee
    Standards Program Management
    Environment and Safety Management
    Ergonomics
    CBEMA/UL Policy
    CBEMA/CSA/ITAC/UL Policy Committee
    CBEMA/ITAC Joint Standards Committee
    North American Open Systems Testing and Certification Policy Council
    Standards Secretariats

Education Councils
    Chief Tax Executives
    Export Controls
    Human Resources
    Service Management

Industry Support
    Industry Statistics Program
    Communications

Sources: Computer and Business Equipment Manufacturers Association, *Annual Report 1992*, p. 5;
    Computer and Business Equipment Manufacturers Association, "Overview," 1992: 1–4.

In sum, CBEMA presents nothing unusual in its organizational structure and decision-making procedures. Since it is a small organization, no elaborate mechanisms are needed to insure member input into decisions.

Table 10.8
CBEMA's Major Policy Objectives, 1992

Intellectual Property Rights in the United States and Internationally

Prevent diminishment of current levels of copyright protection for computer programs as provided within U.S. law and the Berne Convention.

Prevent diminishment of current levels of U.S. patent law; including patent protection for computer-related inventions.

Secure adequate and effective enforcement of protection for copyrighted works in emerging laws, treaties and enforcement measures, including the GATT and the North American Free Trade Agreement (NAFTA).

Prevent diminishment of current levels of international patent law including patent protection for computer-related inventions and, to the maximum extent possible, abolish compulsory licensing provisions that extend beyond those permitted by the World Intellectual Property Organization (WIPO) Paris Convention.

Tax Policy

Enact a permanent extension of the current R&D Tax Credit.

Enact series of international provisions that are revenue neutral but ease our global operations.

Standardization

Achieve worldwide subcontracting and mutual recognition of conformance testing.
Strengthen current U.S. voluntary standards system.

International Trade

Shape Uruguay Round Trade Agreement.

Shape North American Free Trade Agreement.

Enact customs reform legislation to improve performance of the U.S. Customs Service.

Achieve export control legislation mandating a license-free Coordinating Committee (COCOM) zone; supercomputer indexing for export control purposes; export controls on wide area networking equipment consistent with controls on related computer equipment; a prohibition on the imposition of unilateral conditions on high technology exports; multilateral, rather than unilateral, sanctions designed to prevent the proliferation of advanced warfare technology; and a judicial procedure for appealing a commodity classification.

Enact GATT implementing legislation to include adoption of an acceptable Code of Good Practice on Standards.

Enact NAFTA implementing legislation that will ensure full, comprehensive industry participation in both the development and representation of U.S. positions taken within the scope of the NAFTA standards text.

Energy

Initiate voluntary industry program with Department of Energy; establish advisory council; avoid mandatory regulations.

Table 10.8
CBEMA's Major Policy Objectives, 1992 (Continued)

Antitrust

Achieve enactment of acceptable joint manufacturing legislation.

Prevent the passage of any legislation at the federal or state level, including resale price maintenance legislation, which would hinder current legitimate business relationships with legitimate dealers. Defeat any judicial action that would similarly limit current options for doing business with dealers.

Export Control Reform

Introduce export control reform legislation that

- prohibits imposition of unilateral controls and conditions,
- transfers control of mass market software to the U.S department of commerce,
- contains method to ensure that controls key pace with rapidly advancing technology, particularly "super-computers."

Encryption and Wiretapping

Advocate adoption of policies and technologies for encryption that support our customers needs globally, do not reduce U.S. competitiveness, and meet law enforcement needs.

Definition of a "U.S. Company"

Prevent enactment of House-passed provision excluding U.S. multinationals from participating in certain technology programs.

Government Procurement

Shape commercial product acquisition legislation.

Maintain Multiple Award Schedule Program.

Video Display Terminal (VDT) Safety

Oppose unnecessary VDT restriction; support RSI safety.

Environment

By getting out front with voluntary efforts, prevent government energy labeling requirements.

Telecommunications

Maintain competitive telecommunications systems.

National Information Structure

Form CBEMA task force; develop position and prioritization of issues to be addressed.

Antidumping Law Reform

Enact legislation appropriately addressing cost of production methodology, short supply, and anticircumvention.

Table 10.8
CBEMA's Major Policy Objectives, 1992 (Continued)

Standards

Achieve acceptance of DoC/ANSI Memo of understanding to ensure continuation of the private sector operated U.S. voluntary standards process and that the United States speaks with one voice in the international voluntary standards arena.

Gain support of new administration and Congress for the importance of a sound, private sector voluntary standards system and take a strong stand that all private sector groups should

- work together within the system, or
- change it to one within which all can work.

Standards Secretariat

Support improvement of the organizational structure of, and participation within, the JTCI TAG in order to fulfill the new agreement (MOA) between ANSI and information technology (IT) standards developers that puts the focus of efforts to develop a strong U.S. IT consensus in the JTCI TAG.

Maintain high performance levels in administering the X3 program and facilitate the process of harmonized standards within the U.S. information technology community.

Augment and maintain the membership services offered to the X3 and JTCI TAG membership, especially in the areas of leadership training and online information dissemination.

Strengthen and foster existing and newly formed cooperative initiatives with other standards development organizations at the technical and management levels.

Sources: Computer and Business Equipment Manufacturers Association, *Annual Report 1992* (1992): pp. 8–38; CBEMA, "1993 CBEMA Public Policy Priority Issues" (1993); CBEMA, "TPMC Priority Issues 1993" (1993).

Effectiveness

CBEMA's accomplishments parallel its current objectives. The association stressed successful changes in government procurement policy and intellectual property protection. It has succeeded in its support of legislation permitting joint manufacturing, and the association has had long-term influence over the setting of industry standards.[21] Telecommunications, energy, international trade, and taxes were less prominent, with standards occupying a middle position.[22]

American Electronics Association: The Broadest Association

The AEA is by far the largest of the three organizations considered in this chapter. Founded in the 1940s, membership has grown to more than 3,000 electronics firms scattered throughout the United States. The association is organizationally complex, with headquarters shared by its Santa Clara, California, and Washington, D.C., offices with state and regional offices located around the country. Because of its size, complexity, and scope of interests, the AEA provides an interesting contrast to CBEMA and the CSPP, both of which are relatively small and narrowly focused. Because of this basic organizational difference, one would expect the AEA to be somewhat less nimble in terms of choosing policy objectives, on one hand, but potentially more powerful with respect to political influence. This potential trade-off is considered throughout the discussion of the AEA.

Origins and History

The American Electronics Association was formed by 25 electronics firms in 1943, in southern California, under the name West Coast Electronic Manufacturers Association (WCEMA). The original reason for forming the association was to reverse a U.S. War Production Board decision that "prohibited the awarding of contracts to the West Coast because of a perceived acute labor shortage."[23] Initially focused in the burgeoning electronics industry in southern California, the new association consisted of 50 companies by 1950. The association grew with the electronics industry. As more companies sprung up manufacturing various electronics products, the association changed to accommodate them. The speed with which the industry changed is legendary; the fledgling WCEMA kept up. By 1953, membership had reached 100 companies. The association was beginning to move out of California, welcoming the first members from outside the state. At the same time, the WCEMA made a foray into politics as the board of directors met with the California congressional delegation in Washington, D.C. New councils (the association's main organizational subunit) formed in San Diego and the Northwest, and in 1959, the association changed its name to the Western Electronic Manufacturers Association (WEMA).

During the 1960s, membership continued to grow, exceeding 450 firms by 1968. A new council was added in Santa Barbara, California, and the WEMA continued to become acquainted with national politics, holding its first congressional luncheon in Washington, D.C. By the 1970s, the association had become a national organization. Changing its name to the American Electronics Association in 1978, the association established its presence in national politics, lobbying successfully for a reduction in the capital gains tax. The Washington, D.C., office opened, signaling the AEA's intention of maintaining a permanent presence in national politics. By the end of the 1970s, AEA membership was more than 1,500 companies.

During the 1980s, the AEA continued its expansion from its original California base. With members located throughout the country and a permanent base in Washington, D.C., the AEA established an office in Tokyo in recognition of the significance of the Japanese electronics industry in the international market. In the area of public policy, the association worked with the executive branch and Congress to reduce export restrictions. It also began its High-Definition Systems Initiative, aimed at drawing attention to the eroding manufacturing infrastructure. This effort, however, was unsuccessful.

In the first years of the 1990s, the AEA reinforced its public policy program, establishing its strategic "Vision, Goals, and Objectives," which states the association policy positions and underlies its programs. Now an established major player in the business and politics of the U.S. electronics industry, the AEA represents a diverse range of electronics manufacturers on the leading edge of the industry.[24]

Membership

The AEA consists of over 3,000 firms engaged in some aspect of the electronics industry, "from silicon to software, to all levels of computers and communication networks, and systems integration."[25] Member companies range in size from large corporations to small start-ups, with nearly 70 percent of the membership comprised of "companies with fewer than 250 employees and under $50 million in annual sales."[26] Membership dues in 1990 were as low as $330 per year to as much as $50,000 per year, depending on volume of sales.[27] Since its members represent a wide range of industries within the electronics sector, the AEA must accommodate a potentially wide range of policy interests and objectives. Computer manufacturers make up one part—albeit a major one—of the association.

The characteristics of the AEA membership have several important implications and consequences for the extent to which the association addresses the needs, interests, and policy objectives of the U.S. computer industry. First, the association must find ways to deal with conflicts between computer firms and companies in other areas of the electronics industry when they arise. Representing all of these firms' interests requires a decision-making process that allows for the construction of compromise satisfactory to all participants. Second, the sheer number of firms in the association may slow its decision-making process. To the extent that members care about policy objectives and are able to influence them, the association must take time to process their input. Third, the fact that firms from various parts of the electronics industry are members of the same association makes creating coherent objectives and coordinating political activities across industries possible. Presenting a united front on public policy issues affecting the U.S. electronics industries can enhance the association's political effectiveness.

In sum, the characteristics of the AEA's membership present it with some advantages and disadvantages. On the positive side, the association is in the unique position in the U.S. to unify the policy objectives and coordinate the political activities of the U.S. electronics industries. On the negative side, the AEA must deal with a potentially cumbersome decision-making process and obstructive conflicts among members engaged in different parts of the electronics sector.

Structure and Decision Making

The American Electronics Association is a large, complicated organization. With headquarters split between Santa Clara, California, and Washington, D.C., and numerous subunits scattered throughout the country, the association is presented with a difficult administrative task in making decisions and getting member input. As is true for most trade associations, formal authority lies with the board of directors. Consisting of executives of member firms, the board is divided into numerous committees responsible for directing the association's activities in various areas and for developing specific policies (Table 10.9). The AEA's board represents association members through two different paths. Large firm representatives provide the link between the company and the association, while approximately 75 percent of board members are also active at the council level. They connect the local and regional activities of member firms to the national organization.[28]

The board, numbering over fifty directors, is large compared with those of other associations, reflecting the size and diversity of AEA's membership. The committee structure is complex, organized in two tiers. The first tier, consisting of steering and advisory committees, sets policy directions in the areas for which they are responsible, while second-tier committees—the operating committees—are more narrowly focused.[29] This elaborate committee system serves the association in two ways. First, it allows it to deal with a wide range of complex issues simultaneously. Second, through the policy development activities at the steering committee level and operating committee level, the association can build consensus among its members on issues. If consensus cannot be reached at one level, the issue is passed up to the next in hopes of finding agreement.[30]

The AEA maintains eighteen councils in major cities throughout the country. These councils perform three sets of functions for the association. First, they recruit new members and retain current members of the group. Second, they provide services to AEA members within their geographic regions—for example, regular information seminars on issues relevant to member companies. Third, they work with the national organization—for example, organizing grass-roots activities. In addition, the councils provide members a link to the national organization as members active in the councils serve on the national board of directors.[31]

In sum, the AEA is structurally complex, serving a wide range of firms and industries within the general category of electronics. Members can work with the association at different levels, not limited to national issues operating out of a Washington, D.C., base. In this sense, AEA is hardly comparable to CBEMA, which is a small association consisting of large firms, or to the CSPP, a small group of computer companies that claims not to be a trade association per se and has little formal organizational structure.

In addition to its structural complexity, the association is divided along functional lines as opposed to organizational subunits for the industries in which member firms are engaged. This functional orientation focuses the association on

Table 10.9
AEA Committee Structure, 1993

National Competitiveness Steering Committee
Operating Committees:
>   Government Business
>   Tax & Finance
>   Technology, Manufacturing & Infrastructure
>   Environment & Occupational Health
>   Workforce Excellence
>   Human Resources
>   Worker Training

International Competitiveness Steering Committee
Operating Committees:
>   Export Controls
>   Customs
>   Trade & Investment
>   Japan Advisory Committee
>   Industry Committee in Japan
>   Europe Committee

Total Quality Commitment Steering Committee

Member & Council Affairs Advisory Committee
Operating Committees:
>   State Public Affairs
>   Business Services
>   Council/Staff Training
>   Council Chairs
>   Industry Forums
>   Council Organization
>   Membership

Advisory Committee on Public Affairs
Operating Committees:
>   National Public Relations
>   Statistics

Source: American Electronics Association (AEA), *1993 Public Policy Agenda* (Washington, DC: AEA), 28.

policies relevant to the industry as a whole and brings together representatives of different parts of the industry. The potential benefit of this arrangement is that people in various industries have the opportunity to recognize their relationships with other parts of the industry, understand their problems, and find where they have common interests. In this sense, the association's structure can have an integrating effect on the entirety of the highly differentiated electronics industry. A potential cost of this arrangement from the perspective of members is that the immediate, direct needs of their industries cannot be met in full by the AEA. Thus, semiconductor firms, while finding common ground with firms in other parts of the electronics sector by virtue of membership in the AEA, found it necessary to form an association, the SIA, solely committed to their industry. This may also be the case for the computer industry in the formation of the CSPP. However, given that this group does not wish to be considered a formal, permanent trade association, such a conclusion is premature.

Political Strategy

The American Electronics Association takes advantage of its large size and geographic distribution in its efforts to shape public policy. The association produces several publications that keep members constantly apprised of policy developments, changes in government, and AEA positions. In addition to using traditional lobbying tactics out of its Washington, D.C, headquarters, the AEA routinely brings member company executives—particularly CEOs—to the nation's capital to meet with government officials, testify before congressional committees and executive branch agencies, and be briefed on current policy developments relevant to their industries.[32] Like most major Washington-based interest groups, the association keeps a close eye on Congress; for example, it planned to "educate" the 121 new members of the 103rd Congress about the importance and needs of the U.S. electronics industry.[33] The AEA also works with other trade associations and ad hoc groups to influence government officials on particular policies. For example, the AEA joined with the Coalition for Joint Manufacturing, consisting of other like-minded groups, to argue for extension of the National Cooperative Research Act to joint manufacturing ventures.[34]

In sum, the AEA is highly engaged in an effort to shape public policy in the interests of its members. It features a strong lobbying capacity in Washington, D.C., enhanced by routine and regular visits by member company CEOs to government officials. The AEA is certainly not unique in these tactics, but it has carved out a niche for itself in the political representation of U.S. electronics industries.

Central Mission

Like CBEMA, the American Electronics Association includes the information industry in its general statements about its basic purpose. With the importance of high-technology industries to the U.S. economy as the background, the AEA claims the electronics and information technology industries as its clientele, representing their interests in such major policy areas as competitiveness, jobs development, investment, and international trade. Combining electronics with information technology implies a recognition of the inseparability of the two in practical applications. To reiterate a central theme of this volume, with its broad mandate, the AEA attempts to meet the policy and business needs of a large, and getting larger, industry, which includes the computer industry.

The association maintains a sophisticated, active public policy component, operating at the national and state levels. Monitoring and attempting to influence public policy on behalf of its members constitute one part of AEA's central mission. It is also engaged in a considerable range of traditional trade association activities apart from public policy concerns—for example, providing information on employee benefits, business insurance, and support services. AEA councils regularly organize meetings and seminars for members on such issues as manufacturing, quality management, and marketing and sales. Thus, the AEA's central mission may be divided into two parts: public policy and business services.

Policy Goals

Because of the diversity of its membership, the AEA pursues an impressive array of policy goals at the national level. These goals are examined here in three parts: general objectives, examples of specific policy goals, and goals relevant to the new input brought to Washington by the Clinton administration.

The AEA identifies six public policy priorities important to its membership: "a competitive U.S. financial environment, global market access, government excellence in procurement, leadership in technology, manufacturing and infrastructure development, a world-class work force, and a world-class workplace."[35] From the association's perspective, appropriate polices in these issue areas will best meet the economic challenges now faced by the electronics and information technology industry. The AEA recommends actions within each category as part of its basic public policy agenda (Table 10.10).

These broad policy objectives address issues that concern a wide range of high-technology companies. Tax, education, technology, and international trade might be classified as generic issues for leading-edge industries. Government procurement is a constant concern for industries that get much of their income from the federal government. Aerospace firms and electronics firms share this concern, as the Department of Defense and the National Aeronautics and Space Administration have been long-term sources of product development and of major, lucrative contracts. Intellectual property protection is a constant problem for these industries where development and ownership of new products are essential to a company's viability. Overall, this list of policy objectives would serve nicely as the public policy manifesto of the high-technology industry in general.

Table 10.10
AEA's Major Policy Objectives

Competitive U.S. Financial Environment

- Pass a targeted capital gains differential, which will free up the seed and venture capital required by high-tech companies.
- Pass a permanent and improved R&D tax credit.
- Pass a broad-based investment tax credit to support the retooling and investment necessary for U.S. companies to strengthen their U.S. manufacturing base and compete internationally.
- Pass a permanent solution to Section 1.861-8 of the tax code, which discourages companies from locating R&D facilities in the U.S. and encourages them to move jobs offshore.
- Oppose efforts to curtail use of stock options.

Global Market Access

- Initiate major bilateral negotiations with Japan to obtain a fully open market for foreign electronics products.
- Implement a truly multilateral and effective export-control system.
- Complete the Uruguay Round of the GATT and the NAFTA negotiations, taking particular care to protect intellectual property.
- Develop strong export-promotion policies; implement a market cooperator program for industry.
- Participate directly in developing rules for the single European market to promote maximum participation of U.S. companies.
- Pass the Customs Modernization Act.

Government Procurement

- Make certain that military depots, laboratories, and federally funded R&D centers compete fairly with the private sector.
- Remove statutory and regulatory roadblocks to government procurement of commercially available items. Expand use of a new, shorter commercial contract.
- Reduce government's reliance on oversight, audits, and inspections for procurement and R&D.
- Increase the use of "best value" contracting techniques.
- Eliminate government-constructed barriers which hinder the ability of companies to diversify into other markets.

Table 10.10
AEA's Major Policy Objectives (Continued)

Technology, Manufacturing, and Infrastructure

- Refocus federal funds to R&D programs that support industry's efforts to develop and employ critical technology with significant economic potential.
- Create mechanisms for private-sector input in setting federal R&D priorities.
- Develop a federal manufacturing initiative to be implemented by FY 1994.
- Support commercially relevant, pre-competitive generic technology R&D.
- Make the transfer of federal R&D to the private sector a priority of all federal research agencies.
- Support and duplicate federal research initiatives, like the High Performance Computing and Communications Initiative.

Work Force and Workplace

- Raise basic skills through education reform.
- Strengthen school-to-work transition.
- Establish a system of industry-based, voluntary worker training standards.
- Promote incentive-based worker training strategies that take into account the budget constraints of small and medium-size firms.
- Enact technology and manufacturing policies that address workforce training issues.
- Reform national health care to ensure universal access while managing costs and stressing preventive treatment.
- Make environmental and occupational health laws based on good science and realistic risk assessment.
- Determine whether regulations will stifle product innovation or cause delays in production.
- Consider the Japanese and European models for "performance-based" regulations.

Source: American Electronics Association, *1993 Public Policy Agenda*, 9–23.

With these general concerns in mind, the AEA routinely takes positions on pending legislation that affects its members. The issues that concern the association may be roughly divided into international and domestic categories. With respect to international affairs, the AEA has taken clear positions on the Uruguay Round of the General Agreement on Tariffs and Trade (GATT) and on the North American Free Trade Agreement (NAFTA). With respect to the GATT, the AEA has identified six priorities: elimination of duties for semiconductors, computer parts, medical diagnostic equipment, and other telecommunication products; increased deterrence for repeat offenders of dumping regulations; recognition of the "harm of third-party dumping" and the need to "make countries' procedures more open and transparent"; government procurement provisions that "cover all electronics sectors"; harmonization of rules of origin through the Customs Cooperation Council; intellectual property protection provisions that protect software but do not require compulsory licensing; and forcing developing countries like Hong Kong, Singapore, Taiwan, and Korea "to fully adopt international trade rules."[36]

The AEA strongly supports NAFTA and regularly pursues this position in Washington. For example, on July 22, 1993, the "AEA participated in a White House 'High Tech Day for NAFTA' event."[37] Of the 100 top executives attending the event, 70 were AEA members. AEA executives then met with members of Congress to voice their support of NAFTA. These kinds of activities are part of the association's encouragement of AEA members to inform government officials of their desire to see NAFTA ratified.[38] The AEA has carried its case in support of NAFTA to court, joining other U.S. business associations in an amicus curiae brief on behalf of the U.S. government in its appeal of a federal district court ruling that NAFTA requires an environmental impact statement. Other groups joining the AEA in the brief include, for example, the National Association of Manufacturers, the U.S. Chamber of Commerce, and the Business Roundtable.[39]

In addition to successful conclusion of the Uruguay Round of the GATT and NAFTA, the American Electronics Association pursues a wide array of international issues important to its members. Export controls are a high priority among these issues, as AEA member firms seek to develop foreign markets for their products. In general, the AEA supports loosening of export controls so that U.S. electronics firms can increase exports.[40] The association maintains a continuing interest in U.S.-Japan relations with respect to international trade. Its Japan Advisory Group monitors trade flows and government action, offering the association's position to U.S. government officials.[41] In addition, AEA representatives routinely testify before executive branch agencies and Congress on issues connected to the trade relationship between the U.S. and Japan. For example, the AEA spoke out in favor of the "President's [Bush's] decision to obtain enforcement of the Market Oriented Sector Specific [MOSS] Agreements."[42] These examples, of course, do not exhaust the AEA's list of international concerns; they do, however, give a good sense of the association's main concerns, goals, and activities in this area.

The AEA also spends a great deal of energy attempting to influence the direction of public policy related to domestic issues. The association's domestic policy goals cover a wide range of issues, including technology development, taxation, antitrust, work force development, occupational health, and environmental regulations. Among the more prominent of the association's domestic policy goals was its effort to launch a government-funded high-definition system policy initiative. Viewing high-definition television (HDTV) as a critical element to the electronics industry's economic and technological future, the association made it a high priority in the late 1980s. Part of the AEA's proposal included $1.35 billion in federal money to help the industry develop the new HDTV technology, a funding level not greeted with sympathy by all members of Congress.[43] The AEA later made a second, but unsuccessful, attempt to initiate a federal program for HDTV, this time without the original proposal's large price tag. The association's High-Definition Systems task force proposed several recommendations to the

AEA in 1990 that set no funding levels, instead calling for the technology to be given high priority.[44]

Other issues that have occupied the AEA's domestic policy concerns include government procurement, joint manufacturing, restrictions on stock options, and work force skill standards.[45] As in the case of international issues, the association routinely presents its views to government officials in the executive branch as well as Congress. For example, responding to the Financial Accounting Standards Board's (FASB) proposed changes in the accounting of stock options, AEA executives launched a grassroots campaign aimed at Congress in opposition to it.[46] Testifying for the AEA and the Coalition for Joint Manufacturing, Mitchell Kertzman, AEA's 1990 chairman, supported clarification of U.S. antitrust laws to permit greater use of joint manufacturing.[47] Moreover, recently the AEA has spoken out on what it considers to be unfair competition from military facilities. Increased competition from military laboratories and depots caused AEA members to discuss the problems this development presented to their industries with government officials.[48]

These examples suggest the range of domestic issues with which the AEA is concerned. The association typically aims its response at government officials. In both the international and domestic areas, the AEA takes positions that benefit the electronics industry in general. Policy positions are not focused on specific industries within the electronics sector—semiconductors or computers, to name two obvious examples. This reflects both the strength and weakness of the association. As a large, umbrella organization for the U.S. electronics industry, it is able to pursue policies that have sufficient breadth to influence many parts of the industry. In doing so, it integrates the policy initiatives of the electronics sector, giving it a general purpose and direction. On the other hand, the association cannot easily address the specific needs of a particular industry within the sector, perhaps making its policy positions not altogether satisfactory to firms within that industry.

Response to the Clinton-Gore Administration

The Bill Clinton–Al Gore administration included in its campaign a new government commitment to technology development and high-tech industries in the U.S. President Clinton was open to the AEA's input during the campaign and Vice President Gore is a long-time high-tech enthusiast, having worked closely with the U.S. electronics industry to develop the High Performance Computing and Communications Initiative.[49] With the administration's interest in developing an information infrastructure (or an information superhighway), the U.S. electronics industry has a lot to gain from working with it.

The AEA has spelled out a policy agenda to present to the new administration and Congress. The association has prepared positions and recommendations on the environment (linking environmental policies to productivity and competitiveness), technology and manufacturing (a coherent policy recognizing the larger context, like the role of technology in the economy, for example), tax and finance (capital gains tax cut, permanent R&D tax credit, and unlimited use of stock options), international trade (passage of the customs modernization act, the export administration act, NAFTA, market access in Japan, and the multilateral agreement on export controls), and defense (change government's practice of keeping more contracts in-house, and improve policies for buying commercial products).[50] These goals clearly grow out of the association's long-term objectives. The election of Clinton and Gore may give the AEA the opportunity to see many of them realized.

Effectiveness

Keeping in mind the nebulous quality of effective policy influence and the difficulty of measuring effectiveness, the AEA claims several major accomplishments. Speaking in 1990, AEA president Richard Iverson listed the following AEA successes:

- Leading the legislative effort that resulted in cutbacks in capital gains taxes in 1978 and 1981;

- Assisting in the establishment of the Defense Industry Initiative on Business Ethics and Conduct;

- Helping to get the industry committed to alternative solvents to eliminate chlorofluorocarbons by the year 2000;

- Emphasizing the early development of superconductors and convincing the presidential science advisor that the first conference on superconductivity be held;

- Elevating the debate on high-definition and advanced television technologies to a national level;

- Raising $23 million for fellowships to support graduate scientists and engineers who agree to teach at universities for three years or more.[51]

Beyond these achievements, the AEA has succeeded in raising the awareness of government officials—both in the executive branch and in Congress—of the importance of the electronics industry to the U.S. economy, with particular emphasis on such issues as trade, technology development, and education. It is less clear, however, how successful the AEA has been with respect to policies exclusively affecting one industry. Perhaps such a judgment would be unfair, since the association, owing to the nature of its membership, does not claim to be able to achieve such industry-specific policies.

Computer Systems Policy Project—The CEO's Group

The CSPP is the smallest and newest of the three groups. Since its formation in 1989, it has consisted of the CEOs of about a dozen of the top computer systems manufacturers in the United States. It is unusual among groups representing business in national politics. It is not formally a trade association; it prefers to refer to itself as a forum with a Washington-based lawyer, Kenneth Kay, serving part-time as its executive director. It focuses on a limited range of issues with quite specific goals, all of which were spelled out when the group was created. Five years into its life, the group retains its original policy manifesto and organizational form, giving no indication that its members intend it to become a full-fledged traditional trade association for the U.S. computer industry.

What is most interesting about the CSPP with respect to the political representation of U.S. computer manufacturers is its niche among other trade associations of which U.S. computer companies are members. Clearly, CSPP members found that these other associations, while useful for certain purposes, were not up to the task of articulating some of the industry's most pressing policy objectives. In this sense, the CSPP occupies a small but important niche in the political representation of U.S. computer firms.

Origins, History, and Membership

The Computer Systems Policy Project was formed in 1989 by the CEOs of eleven of the top computer makers in the United States. The original members included John F. Akers (IBM), Joseph (Rod) Canion (Compaq), Charles E. Exley, Jr. (NCR), Scott G. McNealy (Sun), Kenneth H. Olsen (Digital), Lawrence Perlman (Control Data), John A. Rollwagon, (Cray Research), John Scully (Apple), James G. Treybig (Tandem), James A. Unruh (Unisys), and John A. Young (Hewlett-Packard).[52] These executives formed the group primarily as a vehicle through which they could voice their views and influence public policy in the areas of technology development and international trade. Their central goal then was "to build a forceful industry presence in the creation and advocacy of technology legislation and to supply pertinent industry data that will illuminate future public policy issues."[53]

Throughout its four-year history, the CSPP has adhered to this twofold policy agenda, issuing position papers and policy recommendations on trade and technology issues affecting the U.S. computer industry. The membership of the group, however, has changed noticeably. By December 1991, Ronald L. Skates (Data General) had joined the group, and Robert E. Allen came on board representing AT&T, the new owner of NCR. Eckhard Pfeiffer replaced Rod Canion at Compaq and took his seat at the CSPP table. By mid-1993, the group's membership had changed still further. James E. Ousley took over the spot for Control Data Systems, John F. Carlson replaced Rollwagon at Cray Research, Robert B. Palmer now represents for Digital Equipment, and Edward R. McCracken represents Silicon Graphics, a relative newcomer to the group. The companies have remained essentially the same, but several executives around just four years earlier at the founding of the CSPP had been replaced at the top spot of their firms.[54]

The key aspect of the CSPP's members is that they are all CEOs; it is not so much that a particular company is a member of the group as it is that its top executive is a member. This gives the CSPP considerable advantage in several ways. First, the group commands attention simply because its members are already highly visible, influential people in the business. If not household names in general, these executives are well known in the computer and electronics industries as well as among top policy makers in Washington, D.C. Second, since CSPP members are top executives, they can more easily and credibly commit their firms to positions taken by the group. This is not to suggest that they can operate completely as free agents; they certainly have responsibilities to their organizations. However, owing to their positions, they speak with recognized and accepted authority. This allows the CSPP to move more quickly than other associations, perhaps, and equally important, to take more finely tuned positions on critical issues. Third, as a "forum" in which ideas and perspectives on the U.S. computer industry may be exchanged, the CSPP offers industry members a unique opportunity to deal with difficult issues directly and at the highest level. Combined, these aspects of CSPP membership give the group some unusual, if not unique, characteristics among business groups, and afford it significant advantages in determining and articulating policy positions.

Structure, Decision-Making, and Political Strategy

The CSPP has very little structure as such. Consisting of thirteen CEOs in 1993, there is no need for an elaborate, or event stated, decision-making process. Staff is also limited; a part-time executive director and minimal staff handle the group's administrative tasks. Thus, the CSPP is distinct from virtually every other business group in its structure. It is more like an ad hoc group than a formal organization. Interestingly, it started out in just this way and has retained its minimalist organization.

Many trade associations and other kinds of interest groups produce a constant flow of paper: reports, position papers, summaries of congressional and executive actions, to name a few. The CSPP specializes in position papers on technology and trade issues. These papers are of unusually high quality, clearly presenting and supporting the group's policy positions. Because the CSPP's policy focus is narrow, its position papers can be equally focused on key issues. Although the effect of these publications would be difficult to determine, it would be reasonable to surmise that they might be relied upon by participants in the policy-making process to give a clear reflection of the U.S. computer industry's perspective.

In addition to these publications, the CSPP has worked with other groups in related industries to develop policy recommendations consistent with the U.S. computer industry's interests. The best example of this sort of activity took place in 1991, when the CSPP worked closely with the Semiconductor Industry Association (SIA) to construct an industry position on the successor to the U.S.-Japan Semiconductor Trade Arrangement of 1986 (STA). Recognizing the different interests of the U.S. computer and semiconductor industries in regard to dumping of foreign-made chips in the U.S. market, the two groups worked out a unified position to present to U.S. government officials in the negotiations of the New Semiconductor Trade Agreement (NSTA).[55] In sum, the political tactics used by the CSPP are hardly revolutionary, but they suit the needs of this unusual trade group.

Central Mission and Policy Goals

The CSPP's original policy goals were limited to technology and international trade. They still are. These two issue areas have been the heart of the group's central mission, which was originally stated to provide "a forum in which the CEOs (of U.S. computer firms) can contribute their views on major public policy challenges that affect their industry and the nation."[56]

Since 1989, the CSPP has developed specific goals within the general categories of technology and trade. Shortly after it was formed, the group set out to identify critical issues affecting technology development in the U.S. The group organized meetings of specialists in relevant fields to determine these factors. The product of these efforts was one of the CSPP's first reports, which detailed and assessed the critical factors (Table 10.11).[57]

This early effort gives a good indication of the direction in which the CSPP wanted to go in terms of technology policy. While not a technology roadmap in the sense of identifying specific technologies that need development, the critical factors listed by the group provide a policy roadmap of sorts, indicating to government officials and industry executives the U.S. computer industry's view of the U.S. needs in technology development. In two subsequent documents, the group outlined problems in technology development more specifically and followed this analysis with pointed policy recommendations.[58] Thus, the CSPP argued that national R&D investment could be strengthened by "improving federal R&D budget review mechanisms through industry input; implementing the High Performance Computing and Communications Initiative; and increasing the interaction between industry and the federal laboratories."[59]

In addition to these technology concerns, the CSPP has identified the development of a National Information Infrastructure (NII) as a top priority. This "information superhighway" will connect individuals in virtually every professional and personal context to one another through some form of telecommunications. Its proponents—most notably, Vice President Al Gore—intend the new communication system to be the basis of as yet unimagined interactions among people leading to economic growth and improved quality of life. The CSPP strongly supports the initiative, contending that it "builds upon the High Performance Computing and Communications (HPCC) Program."[60] The group recommends

Table 10.11
CSPP's Critical Success Factors, 1990

Business Environment

Capital Investment: availability of long-term capital resources

Critical Mass: large scale and structure required to research, develop, and produce competitive products

Large Market Size: significant market size required to sell complex product at a profit

Intellectual Property Protection: worldwide system of laws that protects proprietary interests in all forms of intellectual property

Standardization and Standards: common specifications that simplify compatibility of products and services

Reduced Risk for Large Emerging Markets: availability of early, sheltered markets—such as government procurements—in which emerging technologies can be tested before they are demonstrably viable in the competitive marketplace

Research, Development and Manufacturing

State-of-the-art Manufacturing: manufacturing facilities that include the most advanced tools

Applied Research and Development: R&D focused on specific commercial product areas

Basic Research: exploration of fundamental scientific phenomena not directly related to direct product development

People and Culture

Quality: excellence in all aspects of the enterprise

Excellent People/Skilled Personnel: availability of well-trained personnel

Research, Development and Manufacturing Linkages: concurrent involvement in the product development process by research, development, and manufacturing specialists

Cooperation by Business, Academia, and Government: joint efforts combining talent and resources

Private Sector Cooperation: joint activities within industry enabling sharing of resources and risk

Cultural Characteristics: address issues such as quarter-to-quarter financial perspective

---

Source: Computer Systems Policy Project, *Perspectives: Success Factors in Critical Technologies* (Washington, DC: Computer Systems Policy Project, July 1990), 5–6.

that progress on the NII proceed at a rapid pace urging action in industry as well as in the executive branch and Congress.[61]

Trade policy makes up the second aspect of the CSPP's twofold mission. Market access and antidumping law reform are the two key trade issues that occupy most of the group's time in this area. The CSPP is an enthusiastic supporter of policies designed to open foreign markets to U.S. products. In general, the group prefers multilateral negotiations leading to increased free trade worldwide. But it acknowledges that U.S. computer systems producers "may need, on occasion, bilateral government-negotiated market-access agreements."[62] With increased market access as the goal, the CSPP outlines a four-step process, which "(i) identifies those markets that require bilateral market-opening initiatives, (ii) establishes, through bilateral negotiations, specific actions to be taken to achieve an open market by a date certain, (iii) periodically applies measures of progress, and (iv) uses government imposed sanctions carefully when necessary."[63] The group further opposes "a government guarantee of market share," supporting instead "steady and measurable progress toward open markets."[64]

In light of the increasing use of antidumping laws on high-technology products worldwide, and with the memory of the effects of the antidumping provisions of the STA of 1986 in mind, the CSPP strongly supports antidumping law reform in the United States. The group proposes a four-part approach to the issue: "(i) realistic cost calculations to determine whether there is unfair pricing, (ii) deterrence of injuriously unfair pricing, (iii) measures to combat circumvention of antidumping relief, and (iv) recognition of marketplace realities."[65]

Together, the market access and antidumping law reform proposals constitute a sharply focused set of policy proposals that clearly reflect the interests of U.S. computer systems producers. Because the CSPP is small and because it was chartered with quite specific goals in mind, it has been able to keep its goals untainted by other issues and concerns. This determined effort potentially adds to the CSPP's effectiveness in achieving its objectives.

The CSPP's policy agenda and the 103rd Congress was an extension of its initial concerns for trade and technology issues. Summarized in one of the group's position papers, they included the following:

- take action to increase the nation's return on federal R&D investment;
- expand the research agenda of the High Performance Computing and Communications Program;
- create a new national technology challenge: a national information infrastructure for the future;
- implement policies to open markets and expand trade;
- enhance the ability of U.S. companies to compete globally by modernizing and strengthening U.S. antidumping law and modernizing the U.S. export licensing system.[66]

The CSPP details several specific recommendations within each of these broad categories. For example, in the area of trade policy, the CSPP supports conclusion of the Uruguay Round of the GATT, ratification of NAFTA, and continued efforts to broaden U.S. companies' access to the Japanese semiconductor market.[67] In the area of research and development, the group recommends increased allocations of federal funds to commercially relevant technologies.[68] The key point is that regardless of the level of detail of the recommendation, all are consistent with the CSPP's original concerns with trade and technology policies.

Effectiveness

Measuring the CSPP's effectiveness is a more straightforward operation than it is for either CBEMA or the AEA, mainly because the CSPP's goals are few and sharply focused and because the group represents only U.S. computer systems producers. The CSPP has enjoyed some success in the area of trade policy. Working with the SIA on the New Semiconductor Trade Agreement (NSTA) of 1991, the CSPP was able to get an agreement that did not, in its view, jeopardize its members' access to a reliable source of low cost semiconductors. Owing to the comparatively short period of time during which the CSPP has been pursuing its policy objectives, its goals on trade and technology remain attainable, but the process of achieving them is ongoing. Perhaps more important than specific accomplishments in the group's history is the fact that it has concentrated attention on the specific, at times unique, needs of U.S. computer systems producers. In this way, it has given the major U.S. firms in this industry a voice through which they can articulate their specific concerns. Their membership in other electronics industry trade associations (CBEMA, AEA, and the Electronics Industries Association, to name the major ones) allows them to pursue other policy objectives as well as giving them access to traditional trade association services, but the CSPP focuses their attention on their specific common concerns.

CBEMA, AEA, AND CSPP: COMPARISON AND ANALYSIS

We may now review the evaluations of the three groups seeking to influence public policy on behalf of the U.S. computer industry. By comparing the groups in terms of the criteria used above, the significance of their differences can be drawn out. A summary analysis of the political representation of the U.S. computer industry through CBEMA, the AEA, and the CSPP follows the comparisons.

Origins and History

The three organizations were formed at different times, in different ways, and for different reasons. While CBEMA originated in the early twentieth century to meet the needs of a relatively traditional industry, AEA was formed at the beginning of the postwar, high-technology boom in California. CBEMA changed as the office equipment industry changed, moving with the industry into computers and information technology. The AEA followed the rapid technological development, growth, and geographic spread of the burgeoning high-tech electronics industry. Thus, CBEMA was born and developed in a more traditional environment, initially serving those traditional needs, which eventually included a central role in setting standards. The AEA, in contrast, grew with the industry, attempted to encompass it, and therefore included, and continues to include, firms differing dramatically in size and products. The CSPP, on the other hand, was formed late in the game and with a particular focus. If it is possible to call anything in this industry mature, the CSPP reflects the needs of a "mature" computer-systems producer industry. The CSPP represents the core companies of the U.S. computer systems industry and thereby also most of the U.S. production output.

The upshot is three remarkably different organizations: an established, Washington-based group with a tradition of involvement in policy-making and interaction with government officials; a large group, based in California and Washington, D.C., still embodying the entrepreneurial spirit of high-technology electronics emerging from California; and a small, sharply focused group representing the clear, well-articulated needs of a firmly established part of the electronics industry.

The conditions of these groups' origins and history affect their current structure, membership, activities, and policy objectives. Differences among these factors lead to a rich, diversified, if not altogether unified pattern of political representation of the U.S. computer industry.

Membership

Size most distinguishes the memberships of the three organizations: CBEMA consists of 26 firms and only 13 firms make up the CSPP, while the AEA has approximately 3,000 firms. The AEA's large size forces it to have a complicated decision-making structure to accommodate the interests of its members—or at least of those who are concerned about the association's positions on public policy. Meanwhile, CBEMA can exist with fewer time-consuming procedures, and the CEOs of the CSPP can act most quickly. CSPP and CBEMA consist of large firms, which implies similar general business interests. AEA consists of start-ups to large corporations leading to differences in basic interests. This difference in size makes the AEA's task more difficult, while CSPP's homogeneous membership keeps internal problems to a minimum.

CSPP is the only group dedicated to the U.S. computer systems producers. CBEMA and the AEA include computer manufacturers among their members, of course, but also have companies in a variety of electronics industries in their memberships. CBEMA must respond to the political business interests of such information technology firms as Eastman Kodak and Xerox, while AEA deals with the whole array of the electronics industry—from semiconductors to computer peripherals and software.

The heterogeneity of CBEMA's and, particularly, AEA's memberships in some ways dilutes the interests of the computer industry. These associations clearly cannot act solely in the interests of computer manufacturers, even when they conflict with the interests of member firms in other industries. To retain their members, both associations create ways to accommodate differences, develop policy positions with wide acceptability, and in general, find common ground. The CSPP, of course, is not burdened with the chore of resolving such conflicts.

Certainly there are differences among computer systems producers, but these are likely to be less sharp than those between firms in different industries.

Structure and Decision Making

The main differences among the three organizations have several consequences for how they meet the needs of U.S. computer firms. First, the smaller the organization, the faster it can change policy positions. CSPP has the advantage in this regard, CBEMA follows, and the AEA, of course, has the most challenging decision-making task. The time needed to change policy positions does not mean, however, that the organization is not responsive to the policy-making at the national level. With positions in place, a large staff monitoring government activity, and an elaborate communications network between staff and members, the AEA can respond effectively to shifts in government activity. CBEMA's staff, along with its close working relationship with member companies' Washington representatives, gives it also a credible capability to respond to policy developments. Thus, simple structure and small size may allow quick policy changes, but do not necessarily indicate the ability to monitor and respond to routine government activity.

Second, the comparatively large staffs at CBEMA and the AEA allow the two associations to follow a wide range of policy areas and to provide member firms with regular updates on developments in Washington. The AEA goes one step further; its councils, located throughout the country, allow the association to monitor state government activity. To the extent state policies are important to its members, the AEA provides a service not typically offered by other trade associations.

In sum, the structure and decision-making process of these three groups present a trade-off. While small size and simple structure allow for a certain nimbleness in changing positions on policy issues, large staff allows an association to deal with a number of issues at the same time, giving such arrangements the advantage when it comes to routine activities.

Political Strategies

The strategies chosen by each group reflect its organizational characteristics. The AEA favors direct lobbying in tandem with grass-roots efforts involving member companies in the political process. CBEMA takes advantage of the resources of each of its members, coordinating the lobbying efforts of member company Washington representatives, for example. CSPP uses the visibility and potential political clout of its members, all of whom are CEOs of major computer systems producers, to advance its policy objectives. None of these groups maintains a political action committee. This suggests that partisan politics, at least as far as elections are concerned, is not relevant from the perspective of these groups. Several possible explanations come to mind for this lack of electoral activity. First, the CSPP and CBEMA are too small for significant campaign activity; the AEA, however, is certainly large enough and geographically dispersed enough to realize some political clout by trying to influence elections. Second, member firms may engage in electoral politics on their own, thus finding little need to do so through their trade associations. Third, creating and funding a political action committee may simply be too expensive.

In sum, the AEA, CBEMA, and CSPP use somewhat different strategies to accomplish their political objectives. Each organization approaches policy in a way that suits its organizational character and policy goals. Whether they can work together routinely in some sort of coalition is an open question, however.

Central Mission and Policy Goals

The groups are clearly distinguishable in terms of their central missions and policy goals. The CSPP has the easiest task of the three. Formed for the expressed purpose of influencing trade and technology policies on behalf of a dozen top U.S. computer systems manufacturers, the CSPP has adhered to its original mission and goals.

CBEMA and the AEA have a more difficult challenge in focusing on a central mission and determining specific policy objectives. CBEMA formed in the early twentieth century for purposes that had little to do with the high-technology electronics industry of the late twentieth century. As the office equipment industry changed to include computers, so did CBEMA. Reflecting its history, CBEMA's current members are in the computer industry and other information technology industries, a situation that compels the association to devise a central mission and policy goals that meet the needs of its members somewhat different interests. CBEMA has solved this problem by focusing largely on domestic producers of computer and information technology products, combining the two into one general industry. Its specific policy goals are consistent with this mission as it maintains its historically central position in setting technical standards and pursues objectives consistent with its members' interests. Notably absent from CBEMA's agenda is a technology plan or "roadmap"; the association prefers to pursue a conducive policy environment for technology development, leaving the direction of technological advances to the private economy and industry.

The American Electronics Association has an equally difficult challenge in constructing its central mission and determining its policy objectives. Unlike CBEMA, the AEA began as an association for high-technology electronics companies. Thus, this industry has been the AEA's core since its formation. The problem lies in the increasing diversity of the electronics industry; as new technologies lead to new products, the industry becomes more diverse. This leads to differences in policy interests and goals among different parts of the electronics industry. Since AEA attempts to represent the entirety of the industry and all types of firms—from start-ups to large, established corporations—the association has carved out a difficult task in terms of choosing a central mission and specific policy objectives.

The AEA has responded to the challenge by devising a vague central mission and numerous policy objectives. The AEA features an impressive array of goals and monitors a wide range of government activities, including both Congress and the executive branch at the national level, and state government activity. What the association might give up in the ability to target narrow objectives, it gains in breadth, allowing it to serve a diverse industry.

While the CSPP serves only the computer industry (and only a small part of it, for that matter), the AEA and CBEMA represent broader interests. The CSPP, then, is the only group solely devoted to representing the interests of the U.S. computer industry. While other groups, like AEA and CBEMA, include computer manufacturers, they must balance the needs of this industry with those of the other industries they represent.

Measuring Effectiveness

Measuring an organization's effectiveness in achieving its objectives is notoriously difficult. Two problems make this task difficult. First, determining the extent to which an organization caused a policy to be enacted is methodologically tricky at best. Other factors will likely come into play—other groups, public opinion, or independent policy preferences of government officials—and separating a particular organization's effect is difficult. Second, organizations with multiple objectives may achieve only some of them. For example, a full-service trade association has goals apart from influencing public policy. An association that provides members with good information on the industry, public policy, and technological developments might be considered a success, although it has not accomplished much with respect to altering public policy.

The first conclusion about effectiveness that is impossible to ignore is that there is no single, large, all-purpose trade association at the national level that is solely devoted to the U.S. computer industry. CSPP comes closest to this and, as such, is the most effective in making a difference in government policies, but it is a small, narrowly focused group that does not classify itself as a trade association. CBEMA and AEA represent other industries in addition to the computer industry. At first glance, this state of affairs suggests some limitations on the effectiveness of the political representation of the U.S. computer industry. However, the issue must be considered from a variety of perspectives before settling on this conclusion.

Consider CBEMA, AEA, and CSPP in light of the two basic problems associated with evaluating effectiveness. Because of its narrow focus, it is possible to evaluate CSPP's effect on policy more easily than it is for the other two groups. CSPP has enjoyed some success on trade policy; it successfully influenced the NSTA of 1991 to accommodate the concerns of its members about U.S. anti-dumping policy on foreign-made semiconductors. CBEMA has enjoyed ongoing success in its influence over setting standards. Its importance in this area is historically rooted and continues as a major element of the association's objectives. CBEMA also provides effective political assistance to its members by coordinating their activities, thus helping them respond quickly to relevant policy shifts. AEA presents a somewhat more difficult evaluation problem than the other two groups. It has been effective in monitoring and participating in routine government decisions affecting its members. In this sense, it has been an effective political representative of the U.S. electronics industry.

Expanding the concept of effectiveness to include all group activities, not just efforts to influence public policy, produces a somewhat different picture. CSPP is devoted to public policy; evaluating other activities is irrelevant. CBEMA provides technical information to its members along with a variety of ways for members to exchange information—through trade shows, for example. AEA provides a wealth of nonpolitical services to its members as well—ranging from trade shows to technical information to advice on running a business. In both these cases, then, the associations might be considered effective in terms of the nonpolitical services they provide their members.

Overall, all three groups may be considered effective. Each has enjoyed some policy success, and CBEMA and AEA, the two full-fledged trade associations, effectively provide members with other services. In addition to these two perspectives on effectiveness, providing a constant presence in the national policy process advances members' political interests. Stopping an undesired policy from taking effect is nearly impossible to measure, but nonetheless benefits group members. In this sense, having a competent, professional representative at the national level is an indication of group effectiveness.

Returning to the stark conclusion of the beginning of this section, there may be some advantage to being represented by more than one group. U.S. computer companies can choose from among a number of organizations to influence public policy. Some organizations may be more effective in certain areas than others. Membership in different groups allows the company to work with a different set of colleagues, depending on the issues. This diversity of representation gives computer companies several paths to political influence, something that a single, large, dedicated association would not provide.

SUMMARY

Typical of interest-group representation in American politics, the U.S. computer industry is not represented by one group that handles all its policy needs. Different groups respond to divergent aspects of the industry, reflecting the industry's complexity. The AEA, CBEMA, and CSPP are three of the main organizations representing the U.S. computer industry in national policy-making. Because of the industry's complexity, and because of the rapid changes in the electronics industry as a whole, the political representation of the industry is diverse. Each of the three organizations considered here serves the U.S. computer industry in different ways. The AEA provides representation of U.S. computer firms as part of the larger array of high-technology electronics firms. Its size and scope allow the AEA to forge consensus among different segments of the electronics industry, including the computer industry. The computer industry is one part of a larger collection of similar, but certainly not identical, industries. The negative side of this arrangement, of course, becomes evident when the interests of the computer industry do not match those of other high-technology electronics industries represented by the association. CBEMA is the oldest of the three organizations examined in this study. It serves a more traditional interest of some of the largest of U.S. computer firms growing out of its original focus on office equipment. Now encompassing computers and information technology, CBEMA represents the segment of the computer industry consisting of large, multiproduct companies.

Finally, the CSPP, a new group, targets the specific needs of leading U.S. computer systems manufacturers, keeping its focus on its original twofold goals: trade and technology policies. It appears that the CSPP, in less than five years, has been able to best understand key policy issues, such as the National Information Infrastructure, in the light of national interests. It has also created the credibility and access at the highest policy levels that clearly differentiate it from other interest groups attempting to represent computer systems companies.

NOTES

1. Robert U. Ayres, *The Next Industrial Revolution* (Cambridge, MA. Ballinger Publishing, 1984), 145.

2. McKinsey and Company, Inc., *The 1990 Report on the Computer Industry* (New York: McKinsey and Company, 1990), 1.13, 2.2 –2.6.

3. For the critical technologies list, see Computer Systems Policy Project, *Perspectives: Success Factors in Critical Technologies* (Washington, DC: Computer Systems Policy Project, July 1990).

4. K. P. Julinssen and E. Julinssen, *The 6th Annual Computer Industry Almanac–1993* (Austin, TX: Reference Press, June 1993), 408.

5. Computer and Business Equipment and Manufacturers Association (CBEMA), "A Retrospective," in *Computer and Business Equipment Manufacturers Association: 1990 Annual Report* (Washington, DC: CBEMA, 1990), 54.

6. Ibid., 56.

7. Ibid.

8. Ibid., 58.

9. Ibid.

10. Ibid., 59.

11. Ibid., 60.

12. Ibid.

13. Ibid.

14. Ibid.

15. Joanne Connelly, "CBEMA Restricts Foreign Firms to 30% of Membership," *Electronic News*, 7 May 1990, 1.

16. Interview with CBEMA official, 25 August 1993.

17. Ibid.

18. Ibid.

19. Ibid.

20. Connelly, "CBEMA Restricts Foreign Firms," p.1.

21. Interview with CBEMA official.

22. CBEMA, "A Retrospective," 60–63.

23. Ronald K. Jurgen, "Friendly Adversaries Help U.S. Companies," *IEEE Spectrum*, May 1990, 50.

24. American Electronics Association, *Milestones: 1943–1993* (Washington, DC: American Electronics Association, 1993).

25. American Electronics Association, *1993 Public Policy Agenda* (Washington, DC: American Electronics Association), 26.

26. Ibid.

27. Jurgen, "Friendly Adversaries," 51.

28. Interview with AEA Official, 20 September 1993.

29. Jurgen, "Friendly Adversaries," 50.

30. Interview with AEA Official.

31. Ibid.

32. Jurgen, "Friendly Adversaries," 50.

33. American Electronics Association, "AEA Ready to Get to Work with New Congress, Administration," *Update*, December 1992–January 1993.

34. American Electronics Association, "AEA Speaks Out: Excerpts from Capitol Hill Testimony on Joint Manufacturing," *Public Affairs Bulletin*, 17 July 1990.

35. American Electronics Association, *1993 Public Policy Agenda*, 9.

36. American Electronics Association, "GATT Trade Talks Face More Delays," *Update*, February-March 1993, 12.

37. American Electronics Association, "NAFTA High Tech Day: AEA Members Visit Congress and White House," *Monthly Activities Report*, 1 August 1993, 2–3.

38. Ibid., 3.

39. American Electronics Association, "AEA Intervenes on Behalf of NAFTA in the Court," *Monthly Activities Report*, 1 August 1993, 3–4.

40. American Electronics Association, "Executive Order Loosens Some Export Controls," *International Bulletin*, December 1990, 1.

41. American Electronics Association, "AEA Testifies Before House Ways and Means Subcommittee," *Monthly Activities Report*, 1 August 1993, 1.

42. R. Wayne Sayer, President and CEO of R. Wayne Sayer and Associates, on Behalf of the American Electronics Association, "Testimony before the United States Trade Representative." (document Washington, DC: AEA, 24 May 1989).

43. Peter T. Kilborn, "U.S. Funds Sought for Advanced TV," *New York Times*, 10 May 1989, D1, D6.

44. Jack Robertson, "AEA Task Force Completes New HDTV Request," *Electronic News*, 3 September 1990, 9.

45. American Electronics Association National Competitiveness Steering Committee, *Monthly Activities Report*, 1 August 1993.

46. American Electronics Association, "Unfavorable Stock Options Ruling Spurs 400 CEOs Into Action," *Update*, June-July 1993, 1, 6.

47. American Electronics Association, "AEA Speaks Out: Excerpts from Capitol Hill Testimony on Joint Manufacturing," *Public Affairs Bulletin*, 17 July 1990.

48. American Electronics Association, "Industry Opposes Unfair Competition from Military Facilities," *Update*, February-March 1993, 1, 10.

49. American Electronics Association, "AEA Ready to Get to Work with New Congress, Administration," *Update*, December 1992–January 1993, 1.

50. Ibid., 4-5.

51. Jurgen, "Friendly Adversaries," 51.

52. Diane Crawford, "CEOs Unite to Influence U.S. Technology Policy," *Communications of the ACM*, June 1991, 15.

53. Ibid.

54. Computer Systems Policy Project, "Member Lists" (Washington, DC: Computer Policy Project, 1991, update 1993).

55. The dispute between U.S. semiconductor manufacturers and U.S. computer manufacturers concerning the effect the STA of 1986 had on the price and availability of chips in the U.S. is well documented. For a balanced view of the episode, see Laura D'Andrea Tyson, *Who's Bashing Whom?* ch. 4.

56. Computer Systems Policy Project, [Document], Washington, DC, 1990, 2.

57. Computer Systems Policy Project, "Perspectives: Success Factors in Critical Technologies," 8–24.

58. Computer Systems Policy Project, "Perspectives on U.S. Technology Policy, Part I: The Federal R&D Investment" (26 February 1991); Computer Systems Policy Project, "Perspectives on U.S. Technology Policy, Part II: Increasing Industry Involvement" (Washington, DC, 26 February 1991).

59. Ibid. "Executive Summary," opening page number.

60. Computer Systems Policy Project, "Perspectives on the National Information Structure" (Washington, DC, 12 January 1993), 1.

61. Ibid., 2.

62. Computer Systems Policy Project, "Perspectives on Market Access and Antidumping Law Reform" (Washington, DC, 1990), 1.

63. Ibid., 1-2.

64. Ibid., 2

65. Ibid.

66. Computer Systems Policy Project, *Perspectives on U. S. Technology and Trade Policy: The CSPP Agenda for the 103rd Congress* (Washington, DC, 1 October 1992), 1.

67. Ibid., 10.

68. Ibid., 7.

Chapter 11

Characteristics of American High-Tech Trade Associations

Having looked at descriptions of several American high-technology trade associations and their formation, governance, operation, and activities, some of their general characteristics begin to emerge. Some of these characteristics are similar to those of older trade associations in the United States, while others differ. In addition, the American high-tech associations have some characteristic differences and similarities with those in Germany and Japan.

All the American high-tech trade associations described in the last four chapters were founded by political entrepreneurs. They attempted to combine the resources of individual firms so they may be applied to common issues and have them governed through the mechanism of a trade association. The term *political entrepreneur* seems appropriate for these founders because *entrepreneurs* generally reallocate resources to new endeavors and the term *political* generally relates to obtaining power to govern group activities. Their entrepreneurial resources were allocated to a common association and the entrepreneurial power was utilized for the performance of the associations they founded.

Whether we look at aerospace, semiconductors, biotechnology, or computers, individuals active in the industry's firms were the associations' founders and their companies were the initial members of their association. The impetus for their actions to form associations was either a real or a potential threat to their firms that they also saw as a common threat to all firms. The threat in the case of biotechnology was potential government attitudes and regulations, while in semiconductors it was a foreign industry acting with its government's strong collaborative support. The other associations described in this part of the book had their real and potential threats as well.

In contrast to Japan and Germany, where governments have historically established or encouraged associations (and have even taken an active role as producers in industry itself), the United States government was not a primary factor in the formation of trade associations. American associations were formed by merchants and industrialists and based on voluntary membership. The private and voluntary aspects of U.S. trade associations were greatly impacted by the U.S. government only twice in American history. The first major impact was the antitrust movement at the turn of this century, which halted the use of trade association as major commercial vehicles for anticompetitive behavior. The second time was during the 1930s when the New Deal attempted to achieve industrial economic stability through the use of association cartels allowed under the NRA, (which the Supreme Court later declared as unconstitutional). In both cases, the final result was a lessening of trade association power in the United States at the same time that trade associations were being strengthened and employed in Japan and Germany for broad national purposes.

As a result of the U.S. government actions and federal court decisions, the trade associations in the United States, including any high-tech associations of their day, refrained from overt domestic or international activity related to market position and economic power and turned to serving the internal informational and service needs of the industry. These latter-day activities are relatively pedestrian when compared to those of the pre–Sherman Act days or those envisioned by designers of the Swope Plan. In fact, rather than a strong movement to try to cooperate with government in order to reestablish some of these former activities, many of the industries and their associations from 1945 to 1985 considered the federal government as an adversary. However, since 1985, many trade associations, and particularly those in high-technology industries, have taken proactive roles in assisting government in the formulation of public policies relating to international trade, technology, and other facets of American competitiveness. In so doing, these associations have found a generally sympathetic response from government agencies and officials. The recent willingness to cooperate on the part of both industry and government has been because of the decline of American competitiveness in the world's strategic industries, including those represented by the associations described in the previous four chapters, and its effect on the national economy. The only other post–World War II example of large-scale cooperation between the U.S. government and industry occurred during the Cold War when, because of the Soviet threat, an "iron triangle" was forged through an alliance between defense industries, government agencies (primarily the defense department), and Congress. At the same time that the United States had its "iron triangle," Japan had its own triangle for waging economic war— commercial industry and government agencies, primarily MITI and the Diet (Japan's parliament).[1] Therefore, the U.S. only recently has begun to realize that high-tech industries, their firms, and their associations in cooperation with government are considered of great enough importance in the nation's economic well-being that a nonpartisan, cooperative effort is required.[2] From the standpoint of specific organizations for a partisan political approach, the use of PACs (political action committees) that support specific candidates has been declining markedly, indicating a further use of bipartisan approaches to political action in this as well as other areas. However, regardless of action to support specific candidates or to generally affect public policy in a nonpartisan way, associations tend to be reactive when facing threats to American competitiveness.

Another characteristic of American trade associations is that they may be formed, disbanded, combined, or dissolved with very little effort in terms of legal and public requirements. The story of the associations in the previous four chapters indicates the milieu of changing organizations and strong attitudes by individual firms. Coincident with this occasional internal divisiveness, nonmembers of the association, whose views are often at odds with the mainstream industry views, add to the picture of diverse rather than consensual views.

A contributory element to this diversity of views is the fact that although there is structure *within* the associations, there is a virtual lack of any structure, whether hierarchical or networked, directed or consensual, *between* associations for the resolution of conflicting positions. Consequently, most broad issues related to public policy are primarily left to government agency officials and Congress to reconcile, since no mechanism of reconciliation exists at the level of conflicting associations.

A further characteristic of trade associations in the United States is that their mission is often described by vague general statements. There is generally no description of an association's mission that includes the performance measures of the industry, such as global share of market, technological leadership, profitability, employment, or other benefits sought by stake-holders.[3] Specifically, there are no operational definitions that are measurable and related to any indicators of industry performance. In the previous four chapters, some instances of attempts to do this, such as foreign access to the Japan market by the U.S. chip industry, are described, but even these are only narrow, focused attempts in the scheme of global business affairs. In fact, many industry executives oppose a collective industry strategy or performance measures as a mission of their association, although these measures can be instituted lawfully and are not beyond acceptable competitive marketplace activities. The lack of overall industry performance measures for U.S. associations is evident by reviewing their mission statements and their actual activities. Most activities can be viewed as a menu from which members can select traditional services to assist them by providing industry information or by providing their employees such benefits as insurance or credit union privileges. Other primary association activities involve government relations regarding matters concerning regulations. Both traditional and government-relations efforts appear to be designed to reduce or maintain costs on a narrow, selective basis rather than a proactive program to dramatically impact industry growth in an increasingly competitive global market.

One important characteristic of successful voluntary American trade associations, which is evident in high-tech ones, is the high proportion of the industry's production output represented by the association members despite the fact that membership is not mandatory. Over 80 percent of the industry output is represented by the membership in over two-thirds of manufacturing associations recently surveyed.[4] About three-quarters of the associations surveyed had their membership producing over 60 percent of the total industry production output. The high-tech industries described in the four previous chapters have 70 percent to 90 percent of the total industry output represented by their membership.

Another characteristic of American associations is their tolerance of membership by foreign firms, especially those that manufacture in the United States. According to the survey previously mentioned, 80 percent of the associations will admit foreign manufacturers although, in fact, only about 12 percent of total dues paid into all associations surveyed is derived from foreign members. About 90 percent of the American associations will allow foreign members to vote. By comparison, foreign association members in Japan and Germany do not vote in matters of national or regional policy when related to international competition and trade. The associations described earlier have various treatments of foreign members, although in no case are foreign subsidiaries totally excluded.

The continual restructuring of the American industrial scene has affected U.S. associations. Earlier mention has been made of these impacts and one of them has been the loss of institutional memory.[5] However, only about 35 percent of all associations appear to formally orient their new members and new directors. Less formal methods, such as association committee membership and interaction among peers appears to be the primary means of passing on past institutional experience. None of the associations described have formal orientation sessions for new directors.

In addition to these characteristics, there are others of interest. Although an association may represent up to 90 percent of an industry's overall production, this does not indicate that there are uniform industry opinions. The initial founders are often highly vocal, as well as influential, with regard to association affairs. At the other extreme, there are industry firms which are not members, but who obtain the major benefits of the association's actions. These nonmembers, or "free riders" as they are often called, may also reap the undesirable aspects of association issues as well. Furthermore, they are often quite vocal in opposing their industry's association. Because of this fact, some free riders are consistently used by the media to represent the views that are in opposition to associations. This last fact has been called "skewing the balance" or "coronating the fool."[6] Whether it be vocal, high-profile leading members or free riders, there will be potential divisive factors.

In this day of multidivisional corporations, it is often found that various divisions of corporations belong to different associations or even to the same association. They may also be represented by the same individual or several individuals. A case in point involves the corporations that belong to different associations, such as the computer firms like IBM, which belongs to AEA, CBEMA, and CSPP. This leads to some confusion about the membership roles of such companies. Another case in point involves the semiconductor divisions of firms such as IBM, Digital Equipment Corporation, and Hewlett-Packard, which belong to SIA, while their computer divisions belong to AEA or CBEMA and their corporate CEOs are members of CSPP.

Until recently, the fear of antitrust prosecution lead to self-limiting behavior by the associations. More recently, however, because of various pieces of legislation, associations perform collaborative research and trade exports promotion. They may also participate in joint manufacturing. Moreover, they have joined with the U.S government agencies in national councils, such as the National Advisory Committee on Semiconductors. This is a relatively recent event (since 1980) and legislation is required for each specific council.

Finally, each association previously presented is a state-chartered corporation. In this sense, they are treated generally in the same way as for-profit corporations except with regard to taxation. With regard to public policy, they tend to rely on the congressmen of the association charter state or the states where member firms have some similar type of influence, such as subsidiaries located in their states. The distinction of nonprofit trade associations does not differ greatly from other similar organizations.

The characteristics described here are not designated as positive or negative, nor is the listing intended to be exhaustive. Their exposition is intended to identify some distinct features of America's high-technology trade associations. This knowledge of how associations are structured, how they work, and their most salient features is essential to proposing a reshaping of America's industry associations.

Part 4 of this book is dedicated to formulating new approaches for trade associations in organization, conduct, and behavior.

NOTES

1. "A Softer Triangle: How Japan Inc. Works Will Change Subtly However Voting Ends," *Wall Street Journal*, 16 July 1993, A-1.

2. George C. Lodge, *Perestroika for America: Restructuring U.S. Business-Government Relations for Competitiveness in the World Economy* (Boston: Harvard Business School Press, 1990), 201–209.

3. National Association of Manufacturers, Mission Statements: Reference Guide (Washington, DC: National Association of Manufacturers, 1993).

4. National Association of Manufacturers, *A Survey for Manufacturing Trade Associations* (Washington, DC: National Association of Manufacturers, 1991), Fig. 39, p. 24.

5. Nancy M. Davis, "Restructuring America's Trade Associations," *Association Management* 41, no. 8 (August 1989): 50–61.

6. Dr. Martin R. Stoller, J.L. Kellogg School of Management, Northwestern University, Evanston, Illinois (presentation at National Association of Manufacturers, Association Council Meeting, Traverse City, MI, 29–31 July 1993).

IV

DESIGNING AMERICA'S ASSOCIATIONS FOR GLOBAL COMPETITION

Chapter 12

The Approach to a New Design

The early chapters of this book described the historical foundations of American, Japanese and German trade associations. The conclusions based on these chapters are that trade associations have national differences, which are integral to the different forms of industrial capitalism practiced in each nation.

The German trade associations work in close cooperation with government. Although membership in an industry association is voluntary, over 90 percent of all industrial firms are members of the BDI and over 80 percent of the eligible members belong to the VDA. Furthermore, by law, all firms must belong to the Chamber of Commerce and Industry. It is because of this high degree of industry organization and close cooperation with government that the German form of capitalism was called cooperative capitalism.

The Japanese trade associations' relationship with government is even closer than the German relationship. The Japanese associations build intraindustry consensus and to communicate to both government and industry members. The associations are government supported and, when necessary, are provided with guidance as well as government loans and advance notice to regulatory changes. The mode is one of collaboration, which is one step above cooperation.

The U.S. trade associations have had a history of formation and support by political entrepreneurs rather than by government. The role of trade associations has been to provide commercial benefits to member firms rather than to work toward any national interest in a government partnership. However, there appears today to be a move to bring about a better government-industry partnership in America.

Part 3 then focused on four American high-tech industries and their associations in order to describe how American associations are governed in support of the objectives of their corresponding industries in global competition. These industry associations are part of a highly pluralistic, loosely affiliated, structurally changing and vaguely directed set of organizations that are questionably designed for serving the national interest as well as the interests of the member firms.

Each U.S. industry faces an uncertain future as to its long term world leadership. The U.S. aircraft industry has experienced a continual decline in global share of market. The recently stable global share held by the U.S. computer systems industry was preceded by ten years of decline. Moreover, the recent recovery of the semiconductor industry market share faces an uncertain future, and the prospect of a future decline in share of market for the U.S. biotechnology industry is not out of the question. In every case, U.S. industries are under sustained attack from their Asian and European counterparts. In these global contests the effectiveness of each American industry's trade association, based upon the maintenance and improvement of its industry's global leadership, has not been determined.

In the concluding chapters of this book, the question to be addressed is, based on their American heritage and their current relationship to their corresponding industry, how should the U.S. industry associations be designed in order to be governed, structured, guided, and employed to best meet the challenges faced by their industries' global competition? The closing chapters of this book answer that question.

Chapter 13

American Competitiveness and the Intermediate Sector

WHOSE ELECTRONICS ASSOCIATION?

It was January 1987, and most of the CEOs in the room were members of the American Electronics Association (AEA). The chairman of the AEA board, and chairman of this meeting, was Horace McDonald, the CEO of Perkin-Elmer Corporation, a manufacturer of equipment for the production of semiconductor chips. His largest markets served were American and Japanese chip producers. However, the American chip makers were losing market share rapidly to their Japanese competitors, and McDonald no doubt could see the demand for his products shifting toward Asia. Other meeting room attendees included CEOs from other semiconductor production equipment firms as well as executives from the computer systems manufacturers and the semiconductor device makers. Among the production equipment makers were Applied Materials, and Kulicke and Soffa; the computer systems makers included Hewlett-Packard, Tandem, Apple, and IBM; and the chip makers included Intel, Motorola, and Texas Instruments. The key issue of the meeting was the different perceptions each person held with regard to the newly signed U.S.-Japan Semiconductor Trade Agreement.

The keiretsu firms of Japan, whose subunits produced chips, computers, and semiconductor production equipment, had brought great pressure to bear on their corresponding American customers and suppliers to have the chip agreement scuttled or, at least, ignored. While the Japanese keiretsu firms were all united in their objective, the American industry segments held differing views as to how to treat the government-to-government agreement. Most American production equipment and computer systems makers feared alienating their customers and suppliers. In effect, the American chip makers were causing them a great deal of anxiety. Some American chip makers also believed that their American systems counterparts were, either consciously or otherwise, aiding and abetting the efforts of the Japanese chip makers. On the one side, CEOs of firms like Perkin-Elmer and Hewlett-Packard in the electronics industry who were present believed that their best interests lay in opposing the agreement already in place and in maintaining close ties with their Japanese customers and suppliers. The American chip firms, on the other hand, believed that the Japanese keiretsu would eventually attempt to eliminate the American equipment and computer systems firms, following their destruction of the U.S. chip industry.

The meeting was evolving into a bitter comparison of motives and ideologies. One computer maker stated that his firm was a world marketer and that national boundaries meant little. The single issue became the question, "Should free trade and open markets be the guiding ideology for all American firms, despite protectionist Japan's disdain of free trade and open markets, so that American computer systems and production equipment firms could continue to prosper even at the cost of the eventual demise of a faltering U.S. chip industry?" The belief of many in the room was that, due to a common membership in the AEA, a partial, if not complete, answer could be found to the question. However, rather than a resolution of the issue, the arguments grew more intense and heated until finally, another key question in the debate was formed by Andy Grove, CEO of Intel Corp., the world's leading semiconductor device maker. Andy looked about the room at the executives in the room and stated: "Intel and SIA don't have the national identity problem that some of you apparently have. Maybe the American Electronics Association (AEA) should change its name to the Worldwide Electronics Association."

THE MEANING OF AMERICAN COMPETITIVENESS

The Council on Competitiveness, a private group based in Washington, D.C., is dedicated to proposing public and private policies that will raise the competitiveness of American industries, and therefore, that of the nation as a whole. This group grew out of the frustration of many private sector participants in the President's Commission on Industrial Competitiveness after the Reagan administration ignored most of the proposals in its 1985 final report. In its pursuit of this effort, the council defined competitiveness as "the degree to which a nation, under free and fair market conditions, produces goods and services that meet the test of international markets while simultaneously maintaining and expanding the real income of its citizens."[1]

With regard to "nation" and "citizens," the terms are applicable here to the United States and its American citizens. The key word, "free," in the phrase "free and fair market conditions" relates to the fact that many nations have formal, informal, and gray barriers to their domestic markets. Formal barriers are easiest to identify and refer to regulations, quotas, tariffs, and other regulated means of restricting trade. Informal barriers generally mean those outside normal official government lines, such as secret market and price restriction agreements made between firms in an industry. A third set of barriers are the so-called gray barriers, which are set up by industry with the knowledge and encouragement of their government to restrict trade by a concerted and organized approach while giving the appearance that all lawful means are in favor of open trade. An example of a gray barrier is one whereby several manufacturing firms rationalize their total production with the knowledge of one of their government agencies in order to restrict the penetration of foreign firms. This may be done, although the action may be construed as illegal by the fair trade commission of the same government. In addition to "free," the word "fair" in the same phrase indicates that some competition is not fair. Unfair competition relates to the use of predatory practices of all kinds, including dumping and phantom pricing, rather than only to restrictive practices.

The council's phrase, "produce goods and services," obviously refers primarily to private firms and industries that manufacture for international trade and domestic commerce. The term, "test of international markets," essentially means a firm or industry's ability in the global market to gain share of market, achieve positive sales growth, provide profits, increase the returns to their stakeholders—employees, management, and stockholders—and provide excellent value to their customers. Finally, the term, "real income," refers to the relationship of prices to wages, income, and profits. In effect, it is a measure of the standard of living. It also assumes that the distortions of price inflation and manipulated currency exchange rates are discouraged or countered.

When all the qualifying phrases are subsumed into a single concept, competitiveness is described as a function of American industries' abilities to outperform their foreign competitors. If one measure were to be used above all to compare a nation's industries, it would be their long-term share of market in global competition. This view appears to be supported publicly by the present U.S. administration as represented by a recent statement by Dr. John H. Gibbons, assistant to the president for science and technology, who stated that "the test of national competitiveness is whether or not a nation can retain or increase its market share in the world marketplace."[2]

The council went further by stating that the competitiveness of America's industries is dependent upon each industry's productivity, technology, human resources, and capital. Moreover, government can provide policies that will help maintain open markets (international trade policy), low interest rates (federal budget policy), research and development (technology policy), education and training (human resources policy), and domestic trade policy that would encourage trade such as easing export controls and antitrust regulations.

This general view of the council provides a starting point for the subsequent discussion in which a more detailed view of the roles of the firms, government, and industry will be provided.

THE GLOBAL ECONOMY

This section will provide the reader with the necessary background against which clear and definitive roles of business and government can be drawn. The relevancies of the global economy, the nationality of corporations, national industries, and the interdependencies between national and foreign industries will be covered. The general discussion will be applicable to the roles and the interrelationships of business firms, government agencies, and industry associations.

Before discussing these various roles, however, a look at the meaning of globalization is essential to further discussion. The very high level of international transactions relative to the gross domestic product of each of the world's industrialized nations leads many to describe the collective economies of today as equivalent to a single global economy. However, the term *global economy* does not mean that compatible or common national economic policies or measures have been, or can be, adopted. For example, the United Nations (or any other global body) does not make economic policy, such as fiscal or monetary policy, for all nations of the world. There are trade agreement bodies such as GATT, legal bodies such as the World Court, and investment bodies such as the World Bank and the International Monetary Fund, but there is no single global economic policy-making body. Consequently, global transactions are not governed by a global economic policy but only by many national policies coupled with some degree of influence from multinational bodies, such as the former General Agreement on Trade and Tariffs, now called the World Trade Organization.

If we extend this discussion to corporations, there are no global corporations but rather only national firms with international, transnational, or multinational operations. Corporate activities—design, manufacturing, or marketing—may occur internationally, transnationally, or multinationally and therefore appear global in terms of scope and scale, but corporations are not global in terms of their essential character (as defined by their legal status or primary locale of activity or highest control group). Key corporate activities that add to the perception of the global nature of corporations are their direct foreign investments and their cross-border alliances with foreign firms. However, *foreign* is the common qualifying adjective here with regard to investment and alliances, which merely strengthens the recognition of corporate nationality while emphasizing global activities. The claim, therefore, that the modern corporation has no nationality, although widespread, must be closely questioned and examined.

The contention that corporations are essentially national rather than global citizens can be supported as follows. If all the key elements of a corporation—that is, assets, employment, governance, plant locations, intellectual property rights, and so on—are considered in total, then the overall weight, or center of gravity, appears to be represented in virtually all cases by a single nation. As an example, the assets of a U.S. corporation may be located outside the United States by a proportion greater than 50 percent. However, this does not make the corporation global. The United States may still have a greater proportion of that corporation's assets than any one other single country. The comparison can be made for other measures of corporate nationality. For example, for each corporation—the citizenship of its employees, its legal status in each country, the national jurisdiction for its tax base, the intellectual property patent base, the location of most research and development activity, the location of its manufacturing plants, and the source of diplomatic and military protection—all are elements in the determination of company nationality.[3]

When these elements are defined and applied to specific corporations, their overall effect is the determination of corporate nationality, whether American, Japanese, German, or any other. Any individual familiar with industrial corporations who believes that Hitachi is a global corporation, and not Japanese; that Siemens is global, and not German; or that AT&T is global, and not American, is ignoring the basic fact that any corporation's nationality can be defined by the center of gravity elements described in the previous paragraph. In conclusion, a corporation has a nationality which weighs heavily in all its corporate decisions, and therefore affects its nation as well.

NATIONAL INDUSTRIES AND INTERNATIONAL CORPORATIONS

A firm succeeds in the global marketplace when it has achieved and maintains the market share that is necessary for obtaining adequate returns and long-term survival. Some firms in a given industry will fail, but as the summation of all firms producing the same or similar products, an industry can survive regardless of the fate of individual firms, as long as the industry performs. A nation's industry will also survive as long as its collection of firms has greater capability than its foreign counterparts. Consequently, domestic and international competition will not only influence the survival of individual firms, but also, long-term, the survival of the nation's industry as a whole. American industries, in total, have virtually failed due to international competition. The most quoted example has been the television industry. Only one U.S. firm, Zenith Electronics, now remains from among tens of U.S. firms that existed before 1960. Ninety percent of the television sets manufactured in the United States today are produced in plants owned and controlled by Asian- and European-based firms. More recent examples have been the flat panel display and the silicon materials industries.

National industries and their relationship to national well-being, as described by the council's definition of competitiveness, requires that they be defined and measured in terms of production, financial, and trade as to their impact on the nation's economy and individual citizens' standards of living. Many years ago, the U.S. Department of Commerce defined and classified industries by use of the Standard Industrial Classification system. By employing this system as a means of organizing national data collection, not only can stand-alone industry data be compiled, but also, the interrelation of industries to each other can be determined. Each industry produces goods and services (inputs) that are either used in manufacturing its own, as well as every other industry's, product (outputs) or consumed by government, business, or households as final demand. Inputs to all industries include materials, labor, and capital, and may be sourced domestically or from foreign sources. Outputs may not only satisfy domestic final demand—of government, business, and households—but may also satisfy foreign demand as exports. In turn, inputs may be imported as well as domestically produced. This view of the American economy, based on interindustry relationships whose input and output may be domestic or foreign and which may involve intermediate or final demand products, is best described by interindustry economics.[4] Statistics describing interindustry relationships are available from the U.S. Bureau of Economic Analysis, and these may be used by economists to study American industrial interdependency as well as American industrial dependency on foreign products. International interindustry tables have also been used by the agencies of foreign governments such as MITI in Japan to study the interindustry relationship between America and Japan.[5] This input-output view of the economy provides a great deal of insight as to the interrelationship of industries. It can be used to calculate, for example, the proportion of units of input to units of output, called technical coefficients; the relative size of all industries; the ratio of value-added to outputs; or the ratio of imports to exports for all inputs, as well as outputs, for a specific industry; the ratio of each demand sector to the total demand. In essence, it confirms with great graphic and quantitative power the interdependence of industries and the impact of an industrial structure on the total economy. It also demonstrates clearly the importance of corporate nationality since interindustry values, as well as final demand values, can be identified as to foreign-source dependency as well as domestic sourcing.

The end result of all foreign dependencies—of final demand output as well as intermediate inputs—is the trade balance. The U.S. merchandise trade balance has been negative since the 1970s and can be construed as nothing less than a U.S. debt to foreign nations. As the trade deficit has increased, the result has been a decline in American wages and incomes. An unfavorable trade balance is a sign of a lack of competitiveness in a sufficient number of industries to affect the overall well-being of citizens of the United States.

Thus far, this chapter has focused on the relevancies of the global economy, the nationality of corporations, national industries, and the interdependence between industries, both national and foreign. The discussion appears to be very general and therefore only loosely applicable to the interrelationship of the roles of business firms, government agencies, and industry associations. However, it will have provided the reader with the necessary background against which clear and definitive roles of business and government can now be drawn.

THE ROLE OF THE FIRM

The role of any business firm is to achieve its corporate objectives. These major categories of objectives are well known and can include return on investment, price of stock shares, market share, portfolio of products and services, rationalization of production and distribution, and company image and work conditions. Although the order and relative weight of their importance in any nation-by-nation comparison may be different, the list of objective categories is essentially the same. One 1985 source provides just such a comparison.[6] In achieving their objectives, each firm treats all competitors, both domestic and foreign, as equally threatening to its success. Consequently, as firms perform their role in free and open market competition, there appears to be little room for cooperation between them. Despite this view, however, many alliances do occur for many reasons, and these will include second source agreements, technology licensing, manufacturing agreements, and others.

To accomplish its goals each firm will attempt to best utilize its individual resources, namely, management and employees (people), processes and materials (technology), and its invested funds and fixed assets (capital). The outcomes for each individual firm resulting from this utilization determine its success and survival over time.

THE ROLE OF GOVERNMENT

With respect to the business environment, the role of government is to determine policies that will encourage the success of the nation's business firms while maintaining a balance between businesses' interests and those of the broader community. The community's interest lies in business being able to provide its needs without subjecting the community to adverse effects. The government attempts to balance business success and community satisfaction by the use of financial incentives or laws and regulations, as appropriate.

The policies of government that are generally related to corporations as well as individual citizens are listed as economic policies: fiscal, monetary, income distribution, foreign exchange policies, or regulatory policies, such as those related to health, education, or the natural environment. Other government policies directly and specifically related to industry in a global economic environment are technology, trade, investment, and competition policies.

Technology policy is most often directed toward high-tech industries, which are areas of intensive world competition due to high market growth rates. It covers specific technologies such as biotechnology, microelectronics, and others discussed in this book. Technology policy addresses R&D spending, intellectual property protection, and the supply of trained and educated engineers and scientists, as well as other factors. A recent technology policy issue is the relation of R&D activities of federal laboratories supervised by the Departments of Defense, Energy, Commerce, and Health, to commercial private enterprises.

Trade policy encompasses the issues resulting from imbalances in merchandise trade, the current account balance, predatory practices by foreign entities, regulated duties, quotas, and so on. Investment policy is concerned with the cost and availability of capital for corporate investment, as well as the associated savings rate. Investment policy relates, not only to domestic issues, but also to the regulations concerning foreign ownership and equity holdings. Different nations may treat inward foreign investment differently in a broad sense, and far more extensively than simply setting government rules and regulations. One example of a broad application of investment policy would be instances where local associations of retail stores in Japan block a foreign retailing investor from locating within their locale. Finally, competition policy is related to such matters as antitrust, corporate alliances, interlocking directorates, and utility services. Competition policy includes not only rules and regulations but also how aggressively they are to be enforced.

The role of government, therefore, is to see that business is provided with a set of policies in technology, trade, investment, and competition that meets the needs of business while maintaining the balance with community interests.

THE ROLE OF AN INDUSTRY

The roles of business corporations and government agencies are easier to define than that of an industry. While corporations and government agencies are legally constituted bodies, *industry* is a conceptual economic term. An industry in this context is a collection of firms producing common goods and services while operating within a government's jurisdiction. Firms and governments are legal entities with explicit responsibilities and privileges, whereas, an industry, as only a concept and a nonlegal entity, has no explicitly defined organizational responsibilities or privileges that are subject to review for accountability. The conduct and performance of an entire industry may be the subject of an economic study, but only the firms within an industry are subject to a judicial review and finding. The only means by which a collection of firms can even begin to establish a legal entity that attempts to be representative of an industry is through formation of an industry association. By so doing, firms can then begin to formulate the role of their association (industry), whether with legal implications or as a conceptual context.

The role of an industry as an economic concept can be defined as follows:[7]

1. Efficiently provide product and services that correspond to consumer demand.
2. Progressively add to the improvement of real income per capita by lowering the cost of goods while improving their quality and effectiveness through the full use of science and technology.
3. Fully employing its resources including property, plant, equipment, and especially its human resources, while at the same time not adversely affecting human health, the national habitat, or the earth's environment.
4. Equitably distribute its income among all stakeholders—management, employees, customers, suppliers, and investors.

Since no legal means exists for requiring the overall industry, to perform its role well, it can only be hoped that the individual firms' performance, when aggregated, will achieve the industry objectives. If not, the government will implement policies that, by incentive or enforcement, will result in acceptable industry performance. From either's viewpoint, that of the private corporation or the government agency, an incentive approach is a more welcome one than a regulatory one.

Another alternative, however, is to form an industry association as a legal entity and, through an industry-government partnership, attempt to define and assist in the achievement of the industry's performance goals and objectives. An important consequence of describing the role of industry is to develop a clearer picture of how the member firms and the government, in partnership, may satisfy both the objectives of business and the needs of the community.

Two simple examples will be helpful here. The progress of an industry can be accelerated when governmental steps are taken to accelerate the application of new technology. In partnership with industry, government can provide R&D tax credits, issue grants to industry technology consortia, and also encourage its federal laboratories to share efforts that are commercially applicable to groups of industry firms. All of these kinds of events have actually taken place. Another example relative to the full, nonwasteful, and nondestructive employment of its resources is in the regulation of workers' health in specific industries employing dangerous materials. The role of industry must be to not only fully employ its resources but also to assess the overall needs of all firms so that government and industry can reach appropriate guidelines for the protection of the health and safety of its employees and the conservation of environmental resources.

THE INTERMEDIATE SECTOR AND THE PRIMARY ASSOCIATION

The role of industry may be defined and assisted by an industry association. The association is not a business nor a manufacturing concern; neither does it perform the role of a government. Rather it is located in the middle space between private enterprise and public government agencies. The middle sector is neither a totally private entrepreneurial sector nor a governing public regulatory sector. It is partially both, yet totally neither. How, then, can an industry, which is not a legal entity, provide a form of structure for efficiently and effectively dealing with issues that may have both a private and a public impact, such as global competitiveness, health reform, or natural environmental controls? Only through the use of intermediate organizations, such as the industry trade associations, can issues be resolved that are neither totally private nor public.

It would be appropriate at this point to elaborate, using the semiconductor industry as an example, how the public, private, and intermediate sectors appear to be related. Examples can be constructed for other industries. However, there is an immediate caution which must be taken in reviewing this example. It does not show the degree of overlap between the private and public sector activities. The example in Table 13.1 shows the existence, but not the functions, of the intermediate organizations.

Table 13.1
Private, Public, and Intermediate Sectors as Related to the
U.S. Semiconductor Industry

Government/public	Intermediate	Firms/private
Inter-Agency	*Primary Association*	*Merchant Firms*
National Economic Council	SIA	Intel
National Security Council	*Industry Consortia*	Motorola
Agencies	SRC, SEMATECH	Texas Instruments
Depts of:	*Secondary Associations*	National Semiconductors
Commerce	AEA, EIA	Advanced Micro Devices (AMD)
Defense	*Related Associations*	Others
Energy	CBEMA, CSPP, Semiconductor Equipment and Materials International (SEMI)	*Corporate Parents of Internal Chip Divisions*
State		IBM
USTR	*Advisory Councils*	ATT
Council of Econ Advisors	NACS	Digital Equipment Corporation (DEC)
	NSTC	Hewlett-Packard (H-P)
	Research Institutes	Others
	Economic Strategy Institute	
	Council on Competitiveness	
	Informal Groups:	
	Officials: Congressional Support Group	
	Executives: Business Round Table	
	Associations: Electronic Round Table	
	Academic: Berkeley Roundtable for International Economics	

In Table 13.1 a number of characteristics are evident. The industry firms may be either merchant market firms, namely, their chip business involves selling to all customers in the marketplace; or internal suppliers, whose output is primarily used by other product divisions of their corporations. These captive internal divisions or firms may have ambivalent goals since they are suppliers to internal customers whose goals may not be the same as those of the merchant firm suppliers. The government agencies as part of the public sector affect policy with regard to the industry and generally include interagency organizations and cabinet departments.

The intermediate sector is surprisingly broad and includes primary, secondary, and parallel associations; research consortia; advisory councils; and informal groups. Unless the primary organization—the SIA in this example—can retain control and guidance of the overall intermediate sector effort, the resulting impact on government will be uncertain and even possibly counterproductive. For example, in the case of the SIA-sponsored U.S.-Japan Semiconductor Trade Agreement, between the U.S. government and the government of Japan, a failure to completely convince the computer firms, who were members of AEA and CBEMA, of the need for the agreement resulted in the formation of CSPP, which was dedicated explicitly to contain any negative impact of the agreement on the major U.S. computer firms. In another example related to semiconductor industry firms, alliances between them, inclusive of captives as well as merchants and foreign as well as domestic firms, may result in conflicts of interest before a consensus can be reached on trade policy. Finally, even within government, the Department of State, for example, may appear to be an impediment to U.S. trade policy since the state prefers to maintain good diplomatic relations rather than correct trade relationships with foreign governments. A correct State Department relationship in its broadest context is one that represents all American interests, including trade, defense, and environment, and not only those of so-called diplomatic relations.

Despite the lack of clear consensus between and within all sectors on any given aspect of a specific industry's global competitiveness, the fact is that organizations do exist to address this issue, as well as others. This is a necessary, but not sufficient, condition. In order to reach a consensus on the actions to be taken, the organizations must first assume appropriate roles, responsibilities, representation and, most important, positions and opinions. In this effort, the major driver of the intermediate group is the primary association—in this example, the SIA. The paramount government organization is the National Economic Council and the pertinent group of firms are the merchant firms. Although consensus among sectors must be attempted by all of them, the responsibility for the final resolution of any national- or global-specific industry issue must ultimately lie with the pertinent firms, the primary association, and the paramount government agency.

As one looks at the three sectors—private, public, and intermediate—each has specific characteristics in dealing with separate or joint problems. The public sector, namely government agencies, tends to be more stable, less moved by favoritism, able to broaden its scope, concerned for all interests, a regulator of specific actions, the manager of policy, and a bulwark against exploitation. The private sector appears best able to respond to changing circumstances, innovate, replicate success while abandoning failure, take risks, generate capital, and provide professional expertise and specific knowledge. By comparison, the intermediate sector can reach diverse parties, generate trust, remain committed, promote responsible behavior, and promote the broad industry role.[8] The behavior of the public agencies and the private firms can be modified through the efforts of the intermediate sector as each interacts with the other on various issues. Without an intermediate sector, the means of reaching closure on any given open issue of national, industry, or corporate well-being becomes tremendously more complex—and perhaps virtually unresolvable. The industry association, therefore, plays a crucial role in the solution of major issues such as American competitiveness in the growing global economy.

SUMMARY

American competitiveness, based on American firms and assisted through U.S. government actions, is very important to the country's citizens. In order to ensure that the actions required to maintain competitiveness are forthcoming, the use of intermediate organizations, and especially the primary industry association, is crucial. The complexity of the relationships between firms and government is such that the industry association is the most frequently used means to accomplish a consensus as to the actions and policies required. However, even the intermediate sector has a number of different organizations focusing on different areas, and these must be directed and guided to achieve the goals of the primary association and, consequently, the industry. The successful efforts of an industry's primary association are therefore key to its competitiveness. The structure and function of the primary association is also of extreme importance, which is the subject of the next chapter.

NOTES

1. Council on Competitiveness, *America's Competitive Crisis: Confronting the New Reality* (Washington, DC: Council on Competitiveness, April 1987).
2. "Report on the 1993 Industry Summit, World Economic Forum" (Massachusetts Institute of Technology with Harvard University, Cambridge, MA, 9–12 September 1993), 30.
3. Yao-Su Hu, "Global or Stateless Corporations Are National Firms with International Operations," *California Management Review* 34, no. 3 (Winter 1992): 107–126.
4. W. Leontieff, *The Structure of the American Economy*, 1919–1939, 2nd ed. (New York: Oxford University Press, 1951); W. Leontieff, *Input-Output Economics* (New York: Oxford University Press, 1966).
5. The 1985 Japan-U.S. Input-Output Table, December 1989, Research & Statistics Department, Minister's Secretariat, MITI, Japan.

6. James C. Abegglen and George Stalk, Jr., *Kaisha: The Japanese Corporation* (New York: Basic Books, 1985), 177.

7. F. M. Scherer and D. Ross, *Industrial Market Structure and Economic Performance*, 3rd ed. (Boston: Houghton Mifflin, 1990). The third point of the Scherer-Ross model has been modified to address safety, health, and the environment.

8. D. Osborne and T. Gaebler, *Reinventing Government* (New York: Penguin Group, 1993), 344–349.

Chapter 14

Forming and Focusing the Primary Association

ASSOCIATIONS IN CONFERENCE

Summer weather in northern Michigan can be delightful, and the area around Traverse City is studded with resorts and golf courses, making it a great place for summer relaxation. The Grand Traverse Resort is among the best vacation facilities in the area, and it was the site of the National Association of Manufacturers 1993 Association Council Annual Conference. Chief staff executives of over thirty associations were present for the three days of meetings, which included speeches from experts and roundtable discussions. The speakers had excellent reputations in the fields on which they spoke: namely, crisis management, quality management, product liability, and executive leadership. The most interesting part of the meeting was the series of roundtable discussions held on the last two days.

The Association Council of the National Association of Manufacturers (NAM) is made up of the chief staff executives of industry associations. The council has more than 100 members, and nearly one-third of them were in attendance at the conference. The subjects to be considered for four roundtable sessions of four subjects each were:

Session 1
- Quality Management and Continuous Improvement
- Grass-roots Organizations
- Dues Structure
- Conflict Management and Problem Individuals

Session 2
- Association Downsizing and Mergers
- Current Issues
- Education and Training Programs
- Saving Money

Session 3

• Industry Promotion Programs

• Prioritizing Issues

• Controlling Health Care Costs

• Evaluating Member Needs

Session 4

• Measuring Association Performance

• Mechanisms to Address State and Local Issues

• ISO 9000—International Quality Standards

• Association Benefit Plans

The thirty executives had selected the sessions that they would attend prior to the roundtable meetings. In order to help them decide, the conference booklet provided a description of the questions that the individual sessions would raise, but for brevity here, it is assumed that the subject titles shown above basically imply the kinds of questions discussed. The executives' choices per session were also shown in the conference booklet, and the comparison of the degree of interest by the number of expected attendees is a general indication of the concerns of the association executives in attendance.

The top subjects in each of the four separate sessions in order of highest interest were these:

• Measuring Association Performance

• Evaluating Members' Needs

• Current Issues

• Quality Management and Continuous Improvement

The proportion of associate executives waiting to learn from each other about measuring performance was over 40 percent of the attendees. This high interest level is indicative of the degree of concern for understanding how to measure association efforts. The second highest level of interest (one-third) was in evaluating members' needs. However, it was not clearly stated whether the individual member's needs would coincide with those of the industry. For example, would enough members state a need for an increased level of market share to translate into the industry's market share objectives, or were members' needs a more pedestrian one of lowering dues levels in order to reduce their costs? Current issues, the third topic of interest, could have led to a discussion of objectives (but did not). Rather, it led to a discussion of the regulatory issue of deductions of lobby expenses for tax purposes and a question as to whether an electronics bulletin board was useful. The last of the most important issues was quality management, which appeared to reflect this recent trend in management education.

On considering these attendance intentions, participating at a number of roundtables, and listening to the final summaries for each roundtable, a final conclusion can now be drawn here. Most associations are not clear as to their industry objectives, and even if they are, they are not certain how to evaluate or measure their performance. If this conclusion about the associations represented in Michigan is true, then why were they founded, how were they formed, and where are they focused?

AN ASSOCIATION CHARTER

American associations are usually formed by political entrepreneurs in reaction to a crisis or a need, as contrasted with the situation in Germany and Japan where the government, acting in the national interest, has often been the major association organizer. The American way maintains the traditions of private initiation, voluntary membership, and a choice of several representative groups. Therefore, American associations tend to be unstable, with uncertain membership, to duplicate each other's functions, to form "ad hoc" groups, and in essence to represent American pluralism. Industry associations in America also tend to have many of the characteristics of corporate America because of the entrepreneurial character of their members, despite the fact that a few observers believe that American associations at present have become more like government bureaucracies. One way of eliminating some of the unfavorable characteristics of trade associations is to instill stability through formal means upon the establishment of the association. There may be several ways of doing this, and one specific approach will be proposed here.

Today's organizational approach is to incorporate the association by applying state incorporation laws. This formality provides the status of a legal entity typical of those provided to industrial corporations. It does not, however, provide the kind of stability necessary for the committed collective pursuit of industrial global success. In addition, incorporation in a state does not allow any de facto form of national recognition for debating national public policy or fostering industry cooperation. In this sense, a state incorporation of a society of UFO watchers with national members has as many legal means of input into national public policy as industrial trade associations, while the economic well-being of the nation is far less dependent on the former than the latter. Moreover, national legislation on full employment or import tariffs and other specific economic measures are more closely related to trade associations representing industries than to many other forms of voluntary associations or consumer interest groups. Consequently, in addition to a state corporate charter, with the privileges and responsibilities it bestows, a federal association charter is needed, which bestows national responsibility and privileges as well. Not every association should have a federal charter any more than every bank should be a member of the Federal Deposit Insurance Corporation (FDIC). However, as the public knows there is a significant difference in the responsibilities and privileges of the member banks of this well-known public corporation, as contrasted to nonmember banks.

How would such a federal charter system work, and how would it benefit private firms as well as government agencies? An industry group, namely, a number of firms, forming an association, would apply to the appropriate department (possibly the Department of Commerce), for recognition as a properly constituted industry association. The application would include information as to the SIC code being represented; an estimate of the number of industry firms and their identities; the size of the industry in terms of shipments, production, employment, capital assets, imports, exports, and world share of market; a listing of other industry associations in the same or related fields; the bylaws or intended bylaws of the association; and other pertinent information. It would also include the names of nominees for the association board of directors, the initial dues schedule, names of any part-time or full-time executives of the association, and the intended mission objective and functions of the association. It is very important that the association also be able to show that it clearly represents an industry, in the sense that the members supply essentially the same products and are, therefore, market rivals and competitors; that the technology represented is critical to national interests; that global competition is prevalent in the industry; that foreign governments are active in policy issues affecting industry activities; and that other aspects provide a degree of exclusivity in the qualifications for memberships, for serving the national interests in global economic activity, and being worthy of the privilege of a charter. In addition, the application should propose the functions of government agencies that may, in time, be assumed by the association, in a manner consistent with government practices. As an example, association or industry data could be provided to agencies such as the U.S. Bureau of Economic Analysis for input-output tables, or in place of the Census of Manufacturers. Another example is that the association could provide environmental data of importance to a government agency such as the Environmental Protection Agency to aid in writing new regulations and environmental codes. In effect, the services of the association could include many now undertaken by government agencies, and in greater detail and accuracy, than is generally obtained by the government agencies attempting to act independently. As another example, the association could provide data on its industry's world share of market, its relative global position in technology, and its capacity in relation to other world competitors. In essence, it can provide the data necessary for public policy purposes in a timely and precise manner. Finally, and most important, each chartered association would become a partner with government in determining public policy affecting its specific industry or an intended set of interrelated industries. It would also reduce the number of personnel in the government bureaucracy since industry associations could more effectively perform some of their functions.

In return, the federal government would grant a tax credit or deduction to the member firms, for not only their dues but any direct costs borne by corporations in supporting the association and its activities as they can be related to public policy support. In addition, grants could also be made to the association itself for services provided. For example, industry association offices located in foreign countries to support trade could receive grants for financial support. Any association formed through the usual state corporation laws but without a federal charter would not be allowed to deduct any dues or contributions, in cash or in kind, for tax reasons. Federal charters will not be granted to another association of firms in the same industry if one already exists and performs the activities for which it has been chartered. Exclusivity will apply in the case of federally chartered associations. Any attempt of a group to apply for a charter for a broad set and large number of firms covering many SIC codes, such as the AEA, would only have a charter granted if conditions were met for each SIC code within its membership, as if each were a standalone, chartered association. For example, the general SIC code for electronics is 36; however, if every SIC code within the general code were counted, there would exist over twenty categories. In such a case, an application for a federal charter by AEA to the responsible federal agency would require that AEA provide the necessary informational and corporate aspects of the charter for each SIC code considered to be of strategic importance for national public policy. As an alternative, AEA could apply to be a secondary association, which is made up of individual associations and firms that do not wish to belong or fit any one industry segment. Such a secondary organization can only operate to assist in forming a consensus, but it could not represent a specific segment whose objective might appear to conflict with other segments. The CSPP, on the other hand, could easily, with some modification, fit the requirements for a federal charter.

If a firm is a multidivisional corporation involved in many businesses, each division would be a member of its industry association, as defined by a SIC code. If the total corporation wanted to join an association it should apply to the National Association of Manufacturers (NAM), where manufacturing is the category and which is, therefore, a function-based organization rather than one representing a product or technology segment. As an example, General Motors in total may belong to NAM, but its various product companies or divisions such as its car divisions (Cadillac, Pontiac, etc.), its locomotive division (Electro Motive Div.), its electronic division (Hughes), or its appliance division (Frigidaire) would belong to the appropriate SIC-code industry association. Although General Motors in total could belong to NAM or to the U.S. Chamber of Commerce, the Business Roundtable, or any other functional or broadly based association it chooses, these latter types of associations would not be able to apply for a federal charter represented by a product- or technology-specific association since the overall interests are broader than can be accommodated within an industrially driven public policy structure. The arrangement of overall and divisional memberships would solve many of the dilemmas faced by corporation managements and government agencies in reaching appropriate public policy decisions for specific industry groupings. At the same time that issues related to specific product-related associations are handled as chartered, overall corporate issues related to broad general public policies, for large multidivisional corporations could be expressed through the NAM, the U.S. Chamber of Commerce, or the Business Roundtable. The CEOs of these larger conglomerates could also express their independent corporation opinion as they do today as individual CEOs. With regard to groups of firms that wish to establish associations that are not federally chartered, they may continue to do so; however, they will lose tax benefits, the advantage of close, cooperative relationships with government, the recognition as an industry spokesperson with government bodies, and other possible aspects of government-industry partnerships, such as cooperative agreements in research and development with government laboratories and government grants that partially support technology consortia. However, in order to maintain a charter, an association must, within an agreed-upon period of time, be able to attract to its membership at least two-thirds of its industry's output as member firms. If it fails to do so, it will not be able to represent its industry, or to maintain its federal charter. The installation of a federal charter system for an association with large production representation will, therefore, allow for the structure and means of achieving consensus while making its members key participants in formulating public policy.

By the establishment of a federal charter system, standoffs can be partially avoided. As examples, the gridlock within the Aerospace Industries Association involving aircraft subsidies, and the long and often heated discussions between computer makers, as members of AEA, and chip makers, as members of AEA and SIA, could be avoided and resolutions to problems could be reached sooner. The Biotechnology Industry Association, which may face a third reorganization due to its current diversity, will be able to determine that its manufacturers are the key members of the association, as opposed to other interested groups. Moreover, associations with limited roles will be forced to question their existence since they would not truly represent an industry. For example, CBEMA, which is primarily a standards organization today, would not have a federal charter based on its limited functions and membership. Instead, its members would have to identify themselves within a more appropriate association. In another example, SEMI, whose primary function is to conduct international trade exhibitions for its foreign and domestic members, would not be recognized as a charter organization as long as this function is its largest and most important function, and foreign members sit on its board of directors. However, and importantly in this case, SEMI and other groups could continue to be formed and exist as non-chartered associations.

A question that may be asked, however, is, "Won't a federal charter system result in a rigid system of associations?" It could do so, but it would not if the proper safeguards are in place. One of these safeguards is that corporations would still be free to set up associations that are not federally chartered. In addition, the membership of any association would have the right every few years (perhaps four), to vote on the renewal of an application for a federal charter, and the government would have the right, with appropriate steps, to rescind the charter. Industries no longer deemed strategic may be dropped as a federal charter association yet remain in existence and of importance to their industry as a non-chartered organization. There are ways to allow the system to change as circumstances and conditions change. The final result, however, would be a core set of federally chartered associations representing strategic manufacturing or processing industries, while ancillary associations could continue to exist but would not be the focus of American public policy that is directed at strategic industries.

Another question that may be asked about the use of a federal charter approach to primary associations is whether there is any precedence for the use of a federal charter. Federal charters for national corporations already exist, and the most well known are the public corporations for banks, such as the Federal Deposit Insurance Corporation. Among other national organizations, noncommercial groups such as the Red Cross and the U.S. Olympics Organization have federal recognition. Agricultural organizations with heavy federal influence have existed for many decades, and states such as California have allowed the formation of mandatory marketing organizations supported by state funds. Federal and state charters for specific cooperative efforts that are neither completely private nor public have been awarded in the past, and therefore, the use of a federal charter for primary industry-specific associations is not totally out of the experience of past public-private cooperative organizations.

FOCUSING THE ASSOCIATION

Most associations have published a mission statement that summarizes their major objectives. The National Association of Manufacturers has even published a booklet of mission statements formulated by various specific associations. Some statements in this booklet comprise only a few sentences while others are several pages long. Of the sixty mission statements in the NAM booklet, which represent associations as different from each other as the Synthetic Organic Chemical Manufacturers Association and the Waterbed Manufacturers Association, the shortest and perhaps most relevant in today's global economy is that of the American Gear Manufacturers Association (AGMA). The simple mission statement of AGMA is "to assist its members in competing more effectively in today's global marketplace."[1] If this association represents American firms, then its mission comes as close as any in representing, in an abbreviated form, an industry's American competitiveness. After stating a suitable association mission, an association must next ask about the objectives, functions, processes, activities, and resources that are necessary for an effective association's role in accomplishing its mission.

The objectives of an association fall into three categories: organizational, national, and global. Among the organizational objectives of an association are those related to maintaining membership, revenues, staff personnel, public information, communications, statistics, and other activities that are related to the maintenance of an organizational structure.

The second set of objectives necessary to achieve the association's competitive mission are those related to national or domestic activities and policies. These objectives may be those concerned with federal and state regulations such as antitrust, environmental, safety and health, product approval, taxes, lobbying, political contributions, product and liability standards, manufacturing and processing standards, building codes, restricted use of manufacturing equipment, and many others. Other national objectives, which are unrelated to government, include trade exhibitions, product standards for applications, and other cooperative industry efforts that increases its market presence.

Finally, and most important for high-tech industries in today's global market environment, are those objectives that are related to American competitiveness as measured primarily by market share. These objectives are industry objectives in the global market. Two indications of their importance are that American high-tech industry sales outside the United States are about 50 percent of their total sales and that 70 percent of the wages bill of these global industries is incurred inside the United States. In addition, any list of company standings in the high-tech global marketplace would include firms, not only from the United States, but also from among all its global foreign competitors. Global competition is the foremost competition facing state-of-the-art, high-tech firms. The global objectives of an American high-tech industry must include world share of market as well as the expansion of share in closed foreign markets, technological leadership, capital availability, knowledgeable workers and professionals, and relationships with U.S. government agencies.

It should be noticed that these three classes of objectives—organizational, national, and global—are not the same as the classification of association activities as surveyed by the NAM (shown in Chapter 4) and called "traditional" and "government relations." There is also no attempt here to treat government as separate from corporations with regard to achieving the industry and association mission. The two sectors—private and public—must work together through the intermediate organization, namely, the association, in order to accomplish a mission that will have resulting consequences of benefit to the nation, as well as to the individual firms. It should be noted also that as the objectives expand from organizational to national and then global, the role of government becomes more important in the industry's ability to remain competitive. A systematic treatment of the objectives mentioned here may help in making this point clearer.

If one examines Table 14.1 in light of the activities of a number of associations, it becomes apparent that any association that focuses on organizational objectives, objectives, such as placing a tremendous effort on increasing membership above to all, has little effect on global competitiveness through this activity alone. Membership drives perpetuate the organization and meet the organizational objective. However, these type of organizational objectives are not an end in themselves but rather are necessary for the proper representation and functioning of an association in order to achieve the industry's national and global objectives.

Table 14.1
Specific Objectives by Class

Class of Objective	Specific Objectives
Organizational	Membership
	Financial
	Staff Management
	Public Information
	Legal Requirements
	Industry Statistics
	Exhibition Management
	Committee Management
	Coordination of Activities
	Staff and Member Benefits
	Others
National	Health and Safety Activities
	Environmental Activities
	Product Liability Activities
	Manufacturing Standards
	Others
Global	Market Share
	Capital Availability
	Technology Leadership
	Human Resources
	Government Partnerships
	Others

The second set of objectives (those that are national) are those that the industry performs primarily in order to efficiently meet the product needs of its home country customers and the regulatory needs of the nation's citizens. For example, the implementation of manufacturing standards will eventually reduce costs to the consumer, while product liability standards will also help protect the customer from harm. Product quality standards will also be of benefit to the customer, who thus can be better assured of product satisfaction. All the national objectives are focused on the demands of the customer and the benefits to the nation's citizens as part of the industry's responsibility to them. There may be a domestic share of market objective here in the sense that a domestic industry may be made up of competing firms of U.S. nationality as well as subsidiaries of corporations with foreign nationalities. Domestic share however, is part of the global share objective. However, with regard to other national objectives, both types of firms—indigenous ones or subsidiaries of foreign corporations—are subject to common goals and restraints. It is on this basis that associations often allow domestic subsidiaries of foreign firms to be members of some American association committees and activities. For example, when a U.S. government agency such as EPA sets up regulations for all domestically based manufacturing firms, its regulations are imposed both on subsidiaries of foreign firms and on American firms. It behooves both kinds of firms to work with the EPA to determine the most appropriate degree of regulation. Consequently, there are two ways in which foreign firms located in the United States can be considered with regard to association activities and objectives. First, foreign subsidiaries can be association members only to the degree that their input and activities are restricted to domestic issues and not the broader global objectives; and second, foreign firms have no choice and therefore must be involved at this level if their activities affect the well-being of American consumers and citizens within U.S. boundaries. However, when the well-being of the nation is related to the global marketplace, then the inclusion of foreign firms within a chartered association that recommends national policy with respect to trade or technology should be discouraged.

The real wages, income, and profits of Americans, as individuals or as corporate entities, are not subject to domestic conditions alone. These measures, which are the essential heart of America's competitiveness and well-being, are based to an ever greater degree on events in the global marketplace. The global objectives are, therefore, of even greater importance than national objectives alone. Global economic competition has replaced the military and diplomatic warfare of the Cold War years. The key global objectives of an American industry are world share of market, technological leadership, capital cost and availability, knowledgeable and motivated human resources, and supportive government actions and partnerships. The association's role is to assist the industry in achieving these objectives. The type of assistance that associations may provide include promoting government-to-government negotiations in order to open markets, reducing foreign subsidies, or finding common ground in filing for patent applications. The association can assist in the formation of technology roadmaps, as with the aerospace or semiconductor industries; create research consortia, as in the components industries; or seek a quasi-public corporation for the funding of export sales or in obtaining government grants and loans for specific dual-use technology purposes. The human resources aspect of competition can also be addressed as it was by the Semiconductor Research Corporation when over 600 graduate engineers and scientists, who were grounded in solid-state technology, were eventually provided to the industry by the SRC consortia. The favorable end result may be similar to that in semiconductors where world leadership was recovered by an American industry that had been counted out just a few years ago.

Objectives, including the three given here—organizational, national, and global—must have metrics of performance. To provide objectives and goals that cannot be evaluated by quantitative measures would be meaningless. All the general objectives given in Table 14.1 can be given metrics to measure performance and, in many cases, they have already been applied.

The three classes of objectives (in Table 14.1) were positioned in the order of greatest scope and impact. Global objectives are of greater importance than national objectives, which in turn are of greater importance than organizational objectives. However, each also builds on the other. The hierarchy of importance is related to the direct benefit, as measured in real wages, income, and profits for Americans. Moreover, these three classes are not completely seperate and mutually exclusive. For example, if association membership were to include domestic captive and merchant firms, as well as foreign firms, all with equal voting rights, it is possible that the association's attempt to formulate national antitrust policy objectives could be impossible. This nonresolution of an antitrust issue could compromise a global market share objective and the association would be gridlocked at a position unfavorable to the industry. The importance of achieving consensus in a timely manner cannot be sufficiently emphasized.

It is the responsibility of the highest-level control group of an association, its board of directors, to determine the objective of the association and the roles of its members in attaining them. It is to this subject that the following discussion is directed.

THE ASSOCIATION BOARD OF DIRECTORS

The key policy-making body in American associations is the board of directors. Too often, a board is made up of middle-management executives who have been long-term committee members. (Examples involving the boards of CBEMA and AEA are given in Chapter 10.) Sometimes board members are corporate staff specialists with minimal understanding of the firm's overall business strategy or its industry structure. At times, their only experience with the firm has been in government or external relations or as public relations executives. Despite their best efforts, no group of middle-management executives can truly represent a firm in association board meetings. The best, and perhaps the only, suitable member of any association board of directors is the chief executive officer in cases in which the firm is totally dedicated to the industry that their association represents, or for vertically integrated firms, the highest executive officer of the corporate division that is within the association's industry. Only these chief executives should sit at the board table, and no substitute or alternate be allowed to represent them. The CSPP (described in Chapter 10) has such a rule, and it is perhaps the most effective of all the associations described in being able to reach policy conclusions and to submit them to the highest governmental level in the United States, the president and the White House. Another important aspect of the board of directors is its size. The AEA has over fifty board members, and in order to accommodate an effective decision-making process, it has resorted to the use of a much smaller executive committee which recommends actions to the board for ratification. This governance structure raises the question as to who is really in control—the board or the executive committee.

The governance duties of the board of directors are the most important that can be applied in the association's definition and achievement of its objectives. This also means that association board members must devote a major portion of their time—perhaps as much as 5 to 10 percent—to industry affairs. To devote less would probably result in subcritical performance or the choice of objectives with little meaning requiring very little executive effort. In either case, the results will not be satisfactory. The most important reason to have the highest-level industry executives sitting on the board is the fact that their association's obligations are essential to the industry and too important to be left to lesser corporate authorities. Only the CEO carries the burden of responsibility and the risk-reward perspective that are essential when considering public policy initiatives.

The chairman of the board is generally elected from among the directors to the senior position and is a corporate executive, not a paid, full-time employee of the association staff. The chief staff executive, who is usually called president or executive director of the association, is generally the full-time, paid manager of the association staff and offices. That person should also be a voting member of the board and its chief spokesperson for specific issues unless a board member volunteers to take that role. The role of the president of an association requires knowledge of the industry it represents, the capability of a corporate executive and officer, the skills of a diplomat, and the strength and courage to take a stand among conflicting issues. As George Lodge has stated, "It is no job for a wimp!"[2]

The major role of the board of directors is to determine the policies and the objectives of the association. The first policy document of the association is its bylaws, which is the legal document that provides governance. These bylaw rules generally cover subjects that include qualifications for membership, directors, and officers; and requirements for records, committees, indemnification, fiscal matters, amendments, and meetings.

The second order of importance, if it is not given in the bylaws, is a statement of the objectives of the association. These objectives are the basic reason for the group's existence. They must be categorized into those that are organizational, national, and global. Without these clear-cut objectives being articulated and accepted, differences in views will continue to occur and stymie the progress of the association in the industry. Upon determination of the objectives, which are generally reviewed on a routine, or as-needed, basis, the board can move forward toward delineating the activities of the association so that the private, public, and intermediate organizations can move toward achieving the industry objectives.

THE DIRECTORS AS INDIVIDUALS

The free market system, within which private parties perform their economic transactions, has a unique set of elements. These are self-interest, competitive behavior, profits as the reward, operating principles such as productivity and efficiency, and the free choices of participants, namely, producers, investors, employees and, above all, the customers. The free market system is the concept within which the private-sector American corporate executives perform their major roles. The CEOs of corporations, although members of an association board of directors, still keep their corporate interests first in their mind. Their fellow association directors are still their marketplace competitors, not only domestically but also globally. Each director will consider every association decision, not only in the light of the industry, but also in terms of the effect it will have on his or her company. The transactions of the firm must now not only include the economic transactions of private marketplace, but also the political transactions that take place when reaching the association's final position in regard to its industry objectives. The only board member who has no single company interest and whose position is company-neutral (but industry-directed) is the association's chief staff officer, whose role it is to attempt to balance the board's positions in cases in which it appears to primarily serve the self-interests of a few of the firms represented there, and not the overall association membership. This is a difficult position for any hired staff executive unless given some degree of independence. The means to accomplish this may be varied and difficult. To not fill this role, however, leaves the staff executive to behave as a mere functionary, a role not conducive to the appropriate leadership that is often required.

SUMMARY

The legal foundation on which associations are founded should be modified so that when a strategic industry is identified, it can be properly organized for a national partnership with government. This partnership will have responsibilities and benefits for both the industry, as represented by the association, and the public, as represented by the appropriate government agencies.

The designated associations, being of essential importance to economic security, should have an appropriate set of goals that encompass global competitiveness as well as national issues and organizational requirements. These associations should be governed by a board of directors of the highest industry level and managed by a strong staff executive.

NOTES

1. National Association of Manufacturers, *NAM Mission Statements Booklet* (Washington, DC: National Association of Manufacturers, n.d.).

2. George C. Lodge, *Perestroika for America: Restructuring U.S. Business-Government Relations for Competitiveness in the World Economy* (Boston: Harvard Business School Press, 1990), 148.

Chapter 15

Alliances and Consortia

THE DOOMSAYER AND THE CHAMPION

It was May 1986 and the SIA was holding its spring conference and board of directors meeting in Boston, Massachusetts. At the morning conference session, the most controversial speaker of the day, Charles Ferguson, delivered a speech that shocked an audience made up primarily of American semiconductor company executives. Ferguson was considered a bright, young, academic star at Massachusetts Institute of Technology (MIT). He also claimed to have worked for IBM before joining the academic world. With an attitude that almost seemed contemptuous of his audience, Ferguson stated that under the present circumstances facing the American merchant semiconductor industry—and he did not expect those to change—the American industry was doomed to extinction by its Japanese competitor within five years. It would remain for the very large, integrated American electronics corporations with captive, internal microelectronics operations to maintain any semblance of a presence in microelectronics production for the United States. The mantle of American technological and commercial leadership in chips must fall to IBM, AT&T, Digital Equipment Corporation (DEC), Hewlett-Packard (H-P), and others of their kind. Although the same message had been voiced by others, no one had delivered it as forcefully and condescendingly as Charles Ferguson did that day in Boston.

Ferguson, of course, seemed to have all the industry facts in his favor. Japan had taken control of the DRAM business and was on its way to becoming the largest chip maker and producer in the world. All the actions taken by the U.S. merchant chip makers had failed thus far to blunt the Japanese juggernaut. The American executives left that meeting in a somber mood and convened their board of directors meeting a few hours later.

The board meeting was chaired by Gary Tooker, then president of Motorola's Semiconductor Products Sector (and now CEO of Motorola Inc.). After the usual formalities, the board's conversation turned to Ferguson's comments, and after some discussion two industry members voiced a common concern. George Scalise of Advanced Micro Devices (AMD) and Charlie Sporck of National Semiconductor (NSC) zeroed in on what they believed to be a major American weakness relative to Japan. The major weakness they expressed concerned the manufacturing capability of American merchant chip makers. There was no question in their minds that American designers and marketers could out-compete their Japanese counterparts. It was in manufacturing that Japanese expertise was the most threatening. The outcome of the discussion was that Charlie Sporck, an industry executive with a reputation as a manufacturing specialist, was chartered to determine what could be done to improve manufacturing excellence in the American semiconductor industry.

Several months later, in September, Sporck reported to the SIA board that he had found broad support for some sort of cooperative effort to improve manufacturing excellence within the semiconductor industry. Sporck listed the greatest challenges facing such an effort, including obtaining a working commitment from the participants, funding, staffing, and government participation. The board then agreed to form a committee to meet in late October or November for the purposes of defining objectives, establishing a charter, defining a structure, and assessing potential funding. By November, further progress was presented and by March of 1987 the project had a name, SEMATECH, for SEmiconductor MAnufacturing TECHnology. More important, in establishing the consortium, the SIA board of directors passed some key resolutions, which read as follows:

The SIA would establish a consortium of U.S. semiconductor manufacturers that was structured to include:

- an applied development facility to carry out:

    next-generation development of process, product, tools, and manufacturing science;

    equipment development by and with U.S. suppliers; and

    flexible manufacturing development activity;

- a low-volume manufacturing facility to prove concepts and verify performance;
- establishment of an interface for information exchange on high-volume results of these new concepts when installed in members' facilities; and
- activity to coordinate, cooperate, and advise in research projects and information exchange with universities and federal government–funded/sponsored facilities.

The subsequent board meetings of May and June 1987 covered SEMATECH items that involved the establishment of task forces, member dues and sign-ups, financial plans, obtaining government participation, antitrust rulings, and the search for the SEMATECH CEO and chief operating officer (COO).

The final decision made by the SIA board, on June 5, 1987 (just a little more than one year after the Ferguson speech in Boston), at a meeting in Tokyo, Japan, was that the board would act as the interim board of directors of SEMATECH and that the SIA and SEMATECH board meetings would be held separately. SEMATECH was now afloat under its own power and with a knowledgeable crew aboard.

American industry-led industrial policy had just taken one giant step forward as a strategic, but threatened, national industry formed a consortium with the purpose of improving America's global competitiveness by raising the level of its manufacturing capability.

ALLIANCES

Interfirm alliances have existed as long as American company records have been maintained. The alliances of the late nineteenth century in the United States were held to be illegal in many cases, and the antitrust laws and regulations of later years restricted the types of alliances that could be legally formed. These regulated types of domestic alliances have continued to be formed ever since. However, with the emergence of globalization, alliances have tended to occur between firms of different nationality to a greater degree than ever before. In high-tech industries, particularly since 1950, alliances have been formed, not only between two or more American companies, but also between American companies and the foreign companies of Japan, Germany, France, Italy, the United Kingdom, Korea, and most of the industrialized countries of the world.

The number of alliances between companies in several high-tech fields have been the subject of various papers and reports, one of which indicated that the number of strategic technology alliances per year in the computer industry grew from about ten alliances per year in 1980 to almost forty by 1989; moreover, in microelectronics, the number of alliances born in the same time period grew from twenty to forty. In software, the numbers were even greater—from less than ten to eighty in number.[1] In biotechnology, the number of alliances between 46 U.S. companies and European and Asian companies totaled 161.[2] The fact that there are a large number of multinational alliances in high-technology industries emphasizes the global nature of corporate business activity. These alliances are often based on the mutual cooperation of firms to jointly develop processes, products, markets, and physical facilities.

Not only do the number of international alliances appear to reinforce the concept of a "borderless world" in regard to business, but they tend to be used by observers as evidence that the globalization of industry eventually allows transnational corporations to superimpose their policies upon those of the individual nations in which they operate. The OECD has stated that new alliances focused on R&D and technology grew from about 150 in the mid-1920s to about 2000 annually by the end of the 1980s. Those alliances that were based on development, production, and marketing reached 750 new agreements in 1987 to 1989. A report by the Organization for Economic Cooperation and Development (OECD) stated that alliances are most common in automobiles, electronics, computers, telecom equipment, aerospace, and semiconductors. Interestingly, three of these mentioned are three of the four high-tech industries addressed in Part 3 of this book.[3] Because of the breadth and number of alliances, some observers believe that no form of cooperative effort beyond this mode, such as might be called an association or consortium, are necessary for improving competitiveness. This may be true for many alliances in that the firms involved do gain in competitiveness; however, if the firms are from different countries, no certain conclusions can be drawn as to which country gains the most. For example, in the 1960s and 1970s, many agreements, alliances, and joint ventures were formed in the electronics industry between Japanese and American companies. It should be no surprise to find that many would agree that by the end of the 1980s Japan had gained far more as a nation from alliances than had the United States, although individual American companies may claim that they gained equally from these international alliances. The conclusion that one draws from this logic is that although interfirm alliances may be useful, or even essential, for individual firms, they do not automatically raise the overall level of a national industry. In fact, the Japanese partners in any alliance are probably better organized, not only to utilize the gains internally, but to also share their knowledge within their country through the use of government partnerships and their many forms of associations. Therefore, the contributions of interfirm alliances to national competitiveness, at least in the United States, have not appeared to be a substitute for associated action by many American firms.

However, American high-tech associations should not oppose the pursuit of alliances by member firms. They should, in fact, support their individual members by helping in the strengthening of the contractual obligations of alliances, with the result that American firms will obtain the promised technological knowledge, market results, or operational capability in a timely manner. One approach that federally chartered associations should employ is to catalogue, categorize, and attempt to evaluate the interfirm alliances and the diffusion of knowledge and skills that are the outcomes of the agreements. In this way, interfirm alliances can be evaluated as to their contribution to industry competitiveness overall. The U.S. government publishes no analyses of this kind for any commercial industry.

Alliances can be used to raise or stymie a country's level of competitiveness relative to that of other nations if alliances are treated strategically. The unwillingness to form alliances with the firms of some nations while pursuing them with those of other nations certainly appears to have been a national policy for Japan. For these reasons, associations that claim alliances are merely a private matter are ignoring them as significant factors of American competitiveness and falling short of their industry responsibility. In fact, the industry associations should welcome the responsibility of data collection with regard to alliances as part of their federal charter.

CONSORTIA

While interfirm alliances have long been part of the industrial economy, the development of the concept of consortia is more recent, especially when they are considered as technology organizations intended to improve an industry's competitiveness. Although some consortia of firms existed prior to 1982, the major growth in the number of industry consortia occurred after that time. It has been reported that 123 consortia covering a broad set of industries had registered under the 1984 National Cooperative Research Act (NCRA) by 1989.[4] (This act was discussed in Chapter 3.) The act was put in place so that companies could cooperate in precompetitive research with protection from prosecution under U.S. laws. By so doing, companies could better collaborate to pool their resources for purposes of research and development. A frequently cited example of a successful American consortium is SEMATECH, the organization whose formation was described at the beginning of this chapter. However, this consortium had several characteristics that distinguished it from virtually all the other consortia already in place. Prior to the founding of SEMATECH, other consortia were made up of a few private firms only, with no government funding; moreover, their concentration was on applied research rather than on development, and they did not focus on a specific strategic industry. By contrast, SEMATECH was shielded by antitrust action under NCRA; included firms, both merchant and captive, that represented over two-thirds of the U.S. industry; was 50 percent funded by government grants but not led by government; focused on manufacturing technology rather than product development or pure research; and was organized specifically to raise the level of American competitiveness in response to a highly competent foreign rival. It was also a step in creating advantage in a global competition rather than having natural resources and an imperfect marketplace determine comparative advantage between two countries. SEMATECH was also the first step in an American industry-led industrial policy. The United States has had industrial policies with regard to railroads, agriculture, housing, air transport, and other areas, but this was the first time that industrial policy was intended to affect global competition. With SEMATECH as an example and as background to the remainder of this discussion, an explanation of what a consortium should do, and how it should do so, is now in order.

SEMATECH, as well as an earlier consortium known as the Semiconductor Research Corporation (SRC), were initially organized and funded by the SIA, and both consortia to this day are governed, directly or indirectly, by the SIA board member companies. Consequently, it can be truly said that they are industry-led. Second, they have specific objectives that work to the benefit of virtually all the firms in the industry. The university research conducted by SRC and the manufacturing technology developed in SEMATECH are applicable to the breadth of the chip industry and, in some cases, to other electronics industries such as the manufacturing of flat panel displays. In truth, the semiconductor production equipment industry, through its firms and a special organization called

Semi-SEMATECH, are closely aligned with SEMATECH. This is as it should be since manufacturing technology, by definition, must include manufacturing equipment. It is also true that the newly developed equipment will be available to all industry firms, whether or not they were members of SEMATECH.

Government participation is also an important element, not only in terms of funding, but in terms of the credibility given to the consortia. In addition, SEMATECH was structured as a nonprofit organization with full-time employees as well as loaned engineers from industry companies. Objectives were clearly stated and milestones were established. All these key elements were part of the successful SEMATECH equation.

Abstracting from the experience of SEMATECH, Microelectronic Computer Technology Corporation, SRC, and others, a list of the necessary elements of successful consortia can be drawn up as follows:

1. Sponsorship and oversight by the primary industry association in order to satisfy the industry-led criteria.

2. A set of objectives encompassing enabling technologies and processes of broad benefit to the industry and not narrow goals such as specific products. Another related objective should be the determination of foreign dependency for key areas.

3. Membership that should be as closely coincident with that of the primary association as possible and should include internal manufacturers as well as merchant firms, but association nonmembers should be able to join if they wish.

4. The involvement of government in terms of a partner, but not as an active working participant or a contractor.

5. Funds from industry that should be sufficient to accomplish the tasks, and not merely a token means of support.

6. Management for the consortia with the technological skills and the professional talent necessary for success as well as initial credibility.

7. Consortia structure that should be operated as a horizontal organization, namely, a networked informational flow organization, rather than a hierarchical task-directed one.

In summary, the consortia should be industry-led; state objectives explicitly, obtain broad industry membership, have a partnership with government, have sufficient funds equal to the completion of the objectives, have key management skills, and, finally, operate as a networked-information flow organization. These elements will contribute to successful operation of any industry consortium involved in raising the level of its industry's competitiveness.

BEYOND THE ALLIANCES AND CONSORTIA

Although interfirm alliances often focus on products and processes, while consortia focus on generic precompetitive technology, neither type of arrangement, either alone or together, provides the full scope of an industry's technology progress. One of industry's roles, as distinct from the roles of a firm or government, is progress, and although alliances and consortia contribute to progress, they may not include its entire technological scope. In order to encompass the entire scope of progress in the technological sense, the concept of a technology roadmap was developed by several associations. Among them are the Aerospace Industries Association (as described in Chapter 7), the Semiconductor Industry Association Technology Roadmap (as described in Chapter 9), and a more recent roadmap developed by the IPC and published in 1993.[5] Again, the associations—the AIA and SIA—are the central organizations in the development of roadmaps to guide an industry's technology progress.

In encompassing the entire scope of progress through the use of the technology roadmap, organizations other than the alliances and consortia must be brought into play. These organizations include the university laboratories, various research institutes, and the federal laboratories. When participants from these groups are brought together with technologists from the corporations and the consortia, all can effectively contribute to the final roadmap plan and its work plans. The overall coordination and implementation of a technology roadmap consisting of participants from all groups lies with the primary association.

One aspect of technology progress that must not be forgotten, and cannot be minimized, involves breakthroughs by individual engineers start-up companies. The inventions of the integrated circuit and the microprocessor, the development of biotechnology's pioneering products, and the development of the personal computer would most likely *not* have been able to come from alliances, consortia, or roadmaps. Most of the cooperative approaches tend to be incremental and have made great strides, but thus far, the great breakthrough inventions have been developed not through large cooperative organizations but through independent corporations.

JOINT MANUFACTURING

Most recently, Congress passed legislation that allows firms to jointly manufacture products without being charged with violating the antitrust codes of the United States. However, there are great pitfalls in forming joint manufacturing organizations. Quite often, manufacturing facilities are costly and, although the partners gain by sharing the property, plant, and equipment costs, their distribution of product output and the corresponding unit costs of product manufacturing are not so easily divided. If the demand for product output is not forthcoming or uniform across the requirements of all partners, which firms should pay for the underutilized capacity? Moreover, if the joint facility were to produce an amount greater than aggregate demand of the partners, who should pay for the excess? If product demanded by one partner is distinct from other demands, how should the production development be paid? If market demand is shifting, how should each partner's interests be considered? As the concept of the consortium shifts from basic research to applied research and development to joint manufacturing, the problems change dramatically and a learning process may need to take place, which may not be successful and, in fact, may be more costly than the total cost of establishing separate manufacturing facilities for each intended partner. An example of a failed attempt to establish a joint manufacturing corporation was U.S. Memories, whose story was told in other works on consortia.[6]

GOVERNMENT PARTNERSHIPS IN CONSORTIA

One of the elements of successful consortia is listed as government partnership, but so far there has been little description of what this could mean. A description of this government partnership participation would, therefore, be useful in designing new consortia.

First, the government and its agencies, by their very institutional character, lend credibility to any consortium in that the government believes it sufficiently important to become involved. Government, therefore, provides legitimacy. Further, the government can properly assess the consortium and its objectives with regard to other policy matters of technology, trade, and investment, in which it is continually involved. For example, a multilateral trade negotiation such as GATT may involve a discussion of national subsidies for technology. Without an involvement by the U.S. government in consortia, the government would lack the benefit of valuable experience in how to deal with this issue. Another aspect of government is the activities of government agencies and national laboratories, such as Sandia National Laboratories of the Department of Energy or the National Institute Science and Technology in the Department of Commerce. The government partnership allows an information flow in both directions, to the advantage of government activities as well as consortia activities. The government can also be a supplier of supplemental resources such as funds, personnel, and studies, as well as a coordinator of industry, laboratories, universities, investors, and foreign interests. Government can provide oversight that consortia are operating in the national as well as private interests; that the ongoing benefits are spread equitably; and that no one participant is taking undue influence.

Overall, government partnership provides legitimacy, coordination with other policies, two-way information flow to agencies, supplemental resources, and oversight.

SUMMARY

In high-tech global competition, the phenomenon of alliances and consortia has become widespread. If these new partnership arrangements are to contribute to American competitiveness, they must be treated in a way that their contribution is of great value relative to the costs and efforts expended. The elements of successful consortia have been enumerated, and the data collection and analysis of private interfirm alliances by primary associations has also been suggested. These aspects of alliances and consortia may prove to be essential—and substantial—contributors to American competitiveness.

NOTES

1. John Hagedoom and Joseph Schakenraad, "Leading Companies and Networks of Strategic Alliances in Information Technologies," Research Policy 21, no. 2 (April 1992): 163–190.

2. U.S. Congress, Office of Technology Assessment, *Biotechnology in a Global Economy*, OTA-BA-494 (Washington, DC: U.S. Congress, Office of Technology Assessment, 1991).

3. Organization for Economic Cooperation and Development *Symposium on the Globalization of Industry: Government and Corporate Issues*, Revised Issues Paper, 30 November–1 December 1993 (Paris: Organization for Economic Cooperation and Development, Industry Committee, 1993).

4. George C. Lodge, *Perestroika for America: Restructuring U.S. Business-Government Relations for Competitiveness in the World Economy* (Boston: Harvard Business School Press, 1990), 68.

5. *Technology Roadmap: The Future of the Electronic Interconnection Industry: Full Report, Survey, Summary* (Lincolnwood, IL: Institute for Interconnecting and Packaging Electronic Circuits, August 1993).

6. Laura D'Andrea Tyson, *Who's Bashing Whom? Trade Conflict in High-Technology Industries* (Washington, DC: Institute for International Economics, 1992), 123, 126, 140.

Chapter 16

Operating the Primary Association

FINALIZING THE GATT NEGOTIATIONS

The eleventh hour—December 15, 1993—was fast approaching with regard to the U.S. trade negotiators' sign-off on the GATT agreement in Geneva. Alan Wolff, SIA Washington counsel and a former USTR deputy ambassador, had arrived in Geneva two weeks before the deadline. At the same time, an SIA member company had arranged for a temporary office, fully equipped, to be available at the Intercontinental Hotel, where Wolff and many of the nation's industry and government negotiators were staying, including Ambassador Mickey Kantor, USTR. The Geneva contingent for SIA included members of the Washington representative group, among them government relations executives from Intel and Motorola.

Other links in the SIA network included the SIA staff executives for trade, statistics, and communications in San Jose, California; the Washington office of the law firm (Dewey, Ballentine); key public policy committee executives from various SIA member firms, including Advanced Micro Devices, Harris, Intel, Motorola, National, and others, located in offices spread from Florida to California and high-tech centers in between; and the fourteen SIA directors, who were either located across the United States or traveling abroad.

The SIA faced three serious issues: maintenance of high tariffs for U.S. chip exports into Europe; new GATT rules that could seriously weaken the U.S. laws against foreign firms' predatory or protectionist practices; and finally, GATT proposals that would allow foreign governments to force American firms to license their proprietary technology to their own firms. These GATT proposals posed a severe threat to the health of the U.S. chip industry and were taken seriously enough by the SIA board at its October meeting that it resolved to oppose the U.S. Congress's approval of the GATT treaty if the proposals were not overturned or, at least, modified. The mood among the SIA staff and company members was tense, with the final GATT outcome but two weeks away and the semiconductor industry facing three serious challenges. The first of the three challenges was based on the 14 percent import tariffs that had been the mainstay of European protectionists in chips. Despite continual insistence by the Americans that the tariffs be dropped, the Europeans were adamant and had maintained them. The second challenge was that the new GATT intellectual property codes were written so that the licensing of technology to foreign companies could be mandated by their governments. Several American industries, namely pharmaceuticals and computer systems, supported some parts of the new proposed intellectual property codes, while the semiconductor industry opposed it. The chip manufacturers were concerned that the new text would be used by foreign firms to appropriate highly successful American chip technology and products. Not only did the chip industry face opponents that were represented by foreign governments, they were opposed on this subject by other American industries as well. The third challenge was the new draft (called the Dunkel draft, named after Arthur Dunkel, secretariat of the GATT), which concerned trading practices. The Dunkel draft proposed that bilateral means of countering trade practices such as Section 301 of the U.S. Trade Act, could not be implemented by any country. The Dunkel draft was supported by the Asian countries, which were now becoming large players in international high-tech trade, largely based on acquired American and European technology. All three challenges—tariffs, intellectual property, and trade practices—were formidable, and at the beginning of December 1993, the hopes of winning any gains in these areas appeared highly unlikely.

The SIA legal counsel, member company representatives, staff, key executives, and CEOs, located both across the United States and in Geneva, began an operational approach that they had utilized often in the past. The operational mode was an informational network designed to achieve consensus by the quickest means possible. Information flowed laterally across the equivalent organizational levels of all the groups included, while any one executive or representative could communicate up or down within his or her own firm or SIA function. The physical means were telephone conference calls, fax machines, and overnight mail. The central points for information dissemination were the temporary SIA office at the Intercontinental Hotel in Geneva; the Washington, D.C., offices of Dewey, Ballentine; and the SIA staff headquarters in San Jose, California. The calls regarding GATT negotiations began on December 3, with twelve days to go for the final closing of the GATT meetings. The SIA counsel and industry executives were in touch with the U.S. government negotiating officials in Geneva and Washington, D.C.; with members of Congress in Geneva and in the United States; and with representatives of other industries in Geneva and elsewhere. SIA group conference calls occurred on an average of twice daily, with actions laid out for all participants, including communications to the mass media in the United States and in Europe. The intensity of effort in actions and communication was such that contacts were made at any time of day or night, and in some cases, during the last week of negotiation, the Geneva contingent of SIA were allowed only a few hours of sleep per day.

The negotiations from December 3 to December 13 advanced to the point where progress in favor of the semiconductor industry was finally being made. The European tariffs were partially lowered (though not eliminated) in most chip product categories, and the Dunkel draft on trading practices was modified so as to be found workable by the U.S. industry and government, but the compulsory licensing of technology to foreign firms and foreign governments was still unmodified. The negotiations now had only forty-eight hours to run before the final sign-off by all nations.

The last concerted action by semiconductor company chief executives was a number of telephone calls to key White House staff members with direct access to the president, who was in constant contact with his chief negotiator, Ambassador Kantor. Literally at the eleventh hour of the last day of a seven-year negotiation, the final success of the U.S. government negotiating team, which had worked tirelessly, was the exclusion of the semiconductor industry from any compulsory licensing by foreign parties for commercial purpose, use, or gain.

The *New York Times*, on December 16 (the day following the close of GATT), reported the industry winners and losers with regard to the GATT agreements. Among the eleven industries analyzed by the *New York Times* in its "Business Day" section, five were called draws, two were losers, and four were winners, including the chip makers. The *New York Times* statement on semiconductors was:

> American manufacturers retained the right not to license foreign competitors who would make their products. They also kept the ability to file dumping complaints like those used to fight Japanese competition in the 1980's. There was also a modest gain on European tariffs which will fall from 14 percent to 7 percent on imported memory products after five years.[1]

STRUCTURE

Most associations utilize a committee structure in order to implement the policies of their board of directors. All the associations described in Part 3 of this book have committees populated by the middle level executives of their corporate members. The AIA, for example, has councils and committees, at the level of technology, product, industry functions, and so forth. The committees cover many facets of the industry's concern and cut across all interests rather than merely being divided into government relations committees and traditional activities committees. The IBA, on the other hand, emphasizes government regulatory functions, and virtually half of its committees are primarily government relations committees concerned in some way with government regulations in a domestic market. The SIA committees of Public Policy, the Japan Chapter, and Government Procurement are closely related to government relations. Technology Strategy and Environmental Committee have a strong similar bent. Likewise, the number of committees that are government focused in CBEMA and in AEA are also evident in Tables 10.7 and 10.9. The CSPP, on the other hand, appears to have little structure in terms of supporting committees. Its CEOs have tended to have a few key goals, with the CSPP board being the primary implementers of this group's policies.

Quite often, committees in associations tend to have a number of companies, with various members of the same companies sitting in place at different times. The continuity of committee company and individual members, as well as their attendance at committee meetings, is often poor. Changes constantly take place, and key efforts are often not attended to in such a way that important information is properly passed on to new committee members. The committee structure concept may continue to be an appropriate one for associations; however, the degree of focus, membership continuity and attendance, and communications are open to question. This aspect of association structure requires review on a continual basis.

ASSOCIATION FUNCTIONS

A review of committee names in a number of associations indicates that they are primarily related to specific functions. For example, there are government relations committees, industry statistics committees, communication committees, and so on. The function takes on a life of its own, and the honing of skills, ability, and content tend to be concentrated on the function rather than on the objectives of the association. If the key objective of an association is to obtain technological leadership, then the primary focus of all functional skills should be on the objective—technological leadership—and not on improving functional skills for general results. The function or skills of government relations executives, industrial statisticians, process engineers and scientists, and legal assistants should all be focused on the objective, and not on improving related functional capabilities. Consequently, the major focal activity must be related to the objective and all functions should direct their efforts there. Although a government relations executive is important in approaching government agencies that direct technology with regard to co-investigating with industry a process technology, that functional skill is obviously not sufficient to achieve technological leadership. All functions have specific tasks based on their skills, but they must also be centered on the objective.

If there existed a Global Competitiveness Council to encompass all the global objectives in Table 14.1, then its committees should include one each for trade, technology, capital capacity, and so on. Although government is a major key player in each of these, the government is not the sole key to success, and therefore, the government relations executive is also not the sole key to success. Even in international trade, an area often considered by associations as coincident with government trade policy, the need to foster international interfirm cooperation may be equally important. For example, under the U.S. Export Trading Company

Act, U.S. firms can combine to form trade corporations for trade abroad through the help of a trade association, with no fear of antitrust prosecution. This is not a government action but rather an industry action intended to raise the level of U.S. market share abroad. This approach by industry does not minimize the importance of government agencies such as USTR or the Department of Commerce. It also does not minimize the skills and activities of an association government relations executive. However, the focus on global competitiveness, means the consideration of many kinds of measures, skills, and functions that can be critical to meeting the industry objective and not a government relations overkill.

COMMITTEE MEMBERSHIP

A few years ago, the chair of an association who was uncertain about the number of committees, the corporate membership, and the corporate representative asked his association chief staff officer to construct a committee membership matrix. A matrix was completed in which each row represented an association committee, while each vertical column represented the corporate members of the association. The names of the individuals who were committee members were placed in the intersecting boxes. A matrix of this type showed every committee, every corporate member, and the company representatives assigned. Each association staff member's name was also placed along with each committee activity with which he or she was associated. The results that occur when such a matrix is completed and examined are clear. They answer the questions: of which committee activities are formally recognized, which corporate members are active association participants, which corporate representatives are assigned where, and which association staff members are responsible for coordination. When the matrix was completed to the best knowledge of the chief staff officer of the association, a copy was distributed to each member of the board of directors. That resulting review brought forth the fact that the matrix representation, although 90 percent accurate, still had errors. Some corporations had multiple committee members on most committees with no coordination of the efforts at all. Others had an almost random representation across the committee. In many cases, the corporate committee members also served on the committees of related associations (even those in opposition to their primary associations' goals). The overall result indicates that even if the focus of a council or committee activity is correct, the committee membership may not be proper, either in terms of the corporation members or the individuals assigned.

CONTINUITY

Even when committees' activities are properly drawn and focused and the appropriate individual members appointed, there is no guarantee that continuity will exist. During the 1986 interassociation discussions between the computer systems and the semiconductor industries, a noticeable picture was developing. Although the chip makers kept essentially the same four key industry executives as their spokespersons for every meeting for the period of one year, the computer systems makers' representatives varied a great deal. The computer systems companies' degree of participation and attendance would vary by corporate function and corporate level. The attendance of these participants, even when they were the key spokespersons and not merely industry observers, was also erratic. The computer system attendees, despite their own erratic attendance, also attempted to exclude various invited SIA attendees who were there as observers, not spokespersons, despite the fact that the SIA representatives did not at any time restrict attendance or expression of opinion by any observer from the computer systems side.

One of the primary outcomes of this unsuccessful set of AEA-SIA negotiations with regard to semiconductor trade issues was the formation of the CSPP, a new intermediate organization. The question of whether the new organization was necessary is an important one. It was obviously necessary since no primary computer systems association with CEO membership existed. However, a key to the AEA failure to represent the computer systems industry was the failure to maintain continuity of individual attendance on the part of the computer systems executives themselves.

INTERNAL AND EXTERNAL NETWORKING

With a lack of objective focus, unstable membership, and erratic attendance, the failure of clear, consistent, and continual communication is not to be unexpected. Even if written committee minutes are maintained, including requests for specific actions, there is no guarantee of any real success. The networking capability required in any effective communications among equals also requires that the networked points have continuity if success is to be achieved. The example given at the beginning of this chapter is a model of an effective network in action. The networked communications between members of a network that has existed over a long period of time reduce the delays to reaching a consensus. The longer the experience of networking, and the more frequent the interactions between known parties, the less time required to reach consensus. The time to consensus may be crucial, as it was in the GATT negotiations, and therefore effective networking is crucial.

In addition, to the internal communication among association members in the private sector, an equally important set of communications are those with members of the public sector and of other groups in the intermediate sector. Communication to the media is especially important since the perceptions of all parties outside the primary association can be key to the success of the association in attaining its objectives. The interrelationship between the media and the primary association and its members is necessary in order to shape public opinion and to obtain support among the key organizations and individuals in all sectors. A functionary that exists in many associations is the public relations officer or communications director, whose skills are required often and must be tailored to the existing objective.

THE ASSOCIATION STAFF

Earlier reference was made to George Lodge's quote regarding the strength of character of successful association chief staff executives. The reason for Lodge's statement is that any association's chief staff executive is subject to varying degrees of pressure on issues supported by the association members who serve as board members, committee chairs, or even committee members. The same pressure may also be brought to bear on any member of an association's staff.

The staff of an association is best capable of dealing with such pressures if he or she is aware of the interests of the member corporations themselves. This knowledge of how member corporations do business helps association staff members cope with individual member pressure. However, many association executives are noted as being "staff types," namely, persons who take good meeting notes, provide assistance to the members on a request basis, and act as excellent coordinators but are not leaders or persons willing to take difficult positions when necessary. The association staffs for many industries are populated with such staff types. They may keep their position for long periods, but it is questionable if their existence contributes a great deal to the success of the association. At the other extreme is the staff executive who, because of a knowledge of a broad spectrum of industry activities acquired through the association and other means, gets too far ahead of the membership and tends to be an "hard charger" rather than a consensus builder. Most association staff executives fall somewhere in between and are able to react to pressures from all sides. However, considering the great amount of pressure that individual corporate association members can exert, and this opposing pressure for staff objectivity and nonalignment, it is not difficult to understand the two behavioral poles—staff type and hard charger—that exist on association staffs.

THE GOVERNMENT RELATIONS EXECUTIVE

In the past, American industries believed government to be an adversary that should be closely watched and effectively opposed if any of its steps appear injurious to the interests of industry. In order to accomplish this, many corporations established the positions of government affairs manager, government relations executive, or some other, related title. The job of these individual executives is to represent their corporation's interests in corporate or industry discussions with government. These corporate government-relations representatives often come together within associations and populate the government relations committees of associations or other committees where any relationship to government is in effect. Quite often the government relations executives (GREs) proactively advocate corporate or industry positions, attempt to effect compromises between government and private sector positions, and have, when needed, actively opposed government agency positions by having legislation blocked or modified. Many corporate government relations executives are based within Washington, D.C., or at the headquarters office of their companies. Sometimes they are attorneys or ex-government officials, and often they are more aware of the mechanisms of governmental activity than they are of their corporations' actual business. At times in the recent past, the GRE was told by company headquarters to "keep the government off our backs," that is, until the GRE was later told under different circumstances to get the government to "do something." The GRE acts as a liaison between the government officials and corporate executives on a great number of issues.

The GRE is also faced with the task of interfacing with other GREs within their own industry association or with government affairs managers from a different industry. In a world where the objectives of the corporate employer, the industry association, and the government agencies are not the same, the job becomes extremely difficult. The best possible forum in which GREs can test their opinions and promote a reasonable position is by seeking a consensus with other GREs on the industry association committees. Only here can the best combination of all interests be brought forth, judged, and finally be proposed to both the corporate entities and the government agencies involved. The association provides the GREs with means of conflict resolution that would otherwise not be available.

FUNCTIONAL EXECUTIVES

The work of the government affairs managers involves the interface between the corporation or its industry association and the government, often in a regulatory or legislative sense where regulations or legislation are either to be written, modified, rescinded, or implemented. The emphasis of a GRE's work is on the regulatory or legislative process. However, in the case of the substance of any issue, the association must bring forward other functional corporate or association executives whose expertise may be in technology, production, marketing and distribution, or some other function where the GRE does not have sufficient in-depth knowledge to represent industry's position. Two key areas immediately come to mind: one is technology, where issues such as intellectual property protection or technical and scientific work in federal labs are best understood and conveyed by scientists and engineers employed by the association or the member companies. Another example is in the area of environmental issues. The complexity of environmental issues from a health or social aspect is such that the typical GRE is not likely to capably represent and convey positions on them well.

Consequently, the trade association will bring together sufficient functional expertise so that the best industry position can be determined, represented, and conveyed, not only to government agencies but also to special interest groups and the general public as well.

Regardless of the function involved, a major strength of an association executive is to be able to obtain primary data on issues of interest. For example, since world market share is important for critical industries, a timely and accurate means of collecting data is essential. The data available from routine U.S. government reports is rarely adequate for the task. In addition, analysis of such data is as critical as the data itself. Most trade associations, including several described in this book, have no means of primary data collection or skilled data analysis.

Many associations also utilize outside expertise on an as-needed basis. Among the experts engaged are trade lawyers, environmental and health professionals, economists, technologists, and others. Their assistance is invaluable.

THE ASSOCIATION IN OPERATION

There are several essential elements that have been discussed thus far in regard to association operation. They include the *structural elements* of committees, membership participation, continuity, and communications; and the *human resources element* of directors, staff, governmental specialists, and experts from industry. The last element to be discussed here is the clear assignment of responsibility. The final responsibility for strategic policy lies with an association's board of directors, while the final responsibility for implementation lies with the association staff. It should be made clear to all corporate representatives, whether on councils, committees, task forces, teams, or whatever collective groups are responsible for the completion of tasks, that the staff personnel are not merely a group of highly trained secretaries but rather key executives and specialists responsible to see that the tasks are accomplished with the result that the board's strategic policies are achieved. The staff may not perform the tasks since these are primarily executed by the member company representatives, but the staff must see that the tasks are performed, and are to be held accountable.

RELATING TO THE REST OF THE INTERMEDIATE SECTOR

The role of the primary association is to achieve an effective relationship between the private sector (the companies in an industry), and the public sector (the government agencies). The primary association is also responsibile for the relationship to other members of the intermediate sector. The most important of these intrasector relationships are those between the primary association and the consortia, the secondary associations, and the parallel associations representing upstream and downstream industries.

With regard to the secondary associations, the best relationship is one in which the secondary association can lead on issues of concern to a broader constituency than the companies represented by the primary association. For example, in 1993, two key issues—namely, the imposition of increased taxes by the elimination of lobbying expenses as a corporate deductible item and the new proposed FASB rules on stock options, which would result in high costs to corporations and less benefits to the stock option holder—are two cases in which the secondary association, with its broader base, would be much more effective than the primary association in eliminating the unfavorable aspects of these new rules. These two issues would best be handled by the American Electronics Association for the chip makers rather than by the SIA. They can also be better handled by BIO than they could by the former IBA. In another area, that of product standards, questions among many electronic sectors are best answered within the many standards committees of the Electronic Industries Association (EIA). A tangential question that this discussion brings up remains unanswered, however: does the electronics industry, or any industry, require two secondary or umbrella-type associations, such as the AEA and the EIA? The question itself is indicative of the redundancy among a number of American associations, and the electronics industry is no exception.

With regard to parallel associations, the important fact is that these associations represent the major supplier industry and the major customer industry of the primary association members. In the case of the Aerospace Industries Association, both suppliers of components and subsystems and the airframe manufacturers are part of the same association. Since the aircraft components suppliers provide products for both the U.S. and European airframe makers, their positions on competition and trade issues affecting American and European makers end up being ambivalent. Thus, with an association that is supposed to be representative of all members, the different segments of membership have serious conflicts of interest. Another source of conflict, which is existent within the Semiconductor Equipment and Materials International (SEMI), is the fact that its board of directors has members from both U.S. and foreign companies. International conflicts with regard to the conditions of global competition and trade may, therefore, result in a deadlocked or silent board with respect to the actions to be taken by the American members. Moreover, since the major activity of SEMI involves international exhibitions in U.S., Europe, and Asia rather than public policy, its ability to represent U.S. members' interests in matters of global competition is questionable.

ADVISORY COUNCILS

Advisory councils are legislated by federal law and consist of members of the industry, related government agencies, and other groups such as universities and labor unions. The purpose of an advisory council is to bring together members of the private and public sectors so that the national interest with regard to a specific industry can be considered. Associations are not represented on councils directly. The two councils discussed here are shown in Table 13.1. The National Advisory Committee for Semiconductors (NACS), established in 1988, addressed the difficult competitive positions faced by the U.S. semiconductor industry. It was chartered to make recommendations to industry and government that would help this strategic industry. The NACS was closely observed by the SIA, and communications to the NACS from specific SIA members were also communicated to the SIA membership in general. The more recent council, the Semiconductor Technology Council (STC), was established by federal legislation in 1993 and will direct its efforts towards providing broad policy positions and exercising oversight with regard to technology cooperation between the industry, the universities, and the federal laboratories in the Departments of Commerce, Defense, and Energy.

OTHER GROUPS

Among the other groups within the semiconductor intermediate sector are the research institutes, often based in Washington, D.C., or other major cities and university campuses, which have the ability to study, analyze, and promote various aspects of national and global issues as they relate to various industries. Among them, the Economic Strategy Institute, led by Clyde Prestowitz, a former international trade specialist within the Department of Commerce, often sides with the U.S. semiconductor industry in its differences with Japan. Other institutes may take varying views but can be influenced to take like positions with industry on certain issues.

The informal groups—whether of members of Congress, businesspeople, other association executives, or academics—may provide means of studying, analyzing, and promoting various positions of support for the primary associations. They can be extremely influential in advocating association positions.

SUMMARY

After an association is formed and its objectives determined, it becomes an operational unit and moves towards its goals. The mechanisms that are put in place include committees, functionaries, and staff, who work together in a networking, horizontal organization. In addition to the internal and major interfaces of associations (i.e., companies and government agencies), other intrasectoral groups must also be influenced to support the primary association's position on key issues.

NOTE

1. "GATT: The Effect on Industry," *New York Times*, 16 December 1993, C6.

Chapter 17

Designing the Association

PROVIDING INFORMAL ADVICE

Frequently during the early 1990s, the SIA office in San Jose has hosted persons seeking advice about how to organize a new association or better manage an existing one. The discussions are rarely in depth and the conversation often begins with a tentatively spoken request for some informal advice. The questions posed by visitors seeking advice range from, "At which golf course resorts do you hold your meetings?" (a meaningless question since SIA does not hold combined business-social events at resorts) to more serious questions such as, "Can you help me plan my association's first meeting in Washington, D.C.?"

Requests for information and advice come from consultants, former industry executives seeking to form an association of their former competitors, government officials, directors of foreign associations, academics, research institutes, and others. However, during a five-year period, no one has suggested that an association should be formed according to a plan or a design so that it will be effective after it is established. In one particular case, the visitor stated that only a full six months after the formation of his association did, the founder-directors sit down and ask the important questions about what their association should be and do. A more recent request from an executive director of a foreign trade association was for a copy of the SIA bylaws so that he might review them before writing a similar document for his association.

Over the years, the requests from others for advice in forming and managing an association encouraged the writing of the book of which this is the last chapter. If only a few pages of written material could be provided to those seeking short and simple advice, they would be the ones that follow this chapter introduction.

BRINGING THE ASSOCIATION TOGETHER

In the early chapters of this book, the historical origins of industry associations in the United States, Japan, and Germany were presented. The basic comparison indicated that American associations were initiated by political entrepreneurs, had voluntary membership, and treated government as adversarial. The American associations did not recognize national interests or purpose but rather existed for the general good of the industry. They were not exclusive, nor did they belong to a hierarchy of associations. It was also understood by the American associations that individual company's opinions could be equal to, or even greater than, that of the trade association. American associations tend to be more unstable and have a greater diversity of views, both within the association and between associations, than their foreign competitors. It is not likely for the sake of stability that legislated or licensed associations would be exclusively allowed in the United States. Our cultural heritage, based on our combined social, political, and economic philosophy and a foundation of pluralism, would not allow the compulsory characteristics of government involvement in association formation and affairs such as exists in Japan and Germany. The typical political philosophy today in America is for government to use fiscal, monetary, and other regulatory policies, as well as industry-related policies, to encourage corporations (including associations) to act in a proscribed manner. The use of mandatory directives to construct association objectives is not likely to occur in America. This important aspect of American political heritage—the voluntary formation of associations—is not likely to be relinquished.

However, if the joint interests of industry and the nation are of strategic importance, as in the case of high-tech industries, then an industry-government partnership should be fostered by a form of federal charter that provides mutual goals with corresponding incentives via fiscal, monetary, and other regulatory means. With various industries and government working toward partnership, most of the key strategic industries could eventually be federally chartered. Associations that choose to meet the industry's mutual needs only, without regard to the national interest, would not be allowed the expanded benefits of a federally chartered association. The application for a federal charter would describe the various duties, responsibilities, and benefits to the government agencies and to the industry associations and their members.

After the association has been formed and chartered according to national guidelines, its board of directors must be given the responsibility of determining the major objectives and policies of the association. The redesigned association would have CEO-level representation on its board, with no substitutes or alternates allowed. The board should also be small enough to reach timely conclusions and decisions. The use of smaller boards of CEOs allows for quicker action, greater credibility, less complexity, and faster communication speed than would a ponderous governance structure of lower-level executives with questionable authority. The key role of the board is to provide focus through the determination of explicit objectives. These objectives will be divided into three categories, relating to association organization, domestic industry issues, and global industry issues. The various techniques for achieving a unified member set of objectives that also meet the national interest are no different than would be used by a corporation in determining their business objectives: whether focal groups, communication audits, informal meetings, or tallied polls. The important point is that the objectives must be categorized, enumerated, and communicated to both corporate association members and the cognizant government agencies. In assessing objectives, a board of executives of member firms has the best capability of determining future threats and opportunities in the technological, political, social, economic, and natural environments of global competition. The board will also be able to understand the industry's strengths and weaknesses within the context of these global threats and opportunities.

Once the industry objectives, threats, and opportunities, as well as its strengths and weaknesses, are determined, the association chief staff executive and his staff should be empowered to take the necessary steps to achieve the association goals utilizing the council, committee, task force, or a team of executives from member companies. In determining the objectives and the staff roles, the board of directors must exercise judgment about the final characteristics of the organization. This determination is perhaps one of the most crucial of all steps in defining an association, especially for the application for a federal charter. For example, some associations participate heavily in the development and organizations of exhibitions, to the exclusion of many other activities. Generally, exhibitions, such as those held by SEMI, generate very large revenues and, consequently, the possibility of large profits. Other associations may attempt to provide product catalog services that are priced to obtain revenues and profits. These services as primary activities—exhibitions and product catalogs—may be of value and benefit to members, but it is unlikely that they serve the national purpose to any large degree. Consequently, attempts to carry on these activities—namely, exhibitions and electronic product catalogs—as part of a nonprofit, federally chartered trade association, with fully deductible member expense, is not a major contribution to American global competitiveness. Separating such activities from those performed by chartered associations is far more desirable than confusing the nature of a high-tech strategic industry association, a primary association that is maintaining a partnership with government. On the other hand, the organization and direction of a research and development consortia by a chartered association is realistic provided, again, that the national interest, as well as the mutual benefit of the members, is served.

The next step, and perhaps the most important in the design of a primary association, is to separate the association activities, not by function (i.e., government relations, industry statistics, or industrial relations), but rather by the objectives of the association. As an example, one of the most important objectives of today's high-tech industries and their association is technological leadership, which is an objective and not a function. Technological leadership can be measured in terms of physical parameters in every high-tech industry. Whether the subject is the speed and economy of an aircraft, the size population cured of a disease by biotechnology methods, or the benchmarked performance of various computers or transistors per square centimeter on a chip, all are technology leadership parameters for which objectives and measures of performance can be expressed. In each case, however, the end objective is of greater importance than the exceptional performance of an isolated function of the association.

How, then, should objectives be achieved by utilizing the association structure and functional capability? First, the core processes for attaining each objective should be defined. Assume that technological leadership is the objective. The core processes may involve influencing the government laboratory direction, coordinating the affiliated consortia, regulating the dissemination of intellectual property, publishing and broadly distributing a research finding to member companies, or drawing together in conference experts from all sector participants to develop a technology roadmap. To attain the objective of technology leadership, therefore, requires the delineation of the necessary processes and the ways in which they are linked to the objective. However, general functions such as government relations, data collection, and media communication, are not the keys to achieve global objectives. The line of causality is that objectives depend on processes that may utilize functions in different ways for different results. One can recognize in this organizational philosophy that of the horizontal organization. The functional authority hierarchy does not exist in today's successful association. The successful association is flatter in the sense that the end objective and the process to reach it are more important than the particular function that is used to reach it. Another aspect of the flatter organizations, and one of great importance, is use of the networking mode of communication rather than the hierarchical mode of communication. Networking not only means a greater amount of communication to more people, it also means a broader degree of transmission and reception of messages. Networking provides a consensus-building structure that allows for faster decisions. In fact, the many small decisions that are required to reach a greater and more important decision do not have to be sent up and down a hierarchical organizational staircase in a networked organization. Networking is also iterative, with feedback loops all leading to the evolution of a final consensus. Moreover, since associations have a much weaker authoritative basis due to their voluntary nature than the for-profit private corporation, the networking and consensus-building approach is not only a necessity for making progress, it is also consistent with their character. Consequently, the flattened, horizontal organization is the most appropriate for associations.

There have been many attempts to draw horizontal or networking organizations, and they tend to take many different shapes. However, no single diagram has been presented that is uniformly accepted. The one to be suggested here will probably not be acceptable to all but may be workable for many. An approach that may be useful involves a spreadsheet that organizes processes, objectives, and personnel or skills assignments. The objectives would be as discussed:

namely, technological leadership, market share, and so forth. The processes would include data collection and analysis, regulatory interpretation and negotiation, and technology assessment. Moreover, where the two intersect (i.e., objectives to be achieved and the methods required to achieve them), the personnel or skills should be assigned. The spreadsheet can be changed at any time that circumstances dictate. At the same time, a rearrangement by personnel or resources may be displayed in order to measure the flow of funds, hours, services, other major resources utilized.

With regard to relationships with organizations other than the primary association in the intermediate sector (consortia, secondary associations, parallel associations, etc.), a cooperative rather than confrontational approach is the most productive for the primary association. Not only is this important within a sector, but it should be carried through to other interest groups that may represent consumers, environmentalists, or other parties of even indirect consequence. The cooperative attitude may not necessarily help in reaching a solution to differences, but confrontation will definitely hinder any near-term solution, and possibly negatively affect future solutions.

As the design given in these pages is put into place, one must not forget why it is necessary. The world of today is continually changing. The globalization of industrial activity, advances in technology, health and environmental concerns, and internationalized government roles all lead to the conclusion that present-day organizations, including associations, must change.

FINAL CONCLUSIONS

Every attempt has been made in this book to bring together the historical foundation, the recent practices, and the best innovative thoughts with regard to designing today's industry associations in the global environment. This book is an important beginning for many in association management who wish to analyze the intermediate sector organizations in light of the knowledge brought forth here. It is hoped that the common objective of working for more efficient and effective associations can be better achieved by further development and implementation of the ideas in these pages.

Selected Bibliography

Abegglen, James C., and George Stalk, Jr. *Kaisha: The Japanese Corporation.* New York: Basic Books, 1985.

Alic, K. A., L. M. Branscomb, H. Brooks, A. Carter, and G. L. Epstein. *Beyond Spinoff.* Boston: Harvard Business School Press, 1992.

Anchordoguy, Marie. "Mastering the Market: Japanese Government Targeting of the Computer Industry." *International Organization* 42, no. 3 (Summer 1988): 509–543.

———. "The Public Corporation: A Potent Japanese Policy Weapon." *Political Science Quarterly* 103, no. 4 (Winter 1988): 707–724.

Argue, David A. "Dividing Cartel Profits: The Southern Railway and Steamship Associations." *Essays in Economics and Business History* 9 (1991): 277–293.

Aristarchus Knowledge Industries. *Japanese Industrial Policy: Guided Investment and Anti-Recession Cartels.* Tucson, AZ: Aristarchus Group, 1989.

Armentano, Dominick T. *Antitrust and Monopoly: Anatomy of a Policy Failure.* 2nd ed. New York: Holmes and Meier, 1991.

Armstrong, Philip, Andrew Glyn, and John Harrison. *Capitalism since 1945.* Cambridge, MA: Blackwell Publications, 1991.

Asch, Peter, and Rosalind S. Seneca. *Government and the Marketplace.* 2nd ed. Chicago: Dryden Press, 1989.

Audretsch, David B. "Legalized Cartels in West Germany." *Antitrust Bulletin* 34, no. 3 (Fall 1989): 579–600.

———. *The Market and the State: Government Policy toward Business in Europe, Japan, and the United States.* New York: New York University Press, 1989.

Augustine, N. R. "Public Employees and the Global Landscape." *Public Manager* 21 (Spring 1992): 9–11.

Ayres, Robert U. *The Next Industrial Revolution.* Cambridge, MA: Ballinger Publishing, 1984.

Balassa, Bela, and Marcus Noland. *Japan in the World Economy.* Washington, DC: Institute for International Economics, 1988.

Balmer, John M. T., and Adrian Wilkinson. "Building Societies: Change, Strategy and Corporate Identity." *Journal of General Management* 17, no. 2 (Winter 1991): 20–33.

Barth, H. M. *Berlin Wholesale Electrical Industry in German Politics: Electrical Industry Associations and Parties, 1862–1920.* Berlin, Germany: Free University of Berlin, 1984.

Becker, William H. "American Wholesale Hardware Trade Associations, 1870–1900." *Business History Review* 45, no. 2 (1971): 179–200.

Bellon, Bertrand, and Jorge Niosi. *The Decline of the American Economy.* Montreal, Quebec, Canada: Black Rose Book Company, 1988.

Biddle, Wayne. *Barons of the Sky.* New York: Simon and Schuster, 1991.

Binder, John J. "The Sherman Antitrust Act and the Railroad Cartels." *Journal of Law and Economics* 31, no. 2 (1988): 443–468.

Bingham, Charles F. *Japanese Government Leadership and Management.* New York: St. Martin's Press, 1989.

Bodner, John, Jr. "Antitrust Restrictions on Trade Association Membership and Participation." *American Bar Association Journal* 54, no. 1 (January 1968): 27–32.

Boger, Karl. *U.S. Industrial Policy: An Annotated Bibliography of Books and Government Documents.* Chicago: Council of Planning Librarians, 1986.

———. *Postwar Industrial Policy in Japan: An Annotated Bibliography.* Metuchen, NJ: Scarecrow Press, 1988.

Bolitzer, A. *Nation of Associations.* Washington, DC: American Society of Association Executives, 1981.

Boneo, Horacio. *Interlinkages, Concepts, Characteristics, and Determining Factors.* Austin, TX: Institute of Latin American Studies, University of Texas at Austin, Office for Public Sector Studies, 1986.

Bork, Robert H. *Antitrust Paradox: A Policy at War with Itself.* New York: Free Press, 1993.

Borrus, Michael G. *Competing for Control: America's Stake in Microelectronics.* Cambridge, MA: Ballinger Publishing, 1988.

Bowen, Ralph Henry. *German Theories of the Corporative State, with Special Reference to the Period 1870–1919.* New York: Russell and Russell, 1971.

Bower, Joseph L. *When Markets Quake.* Boston: Harvard Business School Press, 1986.

Boyd, R. A. *Government and Industry Relations in Japan: A Review of Literature.* Washington, DC: Economic and Social Research Council, 1986.

Bradley, Joseph Francis. *The Role of Trade Associations and Professional Business Societies in America.* University Park: Pennsylvania State University Press, 1965.

Brady, Robert Alexander. *Business as a System of Power.* Salem, NH: Ayer, 1972.

Braunthal, G. *The Federation of German Industry in Politics.* Ithaca, NY: Cornell University Press, 1965.

Bright, Charles D. *The Jet Makers: The Aerospace Industry from 1945 to 1972.* Lawrence: Regents Press of Kansas, 1978.

Brock, Malcolm V. *Biotechnology in Japan.* New York: Routledge, 1989.

Bromley, Willard S. "The Making of Forest Policy in Pulp and Paper Trade Associations, 1878–1986." *Journal of Forest History* 30, no. 4 (October 1986): 192–196.

Brouthers, L. E., and S. Werner. "Are the Japanese Good Global Competitors?" *Columbia Journal of World Business* 25, no. 3 (Fall 1990): 5–11.

Brunner, K., ed. *The Great Depression Revisited.* Boston: Martinus Nijhoff, 1981.

Buchholz, Rogene A. *Business Environment and Public Policy.* Englewood Cliffs, NJ: Prentice Hall, 1992.

Buhner, Rolf. "The Success of Mergers in Germany." *International Journal of Industrial Organization* 9, no. 4 (December 1991): 513–532.

Bulmer, Simon, and William Patterson. *Federal Republic of Germany and the EC.* London: Allen and Unwin, 1987.

Burek, Deborah M., ed. *Encyclopedia of Associations.* Vol. 1, part 1. Detroit, MI: Gale Research, 1991.

Burn, Bruno, and S. Fink. *Codes, Cartels, National Planning: The Road to Economic Stability.* New York: McGraw-Hill, 1934.

Burns, Arthur Robert. *The Decline of Competition: A Study of the Evolution of American Industry.* New York: McGraw-Hill, 1936.

Calder, K. E. "Elites in an Equalizing Role: Ex-Bureaucrats as Coordinators and Intermediaries in the Japanese Government-Business Relationship." *Comparative Politics* 21, no. 4 (July 1989): 379–403.

Carrott, Browning M. "The Supreme Court and American Trade Associations, 1921–1925." *Business History Review* 44, no. 3 (1970): 320–338.

Cawson, Alan, Kevin Morgan, Douglas Webber, Peter Holmes, and Anne Stevens. *Hostile Brothers: Competition and Closure in the European Electronics Industry.* Oxford, UK: Clarendon Press, 1990.

Chandler, Alfred D., Jr. *The Visible Hand: The Managerial Revolution in American Business.* Cambridge, MA: Belknap Press of Harvard University Press, 1977.

————. *Scale and Scope: The Dynamics of Industrial Capitalism.* Cambridge, MA: Belknap Press of Harvard University Press, 1990.

Chapman, Gary. "Push Comes to Shove on Technology Policy." *Technology Review* 95, no. 8 (November-December 1992): 42–49.

Cheit, E. "Coming of Middle Age in Business and Society." *California Management Review* 33, no. 2 (Winter 1991): 71–79.

Choate, Pat. *Agents of Influence: How Japan's Lobbyists in the U.S. Manipulate America's Political and Economic Systems.* New York: Knopf, 1990.

Chubb, John E., and Paul E. Peterson, eds. *Can the Government Govern?* Washington, DC: Brookings Institution, 1989.

Cigler, Allan J., and Burdett A. Loomis, eds. *Interest Group Politics.* 3rd ed. Washington, DC: CQ Press, 1991.

Clark, Kim B., Robert H. Hayes, and Christopher Lorenz. *The Uneasy Alliance.* Boston: Harvard Business School Press, 1985.

Cohen, Linda, Susan A. Edelman, and Roger G. Noll. "The National Aerospace Plan: An American Technological Long Shot, Japanese Style." *American Economic Review* 81, no. 2 (May 1991): 50–53.

Cohen, Stephen S., and John Zysman. *Manufacturing Matters: The Myth of the Post-Industrial Economy.* New York: Basic Books, 1987.

Coleman, William D. *Business and Politics: A Study of Collective Action.* Kingston, Ontario, Canada: McGill-Queen's University Press, 1988.

————. "State Traditions and Comprehensive Business Associations: A Comparative Structural Analysis." *Political Studies* 38, no. 2 (June 1990): 231–252.

Constantine, Earl. *Participation of Trade Organizations in a National Emergency.* Washington, DC: Army Industrial College, 1940.

Costello, R. B., and M. Ernst. *Regaining U.S. Manufacturing Leadership.* Indianapolis: Hudson Institute, 1992.

Cravens, D. W., H. Kirk Downey, and Paul Lauritano. "Global Competition in the Commercial Aircraft Industry: Positioning for Advantage by the Triad Nations." *Columbia Journal of World Business* 26, no. 4 (Winter 1992): 46–58.

Cutts, Robert L. "The Construction Market: Japan Slams the Door (Kansai)." *California Management Review* 30, no. 4 (Summer 1988): 46–65.

———. "Capitalism in Japan: Cartels and Keiretsu." *Harvard Business Review* 70, no. 4 (July-August 1992): 48–55.

Davidow, Joel. "The Worldwide Influence of U.S. Antitrust." *Antitrust Bulletin* 35, no. 3 (Fall 1990): 603–630.

Davidson, W. H. *The Amazing Race.* New York: John Wiley, 1984.

Davis, Warren, Thomas R. Howell, and Brent L. Bartlett. *Creating Advantage.* San Jose, CA: Semiconductor Industry Association, 1992.

Day, George, and Robin Wensley. "Assessing Advantage: A Framework for Diagnosing Competitive Superiority." *Journal of Marketing* 52, no. 2 (April 1988): 1–20.

DeBresson, Chris, and Fernand Amesse. "Networks of Innovators: A Review and Introduction of the Issue." *Research Policy* 20, no. 5 (October 1991): 363–379.

Denzau, Arthur T. "Made in America: The Japanese Auto Cartel." *Society* 24, no. 6 (1987): 30–34.

Dertouzos, Michael L., Richard K. Lester, and Robert M. Solow. *Made in America.* Cambridge, MA: Massachusetts Institute of Technology Press, 1989.

deVos, Dirk. *Governments and Microelectronics: The European Experience.* Ottawa, Ontario: Science Council of Canada, 1993.

Diamond, Daniel E., and John D. Guilfoil. *U.S. Economic History.* Morristown, NJ: General Learning Press, 1973.

Dibner, Mark D. *Biotechnology Japan.* New York: McGraw-Hill, 1989.

Dick, A. R. "Learning by Doing and Dumping in the Semiconductor Industry." *Journal of Law and Economics* 34, no. 1 (April 1991): 133–159.

Dietrich, William S. *In the Shadow of the Rising Sun: The Political Roots of American Economic Decline.* University Park: Pennsylvania State University Press, 1991.

Drucker, Peter F. *Managing in Turbulent Times.* New York: Harper and Row, 1980.

———. *The New Realities: In Government and Politics, in Economics and Business, in Society and World View.* New York: Harper and Row, 1989.

Dyer, Davis, Malcolm S. Salter, and Alan M. Webber. *Changing Alliances.* Cambridge, MA: Harvard Business School Press, 1987.

Eisenberg, Carolyn. "U.S. Policy in Post-War Germany: The Conservative Restoration." *Science and Society* 46, no. 1 (1982): 24–38.

Ellison, John N., Jeffrey W. Frumkin, and Timothy W. Stanley. *Mobilizing U.S. Industry.* Boulder, CO: Westview Press, 1988.

Fallows, James. *More Like Us.* Boston: Houghton Mifflin, 1989.

Farr, C. Michael, and William A. Fisher, "Managing International High Technology Cooperative Projects." *R&D Management* 22, no. 1 (January 1992): 55–67.

Feldman, Gerald D., and Ulrich Nocken. "Trade Associations and Economic Power: Interest Group Development in the German Iron and Steel and Machine Building Industries, 1900–1933." *Business History Review* 49, no. 4 (1975): 413–445.

Feldman, Stanley J., David McClain, and Karen Palmer. "Sources of Structural Change in the United States, 1963–78: An Input-Output Perspective." *Review of Economics and Statistics* 69 (August 1987): 503–510.

Ferguson, Charles H. "America's High-Tech Decline." *Foreign Policy* 74 (Spring 1989): 123–144.

Flamm, Kenneth. *Technology Policy in International Perspective.* Washington, DC: Brookings Institution, 1984.

———. *Targeting the Computer: Government Support and International Competition.* Washington, DC: Brookings Institution, 1987.

Florida, Richard, and Martin Kenney. *The Breakthrough Illusion.* New York: Basic Books, 1990.

———. "Organizational Factors and Technology Intensive Industry: The U.S. and Japan." *New Technology Work and Employment* 6 (Spring 1991): 28–42.

Fong, Glenn R. "State Strength, Industry Structure, and Industrial Policy: American and Japanese Experience in Microelectronics." *Comparative Politics* 22, no. 3 (April 1990): 273–299.

Forrest, Janet E., and M. J. C. Martin. "Strategic Alliances between Large and Small Research Intensive Organizations: Experiences in the Biotechnology Industry." *R&D Management* 22, no. 1 (January 1992): 41–53.

Fransman, Martin. *The Market and Beyond: Cooperation and Competition in Information Technology Development in the Japanese System.* New York: Cambridge University Press, 1990.

Freedman, Leonard. *Power and Politics in America.* Pacific Grove, CA: Brooks/Cole Publishing, 1991.

Freeman, E., and Daniel R. Gilbert. "Business, Ethics, and Society: A Critical Agenda." *Business Society Review* 31, no. 1 (Spring 1992): 9.

Fullbrook, M. *A Concise History of Germany.* New York: Cambridge University Press, 1990.

Galambos, Louis. "The Trade Association Movement in Cotton Textiles, 1900–35." *Explorations in Entrepreneurial History* 2, no. 1 (1964): 31–55.

Galambos, Louis, and Joseph Pratt. *The Rise of the Corporate Commonwealth: U.S. Business and Public Policy in the 20th Century.* New York: Basic Books, 1989.

Galbraith, James K. *Balancing Acts: Technology, Finance and the American Future.* New York: Basic Books, 1989.

———. "Let's Try Export-Led Growth." *Challenge* 31, no. 3 (May-June 1989): 37.

Garten, Jeffrey E. "Japan and Germany: American Concerns." *Foreign Affairs* 68, no. 5 (Winter 1989): 84.

———. *A Cold Peace: America, Japan, Germany and the Struggle for Supremacy.* New York: Times Books/Random House, Twentieth Century Fund Book, 1992.

Gerlach, Michael L. *Alliance Capitalism and the Social Organization of Japanese Business.* Berkeley: University of California Press, 1992.

———. "The Japanese Corporate Network: A Blockmodel Analysis." *Administrative Science Quarterly* 37, no. 1 (March 1992): 105–139.

Gilbertson, R. G. *The Spirit of Enterprise.* New York: Simon and Schuster, 1989.

Glen, Maxwell. "Electronics Industry a Reluctant Player in the Game of Political Influence." *National Journal* 17, no. 41 (12 October 1985): 2300–2304.

Gramlich, E. M. "Distinguished Lecture on Economics in Government—Setting National Priorities, 1991." *Journal of Economic Perspectives* 6 (Spring 1991): 3–12.

Gray, Virginia and David Lowery. "The Corporatist Foundations of State Industrial Policy." *Social Science Quarterly* 71 (March 1990): 3–24.

Gregory, Gene. *Japanese Electronics Technology, Enterprise and Innovation.* 2nd ed. Chichester, UK, and New York: Wiley, 1986.

Gresser, Julian. *Partners in Prosperity: Strategic Industries for the United States and Japan.* New York: McGraw-Hill, 1984.

———. "Breaking the Japanese Negotiating Code: What European and American Managers Must Do to Win." *European Management Journal* 10, no. 3 (September 1992): 286–293.

Grinde, Donald Andrew, Jr. "The Powder Trust and the Pennsylvania Anthracite Region." *Pennsylvania History* 42, no. 3 (1975): 207–219.

Groner, Alex. *The American Heritage History of American Business and Industry.* New York: American Heritage Publishing Company, 1972.

Gugler, Philippe. "Building Transnational Alliances to Create Competitive Advantage." *Long Range Planning* 25, no. 1 (February 1992): 90–99.

Gupta, Shiv K., and David R. Brubaker. "The Concept of Corporate Social Responsibility Applied to Trade Associations." *Socio-Economics Planning Sciences* 24, no. 4 (1990): 261–271.

Guth, James L. "The National Cooperative Council and Farm Relief, 1929–42." *Agricultural History* 51, no 2 (April 1977): 441–458.

Hagedoom, John, and Joseph Schakenraad. "Leading Companies and Networks of Strategic Alliances in Information Technologies." *Research Policy* 21, no. 2 (April 1992): 163–190.

Hamilton, W. F., and H. Singh. "The Evolution of Corporate Capabilities in Emerging Technologies." *Interfaces* 22 (July-August 1992): 13–23.

Hannah, Leslie, Norbert Horn, and Jurgen Kocka. "Mergers, Cartels, and Concentration: Legal Factors in the U.S. and European Experience (In German)." In Norbert Horn and Jurgen Kocka, eds., *Recht und Entwicklung der Grossuntemehmen in 19. und fruhen 20 Jahrhundert*, pp. 306–316. Göttingen: Vandenhoeck and Ruprecht, 1979.

Harrigan, Anthony, and William R. Hawkins. *American Economic Pre-Eminence: Goals for the 1990's.* Washington, DC: U.S. Industrial Council Educational Foundation, 1989.

Harris, Martha C., and Gordon E. Moore. *Linking Trade and Technology Policies: An International Comparison of the Policies of Industrialized Nations.* Washington, DC: National Academy Press, 1992.

Harrison, B. "Where Private Investment Fails." *American Prospect* 11 (Fall 1992): 106–114.

Hart, Jeffrey A. *Rival Capitalists: International Competitiveness in the United States, Japan and Western Europe.* Ithaca, NY: Cornell University Press, 1992.

Hawley, Ellis W. *The New Deal and the Problem of Monopoly.* Princeton, NJ: Princeton University Press, 1966.

Hayes, Robert H., and Steven C. Wheelright. *Restoring Our Competitive Edge: Competing through Manufacturing.* New York: John Wiley, 1984.

Hayes, Robert H., Steven C. Wheelright, and Kim B. Clark. *Dynamic Manufacturing: Creating the Learning Organization.* New York: Free Press, 1988.

Hayward, Keith. *International Collaboration in Civil Aerospace.* New York: St. Martin's Press, 1986.

———. "Airbus: Twenty Years of European Collaboration." *International Affairs* 64, no. 1 (Winter 1987–88): 11–26.

Hazewindus, Nico, and John Tooker. *The U.S. Microelectronics Industry: Technical Change, Industry Growth and Social Impact.* Tarrytown, NY: Pergamon Press, 1982.

Heenan, David A. "Why the U.S. Government Should Go to Bat for Business." *Journal of Business Strategy* 11, no. 2 (March-April 1990): 46–49.

Hellwig, Helmu. "Differences in Competitive Strategies Between the U.S. and Japan (Technical Management Note)." *IEEE Transactions on Engineering Management* 39, no. 1 (24 February 1992): 77.

Helou, Angelina. "The Nature and Competitiveness of Japan's Keiretsu." *Journal of World Trade* (Law-Economics–Public Policy) 25, no. 3 (June 1991): 99–131.

Henderson, Jeffrey William. *The Globalization of High Technology Production: Society, Space, and Semiconductors in the Restructuring of the Modern World.* New York: Routledge, 1989.

Hieronymi, Otto. *Technology and International Relations.* New York: St. Martin's Press, 1987.

Hilton, M. "Shared Training: Learning from Germany (Comparison of Investments in Training by U.S. and German Employees)." *Monthly Labor Review* 114, no. 3 (March 1991): 33–37.

Himmelberg, Robert F. *The Origins of the National Recovery Administration: Business, Government, and the Trade Association Issue, 1921–33.* New York: Fordham University Press, 1976.

Hofheinz, Roy, Jr., and Kent E. Calder. *The East Asia Edge.* New York: Basic Books, 1982.

Holcomb, James H., and Paul S. Nelson. "Cartel Failure: A Mistake or Do They Do It to Each Other on Purpose?" *Journal of Socio-Economics* 20, no. 3 (Fall 1991): 235–250.

Howell, Thomas R., William A. Noellert, Jesse G. Krier, and Alan W. Wolff. *Steel and the State: Government Intervention and Steel's Structural Crisis.* Boulder, CO: Westview Press, 1988.

Howell, Thomas R., William A. Noellert, Janet H. MacLaughlin, and Alan W. Wolff. *The Microelectronics Race: The Impact of Government Policy on International Competition.* Boulder, CO: Westview Press, 1988.

———. *Conflict among Nations.* Boulder, CO: Westview Press, 1992.

Hu, Yao-Su. "Global or Stateless Corporations Are National Firms with International Operations." *California Management Review* 34, no. 3 (Winter 1992): 107–126.

Hudson, Pat. *The Industrial Revolution.* New York: E. Arnold, 1992.

Hudson Institute. *The Value of Associations to American Society.* Washington, DC: American Society of Association Executives, 1990.

Huge, Wolfgang. "Promotion of Trade and Professional Education of Craftsmen in the Kingdom of Hanover: On the Educational Activities of the Trade Association for the Kingdom of Hanover, 1828–66." (In German). *Technikgeschichte* 57, no. 3 (1990): 211–234.

Hugh, Patrick, and Henry Rosovsky, Ed. *Asia's New Giant: How the Japanese Economy Works.* Washington, DC: Brookings Institution, 1976.

Israel, Jerry, ed. *Building the Organizational Society: Essays on Associated Activities in Modern America.* New York: Free Press, 1972.

Ito, Takatoshi. *The Japanese Economy.* Cambridge, MA: Massachusetts Institute of Technology Press, 1992.

Japan Fair Trade Commission. *Trade Association Activities and Problems under the Antimonopoly Act* [Survey]. Tokyo: March 1993.

Johnson, Chalmers. *MITI and the Japanese Miracle: The Growth of Industrial Policy, 1925–75.* Stanford, CA: Stanford University Press, 1982.

Johnson, Chalmers, Laura D'Andrea Tyson, and J. Zepman, eds. *The Industrial Policy Debate.* San Francisco, CA: ICS Press, 1984.

———. *Politics and Productivity: The Real Story of Why Japan Works.* Cambridge, MA: Ballinger Publishing, 1989.

Jorde, Thomas M., and David J. Teece. "Competition and Cooperation: Striking the Right Balance." *California Management Review* 31, no. 3 (Spring 1989): 25–37.

———. "Innovation, Cooperation and Antitrust." *High Technology Law Journal* 4 (Spring 1989): 1–12.

Juliussen, K. P., and E. Juliussen. *The 6th Annual Computer Industry Almanac—1993.* Austin, TX: The Reference Press, June 1993.

Kaplan, Eugene J. *Japan: The Government-Business Relationship: A Guide for the American Businessman.* Washington, DC: U.S. Department of Commerce, 1972.

Kash, Don E. *Perpetual Innovation: The New World of Competition.* New York: Basic Books, 1989.

Katzenstein, Peter J., ed. *Industry and Politics in West Germany: Toward the Third Republic.* Ithaca, NY: Cornell University Press, 1989.

Kearns, Robert L. *Zaibatsu America: How Japanese Firms are Colonizing Vital U.S. Industries.* New York: Free Press, 1992.

Kester, Carl W. *Japanese Takeovers.* Boston: Harvard Business School Press, 1991.

Kikkawa, Takeo. "The Electric Power Federation and the Committee on Electricity: The Electric Power Industry, Cartels, and Consumer Regulations." (In Japanese). *Shakai-Keizai-Shigaku* (Socio-economic history) 48, no. 4 (1982): 29–53.

Kimura, Yui. *The Japanese Semiconductor Industry: Structure, Competitive Strategies, and Performance.* Greenwich, CT: JAI Press, 1988.

Kirby, Alison J. "Trade Associations as Information Exchange Mechanisms." *Rand Journal of Economics* 19, no. 1 (Spring 1988): 138–146.

Klepper, G. "Entry into the Market for Large Transport Aircraft." *European Economic Review* 34 (June 1990): 775–798.

Kline, John M. "Trade Competitiveness and Corporate Nationality." *Columbia Journal of World Business* 24, no. 3 (Fall 1989): 25–32.

Kobayashi, Koji. *The Rise of NEC: How the World's Greatest C&C Company Is Managed.* Cambridge, MA: Blackwell Business, 1991.

Kodama, F. "Technology Fusion and the New R&D." *Harvard Business Review* 70, no. 4 (July-August 1992): 70–78.

Komiya, Megumi. "The Japanese Computer Industry: An Industrial Policy Analysis." *Information Society* 6, nos. 1–2 (1989): 1–20.

Krouse, Clement G. "Competition or Monopoly I: Cartelization." *Bulletin of Economic Research* 43, no. 2 (April 1991): 103–125.

Krugman, Paul. *The Age of Diminished Expectations: Economic Policy in the 1990's.* Cambridge, MA: Massachusetts Institute of Technology Press, 1991.

———, ed. *Strategic Trade Policy.* Cambridge, MA: Massachusetts Institute of Technology Press, 1986.

Kudo, Akira. "The International Steel Cartel (1926–32) and the German Steel Industry (In Japanese)." The Proceedings of the Social Science (1982). College of General Education, University of Tokyo (31 March 1983): 1–74.

Kuttner, Robert. *The End of Laissez-Faire.* New York: Knopf, 1991.

Lee, W. R. "Economic Development and the State in Nineteenth-Century Germany." *Economic History Review* 41 (August 1988): 346–367.

Leontieff, W. *The Structure of the American Economy, 1919–1939.* 2nd ed. New York: Oxford University Press, 1951.

————. *Input-Output Economics.* New York: Oxford University Press, 1966.

Levinson, Marc. *Beyond Free Markets: The Revival of Activist Economics.* Lexington, MA: Lexington Books, 1990.

Levy, Hermann, and A. H. Kelley. *Industrial Germany: A Study of Its Monopoly Organizations and Their Control by the State.* New York: Kelly Bookseller, 1966.

Libecap, Gary D. "The Political Economy of Crude Oil Cartelization in the United States, 1933–72." *Journal of Economic History* 49, no. 4 (December 1989): 833–866.

Lincoln, Edward J. *Japan's Unequal Trade.* Washington, DC: Brookings Institution, 1990.

Lindblom, C. *Politics and Markets.* New York: Basic Books, 1977.

Litvak, Isaiah A. "National Trade Associations: Business-Government Intermediaries." *Business Quarterly* 47, no. 3 (October 1982): 34–42.

Lodge, George C. *The American Disease.* New York: Knopf, 1984.

————. *Perestroika for America: Restructuring U.S. Business-Government Relations for Competitiveness in the World Economy.* Boston: Harvard Business School Press, 1990.

Lynn, Leonard H., and Timothy J. McKeown. *Organizing Business: Trade Associations in America and Japan.* Washington, DC: American Enterprise Institute for Public Policy Research, 1988.

Mack, Charles S. *The Executive's Handbook of Trade and Business Associations: How They Work, and How to Make Them Work Effectively for You.* New York: Quorum Books, 1991.

McKinsey and Company, Inc. *The 1990 Report on the Computer Industry.* New York: McKinsey and Company, 1990.

MacKintosh, Ian. *Sunrise Europe: The Dynamics of Information Technology.* Cambridge, MA: Basil Blackwell, 1986.

Magaziner, Ira C., and Thomas M. Hout. *Japanese Industrial Policy.* Berkeley: University of California Press, 1981.

————. *Minding America's Business: The Decline and Rise of the American Economy.* New York: Vintage Books, 1982.

Magaziner, Ira C., and Mark Patinkin. *The Silent War.* New York: Random House, 1990.

Majumdar, Badiul A. "Industrial Policy in Action: The Case of the Electronics Industry in Japan." *Columbia Journal of World Business* 23, no. 3 (Fall 1988): 25–34.

Mann, P. "Gephardt Opens Fight against Airbus Subsidies with Aid Bill for Commercial Aerospace Firms." *Aviation Week and Space Technology* 136, no. 18 (4 May 1992): 24.

Markusen, A., and J. Yudken. "The Birthing of Aerospace." *Technology Review* 95 (April 1992): 28–29.

Matlack, Carol. "Shoestring Success." *National Journal* 21 (20 May 1989): 1239–1241.

Matsui, Taira. "Reorganization of the Coal Cartel and the State Intervention in Weimar Germany: The Rhine-Westphalian Coal Syndicate, 1924-5." (In Japanese). *Tochiseido Shigaku* 90 (1981): 1–20.

Matsuo, Sumihiro. "The Establishment of Coal Mining Cartels in Japan." *Shakai-Keizai-Shigaku* (Socio-economic history; in Japanese) 50, no. 4 (1984): 55–81.

Matsushima, Harumi. "Wartime Economy and the Consolidation of the Government Control of Industries in Japan" *Shakai-Keizai-Shigaku* (Socio-economic history; in Japanese) 41, no. 6 (1976): 70–94.

Matsushita, Mitsuo. "The Role of Competition Law and Policy in Reducing Trade Barriers in Japan." *World Economy* 14, no. 2 (June 1991): 181–197.

Mazlish, Bruce, ed. *The Railroad and the Space Program: An Exploration in Historical Analogy.* Cambridge, MA: Massachusetts Institute of Technology Press, 1965.

Measell, James S. "The Western Flint and Lime Glass Protective Associations, 1874–1887." *Western Pennsylvania Historical Magazine* 66, no. 4 (October 1983): 313–334.

———. "The Pittsburg and Wheeling Goblet Company." *Western Pennsylvania Historical Magazine* 71, no. 2 (June 1988): 191–195.

Merrifield, O. Bruce. "Global Strategic Alliances among Firms." *International Journal of Technology Management* 7, nos. 1–3 (1992): 77–83.

Meyer, Richard. "Preserving the Wa." *Financial World* 160, no. 19 (17 September 1991): 52, 54.

Mezines, Basil J. *Trade Associations and the Antitrust Laws.* Washington, DC: Bureau of National Affairs, 1983.

Michels, Rudolf Karl. *Cartels, Combines, and Trusts in Post-War Germany.* New York: AMS Press, 1968.

Mirow, Kurt Rudolf, and Harry Mauer. *Webs of Power: International Cartels and the World Economy.* Boston: Houghton Mifflin, 1982.

Mokyr, Joel. *The Lever of Riches: Technological Creativity and Economic Progress.* New York: Oxford University Press, 1990.

Mundo, Philip A. "Political Representation of the U.S. Electronics Industries." Paper presented at the annual meeting of the American Political Science Association, Washington, DC, September 1991.

――――. *Interest Groups: Cases and Circumstances.* Chicago: Nelson Hall, 1992.

Nakazawa, Toshiaki, and Leonard W. Weiss. "The Legal Cartels of Japan."*Antitrust Bulletin* 34, no. 3 (Fall 1989): 641–653.

Nanto, Dick K., and Glenn J. McLoughlin. *Japanese and U.S. Industrial Associations: Their Role in High Technology Policy Making.* Washington, DC: U.S. Congressional Research Service, Library of Congress, 26 June 1991.

Nelson, Richard R. *High-Technology Policies: A Five-Nation Comparison.* Washington, DC: American Enterprise Institute for Public Policy Research, 1984.

Nester, William R. *Japanese Industrial Targeting: The Neomercantilist Path to Economic Superpower.* London: Macmillan, 1991.

Noble, Gregory William. "Takeover or Makeover? Japanese Investment in America."*California Management Review* 34, no. 4 (Summer 1992): 127–147.

Norris, Donald M. *Market-Driven Management: Lessons Learned from 20 Successful Associations.* Washington, DC: U.S. Foundation of the American Society of Association Executives, 1990.

Nyrop, R. F., ed. *Federal Republic of Germany.* Washington, DC: Department of the Army, 1982.

O'Brien, Patricia A. "Industry Structure as a Competitive Advantage." *Business History* 34, no. 1 (January 1992): 128.

Ohmae, Kenichi. *The Borderless World: Power and Strategy in the Interlinked Economy.* New York: Free Press, 1985.

――――. *Triad Power: The Coming Shape of Global Competition.* New York: Harper Business, 1990.

――――. "Boundaries of Business: The Perils of Protectionism."*Harvard Business Review* 69 (July-August 1991): 128–130.

Okimoto, Daniel L. *Between MITI and the Market: Japanese Industrial Policy for High Technology.* Stanford, CA: Stanford University Press, 1989.

Okimoto, Daniel L., Henry S. Rowen, and Michael J. Dahl. *The Semiconductor Competition and National Security.* Stanford, CA: Stanford University Press, 1987.

Okimoto, Daniel L., and F. B. Weinstein, ed. *Competitive Edge: The Semiconductor Industry in the U.S. and Japan.* Stanford, CA: Stanford University Press, 1984.

Olson, Mancur. *The Rise and Decline of Nations: Economic Growth, Stagflation, and Social Rigidities.* New Haven, CT: Yale University Press, 1982.

Oppenheimer, Michael F., and Donna M. Tuths. *Nontariff Barriers.* Boulder, CO: Westview Press, 1987.

Organization for Economic Cooperation and Development (OECD). Futures Program. *Strategic Industries in a Global Economy.* Paris: OECD Futures Program, 1991.

———. *Trade, Investment and Technology in the 1990's.* Paris: OECD Futures Program, 1991.

Osborne, D., and T. Gaebler. *Reinventing Government.* New York: Penguin Group, 1993.

Ouchi, William G. *The M-Form Society: How American Teamwork Can Recapture the Competitive Edge.* Reading, MA: Addison-Wesley, 1984.

Ouchi, William G. *Theory Z.* Reading, MA: Addison-Wesley, 1984.

Passant, Ernest. *A Short History of Germany, 1815–1945.* New York: Cambridge University Press, 1959.

Patrick, Hugh, and Henry Rosovsky. *Asia's New Giant: How the Japanese Economy Works.* Washington, DC: Brookings Institution, 1976.

Peter, Lon L. "Are Cartels Unstable? The German Steel Work Association before WWI." *Research in Economic History* (Supplement 3) (1984): 61–85.

———. "Managing Competition in German Coal, 1893–1913." *Journal of Economic History* 49, no. 2 (1989): 419–433.

Phillips, Kevin P. *Staying on Top: The Business Case for a National Industrial Strategy.* New York: Random House, 1984.

———. "U.S. Industrial Policy: Inevitable and Ineffective." *Harvard Business Review* 70, no. 4 (July-August 1992): 104–112.

Porter, Michael E.. *Competitive Advantage: Creating and Sustaining Superior Performance.* New York: MacMillan, 1985.

———. ed. *Competition in Global Industries.* Boston: Harvard Business School Press, 1986.

———. *Competitive Strategy.* New York: Free Press, 1989.

———. *The Competitive Advantage of Nations.* New York: Free Press, 1990.

———. *Capital Choices: Changing the Way America Invests in Industry.* Washington, DC: Council on Competitiveness and Harvard Business School, June 1992.

————. "Capital Disadvantage: America's Failing Capital Investment System." *Harvard Business Review* 70, (September-October 1992): 65–82.

Prestowitz, Clyde V., Jr. *Trading Places: How We Allowed Japan to Take the Lead.* New York: Basic Books, 1988.

Putsay, Michael W. "Toward a Global Airline Industry: Prospects and Impediments." *Logistics and Transportation Review* 28, no. 1 (March 1992): 103–128.

Reich, Robert B. *The Next American Frontier.* New York: Times Books, 1983.

————. "We Need a Strategic Trade Policy: Americans May be Forced to Choose between Balanced Trade and a Higher Standard of Living: They Might Have to Decide Whether They Prefer Profits for U.S. Corporations or Better Jobs for Themselves." *Challenge* 33, no. 4 (July-August 1990): 38–42.

————. *The Work of Nations: Preparing Ourselves for 21st Century Capitalism.* New York: Alfred A. Knopf, 1991.

Reischauer, Edwin O. *The Japanese.* Rutland, VT: Charles E. Tuttle Co., 1977.

Riedl, Erich. "Watershed for German Aerospace Industry." *Interavia Aerospace Review* 45, no. 5 (May 1990): 394–395.

Robert, Michel. "The Do's and Don't's of Strategic Alliances." *Journal of Business Strategy* 13, no. 2 (March-April 1992): 50–53.

Rosecrance, Richard. *America's Economic Resurgence: A Bold New Strategy.* New York: Harper, 1990.

Rosenberg, Nathan, and L. E. Birdzell, Jr. *How the West Grew Rich.* New York: Basic Books, 1986.

Rubenson, David. *Technology Policy in the Federal Republic of Germany.* Santa Monica, CA: Rand Corporation, 1990.

Rugman, Alan, and Michael Gestrin. "EC Anti-Dumping Laws as a Barrier to Trade." *European Management Journal* 9, no. 4 (December 1991): 475–482.

Rushing, Francis W., and Carole Ganz Brown. *National Policies for Developing High Technology Industries: International Comparison.* Boulder, CO: Westview Press, 1986.

Russell, John J. *National Trade and Professional Associations of the United States, 1992.* Washington, DC: Columbia Books, 1992.

Sapienza, Alice M. "R&D Collaboration as a Global Competitive Tactic: Biotechnology and the Ethical Pharmaceutical Industry." *R&D Management* 19, no. 4 (October 1989): 285–295.

Scherer, F. M., and D. Ross. *Industrial Market Structure and Economic Performance.* 3rd ed. Boston: Houghton Mifflin, 1990.

Schlosstein, Steven. *The End of the American Century.* Chicago: Congdon and Weed, 1989.

Schotland, Sara D., and Katherine L. Rhyne. "Product Liability Implications of Trade Associations Activities." *Journal of Products Liability* 7, no. 3 (1984): 215–230.

Schroeder, Wayne E., and Roy L. Butler. *Improving Vocational Education Programming Through Greater Involvement of Trade Associations.* Columbus: Ohio State University, National Center for Research in Vocational Education, 1987.

Schroter, Harm. "Cartels as a Form of Industrial Concentration: The Case of the International Dye Cartel, 1928–39." (In German). *Vierteljahrschrift fur Sozial- und Wirtschaftsgeschichte* 74, no. 4 (1987): 479–513.

Seligman, Ben B. *The Potentates: Business and Businessmen in American History.* New York: Dial Press, 1971.

Semiconductor Industry Association. *Japanese Market Barriers in Microelectronics.* San Jose, CA: Semiconductor Industry Association, 14 June 1985.

Shan, Weijian, and William Hamilton. "Country-Specific Advantage and International Cooperation." *Strategic Management Journal* 12, no. 6 (September 1991): 419–432.

Sherwood-Call, Carolyn. "Changing Geographical Patterns of Electronic Components Activity." *Federal Reserve Bank of San Francisco Economic Review,* no. 2 (1992): 25–35.

Siegfried, John J., and Michelle Mahoney. "The First Sherman Act Case: Jellico Mountain Coal, 1891." *Antitrust Bulletin* 35, no. 4 (Winter 1990): 801–832.

Smith, Adam. *The Wealth of Nations.* Chicago: University of Chicago Press, 1976.

Snyder, D. P., and Gregg Edwards. *America in the 1990's.* Washington, DC: American Society for Association Executives, 1992.

Stevens, John M., Steven L. Wartick, and John W. Bagby. *Business-Government Relations and Interdependence: A Managerial and Analytic Perspective.* New York: Quorum Books, 1988.

Stokes, Bruce. "Multiple Allegiances: U.S.-Based Transnational Corporations, Critics Say, Pursue Strategies That Don't Always Mesh with America's Interests, Complicating Efforts to Cut the Trade Deficit." *National Journal* 21 (11 November 1989): 2754–2758.

———. "High-Tech Tussle: Even Though the Bush White House Is Dead-Set against the Idea, Advocates Say America Still Needs a National Industrial Policy to Help U.S. Firms Compete Worldwide." *National Journal* 22 (2 June 1990): 1338–1342.

Stolper, Gustav. *German Economy, 1870–1940.* New York: Cornwall Press, 1940.

Swann, Dennis. *Competition and Industrial Policy in the European Community.* New York: Methuen, 1983.

Swinbanks, D. "Japan's Largest National Research Project Starts." *Research Technology Management* 34 (July-August 1991): 2–3.

———. "Techno-Globalism and Generation-6 Computers." *Research Technology Management* 34 (September-October 1991): 6–7.

Swope, Gerard. In *The Swope Plan: Details, Criticism, Analysis; Plan by Gerard Swope,* edited by J. George Frederick. New York: Business Course, 1931.

Takeda, Y. "Cooperation of Government, Industry, and Academia in Research and Development Activities in Japan, Looking toward the 21st Century." *International Journal of Technology Management* 6, nos. 5–6 (1991): 450–458.

Takeuchi, Iori. "A Study of the Trade Association in the Early Meiji Era: The Development of the Awa Indigo Trade Association Movement." *Shakai-Keizai-Shigaku* (Socio-economic history) 42, no. 5 (1977): 70–90.

Tatsuno, Sheridan. *The Technopolis Strategy: Japan, High Technology, and the Control of the 21st Century.* New York: Prentice Hall, 1986.

Taylor, Charles R. *Global Presence and Competitiveness of U.S. Manufacturers.* New York: The Conference Board, 1991.

Teece, David J. *The Competitive Challenge: Strategies for Industrial Innovation and Renewal.* Cambridge, MA: Ballinger Publishing, 1987.

Thompson, Donald N. "The Triad, Reciprocity and Alliances: New Realities for Trade." *Business Quarterly* 55, no. 1 (Summer 1990): 25.

Thurow, Lester C. *Head to Head: The Coming Economic Battle among Japan, Europe, and America.* New York: William Morrow, 1992.

Tominaga, Norio. "Cartels and Their Effects between the Wars." *Shakai-Keizai-Shigaku* (Socio-economic history; In Japanese) 47, no. 5 (1982): 66–91.

Towell, Pat. "U.S.-Japanese Warplane Deal Raises a Welter of Issues." *Congressional Quarterly Weekly Report* 47, no. 10 (11 March 1989): 535–537.

Treeck, Joachim, and Jorg-Martin Schultze. "Germany." *International Financial Law Review Supplement* no. 6, (June 1991): 38–37.

Troesken, Werner. "A Note on the Efficiency of the German Steel and Coal Syndicates." *Journal of European Economic History* 18, no. 3 (1989): 595–600.

Turner, Henry Ashby, Jr. *German Big Business and the Rise of Hitler.* New York: Oxford University Press, 1985.

Turner, Louis. *Industrial Collaboration with Japan.* New York: Routledge, 1987.

Tyson, Laura D'Andrea. *Creating Advantage: Strategic Policy for National Competitiveness.* Berkeley: University of California, Berkeley Roundtable on the International Economy, 1987.

———. *Who's Bashing Whom? Trade Conflict in High-Technology Industries.* Washington, DC: Institute for International Economics, 1992.

Tyson, Laura D'Andrea, and John Zysman. *Politics and Productivity: Developmental Strategy and Production Innovation in Japan.* Berkeley: University of California, Berkeley Roundtable on the International Economy, 1987.

United States. Executive Office of the President. Office of Science and Technology. *U.S. Technology Policy.* Washington, DC: U.S. Department of Commerce, 1990.

———. *Report of the National Critical Technologies Panel.* Washington, DC: U.S. Department of Commerce, 1991.

U.S. Congress. Office of Technology Assessment. *International Competitiveness in Electronics.* OTA-ISC-200. Washington, DC: U.S. Government Printing Office, 1983.

———. *International Competition in Services.* OTA-ITE-328. Washington, DC: U.S. Government Printing Office, 1987.

———. *Biotechnology in a Global Economy.* OTA-BA-494. Washington, DC: U.S. Congress, Office of Technology Assessment, 1991.

U.S. Department of Commerce. International Trade Administration. *The Competitive Status of the U.S. Electronics Sector from Material to Systems.* Washington, DC: U.S. Government Printing Office, 1990.

U.S. General Accounting Office. *Competitiveness Issues: The Business Environment in the United States, Japan, and Germany, a Report to Congressional Requestors.* Washington, DC: U.S. General Accounting Office, August 1993.

Vander Meulen, Jacob A. *The Politics of Aircraft: Building an American Military Industry.* Lawrence: University Press of Kansas, 1991.

Van Remoortere, Francois, and Peter F. Boer. "Globalization of Technology: What It Means for American Industry." *Research-Technology Management* 294, no. 7 (July-August 1992): 42.

Van Wolferen, Karel. *The Enigma of Japanese Power: The First Full-Scale Examination of the Inner Workings of Japan's Political/Industrial System.* New York: Alfred A. Knopf, 1989.

Vascik, George S. "What Was the German Sugar Cartel? An Analysis of Interest Group Representation and Industrial Organization, 1850–1934." *Essays in Economics and Business History* 8 (1990): 355–367.

Victor, Kirk. "Step under My Umbrella." *National Journal* 20, no. 17 (23 April 1988): 1063–1067.

Vives, Xavier. "Trade Associations Disclosure Rules, Incentives to Share Information, and Welfare." *Rand Journal of Economics* 21, no. 3 (Autumn 1990): 409–430.

Vogel, Ezra F. *Comeback.* New York: Simon and Schuster, 1985.

———. *Japan as No. 1: Lessons for America.* New York: Simon and Schuster, 1985.

Vogel, Steven. *Japanese High Technology, Politics, and Power.* Berkeley: University of California, Berkeley Roundtable on the International Economy, 1989.

Watson, Philippa, and Karen Williams. "The Application of the EEC Competition Rules to Trade Associations." In *Yearbook of European Law.* Eds. A. Barav and D. A. Wyatt, New York: Oxford University Press, 1989.

Webb, Steven B. "Tariffs, Cartels, Technology and Growth in the German Steel Industry, 1879–1914." *Journal of Economic History* 40, no. 2 (1980): 309–329.

Webster, George D. *The Law of Associations: An Operating Legal Manual for Executives and Counsel.* New York: Matthew Bender, 1975.

Webster, George D., and Arthur L. Herold. *Antitrust Guide for Association Executives.* New York: Matthew Bender, 1975.

Weidenbaum, Murray L. *Business, Government, and the Public.* Englewood Cliffs, NJ: Prentice Hall, 1981.

———. "Business and Government: Fences Make Good Neighbors." *Business and Society Review* 77 (Spring 1991): 22–25.

———. "Business-Government Partnerships Don't Work. Period." *Across the Board* 28, nos. 1–2 (January-February 1991): 52–54.

Wessell, Horst A. "Deutsch Schwachstromkabel-Verband: The Background, Foundation and Development in Its First Years (1876–1917)." (In German). *Zeits, fur Untemehmensgeschichte* 27, no. 1 (1982): 22–44.

Wever, K. S., and C. S. Allen. "Is Germany a Model for Managers?" *Harvard Business Review* 70 (September-October 1992): 36–40.

White, J. W. "Economic Development and Sociopolitical Unrest in Nineteenth-Century Japan." *Economic Development and Cultural Change* 37, no. 2 (January 1989): 231–260.

Whitney, Simon Newcomb. *Trade Associations and Industrial Control.* Berkeley: University of California, Photo Duplication Service, 1982.

"Why the United States Can't Be More Like Germany and Japan." *Harvard Business Review* 70, no. 4 (July-August 1992): 110.

Wise, Paul S. "Friends and Enemies: A Historical Perspective on Trade Associations." *Spectator* 182, no. 10 (October 1974): 24–28, 47.

Wolfe, Archibald J. *Commercial Organizations in Germany.* Washington, DC: U.S. Department of Commerce and Labor, 1914.

———. *Commercial Laws of England, Scotland, Germany and France.* Washington, DC: U.S. Department of Commerce, 1915.

Wright, Gavin. "The Origins of American Industrial Success, 1879–1949." *American Economic Review* 80, no. 4 (September 1990): 651–688.

Yamazaki, H. H., and M. Miyamoto, eds. *Trade Associations in Business History.* Tokyo: University of Tokyo Press, 1988.

Yoffie, David B. "How an Industry Builds Political Advantage: Silicon Valley Goes to Capitol Hill." *Harvard Business Review* 66 (May-June 1988): 82–89.

Zwicker, Dieter G. "Trade Associations in Germany and the United States of America— Antitrust Restrictions on the Ability of Trade Associations to Regulate Themselves." *Antitrust Bulletin* 29, no. 4 (Winter 1984): 775–831.

Index